Music in Time

Music in Time

Phenomenology, Perception, Performance

edited by

SUZANNAH CLARK

ALEXANDER REHDING

Isham Library Papers 9
Harvard Publications in Music 24
Harvard University Department of Music
2016

Distributed by Harvard University Press
Cambridge, Massachusetts, U.S.A. • London, England

ISBN 9780964031777

₃ of America

Typesetting by ꞁꞁꝺꝺꝺꝺꝺꝺ ꝺ ꞃookline, New Hampshire
Printing by Puritan Press, Hollis, New Hampshire

Photograph of Christopher Hasty courtesy of Harvard News Office

Library of Congress Cataloging-in-Publication Data

Names: Clark, Suzannah, 1969- editor. | Rehding, Alexander editor. | Hasty,
    Christopher Francis honoree.
Title: Music in time : phenomenology, perception, performance / edited by
    Suzannah Clark, Alexander Rehding.
Description: Cambridge, Massachusetts : Harvard University Department of
    Music, 2016. | Series: Isham Library papers ; 9 | Series: Harvard
    publications in music ; 24 | Festschrift for Christopher Hasty. | Includes
    bibliographical references and index.
Identifiers: LCCN 2015050821 | ISBN 9780964031760 (alk. paper)
Subjects: LCSH: Musical meter and rhythm.
Classification: LCC ML55. H28 2016 | DDC 781.2/2—dc23
LC record available at http://lccn.loc.gov/2015050821

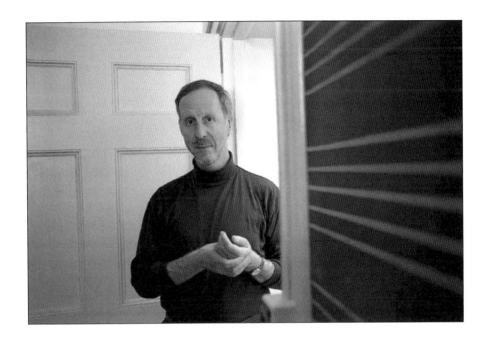

For Christopher Hasty

Contents

Preface · ix

Part I. Experiencing Time

NICHOLAS COOK, University of Cambridge
Time and Time Again: On Hearing Reinecke · 3

LAWRENCE M. ZBIKOWSKI, University of Chicago
Musical Time, Embodied and Reflected · 33

STEPHEN BLUM, City University of New York
Ethnomusicologists and Questions of Temporality · 55

Part II. Knowing the Score

ROBERT MORRIS, Eastman School of Music, University of Rochester
Notation Is One Thing, Analysis Another, Musical Experience a Third: What Can They Have To Do With One Another? · 71

EUGENE NARMOUR, University of Pennsylvania
The Modern Score and Its Seven Modes of Performance · 109

Part III. The Passage of Time, Holding Time Still

SCOTT BURNHAM, Princeton University
On the Last Measure of Schubert's String Quintet · 155

JANET SCHMALFELDT, Tufts University
In Time with Christopher Hasty: On Becoming a Performer of Robert Schumann's Davidsbündlertänze, *op. 6* · 169

JEANNE BAMBERGER, Massachusetts Institute of Technology
Shaping Time · *191*

Part IV. Finding Time: The Body and Parsing Rhythm and Meter

EUGENE MONTAGUE, The George Washington University
Meter, Entrainment, and Voice in The King's Speech · *219*

SUSAN MCCLARY, Case Western Reserve University
Doing the Time Warp in Seventeenth-Century Music · *237*

MATTHEW BUTTERFIELD, Franklin and Marshall College
*When Swing Doesn't Swing: Competing Conceptions of
an Early Twentieth-Century Rhythmic Quality* · *257*

Part V. "Thisness" and Particularities

BRIAN HULSE, College of William and Mary
Off the Grid: Hasty and Musical Novelty in Smooth Time · *281*

MARTIN BRODY, Wellesley College
Theory, as a Music · *293*

NOTES ON CONTRIBUTORS · 315
BIBLIOGRAPHY · 319
GENERAL INDEX · 339

Preface

ALMOST TWENTY YEARS after his groundbreaking study *Meter as Rhythm*, a group of colleagues, friends, and students, came together at Harvard University on October 18–20, 2013 to celebrate Christopher Hasty's work. This book assembles many of the papers presented at the symposium. The title *Music in Time: Phenomenology, Perception, Performance* reflects the key areas in which Hasty has been most active as a musician and thinker, teacher and mentor, author and interlocutor.

Hasty's thinking is boundlessly ambitious: he asks us no less than to take the temporal dimension of music seriously. Just how difficult it is to talk about the passage of time has been clear at least since Augustine of Hippo: "What, then, is time?", asks the Church Father writing in Book IX of his *Confessions*, "if no one asks me, I know what it is; but if I want to explain it to those who ask me, I do not know." These oft-quoted words are far from a simple admission of ignorance, but rather a reflection on the radically subjective nature of our experience of time, and the profound difficulty of communicating this experience to others.

As later thinkers have argued, the passing of time is only experienced thanks to events that occur in temporal succession. By registering these events, which can be as little as the sounding of a new tone in a piece of music, we create a sense of "now"—framed by a sense of the "no-longer" and the "not-yet"—that is to say, we are able to experience a sense of present, past, and future. It is no coincidence that we speak of *passages* of music. Hasty, whose predilection for etymology is well known, never tires of reminding us that the rhythms of a passage of music are related to the Greek *rhein* (= flow). Such rhythms punctuate the flow of time.

Music is sometimes defined as sounds shaped in time, but Hasty encourages us to sharpen this approach by inverting the referents, as time shaped in sounds. In this formulation music can be an answer to Augustine's quandary; it can help us come to terms with the mystery of time.

All the essays assembled here grapple in some way with the questions of temporality that Hasty's thinking challenges us to tackle. They present rich offerings that lead us into various fields of music-theoretical inquiry and that give further impetus to future studies into the temporal nature of music, and the musical nature of temporality.

This volume would not have been possible without the tireless help of various people. The staff of the Music Department at Harvard must be thanked, especially Lesley Bannatyne. Frederick Reece, William O'Hara, and Daniel Walden served as editorial assistants.

Suzannah Clark
Alexander Rehding

Part 1

Experiencing Time

Time and Time Again: On Hearing Reinecke

NICHOLAS COOK

THE DISREGARD OF TIMEKEEPING

CARL REINECKE WAS born in 1824, which makes him quite possibly the earliest born pianist to have been recorded. In the first decade of the twentieth century he made a number of piano rolls for two of the leading reproducing piano companies, Welte-Mignon and Hupfeld. Media Example 1 is a realization of his performance of the exposition from Mozart's F-Major Sonata K. 332 on Hupfeld 50634.[1] It dates from around 1907, and has never been commercially released; I was fortunate to obtain a copy from the collector Paul Tuck. I call it a "realization" because playing a piano roll is significantly unlike playing a CD. Not only do you need the right reproducing piano in good condition, which is asking a lot; you also have to make a number of interpretive decisions, the most important in the case of a Hupfeld roll being the playback speed and the dynamics. I shall come back to this.

Today nobody plays K. 332 the way Reinecke does. The basic issue—to borrow the title of Bonham's debut album—is his disregard of timekeeping: he never settles down to a constant tempo or even seems to make up his mind

[1] Accessible at http://global.oup.com/us/companion.websites/9780199357406/ch4/k332/a15/ (reproduced by kind permission of Paul Tuck). Media examples are taken from the Companion website to Nicholas Cook, *Beyond the Score: Music as Performance* (Oxford: Oxford University Press, 2013); this article expands and develops ideas initially presented in chapter 4 of the book, where I discuss this and other piano rolls recorded by Reinecke in greater depth.

on how fast he wants to play the piece. He hurries through mm. 9–10 in a
way that few piano teachers would—it is as if he could not wait to get to the
cadence—and his unsteady timekeeping becomes more obvious still with
the following passage, which Wye Jamison Allanbrook identifies as the hunt
calls topic (Example 1 incorporates her designations).[2] Reinecke broadens the
tempo a little from the upbeat to m. 13, which is unexceptionable as a way of
marking the new melody, but then accelerates in an apparently uncontrolled
manner through the following two measures before slowing down and returning to something like his original tempo around m. 18. And so it continues.
Blow-by-blow description is unnecessary, but it is striking that he takes much
of the *Sturm und Drang* section (from m. 23) significantly faster than the opening tempo, to which he returns only for the Minuet section (or second subject) from m. 41. Even then his beat remains unsteady, with a sudden slowing
down for the three-against-two texture at m. 49: only when the *Sturm und
Drang* topic returns at m. 56 does Reinecke revert to his faster tempo. At first
the issue is confused by his pendulum-like broadening out at m. 56 and then
contraction at m. 57, which is repeated at mm. 58–9. The effect is to underline
the strong measures as against the weak ones, or perhaps I should say to make
them strong and weak. But at m. 60 there is a sudden lurching forward into
the sequences, and the same kind of vacillations continue to the end of the
exposition.

In using terminology like uncontrolled, unsteady, lurching, and vacillating
I am underlining the difference between Reinecke's playing and assumptions
about how music goes that are nowadays generally taken for granted. If the
playing on that roll seems arbitrary, bizarre, or plain bad to modern listeners,
then it does so against the long taken-for-granted background of post-war
performance practice, as exemplified by Alicia de Larrocha's impeccably consensual recording from 1989 (Media Example 2).[3] With its clean, uncluttered
shaping and melodious textures, it calls for much less detailed commentary
than Reinecke's. Larrocha's playing is more literal than Reinecke's, in the sense
of conforming more closely with the nominal specifications of the score, but it
is not literal in any literal sense. She takes the "Minuet" section a little slower
than the opening (about 135 as against 140MM), though the difference is barely
perceptible as such, and every now and then there are fleeting but quite noticeable inflections: an example is the slight hesitation on the first beat of m. 42,

[2] Wye Jamison Allanbrook, *Rhythmic Gesture in Mozart*: Le Nozze di Figaro *and* Don
Giovanni (Chicago: University of Chicago Press, 1983), 6–7.

[3] Accessible at http://global.oup.com/us/companion.websites/9780199357406/ch4/k332/a4;
released on RCA Victor Red Seal 82876-55705-2.

which creates a moment of reflection (though its purpose is perhaps to make space for the written-out arpeggiation). But these inflections do not disturb the sense of the music's smooth, even flow, and the result is a thoroughly livable version of modernism as against, say, the sharp-edged, industrial feel of Glenn Gould's 1966 recording of the same sonata. Such playing might bring to mind Adorno's description, from as early as 1938, of the "perfect, immaculate performance" that presents music "as already complete from the very first note," and Adorno added: "The performance sounds like its own phonograph

Example 1. Mozart, Sonata K. 332, 1st movement, exposition (Breitkopf & Hartel edition, 1878), with Wye Jamison Allanbrook's topical labels.

Example 1, continued

record."[4] Adorno's point is that what is to come seems already as fixed as what has gone, and Larrocha's performance might well bring to mind the classic image of time as a river that flows evenly past an observer standing on the bank.

[4] Theodor W. Adorno, *Essays on Music*, ed. Richard Leppert (Berkeley and Los Angeles: University of California Press, 2002), 301.

That is an example of what Dedre Gentner and her co-authors call a "time-moving" image of time—as opposed to an "ego-moving" image, where time is stationary and it is the observer who moves across it.[5] The latter is likely to be the dominant image for musicians, because scores and the analytical representations based on them are spatially extended objects that we traverse as we read them. The analogy or cross-mapping between time and space is deeply built into the conceptualization of music, at least of the Western "art" tradition. Robert Morgan has written that "music is apparently unthinkable without the presence of some spatial, extratemporal dimension."[6] Carl Dahlhaus went further: "Nothing would be farther from the truth than to see in the tendency to spatialization a distortion of music's nature. Insofar as music is form, it attains its real existence . . . in the very moment when it is past."[7] As Christopher Hasty has repeatedly argued, it is this kind of thinking that has given rise to analytical models in which time ceases to be of the essence and is instead reduced to a frictionless, transparent medium within which musical objects are located—a musical equivalent of air as it were. And in performance, the correlate of this view of music as a spatially extended object is a style that values clarity, articulacy, directionality, the "long line"—in short, the style of the post-war mainstream, of which Larrocha's recording represents a consummate example. Indeed, Mozart's sonatas have become particularly associated with such playing—or as Nikolaus Harnoncourt might put it, they have been mired in the cult of the "merely beautiful"—to the extent that Dean Sutcliffe characterizes their performance as "stuck in a time warp."[8]

It is against the background of this kind of playing that modern listeners and critics have often responded to early recordings with disbelief; as Daniel Leech-Wilkinson has documented, the first response is often laughter (the second is a feeling of being threatened).[9] One argument that can be deployed in support of such responses is that the technology is not to be trusted. Different

[5] Dedre Gentner et al., "As Time Goes By: Evidence for Two Systems in Processing Space-Time Metaphors," *Language and Cognitive Processes* 17 (2002), 537–65.

[6] Robert P. Morgan, "Musical Time/Musical Space," *Critical Inquiry* 6 (1980), 527–38: 538.

[7] Carl Dahlhaus, *Esthetics of Music*, trans. William W. Austin (Cambridge: Cambridge University Press, 1982), 12.

[8] Nikolaus Harnoncourt, *Baroque Music Today: Music as Speech. Ways to a New Understanding of Music*, trans. Mary O'Neill (Wayne, New Jersey: Amadeus Press, 1995), 135; Dean Sutcliffe, "The Keyboard Music," in *The Cambridge Companion to Mozart*, ed. Simon Keefe (Cambridge: Cambridge University Press, 2003), 61.

[9] Daniel Leech-Wilkinson, "Listening and Responding to the Evidence of Early Twentieth-Century Performance," *Journal of the Royal Musical Association* 135 Supplement 1 (2010), 45–62.

claims have to be made for dismissing the evidence of sound recordings and of piano rolls, of course, but I have already said that realizing a piano roll is not like playing a CD, and I will now briefly enlarge on that. For one thing, piano rolls are like a pre-digital version of MIDI, capturing mechanical actions but not sounds as such: there is no trace, for example, of the room acoustic that might have resulted in a different performance depending on whether the recording was made in a small room or a large hall, while the tonal qualities of the playback instrument may or may not correspond well with the one on which the recording was made. But the most obvious issues are those I have already mentioned. Some systems, including the Welte-Mignon one, captured and played back dynamics, but the system for doing so was much simplified (generally there was one value for the top half of the keyboard, and another for the bottom half). In the case of Hupfeld rolls like 50634, a single dynamic value was captured and printed on the roll in the form of a wavy line: in making his realization, Tuck was moving a small slider while the roll played, using the line as a guide. Most fundamentally, as discussed above, we cannot be sure of the right playback speed and hence the absolute tempo, although the "Tempo 50" marking printed at the beginning of 50634 provides some kind of clue. Given the way Reinecke plays, the idea of a single tempo for this movement is inherently problematical, but at least at the outset that is roughly Tuck's average tempo per measure.

The basic point is that piano rolls, like sound recordings, are historical documents and require the same source-critical interpretation as other historical documents. Whereas there are problems as regards room acoustics, tonal quality, dynamic, and absolute tempo, the *relative* timings on Hupfeld rolls were captured within quite tolerable limits of resolution: that was why I concentrated on timing in my description of Reinecke's playing. Of course there might be a problem with this particular piano roll—perhaps the reproducing piano on which it was made was badly calibrated, or perhaps Tuck's was—but here we can simply make comparisons with other rolls that Reinecke made for both Hupfeld and Welte-Mignon. Reinecke's basic style of playing, including his apparently wayward tempos, is as evident in his other recordings as on 50634. And another of the obvious criticisms—that by the time he made these rolls he was in his eighties and his fingers were no longer in good working order—is strongly counter-indicated by his Welte-Mignon rolls, for which the correct playback speed is known: his tempos are sometimes very fast, and his technique is sufficient to cope with them. In any case it is not just the playing of elderly performers like Reinecke that later twentieth-century critics have sought to explain away. Eugen d'Albert made many piano rolls and sound recordings during the same period, when he was in his fifties, and for Harold Schonberg these recordings "cause nothing but embarrassment . . . . [T]he playing is inexplicable, full of wrong notes, memory lapses and distorted rhythms."[10] Yet this is the same pianist whom, as late as 1931, T. W. Adorno referred to as "still the greatest of all pianists."[11]

At least in the early stages of his career, Heinrich Schenker also had great admiration for d'Albert. He had equal admiration for Reinecke, about whom he wrote repeatedly in 1896–97, when the pianist was already in his mid-seventies. "In his truly virtuoso playing," Schenker writes, "all intentions of the artwork are in balance."[12] It is Reinecke's playing of Mozart in particular that Schenker praises: in his brilliant passagework and his introduction of unnotated ornamentation, Schenker says, Reinecke represents Mozart's music as it would have been played in the composer's time, or even by the composer himself. Perhaps then we should have the sound of Reinecke's playing in our ears when we read Schenker's claim that:

> the performance of Classical works must be shaped freely and expressively. All that contemporaries have reported enthusiastically about the infinitely free and colorful performances of J. S. Bach, C. P. E. Bach, Mozart and Beethoven, Mendelssohn and Brahms, all that should be taken as evidence for this fact. If one adds what can be found in essays and letters by these masters, then one cannot but become convinced that their music is performed correctly only if it is played with the utmost freedom.[13]

Indeed I have argued elsewhere that our understanding of Schenker's writings—about performance, but also about music more generally—is skewed because we read them with an anachronous sound image in our minds.

I will not pursue that here, but the basic point is that written documents reveal much less about ways of playing than we are inclined to think they do. Reinecke is an excellent example: if it were not for the piano rolls he left,

---

[10] Harold Schonberg, *The Great Pianists* (London: Gollancz, 1965), 295.

[11] Theodor W. Adorno, *Gesammelte Schriften*, ed. Rolf Tiedemann et al., vol. 19 (Frankfurt am Main: Suhrkamp, 1984), 314.

[12] Hellmut Federhofer, *Heinrich Schenker als Essayist und Kritiker: Gesammelte Aufsätze, Rezensionen und Kleinere Berichte aus den Jahren 1891–1901* (Hildesheim: Georg Olms Verlag, 1990), 333.

[13] Heinrich Schenker, *The Art of Performance*, ed. Heribert Esser, trans. Irene Schreier Scott (Oxford: Oxford University Press, 2000), 70.

we would not have the least idea that he played as he did. Quite the opposite. If, to modern ears, Reinecke's playing embodies a degree of freedom that verges on downright sloppiness, then he emerges from contemporary documentary sources as the chief exponent of the notoriously conservative Leipzig performance style Liszt was referring to when, in 1884, he told a masterclass student, "you must play that totally carried away as if you were not even seated at the piano, completely lost to the world, not 1, 2, 3, 4 as in the Leipzig Conservatory!"[14] (Reinecke taught at the Conservatory from 1860, becoming Director in 1897.) Though we should bear in mind that piano playing and conducting are by no means the same thing, Reinecke—who conducted the Gewandhaus Orchestra from 1860 to 1895—was lampooned as a latter-day archetype of the North German time beaters against whom Wagner directed so much vitriol: in *On Conducting* Wagner referred to him "Herr Capellmeister *Reinecke*," while in his book of the same name (published in 1906) Felix Weingartner went so far as to refer figuratively to Reinecke's pigtail.[15] In short, there is a glaring contradiction between what we read in the documentary sources and what we hear with our own ears. I shall come back to this, too.

In this article I want to argue that Reinecke plays the music so differently from Larrocha, or modern pianists more generally, because he is working with a different conception of musical time. I am going to take as the starting point of my argument something that lies at the heart of the erratic quality that writers such as Schonberg have heard in the playing of early pianists—something that may indeed go far to explain what Schonberg saw as inexplicable about it. This is what I shall call a principle of density: the denser the music, the longer it needs to work its effect. The principle applies across an indefinite range of different parameters. It might have to do with a melodic feature, for example a large leap, or with harmonic intensity. Or it might have to do with rhythmic or textural complexity: a particularly clear example of this is m. 49, where Reinecke slows down drastically for the three-against-two passage, almost in the manner of a novice pianist who finds cross-rhythms difficult. (In Larrocha's performance this moment is as effortless as everything else: she emphasizes the melody, which continues as if unchanged behind its quaver elaboration, while the left-hand triplets are pushed into the background as textural filler.)

[14] Cited in Kenneth Hamilton, *After the Golden Age: Romantic Pianism and Modern Performance* (New York: Oxford University Press, 2007), 191.

[15] Richard Wagner, *Richard Wagner's Prose Works*, trans. William Ashton Ellis, IV (London: Kegan Paul, Trench, Trübner and Co., 1895), 357; Felix Weingartner, *On Conducting*, trans. Ernest Newman (London: Breitkopf and Härtel, 1906), 9, not mentioning Reinecke by name but referring to the Leipzig Gewandhaus Orchestra's "half solid, half elegant conductor"(8).

Then again, density might arise from less directly technical features, such as the appearance of something unexpected: that would again apply to m. 49—which perhaps goes some way towards explaining why Reinecke does not slow down so much at the corresponding point when he repeats the exposition. Or finally it might be a passage of particular emotional intensity. We might say that Reinecke uses tempo to "bring out" the expressivity of the music, except that such a formulation suggests that the expressivity is locked up in the score, just waiting to be brought out. It might be more accurate to say that, through tempo, Reinecke *creates* expressivity—and expressivity of a quite different kind from that which Larrocha creates through her playing.

Eighteenth- and nineteenth-century performance pedagogues, from Quantz and Türk to Kullak and even Schenker, directed performers to create accentuation under much the same circumstances that I have just described: on high notes, long notes, chromatic notes, dissonant notes, and more generally when something unexpected or particularly passionate takes place. Since one of the principal means of accentuation is prolongation—Riemann's agogic accent—there is some overlap between that and my principle of density, and these historical writers have generally been read as describing momentary nuances within a sustained tempo, in other words, a style of performance more or less along Larrocha's lines. But that is just where the playing of pianists like Reinecke and d'Albert is so different. For them, temporal nuance is not an occasional effect but a permanent condition of the music's being. Indeed, their playing is sometimes so mobile that it makes little sense to think of it having an underlying tempo that is subject to modification. That means time is no longer a neutral medium through which the music flows. Instead, it may at one moment be thick and viscous (as in m. 49 of Reinecke's performance), and at the next offer no resistance at all: as I said, it is characteristic of Reinecke's playing, and that of his contemporaries, that they often let the music run away with them, rushing towards the end of phrases and sometimes across phrase breaks in a way that modern pianists do not. (Reinecke does this in mm. 54–55.) Or perhaps, under such circumstances, it is no longer helpful to think of the music being in a medium at all, or correlatively to think of it as a spatially extended object. Instead, time becomes a dimension of the musical content: rather than being a spatial object that moves in time, the music is intrinsically temporal, temporal through and through. To put it another way, the music is not located *in* time but is rather made *of* time, and in this article I use "*in* time" and "*of* time" as shorthand for the contrasted approaches I have illustrated through Larrocha and Reinecke.

Heard this way, Reinecke's playing is not inherently erratic. The erratic quality results from the encounter between his playing and the mindset of music *in* time, the construal of musical experience that Schonberg took for granted. Construed according to the principle of music *of* time, in which time is a dimension of the musical content, it may not be erratic at all. So much, at least, is implied in the draft papers that Schenker put together around 1911, with the unrealized intention of publishing them as a treatise on performance (which is where he talked about the classical composers' "utmost freedom"). In what Heribert Esser's edition of these papers presents as a chapter on "Tempo and Tempo Modification," Schenker follows in the tradition of the eighteenth- and nineteenth-century pedagogues by prescribing special treatment for chromatic notes, suspensions, arpeggios, repeated notes, and neighboring notes: each, he says, must be handled through "pushing ahead/holding back, holding back/pushing ahead"—a formulation that already suggests something close to the mobile tempos of Reinecke and d'Albert.[16] And he adds that such modification "results in the illusion of a strict tempo." A few pages later, now speaking of the introduction of new rhythmic patterns (as at m. 49 of the Mozart movement), he spells this out:

> if the tempo were maintained with metronomic precision, without considering the listener, the newly introduced motion would prevent his immediate understanding precisely because of the regularity of tempo. It is thus the listener who requires a comfortable moment's lingering in order to comprehend the change of rhythm. If this is not provided for him by the performer, his ear cannot simply adjust; he gets the impression that the performer is rushing. It follows that a performance in the strictest tempo does not seem thus to the listener; for psychological reasons, that which actually was metronomically perfect sounds hasty to him.[17]

What Schenker is saying might be expressed as a paradox: Reinecke is playing in strict time precisely because he is *not* playing in strict time. But what seems like a paradox today may have been a commonplace a century ago. In his contribution to the present volume, Matthew Butterfield cites an essay from 1900 in which Donald Francis Tovey made precisely Schenker's point that "a performance in the strictest tempo does not seem thus to the listener":[18] Tovey

---

[16] Schenker, *Art of Performance*, 54.

[17] Ibid., 59.

[18] Matthew Butterfield, "When Swing Doesn't Swing: Competing Conceptions of an Early

even provided a notation (Butterfield's Example 1) to show how uneven a scale that is played with perfect metronomic accuracy will seem to the listener. And he went on to argue that the artistry of Joseph Joachim—whose regular accompanist was none other than Reinecke—lay precisely in the deviations from metronomic accuracy through which he created the impression of "breadth and detail."[19] Butterfield also draws a parallel with a contemporaneous study of verse rhythm by Warner Brown, according to which—as Butterfield puts it, quoting Brown—"the feeling of rhythm in poetry . . . arises not out of durational equality between accented syllables, but rather 'out of a series of motor performances of alternate vigor and relaxation,' which produces 'the illusion of equality in time,' an equality 'not of time, but of kind, between the elements.'"[20] Here we have all the salient elements of Schenker's thinking: the "alternate vigor and relaxation" corresponds to Schenker's "pushing ahead/holding back," and the "equality . . . of kind" to time as a dimension of the musical content, with the result being an "illusion" of strict tempo.

However that does not explain the paradox away. One of Bruno Repp's many empirical studies of performance investigated how sensitive listeners were to the random prolongation of individual notes within otherwise isochronous eight-measure musical phrases.[21] He found that their sensitivity dipped markedly at those points where lengthening occurs in conventionally expressive performance: because they expected the prolongations, the listeners did not hear them. One might interpret Schenker's and Tovey's arguments about the illusion of metronomic performance in the same way and draw the apparently absurd conclusion that listeners will not be able to hear rubato except when controverts their expectations. But actually this conclusion is not as absurd as it sounds. A listener to Reinecke's roll for whom Larrocha represents the norm is bound to hear m. 49 as a crashing of gears. By contrast, a listener who is enculturated in this manner of performance may perceive the tempo change not directly but indirectly—in the form of sonorous depth, the "speaking" quality to which turn-of-the-century performers and theorists often referred, or emotional engagement. There is a parallel with the cinema, where the traditional criterion of quality is that music should be "unheard," perceived not directly but through the heightening of suspense or

Twentieth-Century Rhythmic Quality," in this volume, 264.

[19] Ibid., 265.

[20] Ibid., 267.

[21] Bruno H. Repp, "Probing the Cognitive Representation of Musical Time: Structural Constraints on the Perception of Timing Perturbations," *Cognition* 44/3 (1992), 241–81.

the deepening of character.[22] In that sense it might be said that one does *not* hear rubato, and when you have become used to Reinecke's playing—when you are listening for the constantly fluctuating content of the music rather than its tempo as such—the degree of jitter that shows up in tempo graphs of his playing can come as something of a shock. The music does not sound as it looks.

That may open up some possible answers to the contradiction between Reinecke in word and deed. Perhaps what sounds erratic and inexplicable to a typical modern listener—one for whom Larrocha's style represents the norm— may have sounded like a steady beat to progressive musicians of the late nineteenth century because they were hearing it in terms of kind rather than time, quality rather than quantity. But then again, perhaps what Reinecke's opponents were talking about was not his beat as such, but rather his reluctance to employ the kind of large-scale tempo articulation favored by conductors in the Wagnerian mold. Reinecke attacked performers who slowed down for the second subject in the first movement of Beethoven's "Waldstein" Sonata, on the grounds that Beethoven had already composed everything into the music ("any perceptible *ritardando*," he adds, "would be a pleonasm").[23] In that case it would be less a matter of the degree of tempo modification than of its nature or the structural level at which it takes place. But all this amounts to little more than informed speculation, and the reason is one of the fundamental problems of musical historiography. Written documents—whether scores or prose descriptions—sit on top of historically specific ways of hearing. They tell us about the effects that were perceived, not about the sounds and actions that elicited those perceptions. The result is that we project present-day ways of hearing into the past, and in this way turn documentary evidence of historical performance into a reflection of the assumptions with which we approach it.

THOSE WERE DIFFERENT TIMES

The paradox of Reinecke playing in strict time because he didn't play in strict time turns, of course, on the distinction between what Adorno refers to as chronometric and phenomenological time, and it is remarkable that in his writings the thinking that underlies Reinecke's and d'Albert's playing—recall his description of d'Albert as "still the greatest of all pianists"—survives into

---

[22] Claudia Gorbman, *Unheard Melodies: Narrative Film Music* (Bloomington: Indiana University Press, 1987).

[23] Carl Reinecke, *The Beethoven Piano Sonatas: Letters to a Lady*, trans. E. M. Trevenen Dawson (London: Augener, 1898), 65.

the 1960s. In his unfinished book *Towards a Theory of Musical Reproduction*, on which he worked during the 1940s and 50s, Adorno baldy states that tempo is "a function of the musical *content*," essentially Schenker's theory in a sound bite; again, his claim that "in a meaningful presentation of a work of thematic music, no two beats will even be chronometrically equal" could easily have come out of Malwine Brée's *The Groundwork of the Leschetizky Method*.[24] In a remarkable encounter between distant artistic worlds, Adorno was still insisting at the 1961 Darmstadt summer school that performance should embody phenomenological rather than chronometric time, and this lies behind his claim that—in the words of Lydia Goehr's summary—Stockhausen's "works are effectively reduced to singular or identically repeatable events. The performances leave or show no remainder in or of the works. From the works are thus removed the possibility (via the performances) of their dialectical undoing."[25] In contrast to phenomenological time—what Alfred Schütz called "inner" time[26]—chronometric time (Schütz's "outer" time) is figured with the negative connotations of administered society, the entertainment industry, and what Adorno condemns as "the dreadful streamline music-making of Toscanini, Wallenstein, Monteux, Horowitz, Heifetz."[27] Adorno's musical values, of course, derived in large part from his association with the Second Viennese School, within which the connotations of chronometricity take on a xenophobic and even racial tinge: "today's manner of performing classical music," Schoenberg wrote in 1948, "derives from the style of playing primitive dance music."[28]

The opposition between chronometric and phenomonological time in Adorno's writing, and outer and inner time in Schütz's, echoes the debates that were raging at the time when Reinecke was making his recordings—most

[24] Theodor W. Adorno, *Towards a Theory of Musical Reproduction*, ed. Henri Lonitz, trans. Wieland Hoban (Cambridge: Polity Press, 2006), 103 and 102; Malwine Brée, *The Groundwork of the Leschetizky Method: Issued with His Approval*, trans. T. Baker (New York: G. Schirmer, 1902).

[25] Lydia Goehr, "*Doppelbewegung*: The Musical Movement of Philosophy and the Philosophical Movement of Music," in *Sound Figures of Modernity: German Music and Philosophy*, ed. Jost Hermand and Gerhardt Richter (Madison: University of Wisconsin Press, 2006), 19–63: 53.

[26] Alfred Schütz, "Making Music Together: A Study in Social Relationship," in *Alfred Schütz: Collected Papers II. Studies in Social Theory*, ed. Arvid Broderson (Den Haag: Martinus Nijhoff, 1964), 159–78.

[27] Adorno, *Towards a Theory of Musical Reproduction*, 6.

[28] Arnold Schoenberg, *Style and Idea: Selected Writings of Arnold Schoenberg*, ed. Leonard Stein, trans. Leo Black (London: Faber & Faber, 1975), 320.

obviously through the writings of Henri Bergson, who insisted on the distinction between the "pure duration" or *durée réelle* that constituted subjective
experience and the measurable, spatialized time of commerce and science,
what is commonly called clock time. However, to call it that is to suggest that it
is a function of technology, straightforwardly mapping temporal change onto
mechanical motion. As Allen Bluedorn explains, this is wrong. The invention
of the escapement, which made the mechanical clock possible, occurred in the
thirteenth century, and in the longer term its effects were transformational:
Bluedorn cites Catherine Gourley's description of Henry Ford's assembly line
as "a giant moving timepiece."[29] But it had a social and linguistic prehistory.
The division of time into units such as hours, minutes, and seconds occurred
much earlier, and this is what prompted the attempts to measure them that
culminated in the escapement. It is to stress this sociocultural rather than
technological grounding that Bluedorn coins the term "fungible" time, "the
term *fungible* referring to things that are substitutable for each other without
restriction": any minute is the same as any other minute.[30] That is essentially
Adorno's complaint about Stockhausen, and music provides an excellent illustration of Bluedorn's point about the independence of chronometric time from
measuring technology. The idea that any crotchet or breve is the same as any
other became built into notation long before a practical device for measuring
them became available in the form of the metronome. And again the technology arguably had a transformational effect: summarizing George Barth,
John Rink refers to the "fundamental changes in musical time-keeping that
the invention of the metronome engendered—specifically, the "'equalization'
of time measure in music' . . . and the abandonment of the pulse of the body
as a guiding principle for one of machinelike regularity."[31]

Bluedorn goes on to remark that categorizations of time usually take the
form of binaries, as exemplified by Bergson, Schütz, and Adorno. In Bluedorn's terminology, fungible time is opposed to epochal or event-based time,
and the way he expresses this resonates with my opposition between music
in and *of* time: as he says, "the time is *in* the events; the events do not occur
in time . . . . When the time is in the event itself, the event defines the time."[32]
Victor Zuckerkandl, who was heavily influenced by Bergson, made a similar

[29] Cited in Allen C. Bluedorn, *The Human Organization of Time: Temporal Realities and
Experience* (Stanford: Stanford University Press, 2002), 12.

[30] Bluedorn, *The Human Organization of Time*, 27.

[31] See John S. Rink, Review of *The Pianist as Orator: Beethoven and the Transformation of
Keyboard Style* by George Barth, *Journal of American Musicological Society* 49 (1996), 157.

[32] Bluedorn, *The Human Organization of Time*, 31.

claim. He insisted that "Time in music is never a neutral background, an empty receptacle of extension:" rather, in Gary Ansdell's summary, "time is a core part of music's *content*. Music works *with* and *on* time, treating it as a force to be shaped and transformed."[33] But the closest analogues to the principle of density that I identified in Reinecke's playing come from psychologists. Paul Fraisse distantly evokes the piano pedagogues when he writes that "the greater the consonance, the easier the organisation of the limiting sounds and the shorter the interval will seem."[34] (The pedagogues put it the other way round: give more time to dissonances.) And this content-based approach to time received its fullest exposition from Robert Ornstein, whose book *On the Experience of Time* demolished older psychological models of multiple internal clocks and instead outlined what he called a "storage size" metaphor. Ornstein traced this approach back to a book published in 1890—at the height of Reinecke's career—by Jean-Marie Guyau, who "felt that time *itself* did not exist in the universe, but rather that time was produced by the events which occur 'in time.'"[35] The basic idea, which Ornstein proceeded to verify experimentally, is that experienced time is a function of information processed: greater complexity translates to the experience of longer duration. The suggestion then would be that through their mobile tempos, pianists like d'Albert and Reinecke allowed for the longer subjective durations entailed by complex musical situations such as those identified by the piano pedagogues. They built the non-linearity of the perceptual process into the stimulus. The result for the listener was the equality of kind rather than of time to which Brown referred.

The distinction between chronometric and phenomenological, or fungible and event-based, time has been invoked as the basis for a number of grand narratives that in effect wrap up changing cultural practices with changing temporal conceptions, in this way privileging time consciousness as the underlying explanation for a wide variety of cultural practices. One such narrative posits event-based time as a basic dimension of human experience, and sees it as having been progressively eroded or corrupted by the measured time of administered society: successive stages in this process might include the church bells of the feudal world, the clocks that conditioned early modernism, and the imposition at the end of the nineteenth century of world standard

---

[33] Victor Zuckerkandl, *The Sense of Music* (Princeton: Princeton University Press, 1959), 131; Gary Ansdell, *How Music Helps in Music Therapy and Everyday Life* (Farnham, U.K.: Ashgate, 2014), 277.

[34] Paul Fraisse, *The Psychology of Time*, trans. Jennifer Leith (London: Eyre & Spottiswoode, 1964), 131.

[35] Robert E. Ornstein, *On the Experience of Time* (Harmondsworth: Penguin Books, 1969), 37.

time. For Raymond Monelle, one of music's functions is to combat this: "Far from reflecting clock time," he writes, music is "devoted to recovering western man from the abyss of clock time."[36] And indeed music fits nicely into such a narrative of progressive standardization. Its story might be told, for example, in terms of the history of notation and the rise of conducting, music's version of the administered society. But it is the history of recorded music that best illustrates it.

The traces of an event-based time consciousness can be heard in the earliest recordings, in the playing not only of pianists like Reinecke and d'Albert but also of ensembles such as the Bohemian Quartet. Robert Philip writes that in their recording of Dvořák's "American" Quartet op. 96, "Each player is functioning as an individual. Each responds to the behaviour of the others, but there is little impression of pre-planned details. . . . They simply were not aiming for our modern notions of ensemble."[37] Rather than being a standardized grid, time is negotiated between the players, or as Bluedorn puts it, the event defines the time: it is rather like the social conception of time in Indian music advanced by Abhijeet Banerjee ("a human being reacts to the other human being, so the beat goes a little bit up and down").[38] According to Philip and many other commentators, the demand generated by recordings for a performance style that stands up to repeated hearings was a key factor in the development of modern notions not only of ensemble but also of musical timekeeping more generally, as illustrated by Larrocha's playing of K. 332: the basic framework of the performance is chronometric, and as I said, the few telling nuances do not disturb the sense of the music's smooth, even flow. Adorno's criticism of "perfect, immaculate performance" that "sounds like its own phonograph record" is just one of a succession of conservative critiques by Roland Barthes and Hans Keller, among others, and seen in this light the use of click tracks and snap-to-beat sound manipulation in today's studio-produced pop represents the triumph of fungible time in its most literal form. According to Philip, this transformation in time consciousness has turned the playing on the earliest recordings into "a lost language which is no longer quite

---

[36] Raymond Monelle, *The Sense of Music: Semiotic Essays* (Princeton: Princeton University Press, 2000), 94.

[37] Robert Philip, *Performing Music in the Age of Recording* (New Haven: Yale University Press, 2004), 120.

[38] Interviewed by Martin Clayton, in Clayton, "The Time of Music and the Time of History," in *The Cambridge History of World Music*, ed. Philip V. Bohlman (Cambridge: Cambridge University Press, 2013), 767–85: 782.

understood"[39]—a point he illustrates by reference to d'Albert, though Reinecke would have done at least as well.

But there is also an equal and opposite narrative, whose starting point is the imposition of world standard time. Driven by governments and the business community, as Stephen Kern explains, this "created greater uniformity of shared public time and in so doing triggered theorizing about a multiplicity of private times that may vary from moment to moment in the individual, from one individual to another according to personality, and among different groups as a function of social organization."[40] Thinking about time that was pioneered in philosophy by Bergson and in literature by Proust came to affect both material and performing arts, including music. Among recent literature reflecting this approach is Emma Adlard's study of how Debussy's music explores ideas of privacy and interiority in terms of both time and space, while Benedict Taylor's approach to cyclic form and memory in the music of Mendelssohn suggests that similar perspectives can lead to an understanding of aspects of earlier music that traditional analytical models have obscured.[41] In this narrative the twentieth century is associated with the development of an oppositional form of time consciousness—that is why I called this an equal and opposite narrative to that of progressive standardization—but the underlying valorization of subjective experience, and hence of event-based time, remains in place.

Both these narratives involve selecting ideas or practices that are overtly temporal and assembling them into a sequence. But there are also narratives that propose specific forms of time consciousness as the underlying explanation of phenomena that might not at first sight be considered temporal at all. For example, Jonathan Kramer, who posits a multiplicity of musical times that correspond to content, suggests that the breakdown of tonality in early twentieth-century music cannot be explained simply in harmonic terms, but was rather a response to new concepts of time.[42] In a similar way, but on a more expansive scale, Karol Berger attributes the complex of stylistic changes that

---

[39] Robert Philip, *Early Recordings and Musical Style: Changing Tastes in Instrumental Performance, 1900–1950* (Cambridge: Cambridge University Press, 1992), 69.

[40] Stephen Kern, *The Culture of Time and Space, 1880–1918* (Cambridge, Mass.: Harvard University Press, 2003), 33.

[41] Emma Adlard, "Interior Time: Debussy, *Fêtes galantes*, and the Salon of Marguerite de Saint-Marceaux," *Musical Quarterly* 96/2 (2013), 178–218; Benedict Taylor, "Cyclic Form, Time, and Memory in Mendelssohn's A-Minor Quartet, Op. 13," *Musical Quarterly* 93/1 (2010), 45–89.

[42] Jonathan Kramer, *The Time of Music: New Meanings, New Temporalities, New Listening Strategies* (New York: Schirmer Books, 1988).

distinguish the music of Bach from that of Mozart to the transition from a circular to a linear conception of time (in the words of his title, from Bach's circle
to Mozart's arrow), and identifies the same transition in painting, literature,
and theology—the transition, as he sees it, to modernity.[43] Even more expansive is Sigfried Giedion's contrast between the classical conception according
to which time and space were ontologically distinct and the modernist conception of space-time—a term that he borrows from the mathematician Hermann
Minkowski (who coined it in 1908), but applies to painting, architecture, and
city planning.[44] For Berger and Giedion a whole complex of cultural practices
are wrapped up into an integrated system that is grounded on a specific mode
of time consciousness, from which it follows that these practices will be mis-
interpreted if not approached accordingly. To that extent their basic position,
and the nature of their interpretive projects, resemble that of the *Annales* historians. Different concepts of time and space are treated as opposed mentalities,
mutually incomprehensible systems of knowledge and belief: in Kern's words,
"even the most seemingly universal foundations of experience as past, present,
and future may themselves vary culturally and historically."[45]

As a way of looking at music history, however, this is problematic. It is not
just that, as Martin Clayton argues, the conception of circular versus linear
time is politically compromised through the association of the former with
primitivism and the latter with colonial modernity.[46] There are much more
specific problems. John Butt and Bettina Varwig have both marshaled impres-
sive evidence to show how concepts of circular and linear time coexist in the
music of Bach:[47] Butt suggests that if circular time predominates in the St.
John Passion and linear time in the St. Matthew Passion, that is because of the
nature of the Gospels on which they are based. Nor was circular time simply
supplanted by linear time: as Adlard makes clear, the idea of circular musical
time is well established in the literature on Debussy, while for Zuckerkandl
the circle and the arrow are simply complementary musical principles found
across the classical concert repertory (he illustrates the circle from Schubert,

[43] Karol Berger, *Bach's Cycle, Mozart's Arrow: An Essay on the Origins of Musical Modernity*
(Berkeley and Los Angeles: University of California Press, 2007).

[44] Sigfried Giedion, *Space, Time and Architecture: The Growth of a New Tradition*, 5th edn.
(Cambridge, Mass: Harvard University Press, 1967).

[45] Kern, *The Culture of Time and Space*, xxiii.

[46] Clayton, "The Time of Music and the Time of History," 775.

[47] John Butt, *Bach's Dialogue with Modernity: Perspectives on the Passions* (Cambridge: Cambridge University Press, 2010), 109–10; Bettina Varwig, "Metaphors of Time and Modernity
in Bach," *Journal of Musicology* 29/2 (2012), 154–90.

and the arrow from Bach).[48] Open up the scope of such approaches beyond music, and Bach's circle and Mozart's arrow map perfectly onto Henri-Charles Puech's contrast between the time consciousness of the ancient Greek world and that of Christianity, not to mention Gerard van der Leeuw's more metaphysical categories of "primordial" and "final" time.[49] All this suggests that any straightforward attempt to locate the ideas of music *in* and *of* time—of fungible and event-based time—within a consistent historical narrative is going to break down sooner or later. In terms of performance I have been framing them within the contexts of the first and second halves of the twentieth century, as respectively represented by Reinecke and Larrocha, but the ideas pop up all over the place.

For example, Monelle's "lyric" and "progressive" time map readily onto the circle and the arrow, but for him—unlike Berger—Bach epitomizes progressive time; in contrast, Reinhold Brinkmann sees the French Revolution as prompting a new temporality that replaced the circular model of "form as architecture" by the arrow-like model of "form as process."[50] Then again, Stockhausen—whose music Adorno saw as governed by chronometric time—repeatedly invoked the idea of an "experiential time" that depended on musical content. In 1955 he wrote that when the content is surprising, time is experienced as passing faster, and so the musical process must be slowed down "if experiential time is to to pass at a constant speed."[51] (There is an echo of Schenker's paradox.) And seventeen years later he contrasted the "traditional concept . . . that things are in time" with "the new concept . . . that time is in the things," the "new" concept representing a reversion to what I have framed as early-twentieth-century thinking.[52] That is like Tristan Honsinger, the classically trained cellist and member of Misha Mengelberg's Instant Composers Pool, who told Floris Schuiling that "in working with Derek Bailey, I realized that *he is not filling time, he's making time.*" In other words, Bailey is

---

[48] Zuckerkandl, *The Sense of Music*, 84.

[49] Henri-Charles Puech, "Gnosis and Time" and Gerard van der Leeuw, "Primordial Time and Final Time," in *Man and Time: Papers from the Eranos Yearbooks*, ed. Joseph Campbell (New York: Bollingen, 1957), 38–84, 324–50.

[50] Monelle, *The Sense of Music*, 99; Reinhold Brinkmann, "In the Time(s) of the '*Eroica*'," in *Beethoven and His World*, ed. Scott Burnham and Michael Steinberg (Princeton: Princeton University Press, 2000), 1-26: 17.

[51] Karlheinz Stockhausen, "Structure and Experiential Time," *Die Reihe* [rev. English edn.] 2 (1959), 64–74: 68.

[52] Robert Maconie, *Stockhausen on Music: Lectures and Interviews* (London: Marion Boyars, 1989), 96.

working not with fungible but with event-based time.[53] But that, like Stockhausen's "new" concept, seems closely aligned with what the choral director and chant specialist Marcel Pérès refers to as "a mentality that treats time differently than we do in the West today": a qualitative time that emerges from the music—in Bluedorn's words, "the event defines the time"—and that cannot be mathematically divided. As Pérès explains, the modern, quantitative sense of time dates from the late thirteenth century, "but the older way of thinking about music co-existed as well."[54] Yet Leonard Meyer, writing in 1963, took a quite different view of how we treat time in the West today: in different genres and in different parts of the world, he claimed, avant-garde artists are jettisoning long established assumptions about the linearity and the teleology of time, and the consequences are profound: as Meyer put it (and the italics are his), "*The Renaissance is over.*"[55]

In the face of so chaotic a picture, the conclusion is obvious, and it applies whether we are talking about chronometric versus phenomenological time, fungible versus event-based time, or linear versus circular time. In each case, one conception or the other may predominate at any particular time or place: as Butt says, "Karol Berger's overall picture of Bach's music as essentially embracing the cyclic principle is undoubtedly correct in its broader historical context,"[56] while the general contrast between pianistic practice from the beginning and end of the twentieth century is self-evident. But that does not mean we are dealing with mutually exclusive mentalities poised in binary opposition. Giedion writes that from the Renaissance until the first decade of the twentieth century perspective "remained a constant element through all changes of style": during this period it "rooted itself so deeply in the human mind that no other form of perception could be imagined."[57] But with the development of cubism and the recovery of premodern art new ways of seeing developed, and we have learned to switch from one interpretive frame to another depending on circumstances. In the same way, hearing early recordings is not *really* like hearing a foreign language, as Philip suggested—or if it

[53] Floris Schuiling, "Animate Structures: The Compositions and Improvisations of the Instant Composers Pool Orchestra" (PhD dissertation, University of Cambridge, 2015), 170.

[54] Marcel Pérès, "A Different Sense of Time," in *Inside Early Music: Conversations with Early Performers*, ed. Bernard D. Sherman (Oxford: Oxford University Press, 1997), 25–42: 39–40.

[55] Leonard B. Meyer, "The End of the Renaissance? Notes on the Radical Empiricism of the Avant-Garde," *The Hudson Review* 16 (1963), 169–86: 186.

[56] Butt, *Bach's Dialogue with Modernity*, 109.

[57] Giedion, *Space, Time, and Architecture*, 435.

is, it is a language that can be acquired quite easily with experience, and that can coexist with other languages.

In short, rather than treating them as mentalities, it makes more sense to think of music being *in* and *of* time as alternative metaphors embedded in perception, and indeed they resemble metaphors in several critical respects: they co-exist within our perceptual apparatus; we can move from one to the other; they can be learned; and we generally become conscious of their operation only when there is a breakdown in communication. It also follows that the metaphors of music *in* and *of* time need not exhaust the available options: for any phenomenon, there is always one more metaphor that will fit it. The construals of music *in* and *of* time are simply two available options in the perception and conception of music.

HYBRID TIMES

The problem with metaphors is that they are too easily mistaken for reality. In a literal sense, it might be argued that in performance—or at least in the performance of mainstream repertory such as I have been discussing in this article—there is no such thing as music *in* time, that is, music in which time is a medium and nothing but a medium. It is not just that humans cannot play in strictly chronometrical time. As I mentioned above, there are traces of content-based time in Larrocha's playing, and the same is true even of the "Darmstadt School" pianists who became a byword for inflexible, objective performance. But to conclude from this that in music there is only event-based time would be to ride roughshod over the phenomenologically very real distinction between playing like Reinecke's, with its mobile, content-based tempo, and playing like Larrocha's, in which fungible time creates the framework within which momentary nuance is incorporated. The metaphors of music *in* and *of* time provide a framework within which we can think about this distinction.

But in music theory the issues of mistaking metaphor for reality run deeper than that. One of Hasty's starting points in *Meter as Rhythm* is the application to music of Bergson's critique of the spatialized time of commerce and science. Theorists have traditionally treated musical time on the model of Newtonian or "absolute" time, a variant of Bluedorn's fungible time in which—to borrow Newton's words, as Hasty does—temporal "Succession" is conceived as isomorphic with spatial "Situation."[58] As Hasty writes a few lines later, "Even though the concept of a mathematical 'flow' of time is not what we usually mean by rhythmic flow, the two are often implicitly conflated in

[58] Christopher F. Hasty, *Meter as Rhythm* (New York: Oxford University Press, 1997), 10.

music theory." It is the same situation that Bluedorn describes in everyday life, where "the distinction between fungible and epochal times has gotten lost or at least blurred to contemporary observers."[59] Bluedorn illustrates this through the idea of lunchtime, which in one sense is a fixed time of day and in another depends on when you get hungry, but people slip from one sense to the other without being aware of it. Through such conflation or elision of ideas, it is possible to combine contradictory beliefs: part of the professionalism of contemporary music performers lies in their ability to create chronometrically correct renditions of rhythmically complex scores, yet this may coexist with a contrary belief in the desirability of a rhythmic flexibility that reflects intuition rather than measurement. Such common-sense conceptual bricolage creates the flexibility to cope with different real-life situations but is clearly inimical to a music-theoretical project that defines itself in terms of conceptual consistency. This means that consistency comes at a cost. As Hasty writes in another publication, theorists have traditionally treated their symbols and concepts as "fixed things referring to a general and persisting state of affairs, as matters of fact," rather than as metaphors or signs that point to experiences that are both situated and transient.[60] And to do this is to "deny the validity of actual experience in all its variety."[61]

Bluedorn speaks of the tendency to see either fungible or event-based time as "the *real* time, or at least the preferred time, and to therefore see all phenomena as representatives of the preferred type or as a distortion of it."[62] That is the substance of Bergson's argument (though his characterization of pure duration as "*durée réelle*" only underlines Bluedorn's point). It is equally the substance of Hasty's. The notation-based concept of meter has distorted the representation of musical experience, just as in the analysis of performance it has given rise to the paradigm of isochronicity and deviation. In contrast, Hasty's concept of projection might be said to admit the possibility of fungibility in the sense of the perceptual salience of successive, temporally equivalent units, but only to the extent that it can be justified in terms of content and context—and even then, as Butterfield observes, projection may be based on equality of kind rather than of time.[63] In short, the metaphor of fungibility embodied in notation is recognized for what it is, and its transference to

---

[59] Bluedorn, *The Human Organization of Time*, 32.

[60] Christopher F. Hasty, "Learning in Time," *Visions of Research in Music Education* 20 (2012), 6. http://www-usr.rider.edu/~vrme/v20n1/visions/Hasty%20Bamberger.pdf, accessed 6.12.15.

[61] Hasty, "Learning in Time," 9.

[62] Bluedorn, *The Human Organization of Time*, 23.

[63] Butterfield, "When Swing Doesn't Swing," 267, fn. 36.

the domain of phenomenological time becomes not an assumption but the outcome of analytical demonstration. This is to say that, in contrast to the tendency to regard either fungible or event-based time as the *real* time, Hasty effectively explores how the two time concepts interact in music and in thinking about it. And here Bergson provides a useful model. This is not however the pure duration that he valorized: it is the spatial time that he denigrated as a "hybrid concept, resulting from the incursion of the idea of space into the domain of pure consciousness."[64] Music, as Derrida and De Man have taught us, is not a pure effusion of human consciousness. But neither is it the purely spatial construction that Dahlhaus came uncomfortably close to describing. It is, rather, an amalgam of fungible and event-based time, an amalgam whose nature varies from one culture, tradition, genre, style, or individual instance to another. In the remainder of this article, I make the point by briefly analyzing three examples of hybrid time.

The performances of K. 332 discussed thus far make the point. I described Larrocha's rendition as creating the sense of an object moving in time, and aspects of this include her treatment of parallel passages: except when a special effect is being made she treats them the same, as do other pianists of the post-war mainstream. The reason for this is self-evident when the music is conceived in terms of the metaphor of fungibility. When the exposition comes back, it is not just a reference to what came before but actually *the same* music in a different place, and so you play it the same. By contrast, Reinecke sometimes plays repeated material the same, but more often he does not. If you think of music in terms of event-based time, then there is no reason why you should play it the same, and several why you should not. While the reasons for Larrocha's interpretive decisions (such as her slight lengthening of the beat to heighten the leap in m. 2) are generally self-evident, many of Reinecke's, when considered in traditional analytical terms, seem quite arbitrary: why for example lengthen m. 14 and, in apparent compensation, abbreviate m. 15, and why for once does he choose to repeat these inflections when the material comes back? What sort of answers might these questions be looking for, and how could they also apply to those instances where Reinecke plays the repeat differently? Consistency is to be found in Reinecke's playing, to be sure, but it is at the level of overall stylistic character rather than that of the musical object.

As her treatment of m. 2 illustrates, Larrocha's playing is not literally chronometric. The point is rather that what I referred to as the telling quality of her nuances derives from the way in which they stand out against a fungible

---

[64] Quoted in van der Leeuw, "Primordial Time and Final Time," 325.

norm. In this way there is in her playing, and that of other modern performers, a memory of the older tradition of content-based playing: if the nuance in m. 2 reflects a leap, then elsewhere she allows a little extra space to accommodate a textural event (the spread chord of m. 25), or to give a particularly emotional note time to work (the G in the melody at m. 42). As compared to the constantly inflected performance style of the older pianists, the content-based dimension—the music *of* time—is now reduced to a succession of momentary intensifications or relaxations that are incorporated within the larger framework of music *in* time. With Reinecke the point can be made in reverse. I characterized his tempos as mobile, but—as with other players of his time—that does not mean that he could not play more or less metronomically when he considered the musical content to call for it: witness the *Sturm und Drang* passages (mm. 27–40 and 60–70) in the first movement of K. 332, which, though fast, are relatively even. One might think of fungible time in his performances being something like projection in Hasty's analyses, a quality that emerges in specific contexts but does not necessarily persist. Similarly, it is not that Reinecke's playing lacks equality but that it is most often an equality of kind rather than of time. Like fungible time for Larrocha, then, event-based time represents not a literal description but a normative metaphor or organizational framework for Reinecke and other musicians of his time—and as Butterfield's chapter demonstrates, it is this that such contemporaries as Tovey and Brown referred to as "swing."

Particularly interesting in this context is the suggestion by another of Butterfield's sources, William Morrison Patterson, that—as Butterfield paraphrases it—"the sense of swing is most active *in the absence of an isochronous pulse* provided from without, because only in such situations is the body itself drawn most explicitly into the process of timekeeping."[65] This is interesting for two reasons. First, the contrast Butterfield draws between this understanding of swing and that of present-day jazz theory, based on the "near-isochrony that is the norm of the underlying pulse of good jazz rhythm,"[66] suggests the same pattern that Hasty has critiqued: event-based time is assimilated into fungible time, with those parts that will not assimilate being assigned to the rag-bag category of deviations (Butterfield cites Charles Keil's "participatory discrepancies" in this context).[67] It also suggests a corresponding development in performance practice, with post-war classical performance and contemporaneous developments in jazz being equally representative of the modernism

[65] Butterfield, "When Swing Doesn't Swing," 272.
[66] Ibid.
[67] Ibid.

that Hasty's approach simultaneously resists and transcends. The point is made
by Paul Berliner's accounts of jazz musicians who practice with a metronome
and internalize the beat "as a series of evenly spaced points."[68] The second
reason is Patterson's emphasis on the body, an emphasis retained in jazz musicians' thinking even as it has been rationalized out of jazz theory. Fred Hersch
practically restated Patterson's claim when he told Paul Berliner, "In order
to swing, not just to approximate swing, the rhythm has to come from your
body."[69] Though it is not a point I will pursue in this chapter, it makes sense to
locate the ultimate source of Reinecke's swing in physical gesture: in the context of performance, better terms than phenomenological, epochal, or event-
based time might be bodily or gestural time. And the contortions into which
this forces music theorists and empirical musicologists prove David Sudnow's
point when he argues that "Mathematics can 'think' body time only by trans-
forming it into an abstracted object with points and measured distances and
measured clock intervals."[70] That is why, as I said, Reinecke's playing sounds
so much more straightforward than the tempo graphs look.

There is another aspect of modern mainstream performance that can also
be described as retaining a memory of pre-war performance practices, but in
a different way. Here we come to my second example of hybrid time. This is
the tradition of phrase arching, the widespread practice—especially in nineteenth-century piano music—of getting faster and louder while playing into
a phrase, and slower and softer while coming out of it. So familiar and taken
for granted is this practice that it has often been seen by pianists, critics, and
psychologists as a "natural" form of musicality: in a well-known study of the
phenomenon, Neil Todd not only asks why it sounds natural, but also proposes
an answer that revolves around the organs of the inner ear.[71] But as is so often
the case with music, what is perceived as natural is in reality historically constructed, and on the evidence of recordings of Chopin's mazurkas I have elsewhere suggested that the modern practice of phrase arching—where tempo
and dynamics are shaped in phase with one another and with the composed
phrasing—became fully established only in the aftermath of the Second World
War. A number of distinct stylistic features found in earlier performance now

[68] Paul F. Berliner, *Thinking in Jazz: The Infinite Art of Improvisation* (Chicago: University
of Chicago Press, 1994), 150.

[69] Berliner, *Thinking in Jazz*, 152.

[70] David Sudnow, *Talk's Body: A Meditation Between Two Keyboards* (New York: Alfred A.
Knopf, 1979), 117.

[71] Neil Todd, "The Dynamics of Dynamics: A Model of Musical Expression," *Journal of the
Acoustical Society of America* 91 (1992), 3540–50.

became synthesized into a coherent, one might say standardized, system.[72] I interpreted this in light of post-war modernism in other areas of culture. For example, phrase arching gives rise to a performance style that is streamlined (Adorno's word), that strips away ornament to reveal form in the same way as the architecture and interior design of the period. In the post-war context it represented a reaction against a now obsolete pianistic style that seemed as fussy and cluttered as Edwardian interiors.

But there is more to it, and this is where ideas of contrasting time enter the equation. Phrase arching also exemplified the same retreat from overt expression—from what was now seen as emotional self-indulgence—that was found across a wide range of cultural practices. It drew on the expressive codes associated with event-based time, the gestural quality that I identified in Reinecke's playing: it referenced the temporal and dynamic ebb and flow so characteristic of the earliest recorded pianists. But it reconstructed and rationalized these codes. Expression was relocated from the moment-to-moment surface to the architectonic level of compositional structure, and in this way transformed from something imposed by the performer—an expression of the performer's own personality—into the expression of the music itself. There was also a change in the relationship between performer and listener that might be linked to timing. The key to music's ability to build social interaction and community is entrainment, through which musicians adjust their timing to one another (that is how ensembles keep together), and through which listeners engage with music, and through music with one another. Entrainment depends on a regular series of time points or beats, with a range of approximately 0.2 to 2 seconds. Most experimental studies of entrainment have accordingly involved people tapping to precisely equal, mechanically generated pulses. But recent research indicates that entrainment is most effective when pulses are not absolutely regular: in Ian Cross's words, "we are biased towards entraining with 'pulse producers' that demonstrate a predisposition to entrain to us."[73] (Recall Banerjee's account of time emerging from the interactions between Indian musicians.) One might then speculate that the mobile and perhaps genuinely arbitrary timing of Reinecke and his contemporaries induced a kind of sociality in listening—a partnership between performer and listener—that was pushed into the background as the phrase-arching style spread, effacing the performer in favor of the listener's solitary communion with the artwork.

The post-war phrase arching style, then, is again organized primarily on

---

[72] Cook, *Beyond the Score*, chap. 6.

[73] Ian Cross, "Listening as Covert Performance," *Journal of the Royal Musical Association* 135 (2010), 67–77: 74–75.

fungible or chronometric principles, but incorporates elements of event-based time. As I suggested, it might be seen as referencing stylistic practices based on event-based time. Or one might see the gestural shaping of event-based time being transferred from the level of surface to that of underlying structure. But perhaps the best way to put it is in terms of Adorno's construal of time as "a function of the musical *content*": this principle applies to the post-war phrase arching style as much as it does to Reinecke and d'Albert, but with the crucial difference that content is now defined as—or reduced to—the abstract and standardized level of the musical phrase. Time is still bent, rather than flowing with the unachievable evenness of a perfect gramophone. But not by the local phenomena of melody, harmony, texture, or emotion. In an almost too perfect analogy with the very twentieth-century idea of relativity, time is instead bent by the gravitational force of a regularly articulated musical object.

My final example of hybrid time might in some ways be compared to Hasty's theorizing of time, in that it can equally well be seen as resisting or as transcending post-war modernism with its prioritizing of fungible time: in other words it might with equal justice be seen as a rehabilitation of the premodern or an expression of the postmodern. Here I return for the last time to the first movement of K. 332—only now not in the time warp of piano performance, but as played on the fortepiano. In reacting against the long line, the singing rather than speaking quality, and the cult of the merely beautiful they impute to mainstream performance, fortepianists—like other historically informed performers—have sought to return to the rhetorical values of eighteenth-century playing. I have already suggested that the attempt to reconstruct period styles on the basis of written documents, whether scores or prose descriptions, is a fundamentally problematical enterprise because such documents sit on top of historically specific ways of hearing. Although it seems to be little recognized by critics or even by fortepianists themselves, what they have reconstructed largely resembles the performance practices of the earliest recorded pianists. One might have guessed as much from the literature associated with those pianists. In his article "Abolish the Phrasing Slur," for example, Heinrich Schenker—that admirer of Reinecke and d'Albert—inveighed against the long line in very much the same way as have fortepianists such as Malcolm Bilson and Robert Levin;[74] in his 1911 papers Schenker repeatedly likens musical performance to speech and asserts that "a nonrhetorical performance . . . is

---

[74] Heinrich Schenker, "Abolish the Phrasing Slur," in *The Masterwork in Music: A Yearbook, Vol. 1 (1925)*, ed. William Drabkin, trans. Ian Bent et al. (Cambridge: Cambridge University Press, 1994), 20–30.

no performance at all";[75] while Harnoncourt's critique of the merely beautiful reproduces Adorno's and Kolisch's attack on the idea of "beautiful tone." This might seem remarkable given the association of Schenker and Adorno with the structuralist principles of "art" musical culture during the second half of the twentieth century, but only goes to show how deeply ideas of rhetoric are embedded within the foundational texts of structuralist music theory.

However, it is through actual performance that the point is best made, and Bart van Oort's 2005 recording of K. 332 (Media Example 3)[76] is a hybrid of the two broadly distinct forms of time consciousness on which I have based this article. I observed that today nobody plays K. 332 like Reinecke, but van Oort comes closer than most. As with Reinecke but not Larrocha, the immediate impression given by van Oort's playing is of a wealth of detail. Again as with Reinecke, this is largely created through flexible timing: in the first few measures van Oort allows a little more time for the leap of a sixth at m. 3, a little extra for the accented passing note at the beginning of m. 4, and a prolongation of the first beat of m. 8 to throw weight onto the trill on the second beat. It is not that he is introducing nuance into an essentially chronometric framework, like Larrocha only more so. At m. 42 he creates the same tiny space for reflection—or for the arpeggiation—as Larrocha did, but whereas in her case it was a single, isolated inflection, it is characteristic of van Oort that he integrates this within a larger gestural pattern. Measures 41–42 and 43–44 are grouped as two-measure, short-long phrases that highlight the melodic leap at m. 42 and the accented passing notes at m. 44, creating an effect a little like the swinging of a pendulum. That is the metaphor I used to characterize Riemann's playing during the *Sturm und Drang* section, and there is in van Oort's playing the same kind of mobile tempo as in Reinecke's, the same sense that tempo is controlled not from the beat but from the gesture, which is to say from the body. Indeed van Oort makes the hunt calls from m. 13 stand out through the simple expedient of playing this passage more or less metronomically, just as Reinecke did at the end of the *Sturm und Drang* section. Yet if all these aspects of van Oort's playing echo the approach to time of the earliest recorded pianists, there are also aspects in which he conforms to modernist values. Like Larrocha, he generally plays things the same way when they come back. That, in turn, can be linked to something deeper: as should be clear from my claims in this paragraph, there is almost always a reason for what he does, which can usually be located in the musical text. After all, Reinecke may have

---

[75] Schenker, *The Art of Performance*, 70.

[76] Accessible at http://global.oup.com/us/companion.websites/9780199357406/ch4/k332/a7.

studied under Mendelssohn, Schumann, and Liszt, but van Oort studied with Malcolm Bilson and is the holder of a DMA from Cornell.

Of my three examples, the last is the most thoroughgoing illustration of temporal hybridity: it is hard to say, and perhaps wrong-headed to ask, whether it is fungible or event-based time that predominates. Because van Oort's performance is dominated by mobile, gestural playing, one cannot really claim—as with the previous examples—that there is a controlling framework of chronometric time. It is rather that his free and colorful performance (to repeat Schenker's words) is disciplined by the values associated with music as object, and hence with the fungible time within which musical objects are located. It is simultaneously fungible and event-based, but in different ways. It brings together different, historically grounded traditions of time consciousness, and thereby gives them new meaning. Perhaps van Oort's playing might be described as Reinecke for twenty-first-century ears.

Musical Time, Embodied and Reflected

LAWRENCE M. ZBIKOWSKI

To SPEAK OF time, in any substantive way, is to court madness. And our purchase on the slippery concepts through which we would grasp time is, if anything, made less secure by differences among our phenomenal experiences of time. There is the present, the time we occupy, which we use to orient ourselves within the world and from which all our journeys through time depart. There is the future, a realm independent of our existence that we know only through inference. And there is the past, which exists for us in wholly subjective memory traces that nonetheless can, to the extent that they are shared with others or anchored in aide-mémoire, serve as a yardstick to measure time and so provide the means through which we can project the present into the future.

Things are hardly made easier by limiting oneself to musical time: restricting the domain only seems to multiply the problems of specification and definition, not least because music, especially as it is experienced through performance, is rarely complete in the moment but is instead a relentless stream within which present, future, and past swirl and bob like so much flotsam and jetsam. Yet I would like to suggest that the force of this experience—the sense of being immersed in an ongoing dynamic process—offers another way to think about time, a way focused less on the limitations of words and more on the resources of music. To paraphrase and re-purpose Augustine, time only becomes a problem when we start to speak about it.

As a way to begin the exploration of this perspective let me turn to a musical example drawn from a set of twelve arrangements of popular songs for classical guitar that Tōru Takemitsu completed in 1977. Example 1 gives the score for the first seven measures of the eleventh song from the set; some of the points I will make in the following pages will be clearer if the reader takes a moment to imagine or play the sequence of sounds captured by the notation.

*Example 1. Measures 1–8 of Song 11 from 12 Songs
for Guitar, arranged by Tōru Takemitsu*

The excerpt begins with a relatively static harmonic field—a quartal harmony on the downbeat of m. 1 that is quickly absorbed into an A-major harmony with an added sixth—over which a languid, predominantly descending melody unfolds. The A-major harmony is replaced, in m. 2, by a G♯-minor eleventh chord, then a C♯-dominant seventh, and then (in m. 3) an F♯-minor harmony, and over all this the melody reverses course, ascending stepwise to arrive on the concert G♯4 of m. 3 (creating a ninth above the bass that resolves to an octave on the second beat). Perhaps with this arch-shaped fragment or with the descending line of mm. 4–5 the name of the song will occur to the listener—"Yesterday," by John Lennon and Paul McCartney—an identification cemented by the melody of mm. 6–7: "Oh, I be-lieve in yes-ter-day." Assuming that this process of recognition has taken place, Takemitsu's arrangement will have drawn the listener away from a focus on the succession of musical events and toward a constellation of knowledge associated with Lennon and McCartney's tune, knowledge that might include the words of the song, memorable performances or recordings, anecdotes about the origins of the song (which, for a long period, existed only as a melody to which the words "scrambled eggs" had become affixed[1]), or random facts connected with the Beatles. Through focusing on such knowledge—knowledge summoned from the strands of memory, stretching to an indefinite extent through one's personal

---

[1] Walter Everett, *The Beatles as Musicians: The Quarry Men Through* Rubber Soul (Oxford: Oxford University Press, 2001), 300.

history—the listener will have stepped away from temporal experience as it is constructed by a succession of musical events and stepped into time as it is constructed by the words, thoughts, and ideas that populate our recollections.

It is, of course, possible that the listener will either fail to recognize Lennon and McCartney's tune or perhaps have no acquaintance with it. Although the latter state of affairs seems unlikely—"Yesterday" is one of the best-known songs of the late twentieth century—in either case the process of recollection I have just described would not take place or would be limited to correspondences between Takemitsu's arrangement and other music with which the listener was acquainted. The listener's musical experience would thus be more firmly guided by the succession of sounds captured by Example 1: the circle-of-fifths harmonic sequence and ascending melodic line of mm. 2–3, which pull the expectant gesture of m. 1 forward before pausing on $\hat{6}$ in m. 3; the continuation offered by m. 4, which takes up and reharmonizes $\hat{6}$ before leading the music toward an arrival on $\hat{3}$ in m. 5 (a contracting gesture that serves as a response to the expansion offered by mm. 2–3); and the completion of the phrase in mm. 6–7, a sequence that introduces longer note values, guides the melody past C♯4 to A3, and concludes with the falling fourth D3–A2 (a set of compositional strategies conventionally known as a plagal cadence). For a listener captured by Takemitsu's rendering of Lennon and McCartney's tune (and, as I have imagined, unaware of its words or history) the experience of time would be one that is molded almost exclusively by the succession of musical events.

Takemitsu's arrangement thus offers two ways to think about temporal experience as it is shaped by listening to (or imagining, or performing) music: on the one hand, that experience might be almost totally shaped by an ongoing sequence of musical events; on the other hand, it might begin with musical events but then shift to a process of recollection quite independent of those events. In the former case, the experience of time would be, of necessity, specific to our encounters with music; in the latter case, the experience of time would be similar to that engendered by a wide range of expressive media. We could also, however, imagine a species of temporal experience that is at first shaped predominantly by a sequence of musical events but then shifts to a focus on a prior moment in that sequence. To illustrate this possibility I would like to turn to another work by Takemitsu, the first movement of his 1987 composition *All in Twilight* (also for guitar), the score for which is given in Example 2. Again, I would encourage the reader to take a moment to imagine or play the sequence of sounds captured by the notation, acknowledging that the first movement of Takemitsu's *All in Twilight* presents a more formidable challenge to the aural imagination or performance than did the first seven measures of his arrangement of "Yesterday."

Example 2. *Tōru Takemitsu,* All in Twilight *(1987), first movement*

Most will find that their encounter with the musical events notated in Example 2 places them on unfamiliar terrain. Gone are harmonies and harmonic progressions shared by a wide range of Western music of the past two

Example 2, continued

hundred years, as well as anything resembling a regular rhythmic or melodic pattern. In their place is an incredibly varied musical surface, one in which fragmentary phrase follows fragmentary phrase, and in which dynamics, timbre, and pitch content are in a constant state of flux. That said, novelty is not the only principle through which the music is organized. For instance, in m. 29 Takemitsu initiates a reprise of musical events first encountered in m. 4;

indeed, mm. 30–43 are a literal reprise of mm. 5–18 (which, for the sake of convenience, I will call the A section). In addition to this out-and-out repetition Takemitsu makes use of partial returns of melodic fragments, sonorities, and gestures within the A section. Examples include the restatement of the melodic passage first heard in m. 7 an octave lower in m. 14; the return of the two-chord sequence of m. 4 in m. 13, a half step lower and without a specified timbral contrast; and the approximate recollection of the gesture of mm. 4–6 in mm. 10 and 11.

On the one hand, these restatements or recollections—whether exact or approximate—point to the ways Takemitsu organized his musical materials. On the other hand, each return has the potential to take the listener out of the flow of musical events to reflect on the larger course of those events: recognition that mm. 30–31 are an exact repetition of mm. 5–6 must come at the expense of devoting one's full attention to the ongoing process of musical events of which mm. 30–31 are a part. Although this interruption may not be as marked as that which follows from identifying Lennon and McCartney's "Yesterday" as the basis for Example 1—the focus of the listener to *All in Twilight* will, after all, remain largely within the domain of musical events—there will still be a moment when the guiding hand of music is stayed by the process of reflection. The first movement of Takemitsu's *All in Twilight* thus offers a third way to think about how temporal experience is shaped by listening to (or imagining, or performing) music: in addition to the possibilities I outlined previously (temporal experience as shaped by an ongoing sequence of musical events, or by a process of recollection independent of musical events), it may be that the ongoing sequence of musical events prompts us to reflect on that very sequence.[2]

In the following pages I explore further the idea that sequences of musical sound have the potential to shape temporal experience in ways that are different from those of language. This exploration will require forays into two topics that might at first seem distant from that of time: consciousness and memory. Understanding some of the key characteristics of consciousness is nonetheless necessary if we are to make sense of temporal experience, as experiences (in the full sense of the term) only come to us when we are conscious.[3]

---

[2] The ideas about temporal experience that I sketch here are similar to those John Rahn developed around the pair of terms "in-time/time-out"; see his "Aspects of Musical Explanation," *Perspectives of New Music* 17/2 (1979), 213–15.

[3] An argument could be made that dreams are a form of experience, but it must be acknowledged that dreams are generally not subject to the kind of rich perceptual input that marks our waking—and conscious—experiences.

Memory is among the cognitive capacities that are central to consciousness, not least because memory is one of the chief means by which we know we are conscious—indeed, the biologist Gerald Edelman's catch phrase for consciousness was "the remembered present."[4] And, as my opening comments suggest, memory is key for the sort of mental time travel that allows us to return to the past and to imagine the future.

It will not, of course, be possible to deal with topics as complex as consciousness or as involved as memory in any detail here, but in what follows I hope to show how our understanding of consciousness and memory can be specified for music. Such a specification can help to explain how sequences of musical sound can shape temporal experience in ways that are different from what is possible with other communicative media, something I shall explore in greater detail through a closer look at aspects of the first movement of Takemitsu's *All in Twilight*.

CONSCIOUSNESS AND MEMORY, MUSIC AND TIME

Consciousness

Let me begin with a slightly obscure but still useful distinction, between *awareness* and *consciousness*.[5] To be aware of something is, in some measure, to take note of it: for instance, you are presently to some extent aware that you are reading a chapter in a Festschrift for Christopher Hasty. Consciousness is quite closely affiliated with awareness—as unconsciousness is typically construed, were you unconscious, you would not be aware that there was a Festschrift for Christopher Hasty to be read, much less that you were reading a chapter from it—but complications quickly ensue. Had you started playing Julian Bream's 1992 recording *Nocturnal* (which includes his interpretation of Takemitsu's *All in Twilight*) and been lulled to sleep by his performance of the sixth movement of Benjamin Britten's *Nocturnal* ("Dreaming [Sognanti]"), some part of your cognitive faculties would continue to register the presence of music in the

---

[4] Gerald M. Edelman, *The Remembered Present: A Biological Theory of Consciousness* (New York: Basic Books, 1989). William James, working from a somewhat different perspective, similarly drew a close relationship between what he called elementary memory and consciousness; see James, *The Principles of Psychology* (New York: Henry Holt and Company, 1890), 646–47.

[5] Portions of the following replicate the approach to consciousness and memory that I took in "Music, Language, and Kinds of Consciousness," in *Music and Consciousness: Philosophical, Psychological, and Cultural Perspectives*, ed. David Clarke and Eric Clarke (Oxford: Oxford University Press, 2011), 179–92.

room. When, a little bit later, the last movement of Leo Brouwer's *Sonata para guitarra sola* got under way ("La toccata de Pasquini"), those same cognitive faculties could set up an alarm at this change in your proximate environment and stir you to wakefulness. You might then become aware that you had dozed off, conscious of a gap in your conscious experience. This points to a special kind of awareness—an awareness that we are aware—that is of the substance of consciousness as it is typically construed.

One of the marks of awareness is that it is under cognitive control.[6] In the case of the cognitive faculties that kept track of aspects of your environment while you dozed, these would not count as awareness for the simple reason that they are not subject to a control mechanism that could direct them elsewhere: you could not shift those faculties from keeping track of Bream's recording, to noting the surface and resistance of the chair in which you slumbered, and then go back to Bream's recording. Awareness, then, involves having various mental images derived from perceptual and prioprioceptual cognitive activity, and being able to in some fashion control which images are at the center of attention. (I should emphasize that "image" in this context is conceived quite broadly, and extends far beyond vision to include any sensory information.) Following the neuroscientist Antonio Damasio, who has written extensively on the issue of consciousness, I call the capacity for this sort of awareness *core consciousness*; the mark of such a capacity is a kind of phenomenological presence that is lacking from unconscious states. In addition to having the sort of awareness that is necessary for core consciousness humans also have the rather more remarkable capacity that they are aware *that* they are aware—that is, they have the capacity to reflect on their own thought processes, to realize that they *have* thought processes. Again following Damasio, I call the capacity to take thought as an object for awareness *extended consciousness*.[7]

One of the crucial cognitive supports for both core and extended

---

[6] Jesse J. Prinz, "Emotions, Embodiment, and Awareness," in *Emotion and Consciousness*, ed. Lisa Feldman Barrett, Paula M. Niedenthal, and Piotr Winkielman (New York: Guilford Press, 2005), 364. See also Endel Tulving, "Varieties of Consciousness and Levels of Awareness in Memory," in *Attention: Selection, Awareness, and Control. A Tribute to Donald Broadbent*, ed. Alan Baddeley and Lawrence Weiskrantz (Oxford: Clarendon Press, 1993), 283–99.

[7] Antonio R. Damasio, "Core Consciousness," in *The Feeling of What Happens: Body and Emotion in the Making of Consciousness* (New York: Harcourt Brace & Company, 1999), 82–106; idem, "Body, Brain, and Mind," in *Looking for Spinoza: Joy, Sorrow, and the Feeling Brain* (Orlando, Fla.: Harcourt Inc., 2003), 183–220. Gerald Edelman, in his extensive writing on consciousness, used the terms "primary consciousness" and "higher-order consciousness"; see Edelman, "Perceptual Experience and Consciousness," in *The Remembered Present*, 91–105; "Consciousness: The Remembered Present," in *Bright Air, Brilliant Fire: On the Matter of Mind* (New York: Basic Books, 1992), 111–23; and "Consciousness, Body, and

consciousness is memory, for it is memory that makes possible the retention of information that can be the focus of awareness. Equally important are a number of distinctive features of the memory systems of organisms endowed with consciousness, for these features shape the kinds of consciousness available to such organisms.

Memory

In what follows I shall sketch four important aspects of memory that connect directly with consciousness and that also inform our temporal experience. My purpose here, as with my discussion of consciousness, is not to provide a comprehensive account of an incredibly complex cognitive process but to draw out those features of the process that shape musical understanding.

Memory within biological organisms

Although it is sometimes convenient to think of memory as a kind of storage system, memories are actually highly dynamic cognitive constructs that are constrained by the biological mechanisms through which they are maintained. Put another way, every time we revisit a memory we change it slightly, strengthening certain of the synaptic connections proper to the memory, weakening others. One of the challenges faced by biological memory systems, then, is to develop means to stabilize memories while still allowing them to change as environmental circumstances change. In general, cultural practices—including those associated with music and language—offer our species an additional means to stabilize memories, a point to which I shall return in my concluding remarks.

Memory levels

For a number of years it has been common to distinguish between three different levels of memory, each with its own temporal frame and cognitive mechanisms.[8] The briefest of these, with a duration of perhaps two to three seconds, comprises various sensory memory systems that function as components of

Brain," in *Second Nature: Brain Science and Human Knowledge* (New Haven: Yale University Press, 2006), 12–22.

[8] A thorough discussion of memory levels within the context of musical listening is offered in Bob Snyder, *Music and Memory: An Introduction* (Cambridge, Massachusetts: MIT Press, 2001).

perceptual processing; there is fairly robust evidence, for instance, for a visual memory store often called iconic memory, and for an acoustic storage system that Ulric Neisser called echoic memory.[9] At the middle level of memory systems is what has come to be called working memory, which is understood to be a limited capacity temporary storage system that provides support for complex human thought.[10] Although specifying the limits of working memory capacity has generated lively discussions there is converging evidence that it extends to approximately four "chunks" of information (a span that could, for instance, accommodate the gesture comprised by mm. 4–6 of the first movement of Takemitsu's *All in Twilight*).[11] There are any number of situations where buffers like this are important, but one ready example is provided by the task of comprehending language, which often requires taking in a certain amount of information, evaluating it, and, subsequent to this process, figuring out what to do with it. The highest level of memory systems (in the sense of being the most comprehensive) is what is typically called long-term storage, although it should be kept in mind that "long-term" is a relative notion and refers chiefly to the sort of changes to synaptic connections that are the biological basis of memory. These kinds of memory are all, of course, intimately related to one another but also appear to involve different brain structures for their support.

Types of long-term memory

The third aspect of memory I wish to consider concerns a distinction made between types of long-term memory. The first type is semantic memory, which is thought to deal with general knowledge of the world not tied to any specific temporal frame. An individual might, for instance, know that Tōru Takemitsu was a Japanese composer of the later twentieth century without being able to specify how or when she came to acquire this knowledge. Episodic memory, by contrast, is connected to a specific temporal framework. Although that same individual might not be able to say when she acquired knowledge about

---

[9] Ulric Neisser, *Cognitive Psychology*, The Century Psychology Series (New York: Appleton-Century-Crofts, 1967).

[10] Alan Baddeley, *Working Memory, Thought, and Action*, Oxford Psychology Series, no. 45. (Oxford: Oxford University Press, 2007), 6–7.

[11] Recent considerations of working memory capacity include that offered in Nelson Cowan, "The Magical Number 4 in Short-Term Memory: A Reconsideration of Mental Storage Capacity," *Behavioral and Brain Sciences* 24/1 (2001), 87–185 and responses to that article. See also Cowan, *Working Memory Capacity*, Essays in Cognitive Psychology (New York: Psychology Press, 2005) and Baddeley, "Individual differences and working memory span" and "What limits working memory span?" in *Working Memory, Thought, and Action*, 175–210.

Takemitsu, she might be able to say with some assurance that her knowledge that Julian Bream recorded Takemitsu's *All in Twilight* was acquired in the course of reading a chapter in a Festschrift for Christopher Hasty while riding on a Metro-North train in early spring. As my example suggests, although episodic memory is oftentimes characterized in terms of being able to provide specific information—the *what, where,* and *when* of a given memory—this identification may be more or less approximate; far more important to the construal of episodic memory is the notion that the knowledge being recollected is associated with a personally experienced event.[12] Episodic memory is regarded by some researchers as providing the basis for mental time travel—that is, the ability to shift awareness from the present moment to a sequence of events in the past or to imagine a sequence of events in the future—a capacity that they have argued is unique to humans.[13] Others, however, have offered evidence that humans are not the only species to be able to imagine a future; were this to be the case it would suggest that language (which is often regarded as one of the key tools through which episodic memories are anchored) is not necessary for some forms of mental time travel.[14]

Memory: Basic systems

The final aspect of memory I would like to explore builds on recent work by the psychologist David Rubin and his colleagues, who have proposed that our model of human memory should reflect what is currently known about both brain and behavior. Rubin notes that one of the striking features of the mind and brain is that they are divided into networks of cognitive operations (or basic systems), "including separate systems for each of the senses, spatial imagery, language, emotion, narrative, and motor output. Each system has its

[12] Endel Tulving, *Elements of Episodic Memory*, Oxford Psychology Series, no. 2 (Oxford: Clarendon Press, 1983) and "Episodic Memory and Autonoesis: Uniquely Human?" in *The Missing Link in Cognition: Origins of Self-Reflective Consciousness*, ed. Herbert S. Terrace and Janet Metcalfe (Oxford: Oxford University Press, 2005), 3–56.

[13] Thomas Suddendorf and Michael C. Corballis, "Mental Time Travel and the Evolution of the Human Mind," *Genetic Social and General Psychology Monographs* 123/2 (1997), 133–67 and "The Evolution of Foresight: What is Mental Time Travel, and is it Unique to Humans?" *Behavioral and Brain Sciences* 30/3 (June 2007), 299–351.

[14] Nicola S. Clayton and Anthony Dickinson, "Mental Time Travel: Can Animals Recall the Past and Plan for the Future?" in *Encyclopedia of Animal Behavior*, ed. Michael D. Breed and Janice Moore (Amsterdam: Elsevier B.V., 2010), 438–42; William A. Roberts, "Evidence for Future Cognition in Animals," *Learning and Motivation* 43/4 (2012), 169–80; in the same issue of that journal, Madeline J. Eacott and Alexander Easton, "Remembering the Past and Thinking About the Future: Is It Really About Time?", 200–208.

own functions, neural substrate, processes, structures, kinds of schemata, and types of errors that have been studied individually."[15] Reflecting this, the model developed by Rubin and his colleagues assumes that each system has its own forms of memory, including subsystems for the storing of sensory information, for working memory, and for long-term memory. One of the results of this approach is a richer view of episodic memory: according to the model, each basic system comprises a separate network of behavioral properties, storage, and neural substrates, which interact to produce episodic memories. Episodic memories are thus constructed "not from a general, abstract, propositional cognitive structure of homogenized information, but rather from sensory, language, emotion, and other systems, each of which uses fundamentally different structures and processes for fundamentally different kinds of information."[16]

As a way to illustrate this perspective on memory Rubin invited his reader to consider six questions:

1. What is your name?
2. What is the color and shape of winter squash?
3. How many windows are there in your home?
4. Is the first note of your national anthem higher than, or lower than, or the same as the second?
5. Where is the letter "a" on your keyboard?
6. How do your feelings when you have a manuscript accepted differ from your feelings when you have a manuscript rejected?[17]

The first question, which requires the retrieval of linguistic information, evokes a paradigmatic memory task. Note, however, the recall process associated with the second question, which seems very different from the first, not the least because it involves tactile and visual information. Of a different sort is the third question—as Rubin notes, while there is a strong visual component to this question, to answer it many people will take an imaginary walk through their home as a way of taking inventory of the windows therein. The fourth question takes us some distance from the first and involves the sort of auditory information with which musicians are quite familiar. The fifth question typically activates motor skills, and many people will answer it by summoning

[15] David C. Rubin, "The Basic-Systems Model of Episodic Memory," *Perspectives on Psychological Science* 1/4 (2006), 277.

[16] Rubin, "The Basic-Systems Model of Episodic Memory," 278.

[17] Ibid., adapted.

an imaginary keyboard on which to enact the solution. The sixth question is of yet a different sort, and engages with a memory for emotion that can be as vivid as it is elusive.

The basic systems model set out by Rubin has two important consequences for our understanding of memory. First, the model pushes to the forefront the notion that long-term memory may include a wide range of information—including that associated with perceptual input, motor systems and the emotions—some of which is but inadequately captured by language. Second, the model suggests an important adjustment to the way episodic memory is construed, as the temporal index for a specific episode may be less important than the part the knowledge associated with that episode plays in the construction of personal identity.

Memory and consciousness

Although consciousness may appear to be a relatively stable cognitive phenomenon, what stability it has is a productive illusion created by cognitive processes designed to anchor and inform behavior. These processes include working memory, which provides a buffer for the evaluation of information from perceptual storage such that it can be integrated into existing knowledge before being transferred to long-term memory. Although consciousness, as an ongoing process, is procedurally occupied with operations that take place in working memory, the substance of thought—that is, the information secure enough that we might call it knowledge—typically involves long-term memory. Some of this information is of a general sort (and associated with semantic memory), some is fundamentally subjective (and associated with episodic memory). Although any absorptive recollection of information from long-term memory will at least temporarily draw us away from the present moment, there is broad agreement that episodic memory makes possible a kind of mental time travel: in focusing our awareness on impressions or experiences gathered by our former selves (or that we can imagine being acquired by our future selves) our consciousness shifts to a temporal frame only tangentially related to that of everyday life. Finally, the different kinds of memory that follow from the basic systems model proposed by Rubin and his colleagues suggests that there are conscious states that are quite different from one another—as different as remembering the color and shape of winter squash is from remembering the opening of the national anthem—and that some of these states may be captured only imperfectly by the resources for conceptualization offered by language.

Musical Memory, Musical Consciousness, Musical Time

In my work over the past couple of decades I have taken the position that
our understanding of music is shaped by cognitive capacities that are quite
general but that can nonetheless be recruited for the rather specialized task
of conceptualizing music.[18] Accordingly, I would propose that the features of
memory I have outlined are not only broadly manifested in human cognition
but—as illustrated by some of the examples I offered in my discussion—also
inform how we think of music. That said, the task of understanding music
may place rather special demands on human memory systems. For instance
(and with respect to the basic systems model offered by Rubin), while memory
systems connected to audition are clearly important for musical understanding, there is good evidence that systems connected with motor function and
emotions are equally important.[19] Put another way, musical practice, especially as a cultural phenomena, includes sounds, and kinesthetic experiences,
and the emotions associated with both. To the extent that memory processes
shape consciousness, then, conscious states that are structured by sequences
of musical events may be markedly different from those structured by other
communicative media.

I can expand on this last point by making recourse to some of my recent
work in which I have put forth distinctions between the basic functions of
language and music in human cultures.[20] Drawing on the work of the developmental psychologist Michael Tomasello, I have taken the position that the
basic function of language within human culture is to direct the attention of
another person to objects or concepts within a shared referential frame.[21] The

---

[18] The fullest statement of this position is provided in Zbikowski, *Conceptualizing Music:
Cognitive Structure, Theory, and Analysis*, AMS Studies in Music (Oxford: Oxford University
Press, 2002).

[19] I have discussed the role of motor function in musical understanding in Zbikowski,
"Music, Dance, and Meaning in the Early Nineteenth Century," *Journal of Musicological
Research* 31/2–3 (2012), 147–65 and "Music and Movement: A View from Cognitive Musicol-
ogy," in *Bewegungen zwischen Hören und Sehen: Denkbewegungen über Bewegungskünste*, ed.
Stephanie Schroedter (Würzburg: Königshausen & Neumann, 2012), 151–62. I have offered
my perspective on the way the emotions shape musical understanding in Zbikowski, "Music,
Emotion, Analysis," *Music Analysis* 29/1–3 (2011), 37–70.

[20] Zbikowski, "Dance Topoi, Sonic Analogues, and Musical Grammar: Communicating with
Music in the Eighteenth Century," in *Communication in Eighteenth Century Music*, ed. Kofi
Agawu and Danuta Mirka (New York: Cambridge University Press, 2008), 285–92.

[21] Michael Tomasello, "Linguistic Constructions and Event Cognition," in *The Cultural Origins of Human Cognition* (Cambridge, Mass.: Harvard University Press, 1999), 134–60.

basic function of music, by contrast, is to represent through patterned sound various dynamic processes that are important within human social interactions. Chief among these dynamic processes are the sequences of physiological and psychological events associated with the emotions, the spontaneous gestures that accompany speech, and the movements of bodies—including our own—through space. The patterned sound of music offers sonic analogs for these dynamic processes, and these analogs provide the basic components of musical grammar.

For an example of a sonic analog let me return once more to the opening of the first movement of Takemitsu's *All in Twilight*. In my initial discussion I noted that the gesture comprised by mm. 10 and 11 recalls, if imperfectly, the gesture of mm. 4–6. My use of the term "gesture" is, of course, purely metaphorical—performing the sweeping ascending passage of m. 5, for instance, requires hardly any movement of the guitarist's left-hand fingers—and yet the musical events of these passages do provide an apt sonic analog for the sequence of motor actions that make up a physical gesture.[22] Perhaps more importantly, sonic analogs such as these can also summon our own sense of making such gestures: our understanding of these passages is to some extent grounded in our embodied experience of making physical gestures.[23]

My broader proposal, then, is that language and music draw on different communicative resources to realize their functions within human cultures, and that these resources are supported by equally different memory systems. To the extent that consciousness is shaped by memory, the kind of consciousness that is created through language will be markedly different from the kind of consciousness that is created through music. And to the extent that different kinds of consciousness shape our experience of time, music and language will lead us toward different ways to experience time. Language is particularly good at capturing objects and relations, and so leads us toward places in time: a present that is coextensive with our interpersonal space, a future that is ahead of us, and a past that is behind us.[24] Language is less good at capturing the

---

[22] I discuss correlations between musical materials and physical movement in more detail in Zbikowski, "Musical Gesture and Musical Grammar: A Cognitive Approach," in *New Perspectives on Music and Gesture*, ed. Anthony Gritten and Elaine King, SEMPRE Studies in the Psychology of Music (Farnham, U.K.: Ashgate, 2011), 83–98.

[23] Zbikowski, "Music and Movement," 154–57.

[24] Rafael Núñez and Kensy Cooperrider, "The Tangle of Space and Time in Human Cognition," *Trends in Cognitive Sciences* 17/5 (2013), 220–29. It is worth noting that it is possible to characterize time in terms of space in other ways—among Aymara speakers in South America, for instance, the past is in front and the future is behind. For a discussion, see

phenomenal experience of an ongoing dynamic process. We can, of course, use language to *describe* an ongoing process, but if we really want to summon, say, the phenomenal experience associated with the descent of a falling body we typically resort to physical gestures or to sonic analogs of the sort that are regularly exploited by music.

I should hasten to add that the view I have sketched here leaves out much, not least because it gives the impression that the cultural practices associated with language and music are as simple and straightforward as the two-syllable words we use to conjure these practices. This would be wrong: both language and music involve a complex mosaic of cognitive and social skills, collocations that are anything but simple. That said, the view I have offered gives some sense why temporal experience that is shaped by listening to (or imagining, or performing) music is different from that created by other communicative media: music's sonic analogs provide representations of dynamic processes that can be correlated with physical movements and emotional processes, activating memories of embodied experience that shape consciousness in a distinctive and compelling way.

EMBODIED AND REFLECTED TIME IN THE FIRST MOVEMENT OF TAKEMITSU'S *ALL IN TWILIGHT*

As I observed in my initial comments, the first movement of Takemitsu's *All in Twilight* offers two distinct ways to think about how music shapes temporal experience: as shaped by an ongoing sequence of musical events (the sonic analogs of which would provide an opportunity for embodied immersion); and as shaped by a process of reflection prompted by that very sequence. Indeed, among the things I find striking about the movement are the range of opportunities it offers for both embodied immersion and (momentary) detached reflection. An example of this range is provided by mm. 4–6, which offer a holistic structure that could serve as a sonic analog for the dynamic process of a physical gesture. This potential is a consequence of the coordination of three features: (1) the passage begins and ends with two-chord sequences, in which the first chord is longer than the second, (2) there is a smooth continuity to the melody, which opens with a descending major third (E4–C4) and continues with a sequence of sixteenth notes that stretches from D3 up through E4 to arrive on the repeated G4s of m. 6, and (3) the passage ends

Rafael Núñez and Eve Sweetser, "With the Future Behind Them: Convergent Evidence from Aymara Language and Gesture in the Crosslinguistic Comparison of Spatial Construals of Time," *Cognitive Science* 30/3 (2006), 401–50.

with a kind of harmonic stasis in that the second chord of m. 6 is simply a revoiced version of the first chord. Together, these features provide analogical correlates for the preparation, stroke, and retraction typical of the spontaneous gestures that accompany speech.[25] I should also note that the sonic analog offered by mm. 4–6 could correlate equally well with the movements of a physical body through space or with a sequence of emotions. While all of these options would connect with embodied experience, the specifics of these connections—whether they involve physical movements we could make ourselves or emotional states we might experience—will of necessity be different.

As I noted earlier, the passage comprised by mm. 10–11 is very similar to that comprised by mm. 4–6 and indeed replicates a number of its distinctive features: it opens with a two-chord sequence, the melody begins with a descending major third followed by a rapid sequence of shorter note values that sweeps upwards, and the passage concludes with a sustained chord (here colored by harmonics). Were these similarities to be noted by a listener, mm. 10–11 could be heard as an approximate recollection of mm. 4–6; if we assume this recollection informs consciousness it could lead to the kind of mental time travel associated with episodic memory, although in this case the span traversed would only be a handful of seconds. It is of course also possible to imagine a listener who does not notice the similarities between the passages and who thus accepts mm. 10–11 as unique, and whose temporal experience is, at least at this point, not transformed through reflection.

A similar set of possibilities is offered by the restatement of the two-chord sequence of m. 4—a half step lower, and with its rhythmic and timbral character changed—in m. 13. The held chord is followed (as it was in m. 5) by an ascending passage in sixteenth notes that terminates in a sustained chord, but here the melody is borrowed from m. 7. On the one hand, Takemitsu arranges his material to call attention to the moment: it comes close on the heels of mm. 10–11 and begins, in m. 12, with what could be taken as a false start; on the other hand, the passage is different enough from those of mm. 4–6 and 10–11 (in its timbre, halting beginning, and conclusion on a recognizable diatonic chord) that it could be regarded less as a reference to the earlier passages and more as a distinct utterance.

The potential for hearing these passages as referring to one another (or as manifestations of some more general prototype) expands with the repetition of the A section in mm. 30–43. Although one could imagine an attentive listener

[25] David McNeill, *Hand and Mind: What Gestures Reveal About Thought* (Chicago: University of Chicago Press, 1992), 15.

coming to an appreciation of the importance of these passages (and the sonic analogs they offer) for the rhetoric of the movement, one could also imagine a listener becoming lost among the multiple statements. I would propose that each of these alternatives would have an influence on the listener's temporal experience: appreciating the importance of the passages to Takemitsu's larger design could lead to a more reflective (and less engaged) stance, but one that also affords an opportunity to view the whole from a point of remove; becoming lost could lead to a feeling of being guided only by the whim of the composer.

A somewhat different, and slightly more abstract, set of references is provided by the E-minor ninth chord first heard in m. 21. The chord appears near the beginning of what will ultimately serve as contrasting material (in that almost all of the material of mm. 20–28 is unique to those measures) and reappears in m. 44—now in shimmering, languidly unfolding harmonics—to interrupt the completion of the A section. The arpeggiated melody that results is then restated, an octave lower, in m. 46 and leads to the steady succession of sixteenth notes of mm. 47–54. The minor ninth harmony returns in m. 52 (where it is followed by the same angular pentatonic material used in m. 47) and then—transposed up a major third to create a G♯-minor ninth—appears again in mm. 54–55 and brings an end to the succession of sixteenth notes. Measures 56–58 then gather the threads lost when the A section was interrupted, only to have the E-minor ninth reappear—first in harmonics (replicating the voicing of the G♯-minor ninth in m. 55), then voiced low in the guitar's tessitura—to conclude the movement. This concluding passage brings into prominence a passing detail of the end of the A section that goes almost unremarked the first time—the incomplete C-minor ninth chord at the end of m. 18 (lacking a seventh) leading to the sustained chord of m. 19—whose restatement in m. 43 is interrupted by the E-minor ninth of m. 44 and which is then recovered in m. 56.

What unites these events is not similarity of pitch contour or rhythmic figuration but their belonging to the same class of sonorities ("minor-ninth chord"). The basis for similarity among these events is thus markedly different from that which might apply to the passages comprised by mm. 4–6, 10–11, or 13–15, for what is relevant is the intervallic content of the events rather than the way that content is activated through the disposition of its constituent pitch classes in register and time. Put another way, the sonic analogs that comprise the different statements of minor-ninth chords over the course of the movement are quite various. This variety would seem to indicate that the identification of the sonorities as members of the same class is more a product of detached reflection than embodied immersion, and yet the intervallic resources shared by these sonorities suggest that the sonic analogs produced from them would belong to a common topography. The effect is more marked with the pentatonic material first heard in m. 47, which returns (with the same pitch-class content) in different guises in mm. 50–51 and 53: although the uniformity of this material owes something to the pattern of quasi-arpeggiated sixteenth notes over a sustained bass note shared across these instances, there is also a sense that each iteration is an exploration of a common harmonic topography. In both cases, the focus on this topography at the expense of its activation through sequences of pitches would tend to attenuate engagement with sonic analogs, but it would also provide a spatial correlate for those analogs—a kind of "where" that could inform the recollection of musical events.

A set of relationships more abstract still circulates around the sonority that concludes the introductory material set out in mm. 1–3. The pitches sustained into m. 3 create an [0257]-type tetrachord, a collection that becomes a touchstone for the movement as a whole. Table 1 gathers the more prominent instances of this tetrachord, indicating the measures in which they occur, the pitch-class content of the sonority, and the transposition level relative to the first instance. What is immediately evident on surveying the pitch-class content of these instances as well as their realization over the course of the movement is their diversity: Takemitsu insures that each instance has a distinctive character such that they sound as individuals even when juxtaposed with one another (as they are in mm. 16–18/41–43). (One exception is provided by the arpeggiated instances that occur in mm. 26 and 28, which are identical save that the latter is a T_2 version of the former. I would propose that the sonorities here are part of a compositional strategy analogous to that of a semi-cadence that plays out over the course of mm. 25–28. Indeed, [0257]-type tetrachords participate in similar quasi-cadential strategies in mm. 16–19 and—interrupted by the contrasting material of mm. 44–55—mm. 41–43 and 56–58.) It must be admitted that, while these diverse instances of [0257]-type tetrachords are touchstones, they are of a rather ephemeral sort, emerging from the cloud of sonorities that make up the movement only to disappear once again. That said, few other sonorities within this cloud replicate the intervallic content that distinguishes this tetrachord (save for the pentatonic collections of mm. 47–53), which suggests that instances of the tetrachord could provide a kind of topographical marker—perhaps known through reflection, but perhaps simply felt as an essential constituent of the sound world created by Takemitsu—within the overall landscape of the movement.

*Table 1: Instances of [0257]-type tetrachords in the first
movement of Tōru Takemitu's* All in Twilight

Measure	Pitch Classes	Transposition
3	(1,3,6,8)	T0
7–8 / 32–33	(4,6,9,11)	T3
10 / 35	(2,4,7,9)	T1
16 / 41	(6,8,11,1)	T5
17 / 42 / 56	(9,11,2,4)	T8
18 / 43	(6,8,11,1)	T5
19 / 57–58	(0,2,5,7)	T11
26	(9,11,2,4)	T8
28	(7,9,0,2)	T6

Again, the range of opportunities for embodied immersion or detached reflection offered by the first movement of Takemitu's *All in Twilight* is striking. This range is due in part to the novelty of the musical events comprised by the work—at times it is all we can do to hang on to the current sequence of events, never mind relating that sequence to others—but it is also due to the compositional strategies Takemitu employs. These include his practice of presenting the listener with passages that might or might not sound quite similar to ones heard a moment or two before, a practice in evidence both within the A section and in the reprise of the A section. It is good to keep in mind that, while it is easy enough to see this reprise on the printed page, most listeners would not have access to visual aids of this sort. In consequence, the similarity of passages both within and across the A sections complicates the listener's identification of individual passages: is what I am hearing now the same thing I heard earlier, is it an oblique reference to what I heard, or is it something entirely different?

I have, of course, proposed that the contrast between embodied immersion and detached reflection is linked to a contrast in conscious states, and thus to a contrast in temporal experience. Temporal experience, as it is shaped by music, is of necessity multiple rather than unitary, and conditioned in part by resources for communication—sonic analogs for dynamic processes—uniquely exploited by music. That said, reflection on certain aspects of musical events, such as the similarity of one sonority to another, may lead to a regard of musical materials that approaches the classificatory systems facilitated by language. Such a regard is certainly not to be disparaged—it is, after all, one of the strengths and pleasures of the systematic perspectives on musical organization that distinguish work in music theory—but it is one that of necessity stands apart from the work of music and from an embodied immersion in sequences of musical events.

MUSICAL TIME, EMBODIED AND REFLECTED

My focus in this chapter has been on humans' experience of time, and on ways music shapes that experience. There are, of course, other ways to approach the topic of time that leave humans more or less completely out of the picture—the inquiries of the physicist or cosmologist must set aside humans' blinkered view of time if they are to make any progress—but such perspectives are of limited application to human cultural practices such as those that give rise to music, practices that only exist within and for human experience.

As I have tried to show here, human experience is shaped by the resources of human consciousness, and consciousness is shaped by cognitive processes related to memory. The memories of humans are also shaped by cultural practices, through which groups of humans structure and stabilize knowledge that is important to their societies.[26] I should emphasize that "knowledge" here extends beyond those concepts that can be captured through language to patterns of physical movement and to privileged emotional states. The representation of such movements and states is one of the functions of the sonic analogs that I have proposed are basic to musical grammar, and that in turn shape our experience of time.

As I endeavored to illustrate through my analysis of aspects of the first movement of Takemitsu's *All in Twilight*, our reception of a musical work can range from embodied immersion in its constituent sonic analogs to reflection on the materials comprised by those analogs, with both shaping our temporal experience of the work. And, returning to Takemitsu's arrangement of Lennon and McCartney's "Yesterday," our reception may also be informed by knowledge or events that are only tangentially related to the musical work, excursions into which can further shape our experience of time.

Perhaps it is madness to attempt to speak of time—to attempt to capture that which provides the metric for every dynamic process and is thus the essence of such processes—and yet, linguistic beings that we are, speak we will. Nonetheless, we are also beings that have developed other means to communicate about our experience of the world, means that include painting,

---

[26] The relationships between cultural practices and memory is given careful consideration in Paul Connerton's *How Societies Remember* (Cambridge: Cambridge University Press, 1989).

sculpture, dance, and music. Through such media we may add to and enrich our experience of the world, and also find a slightly more secure grasp on those elusive things that add both mystery and meaning to human life.

Ethnomusicologists and
Questions of Temporality

STEPHEN BLUM

REFLECTING ON HOW the three nouns in the subtitle of this volume—phenomenology, perception, performance—relate to the musical scholarship of the past century, we may remember complaints that perception and performance were not receiving the scholarly attention that their centrality in musical experience demands. Only two decades ago, Regula Qureshi described "the place of performance in the study of music and time" as "conspicuous more by its absence."[1] A history of the engagement of music scholars with phenomenology, a term whose highly variable usage was already noted by Ernst Kurth in his *Musikpsychologie* of 1931,[2] might prove a more rewarding inquiry than a reckoning with the neglect of perception and performance through most of the twentieth century, a situation that, happily, no longer obtains.

Besides examining explicit responses, positive and negative, of music scholars to arguments of phenomenologists, such a history might also probe affinities in method like those some scholars have posited, and others have questioned. Examples are Leslie Blasius's comparison of "descriptive protocol" in Husserl, Freud, and Schenker,[3] Nicholas Cook's comment on Schenkerian

---

[1] Regula Burckhardt Qureshi, "Exploring Time Cross-Culturally: Ideology and Performance of Time in the Sufi *Qawwālī*," *Journal of Musicology* 12/4 (1994), 498.

[2] Ernst Kurth, *Musikpsychologie* (Berlin: Max Hesse, 1931), 54 n. 2.

[3] Leslie Blasius, *Schenker's Argument and the Claims of Music Theory* (Cambridge: Cambridge University Press, 1996), 35.

reduction in relation to Husserl's *epoché*,[4] and Cook's observation that "Schenker's thought comes close to Husserl's" in positing a "covert retention, by the ear, of the consonant point of departure" when we hear a dissonance.[5]

Those who undertake histories of musical scholarship in relation to phemomenology will need to discuss at some length the work of Christopher Hasty and that of his distinguished predecessor at Harvard, David Lewin. In the final section of his 1986 essay on "Music Theory, Phenomenology, and Modes of Perception," Lewin interrogates "an assumption that music theories are, or should be, fundamentally perceptual in nature or purpose," adhering to "a paradigm in which a 'listener' X is 'perceiving' some music Y that is demonstrably other-than-X." He found that this "X/Y paradigm . . . fits very poorly with the present-tense activities of composers and performers," even if it "can accommodate without undue strain the apparatus of Husserl's phenomenology."[6] Lewin presumably regarded perceiving as but one of the present-tense activities of composers and performers, and his wording leaves open the possibility that other paradigms might likewise "accommodate without undue strain the apparatus of Husserl's phenomenology."

Ethnomusicologists have no choice but to agree with Lewin that music theory should not be limited to works conceived within a Y-is-other-than-X paradigm, if only because the theorizing of the musicians we study addresses relationships of other types, such as *As performers of Y, we may become X;*[7] *The path we follow in this performance genre is defined by coordinates x and y,* where the coordinates may refer to movement in time *and* in space; or *X is now engaged with Y in performing, or preparing to perform, Z,* where Z refers to a composition, a genre, or some other mode of performance with which X

[4] Nicholas Cook, "Epistemologies of Music Theory," in *The Cambridge History of Western Music Theory*, ed. Thomas Christensen (Cambridge: Cambridge University Press, 2002), 96.

[5] Nicholas Cook, *The Schenker Project: Culture, Race, and Music Theory in Fin-de-siècle Vienna* (Oxford: Oxford University Press, 2007), 282–83. John Rothgeb's and Jürgen Thym's translation might be more suggestive of Husserl than the original. Compare "ein seltsamer Einschlag von Vorgestelltem: er besteht in der geheimnisvoll wirkenden Erinnerung an den konsonanten Ausgangspunkt" (Heinrich Schenker, *Kontrapunkt*, 2: *Drei- und mehrstimmiger Satz. Übergang zum freien Satz* [Vienna: Universal Edition, 1922], 59) with "a curious intrusion of the imaginary: it consists in the covert retention, by the ear, of the consonant point of departure" (Schenker, *Counterpoint*, vol. 2 [New York: Schirmer, 1987], 57).

[6] David Lewin, "Music Theory, Phenomenology, and Modes of Perception," *Music Perception* 3/4 (1986), 375; repr. in Lewin, *Studies in Music with Text* (Oxford: Oxford University Press, 2006), 94.

[7] For examples of this format see Stephen Blum, "Modes of Theorizing in Iranian Khorasan," in *Theorizing the Local: Music, Practice, and Experience in South Asia and Beyond*, ed. Richard K. Wolf (Oxford: Oxford University Press, 2009), 219.

and Y are familiar. That type of relationship was addressed by the sociologist Alfred Schütz (1899–1959) in his classic essay of 1951, "Making Music Together," one of many writings in which Schütz treated Husserl's phenomenology in relation to Max Weber's theory of social action.[8] A major sociologist of the generation preceding that of Schütz, Maurice Halbwachs (1877–1945), likewise found it necessary to confront the thought of Husserl's exact contemporary, Henri Bergson, with that of Émile Durkheim. Although Halbwachs's 1939 essay on "The collective memory of musicians" (included in the unfinished book on collective memory published five years after his death in Buchenwald) treats the collective memory of musicians as dependent on notation, it is not difficult to imagine alternative sources of support, as Simha Arom has done in a short article on "Collective Memory in the Traditional Musics of Central Africa."[9]

American ethnomusicologists with an interest in phenomenology like- wise make reference to larger configurations of social theory, citing Schütz more often than Halbwachs. Harris M. Berger's phrase "the practice of percep- tion" acknowledges his interest in the practice theory of Pierre Bourdieu and Anthony Giddens alongside Husserl's writings on internal time-consciousness and Merleau-Ponty's 1945 *Phenomenology of Perception*.[10] Berger maintains that "the fundamental insights of [phenomenology] have not yet been fully absorbed" by ethnomusicologists.[11] A more sustained engagement of music theorists with phenomenology is suggested by Judy Lochhead's observation that "the music theoretical focus on musical experience and cognition through the lens of Continental philosophy has had a significant impact on who writes theory."[12]

[8] Alfred Schütz, "Making Music Together: A Study in Social Relationship," *Social Research* 18/1 (1951), 76–97; repr. in Schütz, *Collected Papers, 2: Studies in Social Theory* (The Hague: Nijhoff, 1964), 159–78.

[9] Maurice Halbwachs, "La mémoire collective chez les musiciens," *Revue philosophique de la France et de l'Étranger* 127/3–4 (1939), 136–65; repr. in Halbwachs, *La mémoire collective: Édition critique*, ed. Gérard Namer (Paris: Albin Michel, 1997), 19–50; Simha Arom, "La 'mémoire collective' dans les musiques traditionnelles d'Afrique Centrale," *Revue de Musicologie* 76 (1990), 149–62.

[10] Harris M. Berger, "The Practice of Perception: Multi-functionality and Time in the Musi- cal Experiences of a Heavy Metal Drummer," *Ethnomusicology* 41/3 (1997), 464–88; *Metal, Rock, and Jazz: Perception and the Phenomenology of Musical Experience* (Hanover: Uni- versity Press of New England for Wesleyan University Press, 1999), 200–48; *Stance: Ideas about Emotion, Style, and Meaning for the Study of Expressive Culture* (Middletown, Conn.: Wesleyan University Press), 6.

[11] Berger, "Theory and Practice 8: Contemporary Ethnomusicology in Theory and Practice," *Society for Ethnomusicology Newsletter* 47/4 (2013), 5.

[12] Judy Lochhead, "Music Theory and Philosophy," in *The Routledge Companion to Philoso- phy and Music*, ed. Theodore Gracyk and Andrew Kania (New York: Routledge, 2011), 514.

My own interest in phenomenology stems from a desire for histories of musical scholarship that would avoid temptations to advertise progress, or deplore decline, or chronicle a succession of paradigms, each said to have reigned for a limited time. The field of inquiry that began to be known as ethnomusicology in the 1950s drew upon several existing areas of research, among them musical folklore, musical ethnography, social and cultural anthropology, and comparative musicology. In the writing of the founding fathers of comparative musicology, Carl Stumpf (1848–1936) and E. M. von Hornbostel (1877–1935), we can recognize the language and concerns of the philosophers and psychologists who are now identified as phenomenologists. Stumpf, like Husserl (1859–1938), was a student of the philosopher and psychologist Franz Brentano (1838–1917). After Stumpf was called to the chair of philosophy at Halle in the mid-1880s, he accepted Husserl as a student on Brentano's recommendation and later appointed him *Dozent*.[13] In his *Vorlesungen zur Phänomenologie des inneren Zeitbewusstseins*, first published in 1928, Husserl acknowledged a passage in Stumpf's *Tonpsychologie* as one means of access to Brentano's unpublished ideas on the subject.[14] The 1928 publication, presented as "lectures from the year 1905" with additions from the next five years, is in fact a composite made in 1917 by Edith Stein from texts written as early as 1893, though largely in the first decade of the twentieth century.[15]

More than one passage in Husserl's *Vorlesungen* resonates, to a degree, with passages on *Aufmerksamkeit* ("attentiveness") in Hornbostel's publications of the first years of the past century, such as a 1905 lecture on "The problems of comparative musicology" offered to the Vienna chapter of the

[13] Edwin G. Boring, *A History of Experimental Psychology*, 2nd edn. (New York: Appleton-Century-Crofts, 1950), 365.

[14] Edmund Husserl, *Vorlesungen zur Phänomenologie des inneren Zeitbewusstseins*, ed. Martin Heidegger, vol. 9 of *Jahrbuch für Philosophie und Phänomenologische Forschung* (Halle: Max Niemeyer Verlag, 1928), 367–496; repr. in *Husserliana*, vol. 10 (1966), which includes additional texts written between 1893 and 1917. The full translation of the texts in *Husserliana* 10 by John Brough (*On the Phenomenology of the Consciousness of Internal Time (1893–1917)* [Boston: Kluwer Academic Press, 1991]) is more accurate than James Churchill's translation of the 1928 publication (*The Phenomenology of Internal Time-consciousness* [Bloomington: Indiana University Press, 1964]). Stumpf remarked that Brentano, in his lectures, had been the first to describe "eine inhaltliche Veränderung der Vorstellung," which in Stumpf's summary involved "die Vorstellung der bereits vergangenen zeitlichen Empfindungsstrecke als einer vergangenen, mit diesem Merkmal behafteten, sodass der Eindruck, während er im Bewusstsein erhalten bleibt, zugleich eine immer grössere zeitliche Ausdehnung gewinnt" (Carl Stumpf, *Tonpsychologie*, vol. 2 [Leipzig: S. Hirzel, 1890], 277).

[15] Rudolf Boehm, "Einleitung des Herausgebers," *Husserliana* 10 (1966), xix–xxiii.

International Musical Society.[16] Speaking of a tone as a "hyletic datum," Husserl remarked that "Ich kann die Aufmerksamkeit auf die Weise seines Gegebenseins richten. Er und die Dauer, die er erfüllt, sind in einer Kontinuität von 'Weisen' bewusst, in einem 'beständigen Flusse.'"[17] I read Husserl's *Weisen* "modes" as a term that can accommodate whatever changes may be "given" from a tone's beginning through its decay, or until a new beginning. Husserl's *Zeitpunkte* ("time-points") are not durationless instants; each "actual now-point" is "somehow or other continually filled": "die abgelaufene Dauer sich vom aktuellen Jetztpunkt, der immerfort ein irgendwie erfüllter ist, entferne, in immer 'fernere' Vergangenheit rücke."[18] After 1917, the year when Edith Stein stitched together the texts that became the 1928 publication, Husserl no longer used the term *aktuellen Jetztpunkt*,[19] a change which is compatible with Hasty's suggestion "that now might be regarded as a continually changing perspective on becoming."[20] Eugene Montague speaks accordingly of "gestures, interacting through retention and protention."[21] Interaction of retention and protention can be understood as a general category that includes such carefully defined relations as that between Hasty's *projected duration* and *projective potential.*[22]

Remembering Lewin's appropriate concern with "present-tense activities of composers and performers," we can easily enough understand the "actual now-points" of Husserl's early texts, Hasty's "continuous durational quantity that begins and ends,"[23] or Montague's "interactions of retention and protention" as continually filled with many kinds of action and preparation

---

[16] E. M. vom Hornbostel, "Die Probleme der vergleichenden Musikwissenschaft," *Zeitschrift der Internationalen Musikgesellschaft* 7 vol. 3 (1905), 85–97; repr. in *Hornbostel Opera Omnia* 1 (The Hague: Martinus Nijhoff, 1975), 247–70.

[17] Husserl, *Vorlesungen*, 385. In Brough's translation (25), "I can direct my attention to the way in which it is given. I am conscious of the tone and of the duration it fills in a continuity of 'modes,' in a 'continual flow.'"

[18] Ibid., 387. In Brough's translation (27), "that the elapsed duration moves away from the actually present now-point, which is constantly filled in some way, and recedes into the ever more 'distant' past."

[19] Lanei Rodemeyer, "Developments in the Theory of Time-Consciousness: An Analysis of Protention," in *The New Husserl*, ed. Donn Welton (Bloomington: Indiana University Press, 2003), 128.

[20] Christopher F. Hasty, *Meter as Rhythm* (Oxford: Oxford University Press, 1997), 76.

[21] Eugene Montague, "Phenomenology and the 'Hard Problem' of Consciousness and Music," in *Music and Consciousness: Philosophical, Psychological, and Cultural Perspectives*, ed. David Clarke and Eric Clarke (Oxford: Oxford University Press, 2011), 38.

[22] Hasty, *Meter as Rhythm*, 84.

[23] Hasty, "Just in Time for More Dichotomies: A Hasty Response," *Music Theory Spectrum* 21/2 (1999), 280.

for action, in performance as well as in perception.[24] This affinity of perception and performance comes to the fore in the paragraphs on an ecological perspective that conclude the chapter on "Meter as projection" in *Meter as Rhythm,* which seem consistent with Lewin's interest in present-tense activities of composers and performers, best understood as including but not limited to actions of perception.[25] In an introduction to the *nō* drama of Japan, Takanori Fujita speaks in this connection of *somaticity,* in his words, "the bodily perception in a performance, which is fulfilled and shared by all the players and spectators."[26] Fujita notes that drummers learn how to perform actions of the other participants in order to retain precise memories of how singers, dancers and flutist time their actions.

When Hornbostel and his co-author Otto Abraham spoke of *Aufmerksamkeit* with reference to tones, they had little to say about the succession of nows constituted by Husserl's temporally intending subject.[27] They were concerned, rather, with the multiple ways that the distinctions humans learn to make among tones are "rhythmicizing," the key term in the 1905 lecture:

> Das psychologische Experiment hat uns darüber belehrt, dass nicht nur Stärke und Dauer (dynamischer und temporaler Akzent) rhythmisierend wirken. Jede Eigentümlichkeit, die einen Ton von anderen unterscheidet, also auch Tonhöhe, Klangfarbe usw., vermag die Aufmerksamkeit gefangen zu nehmen und dem betreffenden Ton einen (subjektiven) Akzent zu verleihen (psychologischer Akzent). Diese verschiedenen Betonungsmöglichkeiten können nun sehr verschiedene Grade der Wirksamkeit haben, je nachdem wir gewöhnt sind,

---

[24] Richard Wolf makes this point with reference to Bergson and Hubert: "duration is given content through the nature of activities which compose it"; see Review of Martin Clayton, *Time in Indian Music* (Oxford: Oxford University Press, 2000) in *Asian Music* 34/2 (2003), 138. Compare Montague's remark ("Phenomenology," 37) that "the physical gestures of a performer offer . . . an opportunity to discuss the experience of music as a continuous event, structured in a Husserlian sense by the interactions of protention and retention."

[25] Hasty, *Meter as Rhythm,* 94–95.

[26] Fujita Takanori, "Structure and Rhythm in *nō*: An Introduction," in *The Oral and the Literate in Music,*" ed. Tokumaru Yosihiko and Yamaguti Osamu (Tokyo: Academia Music, 1986), 91.

[27] For discussion of Husserl's treatment of this topic, see Randall H. Jacob, "Husserl's Concept of the Temporally Intending Subject: Phenomenological Reflection and Living Present" (PhD dissertation, State University of New York at Buffalo, 1999).

auf dieses oder jenes Moment der Gesamtempfindung besonders zu achten.[28]

Hornbostel would have agreed with Georg Simmel's observation, in a 1903 essay, that "Der Mensch ist ein Unterschiedswesen," though Simmel was specifically referring to urban life, where our perceptual habits are challenged by dense sequences of sharply contrasting sensations and representations.[29]

Hornbostel's observation that we habitually direct attention to certain distinctive features of tones while neglecting others can be read as an invitation to set aside those habits and turn our attentiveness toward distinctions that may prove more pertinent in a given situation—an essential skill for those studying practices in which they have not yet been socialized. Twentieth-century composers, in all parts of the world, have extended essentially the same invitation many times over, as have those music theorists who kept closely in touch with developments in composition, such as Lewin and Hasty. It is regrettable that so few ethnomusicologists have been interested in learning what we can from the innovative work of composers and choreographers.

I wish to read the Hornbostel passage in a manner that does not merely assign each tone an identity composed of such attributes as pitch class, timbre, duration, and intensity, but also focuses attention on modifications in their interrelationships as performers and listeners constitute the living present of the tone. Hence I am in sympathy with Ildar Khannanov, who supports

---

[28] Hornbostel, "Probleme," repr. in *Hornbostel Opera Omnia* 1, 265. Modifying the translation provided with the reprint, "Psychological experiment has taught us that it is not only intensity and duration (dynamic and temporal accent) that are rhythmicizing. Any feature that differentiates one tone from another—hence also pitch, timbre, etc.—may capture attention and endow the relevant tone with a subjective accent (psychological accent). These diverse possibilities of accentuation can be effective to very different degrees depending on the habits we have acquired of attending to this or that feature of the total sensation." Hornbostel defined sixteen attributes of sounds in "Psychologie der Gehörserscheinungen," in *Handbuch der normalen und pathologischen Physiologie*, ed. A. Bethe *et al.*, vol. 11 (Berlin: Springer, 1926), 701–30.

[29] Georg Simmel, "Die Grossstädte und das Geistesleben," in *Brücke und Tor: Essays des Philosophen zur Geschichte, Religion, Kunst und Gesellschaft*, ed. Michael Landmann (Stuttgart: K.F. Koehler, 1957), 228: "Der Mensch ist ein Unterschiedswesen, d.h., sein Bewusstsein wird durch den Unterschied des augenblicklichen Eindrucks gegen den vorhergehenden angeregt; beharrende Eindrücke, Geringfügigkeit ihrer Differenzen, gewohnte Regelmässigkeit ihres Ablaufs und ihrer Gegensätze verbrauchen sozusagen weniger Bewusstsein, als die rasche Zusammendrängung wechselnder Bilder, der schroffe Abstand innerhalb dessen, was man mit einem Blick umfasst, die Unerwartetheit sich aufdrängender Impressionen." First pub. in *Die Grossstadt: Vorträge und Aufsätze zu Städteausstellung*, vol. 9 of *Jahrbuch der Gehe-Stiftung zu Dresden* (Dresden: Jahn & Jaensch, 1903), 185–206.

his thesis that an "ever-changing view of moments of time . . . characterizes nomadic time-perception" with a citation from Husserl's text of 1904 or early 1905 on "The Identity of the Tone" that was not included in the 1928 publication: "The momentary phases of perception constantly 'sink'; they continuously experience modifications . . . Any time-object sinks back into time, i.e. newly presented content constantly modifies itself."[30]

Experiences of newly presented content constantly modifying itself are available to any of us, whether or not we lead a nomadic way of life. Countless musicians the world over have experienced what Morton Feldman described as "the discovery that sound *in itself* can be a totally plastic phenomenon, suggesting its own shape, design and poetic metaphor."[31] Compare Helmut Lachenmann's conception of a sound as at once *Zustand* "state" and *Prozess*: "Klang als beliebig lange, in ihrer Dauer von aussen her zu begrenzende *Gleichzeitigkeit*, und Klang als zeitlich aus sich selbst heraus begrenzter charakteristischer *Verlauf*."[32]

Feldman and Lachenmann are but two of the major composers whose musical thinking clearly shares some of the concerns we recognize in Hasty's "attempt to replace the concept of durationless beat with continuous durational quantity that begins and ends."[33] While *Meter as Rhythm* is rightly praised as highly original in our current academic context, for that very reason it opens avenues toward a more adequate interpretation of theoretical statements from many times and places, including the philosophical and literary texts pertinent to the work of music theorists. It would be good if students in history of theory surveys were increasingly asked to read Whitehead, a peerless guide to the history of Western thought.

Much of the theorizing studied by ethnomusicologists is focused on

---

[30] Ildar Khannanov, "Line, Surface, Speed: Nomadic Features of Melody," in *Sounding the Virtual: Gilles Deleuze and the Theory and Philosophy of Music*, ed. Brian Hulse and Nick Nesbitt (Farnham, U.K.: Ashgate, 2010), 258, translating *Husserliana* 10, 213–14: "Die Momentanphasen der Wahrnehmung 'sinken' stetig, sie erfahren fortgesetzt eine Modifikation. Sie erhalten sich nicht, sondern sie ändern sich stetig. Irgendein Punkt des Zeitobjekts sinkt stetig in der Zeit zurück, d.h. zunächst der präsentierende Inhalt modifiziert sich stetig."

[31] Morton Feldman, " . . . Out of 'Last Pieces,'" liner notes to *Leonard Bernstein Conducts Music of Our Time*, Columbia Records ML6133/M6733 (1965), repr. in *Give My Regards to Eighth Street: Collected Writings of Morton Feldman*, ed. B. H. Friedman (Cambridge, Mass.: Exact Change, 2000), 19.

[32] Helmut Lachenmann, "Klangtypen der neuen Musik," *Zeitschrift für Musiktheorie* 1 (1970), 20; repr. in Lachenmann, *Musik als existentiele Erfahrung: Schriften 1966–1995* (Wiesbaden: Breitkopf and Härtel, 1996), 1: *both* "a simultaneity of any length desired whose duration is externally delimited" *and* "a distinctive passage temporally delimited from within outward."

[33] Hasty, "Just in Time," 280.

process and passage, including capsule analyses, or templates, like the syllables used in many regions of Africa, the Middle East, and Asia to teach and remember sequences of sounds and the motions that produce them. For over a millennium, countless performers of sung poetry in Arabic and Persian have used two sets of syllables to represent continuous quantities that begin and end. The musical sequence voiced as *ta nan ta nan ta na nan tan / ta nan ta nan ta na nan* corresponds to the prosodic sequence *ma-fā-e-lon fa-e-lā-ton / ma-fā-e-lon fa-e-lon*. Both are needed because the first strongly implies that syllables ending with *n* have twice the duration of the others and the second allows performers to determine in the course of performance the duration of each constituent, usually a group of two, three, or four syllables.

In performances of Persian classical music an instrumentalist responds to a singer in two different ways: first, recognizing the projective potential of the singer's performance of a few syllables in order to respond in a slightly different manner before the singer articulates the next group of syllables with its own projective potential, and so on. Then, once the singer completes half of a verse, the instrumentalist responds by connecting all the earlier constituents within the projected longer duration. While this manner of performance is often described as "non-metric" and "monophonic," neither term is appropriate. The dialogic interplay among performers should not be perceived as "one voice," and the measuring of events deserves to be described in its own terms.

One of the greatest obstacles that ethnomusicologists face in addressing questions of temporality is the ready availability of conventional terms like these, which many feel obliged to use in teaching surveys of so-called "world music." Yet if I follow Hasty's recommendation to cultivate, in his words, "a sensitivity to the metaphorical character of the language and concepts we have—and a resistance to their constraints,"[34] I must ask what is implied when "time" becomes the object of the verb "organize"—as when Bonnie Wade describes one chapter of her textbook *Thinking Musically* as an exploration of "the ways in which musicians organize time in music."[35] Discussion of different "kinds of time" raises a similar problem, as Richard Wolf has observed, citing the anthropologist Alfred Gell, and suggesting that "kinds of time" be replaced

[34] Christopher F. Hasty, "If Music Is Ongoing Experience, What Could Music Theory Be? A Suggestion from the Drastic," *Zeitschrift der Gesellschaft für Musiktheorie*, Sonderausgabe (2010), 207. www.gmth.de/zeitschrift/artikel/546.aspx

[35] Bonnie C. Wade, *Thinking Musically*, 3rd edn. (Oxford: Oxford University Press, 2013),71. Michael Tenzer glosses the expression "time organization" as "mental constructions of time through which we cognize musical rhythm" in "A Cross-Cultural Topology of Musical Time," in *Analytical and Cross-Cultural Studies in World Music*, ed. M. Tenzer and John Roeder (Oxford: Oxford University Press, 2011), 419.

by "contrastive categories through which individuals have proposed differences in human experience."[36] How are we thinking of time when we make it the object of the verb "organize" or distinguish its various "kinds"—linear and cyclical, for instance?[37] Jeanne Bamberger's "shaping time" seems more broadly applicable to human activities than "organizing time"; in her textbook, *Soundscapes*, Kay Shelemay likewise speaks of how music "shapes time."[38]

The discomfort felt by some ethnomusicologists about the gulf between the terms and metaphors used by the musicians we study and conventional categories of academic analysis has caused more than a few to avoid analytical work, which is a terrible mistake. As the daughter of missionaries, Ruth Stone learned the Kpelle language of Liberia early on, and she later interpreted Kpelle metaphors for performance actions with reference to Bergson's distinction between "inner" and "outer" time, as elaborated by Schütz in "Making Music Together."[39] She did not probe the implications of those metaphors for analysis.[40]

Much of the best work addressing questions of temporality has been produced after many years of experience with a set of related practices that included intensive analytic work as well as performance experience, enabling the scholar to effectively relate the metaphors of our analytic practice to those used in other languages for discussion of musical performance. Two strong examples are Regula Qureshi's 1994 essay cited above in footnote 1, and the chapter on "The Cognitive Study of African 'Rhythm'" in the second volume

[36] Alfred Gell, *The Anthropology of Time: Cultural Constructions of Temporal Maps and Images* (Oxford: Berg, 1992); cited in Richard K. Wolf, *The Black Cow's Footprint: Time, Space, and Music in the Lives of the Kotas of South India* (Delhi: Permanent Black, 2005), 227, 260 fn. 7.

[37] Tenzer aptly notes that "old categories like linear and nonlinear time emerged from obsolete distinctions between the West and 'the rest' and are based on misleading analogies to the physical world" ("Temporal Transformations in Cross-Cultural Perspective: Augmentation in Baroque, Carnatic and Balinese Music," *Analytical Approaches to World Music* 1/1 [2011], abstract).

[38] Kay Kaufman Shelemay, *Soundscapes: Exploring Music in a Changing World*, 2nd edn. (New York: Norton, 2006), 27.

[39] Ruth M. Stone, *Let the Inside Be Sweet: The Interpretation of Music Event among the Kpelle of Liberia* (Bloomington: Indiana University Press, 1982), 67–78.

[40] Reviewing Stone's monograph on the Kpelle Woi epic, David Locke found that "The book . . . seems hostile to musical analysis," noting that "musical elements such as texture, form, mode, and rhythm are not described and interpreted." See Locke, Review of Ruth Stone, *Dried Millet Breaking: Time, Words, and Song in the Woi Epic of the Kpelle* (Bloomington: Indiana University Press, 1988), in *Ethnomusicology* 34/1 (1990), 174.

of Gerhard Kubik's *Theory of African Music.*[41] Kubik's chapter includes a rich account of oral formulas used in teaching and remembering rhythmic patterns in several regions of Africa, such as *koŋ koŋ kele koŋ kele.* Qureshi's earlier analysis of *qawwālī* had shown the effectiveness of "a multi-channeled code capable of conveying different message dimensions simultaneously."[42] She begins the 1994 essay by tracing her "journey of discovery" from "a complex of time notions absorbed and distilled from Western experience and concepts" through "participation in the time world of Sufis and their music" which "expanded and challenged these notions at many levels." Recognizing that such journeys are not quickly accomplished, Qureshi described her understanding of Sufi "performance of time" as "uneasy and tentative: as yet an ongoing translation."[43]

A larger body of work initiated by Catherine Ellis deserves notice in a discussion of phenomenology, perception, and performance. In a 1984 essay on "Time Consciousness of Aboriginal Performers," Ellis drew on more than two decades of experience and analysis of Australian Aboriginal singing, work that continued for the remaining twelve years of her tragically short life.[44] Two of her students, Linda Barwick and Guy Tunstill, contributed significantly to Ellis's analytical work, and toward the end of her life she collaborated with Udo Will, a leading advocate of what he calls cognitive ethnomusicology. Ellis's reading of Husserl, Merleau-Ponty, and others seems to have encouraged her to pursue analytical study in which performance experience and attention to questions of perception were crucial. One of her early insights was confirmed and slightly modified through the detailed work with Will: Central Australian melodies do not pass from one discrete interval to another but superimpose a melodic contour (*mayu* "scent") on a set of recurrent frequencies, each of which singers reproduce with remarkable accuracy.[45]

Ellis's 1984 essay on "Time Consciousness" concentrates on Pitjantjatjara "small songs" (*inma tjukutjuku*), or "namings," each of which has a duration of about 30 seconds and is associated with a place or event within a "songline"

---

[41] Gerhard Kubik, *Theory of African Music*, vol. 2 (Chicago: University of Chicago Press, 2010), 1–84.

[42] Qureshi, "Exploring Time," 499.

[43] Ibid., 491.

[44] Catherine J. Ellis, "Time Consciousness of Aboriginal Performers," in *Problems and Solutions: Occasional Essays in Musicology Presented to Alice M. Moyle,* ed. Jamie C. Kassler and Jill Stubington (Sydney: Hale and Iremonger, 1984), 149–85.

[45] Udo Will and Catherine J. Ellis, "A Re-Analyzed Australian Western Desert Song: Frequency Performance and Interval Structure," *Ethnomusicology* 40/2 (1996), 187–222.

(*mainkara wanani*). She suggested that a thesis of Brentano's, as recalled by Husserl, "may be more common to Aboriginal musicians" than to Western listeners: our internal consciousness of a whole whose parts are successive is possible "only if the parts combine in the form of representatives of the unity of the momentary intuition."[46] Ellis found Husserl's discussion of "the unity of what is remembered" (*die Einheit des Erinnerten*)[47] to be consistent with her understanding of "the nature of accuracy of retention and manipulation of temporal-musical structures" in this practice, which involves "manipulation of patterns in proportions of their total duration."[48] Thus, like Khannanov, Ellis cited Husserl in an effort to describe perceptual habits that differed from those in which she had been socialized. That was not Husserl's intent.

The basis of a Pitjantjatjara small song is what Tunstill terms a "rhythmic-textual cycle,"[49] perhaps as short as 5.5 seconds or as long as 10, sung to a melody that generally calls for three, four, or five iterations of the rhythmic-textual cycle, the first and last of which need not present the full text. The rhythmic pattern of the cycle "assigns specific duration and accentuation to each syllable of the text" and is normally composed of four segments in which shorter durations precede one or more longer durations. A singer, in Ellis's words, "must correctly present all the interlocked rhythmic, melodic and textual structures" in order to release the power that can be made available through correct performance.[50] Her account of Pitjantjatjara singing is a strong example of what Janet Schmalfeldt elsewhere in this volume calls the mental multi-tasking needed to convey inner time.[51] While the duration of a single rhythmic pattern may change as one small song is followed by another,

---

[46] Ellis, "Time Consciousness," 157–58, quoting Churchill's translation of Husserl, *Vorlesungen*, 383: "Es erscheint überhaupt als Selbstverständlichkeit, dass ein jedes Bewusstsein, das auf irgendein Ganzes, auf irgendeine Vielheit unterscheidbarer Momente geht (also jedes Relations- und Komplexionsbewusstsein) in einem unteilbaren Zeitpunkt seinen Gegenstand umspannt; wo immer ein Bewusstsein auf ein Ganzes gerichtet ist, dessen Teile sukzessiv sind, kann es ein anschauliches Bewusstsein dieses Ganzen nur sein, wenn die Teile in Form von Repräsentanten zur Einheit der Momentanschauung zusammentreten."

[47] Husserl, *Vorlesungen*, 410: "und dadurch, dass diese reproduktiven Modifikationen eine Intentionalität bedeuten, schliesst sich der Fluss zusammen zu einem konstituierenden Ganzen, in dem eine intentionale Einheit bewusst ist: die Einheit des Erinnerten."

[48] Ellis, "Time Consciousness," 158.

[49] Guy Tunstill, "Melody and Rhythmic Structure in Pitjantjatjara Song," in *Songs of Aboriginal Australia*, ed. Margaret Clunies Ross, Tamsin Donaldson, and Stephen A. Wild (Sydney: University of Sydney, 1987), 125.

[50] Ellis, "Time Consciousness," 152–53.

[51] Janet Schmalfeldt, "In Time with Christopher Hasty: On Becoming a Performer of Robert Schumann's Davidsbündlertänze, op. 6," in this volume, 187–88.

melodic movement transpires over the same proportion of each duration. The beating pattern, with main beats and echo beats realized by various means, remains constant through all the small songs in a Pitjantjatjara songline, and syllables are articulated at different speeds so that certain syllables will always coincide with beats, though it may happen that no text accents coincide with main beats or echo beats.[52]

Eight years after Ellis's death Udo Will published what he called "a cognitive ethnomusicological perspective" on "oral memory in Australian Aboriginal song performance," which greatly enriches Ellis's analysis of "retention and manipulation of temporal-musical structures." Will saw the Australian data as a strong example of accuracy in transmission resulting, in his words, from "a set of interlocking constraining and cueing factors provided for by nondeclarative memory processes like habit learning, motor learning, sensory-motor control, pattern extraction and serial pattern recall."[53]

No musical practice could be more powerfully motivated by bonds with ancestors than is the performance of Central Australian song lines, which are composed of items believed to have been uttered by ancestors as they emerged in the time of the Dreaming. Hence Ellis's and Will's work exemplifies one of the primary questions addressed by ethnomusicologists with respect to temporality: how does moment-to-moment musical experience relate to a community's understanding of time as a whole?

[52] Ellis, "Time Consciousness," 168 and Figure 6. Parts of the Pitjantjatjara *Langka* cycle discussed by Ellis and Tunstill in the publications cited can be heard on the audiocassette *Songs from the Northern Territory, Recorded and Edited by Alice M. Moyle* (Canberra: Australian Institute of Aboriginal Studies, 1997; first issued 1967).

[53] Udo Will, "Oral Memory in Australia Aboriginal Song Performance and the Parry-Kirk Debate: A Cognitive Ethnomusicological Perspective," in *Studien zur Musikarchäologie IV: Musikarchäologische Quellengruppen: Bodenurkunden, mündliche Überlieferung, Aufzeichnung, 9–16 June, 2002*, ed. Ellen Hickmann and Ricardo Eichmann (Rahden: Marie Leidorf, 2004), 176.

Part II

Knowing the Score

Notation Is One Thing, Analysis Another, Musical Experience a Third: What Can They Have To Do With One Another?

ROBERT MORRIS

1.

JOHN CAGE ASKED a similar question in 1955: "Composing's one thing, performing's another, listening's a third. What can they have to do with one another?"[1] In the context of Cage's work the question is rhetorical: the three activities have no inherent relation with each other. In this, he aligns himself with theories of music such as Jean-Jacques Nattiez's tripartition of musical discourse into the poietic, aesthesic and neutral planes in which what composers do, listeners hear, and analysts find, may be studied completely independently of each other.[2]

But Cage doesn't take into account musical notation (which is used in all three of his activities, and in which he was a pioneer). While notation is unnecessary in or irrelevant to many forms of music, that doesn't mean it is superfluous, for, when it is used, different forms of notation may lead to very different kinds of musical experiences.

---

[1] See John, Cage, *Silence: Lectures and Writings* (Middletown, CT: Wesleyan University Press, 1961), 15.

[2] See Jean-Jacques Nattiez, *Music and Discourse*, trans. Carolyn Abbate (Princeton: Princeton University Press, 1990).

Moreover, the measurable quantities expressed in music notation often serve to enrich the seemingly ineffable qualities of musical experience. The purpose of this essay, then, is to look at many of the ways musical notation influences and even forms aspects of musical phenomenology. I will also develop an analytic orientation I call *parametric dynamics* that is designed to highlight how musical notation influences musical qualia such as mobility and heft.[3]

Professional Western musicians and those who study "classical music" are familiar with traditional music notation; this system of signs, symbols and icons embodies a set of visual, sonic, and motor skills that facilitate composition, performance, and aural perception, and, as such, it provides a basis for various theories of the music. But musical notation does much more than simply describe musical features or prescribe musical action. When thoroughly mastered, such notations become largely transparent, automatically drawing attention to certain entities and processes and making them salient at the expense of other aspects of musical experience.

Because of this—as well as social and historical factors—there have been many innovations in music notation in the 20th century as composers have found traditional notations increasingly inadequate to communicate the musical objects, ideas, and practices that interest them. Similarly, an array of special notations used in music analysis and theory has been invented to better describe, explain, and model musical processes that are hardly captured in traditional music and/or music theory. But beyond these innovations there is a larger question: how does notation affect music perception and phenomenology?

This is an enormously difficult and complex question, but to begin to answer it we need to understand that notation is the nexus for communication between the intersubjective and objective aspects of (musical) experience. It translates between the qualitative and quantitative modalities, between qualities such as sound, gesture, and motion and measurable, notated quantities that stand for these qualities. It is important to see this as a two-way relation— that salient aspects of musical experience can be mapped into a graphic symbol system and that the latter can be translated (back) into musical experience. The

---

[3] Before I proceed further, I wish to acknowledge the work of Joshua Banks Mailman, whose research on what he calls *dynamic form* has had helped advance and coalesce my own thinking about experience and form in new music. See "Seven Metaphors for (Music) Listening: DRAMaTIC," *Journal of Sonic Studies* 2/1 (2012) http://journal.sonicstudies.org/vol02/nr01/ a03 and "Temporal Dynamic Form in Music: Atonal, Tonal, and Other" (PhD Dissertation, University of Rochester, Eastman School of Music, 2010).

translation is never exact, losing information in both directions, but effective enough for it to be useful for many different functions. Working with musical notations can therefore reify the transient and ephemeral nature of music so it can be documented and studied, as well as provide a graphic language that enables the creation of new musical qualities and expressions.

2.

In an attempt to characterize some of the effects of notational systems on music perception and phenomenology, I will evaluate them from a number of polar oppositions: analog/digital, description/prescription, structure/infrastructure, emic/etic, neutral/context-sensitive. None of these modalities are crisp or absolute, and any of them may be deconstructed in certain cases.

To get started, let us consider a page from a score in Western notation, such as the Brahms symphony in Example 1. We see an organized system of symbols, signs, words arranged in various ways. We may assume that everything in the score corresponds to some musical entity in the performance of the work, and that this correspondence works both ways—from notation to sound and sound to notation. Thus, the score tells the players what to play; in this sense it is prescriptive. It also enables a conductor to read the score so she can hear it in her head and know how the music will sound; in this is way it descriptive. But upon closer examination, the graphic signs and/or their spatial configurations in the score do not necessarily each correspond to some sound in the performance. While a note on the staff designated for the oboe will refer to an oboe sound, what of a rest in that part? And what of the bar line between measures? Here the score indicates a logical function, not a sound—a (mental) grouping or partitioning of sounds. A dynamic sign stands not for some sound entity, but for an attribute of a sound. We could say the dynamic sign is like an adjective and a note is like a noun, but any correspondence between grammatical notions and musical notations breaks down very quickly: for instance, is an interval between two notes a noun or a verb?

Indeed, consider intervals. "Interval" is a musical concept of pitch distance supported by notation, and built into the notational system. The number of stave lines and spaces plus one between two notes gives the interval number, and the number of chromatic steps gives its type. A difference of two lines and spaces makes the interval a third, and if there are five chromatic steps, it is an augmented third. Note that in order to count the semitones the notation introduces accidentals that alter the pitch of a tone up or down a semitone. In this way, the notation shows both the diatonic and chromatic distance between notes. Intervals are not notated as signs in the score, but recoverable from it by operating on the symbols (the notes) with some algorithm. Interval identification quickly becomes a habit so that expert score readers immediately can tell and hear the intervals in the score, a skill that is completely transparent to the user.

Example 1. Score to Brahms's Symphony 1, first page

I could continue in this vein to describe the way time signatures and meter are coded in traditional notation, but space does not permit it. In any case, temporal sequences are not simply one-to-one relations between sound and symbol but complex, context-sensitive rule systems, which when mastered become second nature. If score reading is rule-based, then notation serves in the function of language whose semantics is inherent in the way the score corresponds to the musical sound.

There is of course much more to say about how the notational symbols—which we will call henceforth call *graphemes*—correspond to the sounds (phonemes) and other features in the sounding music. First of all, as implied above, some graphemes notate primary "parameters"[4] of traditional music: pitch, pitch-class and duration. Other symbols notate secondary "parameters" such a loudness, timbre, and articulation. This sets up ontology for some traditional Western music that may not be shared by other types of music. For instance, pitch need not always be primary and loudness secondary, but traditional notation favors this hierarchy so that the primary parameters are notated with a certain grapheme in the score, while secondary parameters are shown by adjoining other graphemes to the primary ones by spatial proximity. Older scores from as far back as the thirteenth century notated only the primary parameters of pitch and duration. Performers added the secondary parameters following various performance practices not notated in a score, but passed down from teacher to pupil over time. The notation of secondary parameters becomes prevalent after *ca.* 1600, and by the twentieth century the number of graphemes of secondary parameters more or less outweighs the number of primary graphemes. Each note or group of notes has a dynamic indication (like *forte* or *sforzando*, or *cresc.*), an articulation (slurs, dots, and words like *dolce* or *ben marcato*), and a timbral indication (like tremolo slashes, *mute, sul pont., pizz., flutter tongue*). In general, unlike the graphemes that notate the primary parameters of pitch, duration, and some aspects of articulation, other parameters are shown by the use of words or abbreviations.

This division of labor between primary and secondary parameters, supported by the way in which they are notated—by grapheme or word, respectively—supports traditional music theory. Pitch and time relationships are structural, where loudness, articulation and timbre are structural only in as much as they show differences in salience and priority between and among the primary parameters. Primary parameters provide coherence and logic,

---

[4] *Parameter* is a term used in certain strains of music theory to stand for some perceivable attribute of musical sound. For instance, a heard musical entity, such as a note, has a number of parameters: pitch, pitch-class, duration, timbre, loudness, all of which are indicated in various ways in musical notation. An entity such as a glissando between two notes, or a phrase or musical gesture, has other (global) parameters, such as velocity, bandwidth, and density. In general, "parameter" is roughly equivalent to "psychological dimension."

and secondary parameters promote difference and character—we might say they bring the music to life. From this we see why musical notation changes over time—innovations bring changes in what is considered primary and secondary; and in the twentieth century, when composers began to question the traditional functions of music, traditional notation became inappropriate and even useless for notating the ontologies and phenomenologies that new music discovered and invoked.

Returning to our Brahms score, we can note an important contrast between the use of graphemes in musical notation: the *analog/digital* distinction. Some aspects of music may change continuously between a starting and ending value such as pitch (from low to high) and possibly time (from a beginning to ending timepoint). Such changes can be mapped geometrically so that variation in pitch and time corresponds to spatial variations from the bottom to top or left to right on a page. This is called analog coding. When a musical thing or aspect is not continuously variable in one musical dimension, such as timbre or articulation, it is coded by some graphic symbol including a word or letter whose shape or position bears no analogy with the item being coded. This I call digital coding. The word *crescendo* is digital, but the hairpin sign for a crescendo is analog. Digital coding is by definition discrete, but analog coding may be either continuous or discrete. In the later case, the thing coded comes in steps or quanta forming a completely ordered set of discrete states.[5] These steps might be samples taken successively from otherwise continuous change. Such discrete but analog coding is the way pitch is coded in traditional scores.

While we usually code events in time from left to right in a score, the spacing of the note values of various durations such as quarters and half notes are represented discretely—digitally—in the score. There is no relationship between the shape of a half note and the duration to which it corresponds. Moreover, the placement of a quarter grapheme followed by an eighth-note grapheme may be placed horizontally on the page in any way providing the quarter grapheme is always to the left of the eighth. Thus timing and horizontal

[5] The difference between discrete and continuous analog notation is illustrated by the use of the glissando in various contexts. In a piano score, a glissando is notated by a series of successive notes given by a starting and ending pitch connected by a wiggly line—one glides one's fingers (using the fingernails) over successive keys. The same notation in a violin part indicates continuous pitch change produced by sliding a finger from one pitch position to another on the fingerboard. (The term *portamento* for bowed string instruments indicates a certain trajectory for a glissando—roughly, to linger on the first note, then near to the end of its duration, to slide to the second.)

space do not correspond. Digital and analog coding can interact as in the use of accidentals that ask for notes to be raised or lowered by a semitone or more without changing vertical position of the note on the staff. Thus the interval between F♭ and G♯ is actually larger than the interval between between E and G, contradicting the analog ordering of pitches on the staff. And while analog coding of pitch applies to the notes on a staff, it may not apply to music on two or more staves, where the selection of clefs or transpositions may contradict the pitches' vertical order on the page.

From this and many other complicated features of traditional notation that may come to mind, reading a score at sight is no easy task. Moreover, reading music in some other notation renders many of the habits used in reading traditional music relatively useless, so the new notation will no longer be transparent to the reader; this sets up a different ontology of musical entities and relations that have to be learned in order to be appreciated as such.[6]

Let me now turn to some other of the polarities I mentioned above. Although traditional Western music notation is both prescriptive and descriptive, the balance between these two functions varies in different notations. Guitar tabs in the notation of popular music are largely prescriptive. They tell the player where to put her fingers on the frets of the fingerboard. However, one can recover which notes are being played if one knows how the strings are tuned, so tabs can be used descriptively if necessary. A more definitive example of a prescriptive notation is the way harmonics are notated for string instruments. Two simultaneous notes are written on the staff with the higher written with a diamond note head. This tells the player to play the lower note, while touching the place where one would normally play the higher note. This produces a higher harmonic pitch than the pitch notated by the diamond-headed note. The notation tells the player what to do, without notating the desired pitch. By contrast, an alternative description notation is also used; a pitch may be notated with a circle over it indicating that it is a harmonic. This notation does not tell the player what to do to produce the desired sound.[7]

Completely prescriptive notation came into its own in the 1950s with the indeterminate music of John Cage and Christian Wolff. A more recent example

---

[6] Learning a new language such as Russian or Arabic using a different character set poses a similar challenge. And in the case of Chinese, things are even more difficult, for there is no analog relation between the sound of a word and the symbol that stands for it.

[7] It is interesting to note that the prescriptive notation for harmonics is more precise than the descriptive notation; it enables distinctions between the different sounds of different harmonics producing the same pitch.

Example 2. Aaron Cassidy, String Quartet (2000)

is the String Quartet (2002) of Aaron Cassidy in Example 2, where the motions and placements of each finger on the string, and the position and motions of the bow are specified without notating the pitches and rhythms that may result when these actions are carried out in performance.

The use of texts as scores is another sort of prescriptive notation. Such a "score" might include the following statement: "Play a high, soft note, holding it for at least ten seconds, letting its pitch slightly and gradually fall." In general, the more prescriptive the notation, the more indeterminate or unpredictable the musical result. Completely descriptive notations were also developed in the mid-twentieth century including graphic scores of electronic music, and sonograms, plots of FFT, and so forth.

Let us now turn to *structure/infrastructure*. I suggested above that traditional Western musical notation provides a general infrastructure to support specific structural musical relationships; nevertheless, the distinction is blurred, especially in new music in many ways. Notation may enable higher level infrastructural relations to be composed as in music composed by chance, where the arrangements of musical entities is not meant to code structure, but just allow the notation of flowing sound. Stockhausen's concept of a field, a collection of sounds that merges irreducibly together into a higher gestalt provides a second example. Many composers use traditional notation to specify all the components of a field, but these components will not be heard as distinct, even though each sound is clearly notated in the score.[8] However, a change of notation can separate the infrastructure from the structure.

Compare the scores of Ligeti and Penderecki in Example 3. It is clear, on the one hand, that the note as found in the Ligeti score (Example 3a) is not a unit of musical progression; on the other hand, the Penderecki score (Example 3b) directly notates what is basic; dynamic sonic streams of clusters of sustained tones. But even in the various forms of serial music notated with discrete pitches and time points, the literal use of traditional notation obscures the serial structure. So some traditional notational rules have to be changed: key signatures are avoided, inharmonic differences are ignored, the rules for using accidentals are modified, and, most importantly, rhythmic notations are reinterpreted and/or differentiated from the traditional use of time signatures that support periodic or cyclic meter. Otherwise, the serial structure may be confused with the type of composed infrastructure associated with chance and stochastic music. Of course, some composers do not want the serial units and configurations they compose to be heard as structure *per se* in the first place.

Even in the case where traditional notation completely supports the structure of the music written within it, the reduction of a structural item to its

---

[8] Traditional examples of fields are the singular sound that arises when many instruments or voices play a trill or tremolo. A similar situation is the *choric effect* produced by a group of instruments or singers playing (or singing) the same musical line or holding a chord. Another example of a field occurs when an orchestral simultaneity is heard as an irreducible unit.

8

Example 3a. Violin 1 divisi extracted from György Ligeti, Atmospheres, *m. 48*

VI. I

notation is not definitive. This is because the relation of the notation to different musical structures and their theories is one to many, not one to one. So
the item notated in Example 4 can have many different structural descriptions:
a dissonant simultaneity in Renaissance counterpoint; a $^6_5$ seventh-chord in
common practice music; a major chord with added sixth in jazz; a 4-26[0358]

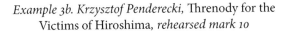

Example 3b. Krzysztof Penderecki, Threnody for the
Victims of Hiroshima, *rehearsed mark 10*

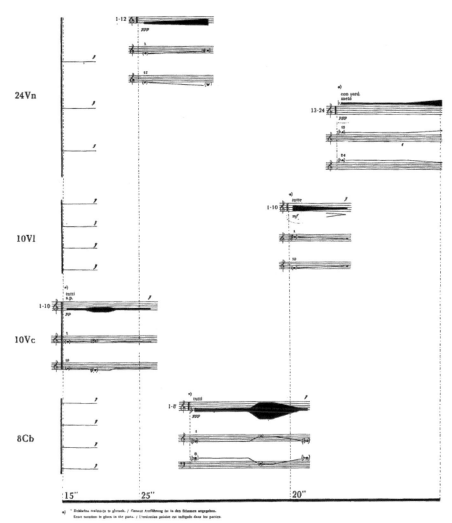

sonority in post-tonal music; a vertical acrostic of John Cage's last name; and
so forth.

The terms "emic" and "etic" were coined in analogy to the linguistic terms
"phonemic" and "phonetic." The emic perspective identifies the intrinsic distinctions that are used by members of a given community, just as phonemic

analysis identifies the intrinsic phonological distinctions used by speakers of a given language. The etic perspective depends upon the extrinsic distinctions that can be used by observers outside the community; this parallels phonetic analysis, which depends on sonic distinctions that have been identified by linguists. With respect to musical notation, emic notations are used by musical communities to notate their own music, while outsiders to a particular community of musical experts may be obliged to use etic notations to notate that community's music. From the point of view of the classically trained musician, the emic notations used in jazz, such as lead sheets and chord symbols, seem incomplete and sketchy, whereas within the jazz community, such notations

Example 4. A chord from a score

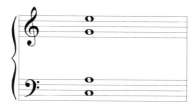

are completely adequate for the purpose of performing, arranging, and improvising music. Such emic notations depend on the musical knowledge that all of the practitioners share; in this way emic notations depend upon implicit musical knowledge. In contrast, etic notations must be explicit. To illustrate the difference between emic and etic notations, see Example 5, where I have notated a line from a south Indian composition in three ways. The top part of the example is the emic Indian "solfeggio" notation of the passage, and the bottom part consists of two systems of three staves; the Indian notation above is translated symbol for symbol into Western notation on the top staff; the other two staves notate how it is sung using the solfeggio (middle staff) or the text (lower staff). There is no improvisation involved, so that Indian musician reads the emic notation exactly in the same way from one performance to another. This is possible because an Indian musician knows the raga, style, and context of the composition and fills in all the additional information, which for him or her is implied by the notation. For the outsider, having none of this insider information, the only recourse in order to produce a reliable transcription is to notate it as completely as possible using Western notation, sometimes equipped with special symbols, signs, and extensions.

Example 5. Etic and emic notations of a south Indian composition

Emic notation for Indian musicians

Pallavi:

Ṡ	Ṡ	,—	Ṡ		N	D—	Ṙ	Ṡ		N—	N	D—	D		P	M	G	M
Va	na	—	jă		—	—	kshi	—		—	rō	—	—		—	—	ee	—

P	D	N	D		,—	Ṙ	Ṡ	N		D	P	M—	G		M	P	D	N
vi	—	—	ra		—	ha	—	—		mō	—	—	rva		—	—	—	nē

Etic transcription for study

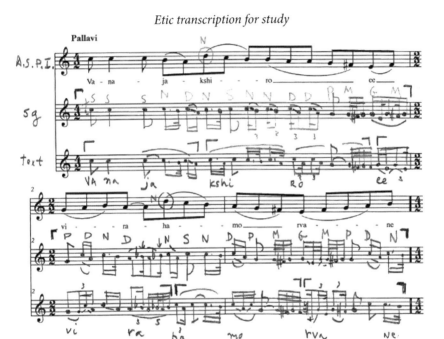

But every form of musical notation depends upon a mix of implicit (emic) and explicit (etic) musical knowledge. The term performance practice stands for the emic knowledge that performers bring to the explicit notation in the score. Adequate and appropriate performances of Baroque versus Romantic music depend upon knowing the corresponding performance practice that is not notated or directly notated in the music. However, performance editions may actually notate some aspects of the performance practice.

We may ask why adaptions of traditional emic Western notation can function as etic notations for jazz, Indian, and other world musics. The reason is that over the history of Western art music, musical specification has gradually become more complex, musical expression has become more diverse, and improvisation has died out. Thus, musical notation has had to become increasingly etic to accommodate musical innovation. Two hundred years ago, scores only specified pitch and time information; today, notations for time and pitch have become nuanced and refined, bolstered by articulate specifications of loudness, instrumentation, timbre, expressive indications, explicit directions for performance and new instrumental techniques. This trend increasingly limits the creative role of the performer so that its end point lies in the composition of electronic and computer music where the performer is altogether removed from the presentation of music. Some composers and musicians have responded to this development by turning or returning to simpler notations, often employing improvisation and indeterminacy, with which the performer has a vital new or renewed role in musical performance.

This turn to simpler notations brings me to the last of my contrasting terms: *neutral/context-sensitive.* We have seen how traditional notation is quite context-sensitive; graphemes modify other graphemes in the variable contexts of still other graphemes. When the music being notated is not of the kind supported by its notation, new complications develop since some of the context-sensitive aspects of the notation have to be ignored (as I explained in the case of serial, aleatoric, stochastic, and spectral musics). Thus the music fights against some of the features of its notation. (As an example, consider the questions about accidentals that traditional performers invariably ask about the pitch notation of twentieth-century music.)

Again, modern composers have used notations that eschew context-sensitive relations between graphemes; what you see is what you get. Scores where "time equals space"—a completely analog notation—present one example. See Example 6. Such scores may employ staffs or just a rectangle of space were notes are inserted as needed; these scores often show duration by extended braces or thick lines extending a note head; glissandi are easily drawn. However, such scores do not notate rhythmic nuance or simultaneities very precisely so that some traditional rhythmic graphemes may be employed as well. These scores also allow performers to have a greater role in interpreting the music—a performance practice that often has to be taught to novices without experience in new music or improvisation.[9]

[9] This preference for context-free or neutral notations resembles a similar trend in American literary criticism in the 1920s/30s. William Carlos Williams put it this way, describing

Example 6. Analogue time notation in Earle Brown,
9 Rare Bits for 1 or 2 harpsichords *page 3*

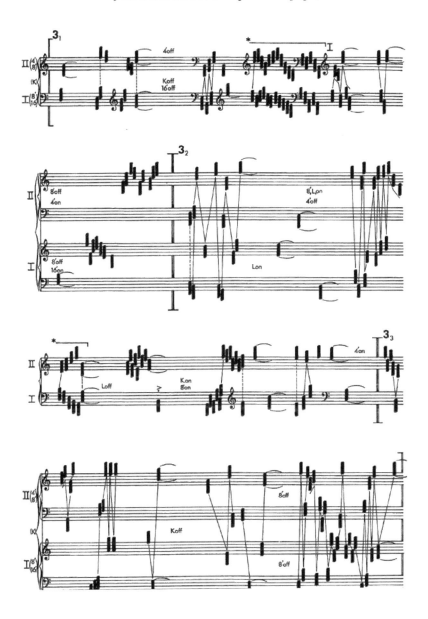

A concomitant desire on the part of some progressive composers has been to concentrate on the visual "look" of a score, so as to suggest the character of the music. Sometimes this makes the music much more difficult to read and play. Some composers suggest that such scores should be renotated, making them more "performance friendly," but at the expense of aesthetic appeal.[10]

3.

Having shown that musical notation is complex and context-sensitive in many different modalities, I wish to think about notation in another way. While I will be interested in notational function, I will purposely disregard those descriptions and explanations that show how a composition's identity depends upon theories of pitch, rhythmic, and/or timbre. Rather, I want to focus on the way the music moves in time, and specifically on the qualities of those moves. In traditional music, this means a focus on the secondary parameters, but also on the aspects of the primary parameters such as pitch and time that are independent of their structural description. This also entails disregarding those musical features and qualities that depend on repetition and reach of reference, putting aside fixed forms such as ABA or rondo forms.[11] Put another way, I want to study how the notation can help us to attend to a piece's moment-by-moment flow so we are listening *to* the music, not *for* something within it. This may seem strange, since many people like to listen to music without a score because that brings them nearer to the experience of music (not to mention music lovers who cannot read notation). Nevertheless, I will show how musical notation can be used to heighten our appreciation of musical flow as well as neutralize the aspects of structural descriptions that take us away from the musical flow to abstraction. However, permit me to offer a disclaimer: the study of musical structure should not remove us from the experience of music, but serve to heighten it in its explanations of process and form. Furthermore,

Gertrude Stein's work in 1935 as "systematically . . . . smashing every connotation words have ever had, in order to get them back clean" ("A 1 Pound Stein," in *Selected Essays of William Carlos Williams* (New York: New Direction, 1969), 163.

[10] Before the advent of computer engraving software, scores were copied by hand, distinguishing composers by their musical handwriting. Current programs like Finale and Sibelius with their defaults supporting traditional music notation tend to suppress a score's visual individuality; moreover, they make it painfully difficult to notate scores in new, innovative ways, which includes the scores of many important composers over the last fifty years. Such engraving programs therefore may be said to represent a reactionary position to new music. Fortunately there are alternatives.

[11] Some process forms such as the fugue are also disregarded since the return of the subject is not part of the sonic design.

Example 7. George Crumb, Makrocosmos I

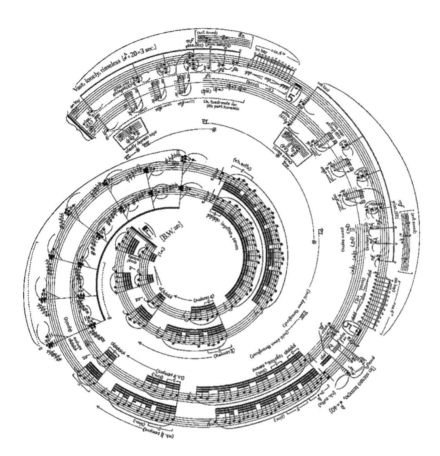

the kind of listening I am trying to describe often supports structural hearing, but in ways that are usually not acknowledged by theorists and analysts.
Indeed, secondary parameters are usually only mentioned if they function
to bring out relationships among structural items. For instance, register and
dynamics can help distinguish polyphonic strands and important beats.[12] If

---

[12] In fact, in even completely homophonic passages, what is in the soprano and bass of a
series of chords defines the melodic and harmonic function of each chord. This is the use of
pitch as a secondary parameter, defining the function of pitch-class, a primary parameter
in tonal music.

they do not function in this way, they are either not mentioned or consigned to the fuzzy categories of accent and syncopation.

To illustrate musical flow, let us examine a passage by Beethoven, from his *Sonata Pathetique* in C minor, op. 13, first movement. See Example 8a. The passage is from the closing theme area of the exposition, notable because it has such a climatic effect. From the point of view of tonal structure, the passage falls into two almost identical parts, each 12 measures long.

Before I broach the musical flow in this passage, I will discuss the tonal structure using a special analytic notation to show structural levels. These voice-leading graphs prune all aspects of the music that are not of tonal significance. To this end, secondary parameters and even some aspects of the pitch and rhythmic surface are removed. Unlike the graphs I shall use later, these graphs are explanatory and reductive; they hierarchize the events in the tonal pitch structure.

On the top level of the graph in Example 8b, we see the chord progression written to show voice leading connections. Chord functions are not given at this level, which is mainly descriptive. The middle level omits passing chords and we see that the bass moves down by thirds until measure 98 (or 110). There the two parts of the passage diverge into two different versions of a perfect authentic cadence. See also that the bass third progression supports a I-IV-ii-V-I progression, but the last chord is in first inversion. The bottom level of structures shows that the entire passage twice passes through a tonic—dominant-preparation—dominant—tonic functional progression with the opening tonic function prolonged by the descending third progression.

The tonal structure revealed in the graph is hardly adventuresome. First, it has only three levels; second, the surface harmonies are mainly diatonic with a few chromatic tones to facilitate the voice-leading; third, the chord sequences at any of the levels (considering other progressions in Beethoven's work) are, in fact, somewhat ordinary.

So what causes the climactic effect of the passage? This is not hard to discover—it is based upon on the play of secondary parameters—but because the tonal structure is not concerned with climax or other aspects of musical character, the music's dynamism is ignored in the structural description and the notations that disclose it.[13]

First of all, the oscillatory eight-note rustling of the inner voices of the

---

[13] One can make the point that the teleology of tonality drives the music forward as the chord and voice-leading progress to their goals, and that this occurs on multiple levels of structure, and further, that the delay of these goals heightens the tension. Still the character of the tension and other features of the music remain unaddressed. The only aspect

chords produces a sense of turbulence and urgency. The staccato signs on the first and second beats of each measure from 93–99 (105–112) helps make the rush seem almost reckless. The lack of eight-note activity in the bass of measures 99–100 and 111–112 produces a sense of release and marks the two perfect authentic cadences (PACs) at the end of each together with the lack of accent of the two parallel parts.

Second, in the two parallel parts, the music starts at piano and crescendos to forte. The cadence at measure 101 is made almost deceptive—a sort of fake-out—by the *subito* return to piano at the resolution, eliding with the start the second part. Beethoven marks the end of the crescendo at the onset of the two PACs.

Third, the sense of climax is highly dependent upon changes in pitch register; each parallel part starts out in the middle register and fans out inexorably to the edges of the piano keyboard. This leaves a registral gap between the two hands as they separate, to be only explicitly filled in at the end of the first part in measures 100–101. (I should point out that this gap is more of a notational artifact than heard as a gap, *per se*; the harmonics of the lower notes possibly aided by the damper pedal fills in the registral space.[14]) Returning to measure 98 as shown in Example 8a, the upper voice has reached the high tonic note E♭6 at which point a middle voice starting on B♭5 starts a scale progression from scale degree 5 to 8. However, the registers of these notes is changed[15] so while the B♭5 travels up to B5-♮ and then C6, the next pitch-class D is placed an octave lower, so it can progress by step to the E♭5 at the onset of the second part. This takes a bit of wind out of the PAC, but closes the registral gap and helps prepare the next part. In addition, the change of register sets up the otherwise unexpected *subito* piano I mentioned above.

The wedge in the first part progresses from E♭5 to E♭6 while the bass moves from E♭3 to low G1. In the second part, the wedge is even wider due to use of F6 (the highest note on Beethoven's piano) in measure 111. This transcends first part's highest note and the registral descent in measure 100, continuing the chromatic ascent from measure 109 to 111—from D♭6 through D6 to E♭6 further through E6-♮ to F6. The change of chord in the PAC of the second part vis-à-vis the first PAC helps also to surpass the motion and resolution in the first part.

---

of musical experience that is recognized is desire and resolution. Moreover, this example shows how notation (in this case, a voice-leading graph) can influence the character of music experience.

[14] The pianist, of course, will notice the gap as her hands separate.

[15] This change of register also hides a parallel fifth, which is exposed in the voice-leading graph.

Example 8a. Beethoven, piano Sonata no. 8 in C minor, op. 13 (Sonata Pathétique), 1, mm. 88–115

Example 8b. Analytical sketch of the Beethoven

Finally, the pacing of the two parts is identical. The first two measures of each (89–90 and 101–102) sustain an E♭-tonic chord, followed by another two measures of an E♭-based sonority, but an unstable one—a I_2^4 with D♭ in the bass. The music then progresses by two chords a measure until the one-per-measure chord changes at the end of each part (99–100, 111–112). However, we can hear measures 96–97 (108–109) as united, as basically projecting a dominant function.

A nice detail in the first two measures of each part (89–90/101–102) is syncopation on the second half of each measure. The soprano voice attacks on the second beat of both measures, while the bass joins the soprano on the second measure, having played its pitch on the downbeat of the first measure. This pattern repeats in the next two bars (91–92, 103–104). The effect seems to me to be one of panting, followed by quicker breaths in the next measures.[16] This emphasis on the second half of a measure is followed up by putting a passing chord on the second half of subsequent measures; notice also that the notes of the passing chords are higher/lower than the notes on the downbeats (until measure 98, as pointed out above). In the last pairs of measures in the two parts (99–100, 111–112) the bass plays on the downbeat, and the high note in the right hand is placed on the second beat.

These secondary parameters, which are clearly notated in the music, significantly contribute to the turbulent climax of the passage. I have spent some time on these perhaps obvious features to point out that they are doing the emotional heavy lifting, not the tonal structure;[17] however, some of the secondary parameters support the structure, others deviate from or contradict it, and it is this incongruity of function that gives this music a sense of conflict. Generalizing, perhaps mightily, if there is a sense of conflict and resolution inherently built into tonality—something that can be debated—it can be heightened or diminished by the play of densities, registers, dynamics, and timbres that occur concomitantly in the music. This also shows that various

---

[16] This "panting" suggests a narrative for the passage: a 50-meter dash. At measures 89–92, the runners are lined up at the starting line, ready to go. At measure 93, the gun is fired and the athletes race to the finish line reaching there at measure 98, after which each runs a bit more to shake off their momentum; however, the race has been called a tie, so they must start again and line up at measure 101 for the second deciding dash. They are off in measure 105, and reach a finish line at 111, at which point one of them has clearly won, and s/he runs jubilantly around the course from measure 113 on. I consider such narratives as benign, and they may or may not be suggested by the play of parameters in a passage of music.

[17] A Marxist interpretation might be suggested here. The primary parameters control the music but are supported by the *sub rosa* workings of the secondary parameters just as the upper class of a society is supported by the unacknowledged labor of the proletariat or even slaves.

forms of post-tonal music can enjoy forward motion or teleology due to the compositional coordination of any parameters whatsoever.[18]

4.

There are some analytic tools in the literature that address musical flow in direct ways with or without invoking structural theories of pitch, or rhythm/meter. I shall refer to these tools as "sonic profile tools." Many of these tools were invented by composers who wished to write music in which they sought to make dynamic flow the most important aspect of music experience.

I will not describe any of the sonic profile tools in any detail here, but some of them are graphically analog, as in the sonograms of Robert Cogan or the graphs of Fast Fourier Transforms used in computer music. Others use digital methods, in the form of short musical figures, together with charts, text, and/or mathematical expressions.[19] Most of these tools segment the musical flow and/or show accents within it; this may be accomplished by attending to gaps between musical entities or changes in local direction or contour.[20] Moreover, they can be used recursively to show hierarchic, well-formed partitions in a piece. Most of these tools are insensitive to anything but generic musical repetition; they do not detect the return of particular themes or motives. What

---

[18] However, I should say that the interplay of syntactic pitch and time structure with sonic structures such as register, contour, dynamic, timbre, and the rest can produce even richer experiences than with the sonic factors operating alone.

[19] See Christopher F. Hasty, "Segmentation and Process in Post-Tonal Music," *Music Theory Spectrum* 3 (1981), 54–73; Dora Hanninen, *A Theory of Music Analysis: On Segmentation and Associative Organization* (Rochester, NY: University of Rochester Press, 2012); David Lefkowitz and Kristin Taavola, "Segmentation in Music: Generalizing a Piece-Sensitive Approach," *Journal of Music Theory* 44/1 (2000), 171–229; Robert Morris, "New Directions in the Theory and Analysis of Musical Contour," *Music Theory Spectrum* 15/2 (1993), 205–28; Larry Polansky, "Morphological Metrics: An Introduction to a Theory of Formal Distances," in *Proceedings of the International Computer Music Conference* (San Francisco: International Computer Music Association, 1987), 197–205; John Roeder, "A Calculus of Accent," *Journal of Music Theory* 39/1 (1995), 1–46; James Tenney, *META + HODOS and META Meta + Hodos,* 2nd edn. (Lebanon, NH: Frog Peak Music, 1988); James Tenney and Larry Polansky, "Temporal Gestalt Perception in Music," *Journal of Music Theory* 24/2 (1980), 205–41; Yayoi Uno and Roland Hübscher, "*Temporal Gestalt* Segmentation: Polyphonic Extensions and Applications to Works by Boulez, Cage, Xenakis, Ligeti, and Babbitt," *Computers in Music Research* 5 (1995), 1–38.

[20] Indeed, Hasty's "Segmentation and Process" was written in part to address a question in set-theory: which pitch-class configurations were likely to be heard as such in post-tonal music?

they do show is the interplay of various unhierarchized parameters, what I have been calling musical flow.[21]

Clearly, sonic profile tools are exactly what we need to help show how the climax is constructed in the Beethoven example. They will systematically help to reveal what (especially traditional) musical notation tends to conceal or camouflage: that is, the dynamics of contour, density, segmentation, and gesture.

I have adapted aspects of these tools, which I will use to show more clearly and systematically what I have just informally discussed in the Beethoven example. In this paper, I will call this approach *parametric dynamics*, which is derived from the sonic profile tools I cited above.[22] Parametric dynamics partitions music into contiguous segments and examines distinct attributes or parameters of each segment. Then I follow the progress of each parameter over the series of segments. The progress of different parameters has to be described in similar ways so that their contribution to the musical flow can be meaningfully compared. However, I am not interested in fusing the various attributes together to provide a series of single numbers that presumably summarizes the flow. That is too reductive, and ignores the way the parameters interact to create the qualities of the flow.[23]

I take the parameters of a segment in the Beethoven to be: 1) its duration; 2) its highest pitch; 3) its lowest pitch; 4) its number of distinct pitches; 5) the mean or average of all its pitches; and 6) the bandwidth or interval from the lowest to highest pitch.

The reader may wonder why I do not use the center pitch of the bandwidth. This is because I want to reflect the vertical distribution of the pitches in the analysis. In Example 9 I show three chords that have the same bandwidth and center pitch, but are differentiated according to spacing as measured by the mean pitch. (Note that a two-note simultaneity's pitch mean equals its center pitch.)

---

[21] While all of the aforementioned tools are quantitative, there are yet other approaches that are more qualitative, such as the expectation theories of Leonard B. Meyer and the plus/minus notations of Stockhausen. Nonetheless, on the one hand, sonic profile tools may seem useful, but inadequate in the presence of music that can be described within the context of some theory, such as tonality or twelve-tone theory. On the other hand, much contemporary music is not composed according to explicit structural rules and in these cases sonic profile tools may be sufficient.

[22] Parametric dynamics is but one incarnation of many diverse formal strategies in Mailman's work on dynamic form. See fn. 3 above.

[23] Stockhausen's prescriptive plus/minus notation, used to guide free improvisation in his works of the 1960s such as *Prozession*, is one of only a few examples of a sonic profile notation that permits the counterpoint of parameters.

In order to determine the duration of each segment, in the Beethoven I use surface harmonic rhythm so that each segment contains one and only one chord. Segments are therefore two measures, one measure, or half a measure in duration.

Example 9. Three chords with bandwidth = 11 and center pitch = 5.5

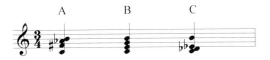

chord A: pitches 0 6 8 11. mean pitch = 24/4 = 6.25

chord B: pitches 0 4 7 11. mean pitch = 22/4 = 5.5

chord C: pitches 0 1 3 11. mean pitch = 15/4 = 3.75

Example 10. Chart of parameter change from measure 96a to 96b

measure	96a		96b
high pitch	22		24
mid pitch 1	-19		-19
mid pitch 2	-10		-12
mid pitch 3	10		12
mid pitch 4	17		17
low pitch	-22		-24
mean pitch	-0.33 ...		-0.66 ...
#dif pitches	6		6
BW	44		48
Top pitch int		+2	
low pitch int		-4	
Mean pitch int		+0.33 ...	
Dif pitch int		0	
Bw int		6	

Some important parameters not among the five used in this analysis are loudness and the number and density of attacks in a segment. Loudness is omitted since it follows and supports the changes in other parameters closely, and the number and density of attacks is omitted because it is invariant in the Beethoven passage—four attacks per beat. After determining the numerical values of the parameters of all the segments, successive values in a given parameter across the segments are compared by examining the successive values in pairs. This is equivalent to taking the interval between pitches. A chart such as the one shown in Example 10 can show the result of the analysis.[24] Here only the parameters of two segments are analyzed; they are from measure 96, the music for which is also given in the example. Pitches are numbered, so middle C is 0.

Example 11 graphs the parametric values over the entire passage, from measure 89–101 to show the changes much more vividly than the chart, since it visually portrays the data in analog coding. The graph shows the progression of the five pitch parameters. Zero on the y axis is middle C. The high and low pitch diverge with the mean pitch fairly low since the right and left hands are both articulating chord tones, and the bandwidth gradually increases in tandem. The parameters converge back to their initial values from 99 to 101. Measure 101 is the same as measure 89. Thus there is nothing in this graph that should surprise.

But when we graph the changes of intervals between adjacent values of the five parameters, things are different. To make this kind of graph, I convert the pitch notation to frequency and take the ratios between successive frequencies. This is so I can compare pitch change to other non-pitch changes like duration and loudness, whose intervals are represented by ratios in the first place. For example, the interval between the two durations 5 and 8 is not their difference 3, but their ratio 8/5 or 1.6.

The graph in Example 12 shows the changes of intervals or ratios between the parameters of each pair of sections. Note that it is relatively flat excepting the duration ratio at its onset,[25] until measure 99 where it becomes quite discontinuous. This does not indicate that the music is not changing from measure 93 until 99; it *is* changing, but at roughly the same rate. This graph is analogous to the first differential of a function in calculus—or more accurately, to the first difference in the difference calculus. Taking the ratio of the ratios

---

[24] Examples 10–13 and 16–17 can be found in color at http://lulu.esm.rochester.edu/rdm/pdflib/NOTATION.pdf

[25] This is because the duration of segments changes from two measures to a half a measure at 93a; after that, sections stay at half a measure and the durations ratios are 1.

Example 11. Graph of pitch parameter values in measures 89–101

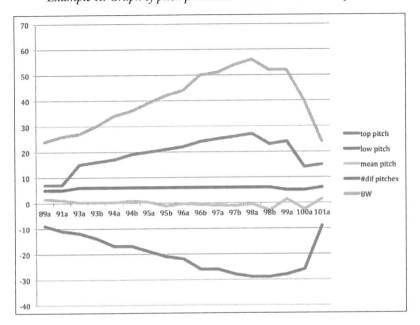

Example 12. Ratio graph of pitch parameters from measures 89–101

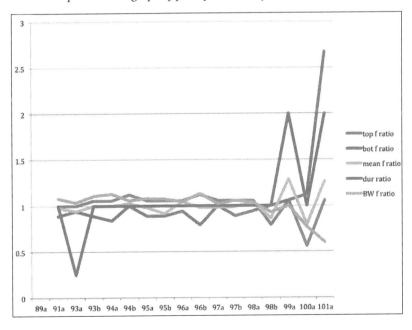

would be like taking the second differential.[26] At measure 98 the changes of interval cause spikes in the graph, which signal that many things have changed from measure 98b to 99 and beyond that timepoint: duration and bottom pitch change by much larger factors than before, as much as ratios of 2 to 1. The reason for the great change from 100 to 101 is that the music returns to the state of measure 89, and the changes are radical in many of the parameters. This is compensated by a change to piano from forte at that point.

Now let us look at the difference between the ratio graphs of the last four measures of the two parts of the passage. The two selections of music and their graphs are given in Example 13. The second graph is less dramatic than the first because at measure 110 Beethoven does not reduce the range of the upper pitches nor does he return to the opening of the passage. Thus change is smoother in 110–113 than in 98–101. It is important to see that a ratio graph will show points of change vividly, but the character of these changes may be negative or positive (up or down in the graph) as the case may be. The most important feature of the ratio graph is that it shows how all the parametric changes relate to each other to influence the experience of the music.

5.

When we apply parametric dynamics to more recent music, there may be no structural theory of pitch or rhythm that can help partition the music into sections. (In the Beethoven we had harmony and meter to help us.) We then have to rely on one of the methods that partition a composition into successive sections. For my purposes I choose the Tenney/Polansky algorithm, which invokes the temporal gestalt theory of James Tenney.[27] The algorithm partitions a stream of music into successive *temporal gestalts*—my sections. Tenney's theory is based on proximity and grouping.

The algorithm looks at a series of intervals derived from some parameter. See Example 14. Taking four successive parameter values, we have three successive intervals, x, y, and z. These intervals are interval-classes, so only the size or distance of each interval is registered. If interval y is larger than x and z, then we can partition the four values after the second value. For example, if we have four pitches 0, 2, 8, 7, then interval x = 2, interval y = 6 and interval z = 1. Since interval y is larger than the others, we can partition the pitch succession as 0, 2 | 8, 7. In the case of ratios as interval-classes, we have to compare absolute

---

[26] Roeder, "Calculus of Accent" uses a similar methodology.

[27] See Tenney, *META + HODOS*.

Example 13. Comparison of ratio graphs from measures 98–101 and 110–113

mm.98-101

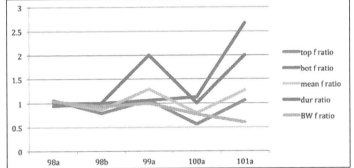

mm.110-113

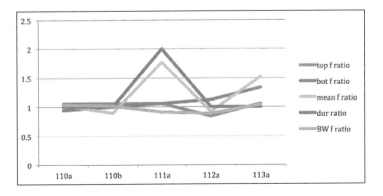

Example 14. The Tenney/Polansky algorithm

> Given four successive parameter values A, B, C, and D, we take
> the unordered intervals x, y, z between the three pairs as shown
> below.
>
>
> A   B   C   D
>   x   y   z
>
> If y is greater than x and z, a partition is placed before C
>
> Pitch example
>
> Pitch: 0   2   8   7
> Interval –class: 2   6   1
>
> ic 6 is greater than ic 2 or 1; Partition before pitch 8.

ratios.[28] Given a ratio that is less than 1, we take its reciprocal as the absolute
ratio. Given ratios .6 and 1.1, we compare absolute ratios 1.666 . . . with 1.1, and
find that the first absolute ratio is "larger" than the second.

Now we are ready to apply parametric dynamics to Arnold Schoenberg's
Piano Piece op. 19, no. 4. Since its pitch and rhythmic structure are contended,
or perhaps even inherently unclear, we use the Tenney/Polansky algorithm to
partition it, operating on the series of durations between its successive time
points. Example 15 shows the piece segmented into fourteen numbered sections. The sections 5a and 5b are actually one according to the algorithm,[29]
but I have divided section 5 into two parts according to the same algorithm
operating on mean pitch and/or low pitch. The partitioning seems intuitively
reasonable—to me at least.

Now that we have sections, we determine the parametric values of each.
Unlike in the Beethoven, the duration and number of attacks vary. This produces another parameter, density, which is the number of attacks divided by
the duration. We also treat loudness as a parameter, which we omitted in the
Beethoven analysis. Examples 16a and 16b respectively show the graph of four
non-pitch parameters and of the five pitch parameters.

The graph in Example 16a shows duration varying in a zigzag pattern,

---

[28] Absolute ratios are defined in analogy with absolute differences, which is the way interval-
classes are defined.

[29] Schoenberg might have approved of my numbering due to his triskaidekaphobia.

Example 15. Schoenberg partitioned according to Tenney/Polansky algorithm

but with the higher values in the middle of the piece. The number of attacks zigzags in tandem with the duration. This causes the density to remain more or less invariant, since it is density determined by the number of attacks divided by the duration. This means the longer a section, the fewer the attacks. The loudness at first contradicts duration especially in sections 4 and 10, so that short sections are generally louder than longer ones.

The graph of pitch parameters in Example 16b shows more zigzag patterns.

Example 16. Non-pitch and pitch parameter values in the Schoenberg

16a. Non-pitch values

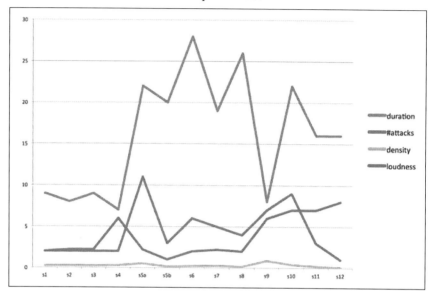

16b. Pitch values

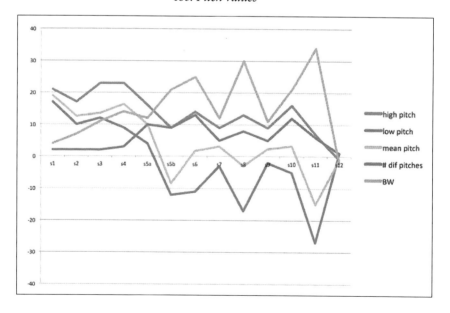

In the first few (and short) sections the parameters more or less agree. After that, the low and high pitch change in contrary motion, but mean pitch does not remain level due to the chords that interpolate or accompany the recitative-like melodies. The mean pitch gradually falls until the nadir at section 11. At section 12 all parameters meet since that section is the single note B below middle C.

Example 17a and 17b show the ratios (or intervals) between the values plotted in Example 16a and Example 16b, respectively. Example 17a shows that the changes between values in the non-pitched parameters are actually more stark than in the graph of the values of these parameters. The number of attacks shoots up in section 5, where the music moves along in constant sixteenth notes. Similarly, the density ratio peaks in section 9, the place where the loud thirty-second notes commence. In general, the nice correspondence of parameter values we saw in Example 16a is more complexly depicted in the ratio graph in Example 17a. Thus, this graph of ratios shows once again that examining the parameter values alone does not give as vivid a picture of the dynamics of a passage as implied by the parameter value graph.

However, in Example 17b, the ratio graph of the changes in pitch parameters are more or less like those we inferred in the pitch value graph in Example 16b. What is different is that the ratios between the parameter values are in the same range rather than situated in different registers. Note how the bandwidth ratios move in opposite direction with the low pitch. Since the music stays in the middle register while the lowest notes of sections alternate, the lower the note, the larger the bandwidth. Further contemplation of these graphs will reveal other aspects of the piece that will have quality-correlates as we listen to it.[30]

6.

Let me conclude with some observations about parametric dynamics and notation. Traditional notation actually provides much more information about musical flow than we usually use when we do analysis. We operate upon the notation to look for patterns of change, just as we operate on pitches to find the intervals between them. However, a list of the parameter values does not show how they change or interrelate to each other very well since the list is digital. Making a graph—an analog coding—which, as score readers we can understand almost immediately, portrays the value change vividly.

[30] As in the Beethoven, the play of parameters might suggest a narrative interpretation for the piece—perhaps an intense conversation that ends with an angry outburst.

Example 17. Ratio graphs of non-pitch and pitch-values in the Schoenberg

17a. Non-pitch

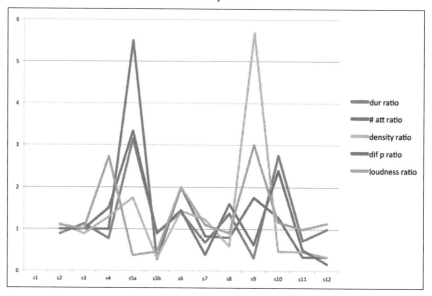

17b. Pitch

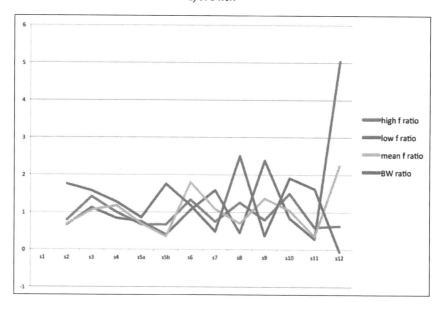

Nonetheless, the precision of parametric dynamics goes only so far. The method is heuristic—meant to discover or draw attention to the changes in music notation that affect musical experience. As I said at the outset, the matching of quantity to quality will always be less than perfect. Analysts will have to make small adjustments, just as musicians do when they perform.

Example 18. Processes of change in mean pitch and bandwidth in sections 5a and 5b in the Schoenberg

I should also point out some issues with parametric dynamics, and these apply to many of the other sonic profile approaches I have mentioned before. The division of music into sections is analeptic rather than proleptic. This means we must wait until the end of a section to determine the values of its parameters. Of course, we listen to music this way when we do not know what will come next.[31] We can nevertheless capture the process of unfolding that occurs within a section by applying parametric dynamics to each event in the section and see how the values change over time. For instance, let us look at sections 5a and 5b, as shown in Example 18. We see how the mean pitch and bandwidth change as we hear new notes come into the music. Thus, the immediate experience of music flow can be portrayed by parametric dynamics. However, when we determine parametric dynamics among sections, choosing one value out of many for each parameter implies that the phenomenology of hearing local process and attending to processes as larger scales of time is different in kind, not degree.

It would seem that parametric dynamics and any of the other sonic profile

---

[31] However, once we have heard a piece a few times we can listen proleptically, anticipating what will occur next. Analeptic and proleptic listening can alternate and intertwine as we hear new aspects and relations on subsequent occasions.

tools seem only suitable to show music that moves forward in one stream. What about polyphonic music or music in which there are multiple simultaneous, uncoordinated processes going on? This is indeed a limitation, but we have seen that parametric dynamics reveals how various parameters engage in a kind of counterpoint with each other. In older music, primary and secondary parameters often contrast with each other.

Another problem plagues any model of music that invokes independently changing parameters: how should one weight each parameter? Lefkowitz and Taavola address this issue by making a first pass over a composition to determine appropriate weights for each parameter, and then do the analysis on a second pass.[32] But the idea that the parameters need to be weighted suggests there is an intention that they could be combined to produce a single series of numbers representing the musical flow; this is reductive[33] and hence defeats my goal to draw attention to the character of musical flow, which has many varying aspects as music moves through time.[34] Still, the parameter changes should have some degree of commensuration. For instance, parametric analysis uses ratios, not differences, for the "intervals" between values to achieve some consistency in comparing parameter change.[35]

Then there is the question of hierarchy; can the sections be grouped to form higher levels of organization? Partitioning the sections into groups of sections, taking the average of each different parametric value over the groups of sections, and doing the dynamics on the series of group averages, etc.to higher levels easily accomplish this. This way of building hierarchic form was first described by Tenney; Benjamin Boretz also discusses converting a series of values into an unordered set and taking a representative of the set to produce a unit at the next level in the hierarchy. Does this take us away from the

[32] Lefkowitz and Taavola, "Segmentation in Music."

[33] A distinction might be made between pre-reduction and post-reduction. The former term indicates that a notation is omitting aspects of the composition or its notation; prescriptive notation and sonic profiling tools are pre-reductive. Post-reductive means that an analytic tool is reducing features of a notation that the tool receives as an input. The output is simpler and often implied to be essential. All notation tends to be pre-reductive, where some analytic tools are post-reductive as in sonograms or the notation of structure that results from Schenkerian analysis.

[34] This desire to have one number stand for many different things is found in the use of letter grades or percentages to grade students. The student's different degrees of success in different aspects of learning are weighted and averaged to determine his/her grade. We can contrast this with letters of recommendation that are far more nuanced than the reduction of the record of a student's progress to a number.

[35] Logarithms could be used just as well. Then we would use the differences between pitches, but take the log of time and dynamic ratios.

immediate flow of the music? I think it might, as I implied before, but I submit that we can listen in many different ways to music, if not at the same time, then at different times.

Let me also put to rest the idea that I consider parametric analysis to be able to uncover or discover universals in music. First of all, the parameters one choses to examine can be different for the same or different pieces and repertoires. The fact that polyphonic music is not well served by one-stream accounts of music experience makes my point in another way. In addition to pre-common-practice music, a good deal of new music involves independent multiple streams, as in music by composers as diverse as Ives, Carter, Cage, and Babbitt. Indeed, how does this music work?

Parametric dynamics is not about analyzing or reducing music to its structure. It is to sensitize the listener and performer to music as flow—the flow of sound and flow of experience. We do this by looking closely at the music notation. Parametric dynamics is both descriptive and explanatory. It seeks to describe how the heard experience of music changes from moment to moment; it also partially explains how musical notation induces particular types of music experience. This follows from the assumption that in music quantity maps to quality and vice versa. In this assertion lurks a challenge to those philosophers of mind who assert that qualia are illusory, and/or have no purpose.

In summary, scores—and how one reads them—differ. Different ontologies are set up by these differences and the phenomenology that arises within these worlds is only internally stable. This is not a gloomy remark, for difference—especially in music experience—is a good thing.

The Modern Score and Its Seven Modes of Performance

EUGENE NARMOUR

IN THE HANDS of great performers, music is always in the process of becoming something emotionally new, a topic central to Christopher Hasty's research. Musicians love to perform because different interpretations afford limitless experiences of auditory arousal. No matter what the valence, performance is personally exciting, and it is exhilarating to share with listeners. To probe music's moods—abstract affects, quixotic expressivity, tensions (with and without resolutions), and other concrete feelings concerning intellect, modeled movement, and temporal explorations of myriad styles and structures—all these fill musicians and their audiences with sonic joy.

The modern score inscribes and encodes all such feelings and attributes. To sophisticated music readers it thus communicates a tremendous amount of performing information that models human interests and passions. As we shall see, however, the score remains only partially and variably formalized, and thus depends on many extramusical sources to realize its full potential.[1]

[1] Caroline Palmer, "The Role of Interpretive Preferences in Music Performance," in *Cognitive Bases of Musical Communication*, ed. Mari Reiss Jones and Susan Holleran (Washington, D.C., American Psychological Association, 1992), 249–62; L. Henry Shaffer, "Intention and Performance," *Psychological Review*, 83/5 (1976), 375–93; John. A. Sloboda, "The Communication of Musical Metre in Piano Performance," *Quarterly Journal of Experimental Psychology*, Section A 35/2 (1983), 377–96; Johan Sundberg, "Music Performance Research: An "Overview," in *Music, Language, Speech and Brain*, ed. Johan Sundberg, Lennart Nord, and Rolf Carlson (London: Macmillan, 1991), 173–83.

In addition, the score-based frame (S) competes directly with the norm-based frame (N), the latter of which organizes interpretations similarly yet relies on *unwritten* scripts.

THEORY (PART 1): THE SCORE FRAME (S) AND ITS SEVEN MODES OF PERFORMANCE

Figure 1 displays seven musical modes that posit an infinite number of basic procedural interpretations vis-à-vis notated scores (S) and written or unwritten scripts (s). These carry with them performing traditions (T) and conventions (C) *currently associated* with the music at hand (traditions = "customs" and conventions = "habits").

Scores (S) and written scripts (s) are two of the grounded frames in music from which we can hypothesize a theory of seven score-based musical interpretations. With formalism (*fm*) as the capstone (capitalized in bold in the Figure), six other modes derive from it and occupy differentiated positions with respect to one another (note the cross-colon correspondences). The oval thus spatially portrays seven related types of musical interpretations.

Above the center box at the top of the oval are six *frames*—tradition, convention, norm, script, score, and recording (TCNsSR). T, C, and N are a conceptual threesome in that they are not dependent on notation, whereas the material sources of sSR are. These six frames constitute the generative constraints that organize the seven modes of interpretation.[2]

The left-to-right order of the symmetrical abbreviation TCNsSR is meant to suggest a possible synchronic, scalar development of the six frames. Unwritten (oral/aural) musical traditions (T) are first consciously established and regulated. These are gradually converted to and regulated by unconscious conventions (C). Unwritten Ns (norms) follow, and eventually written scripts (s) occur, then scores (S), and then recordings (R)—the latter a relatively recent electronic technology that appears in many different media and which today strongly influences interpretation, regardless of mode, norm, or style.[3] (I shall return to the topic of frames later.)

Scripts (s) can be unwritten (aides-memoires orally transmitted), written

[2] T, C, and N that impinge directly on music need to be studied in their own right as a prelude toward understanding the motivations for performance change in cultural history. When unwritten Ts, Cs, and Ns become notated, they become, strictly speaking, part of the score. But the score's notation never completely absorbs the unwritten T, C, and N associated with it. Some unwritten, unnotable properties always remain outside the score, ensuring that every interpretation is contextualized.

[3] I have omitted discussing *sketch* (sk) here, whose rank precedes written script (s). Sk's are work sheets, preludes to a composition and thus eventually morph into S-generated

Figure 1. *The score-based system and its seven modes of performance (around the oval and in the square) arising from six TCNsSR frames (heading list above the oval). Applicable to any musical style, inscribed scores (S) compete with unwritten norm-based (N) frames (apex of oval; compare Fig. 6). Colons in the figure show contrapositional pairs. Transformation at the bottom along with its arrows refers to congruent modal variances (plusses) and noncongruent discrepancies (minuses). These pressure current isms (thus transformation is processive and not a mode). Outside the box lie the forces of reformalisms (left sector) and informalism (right sector).*

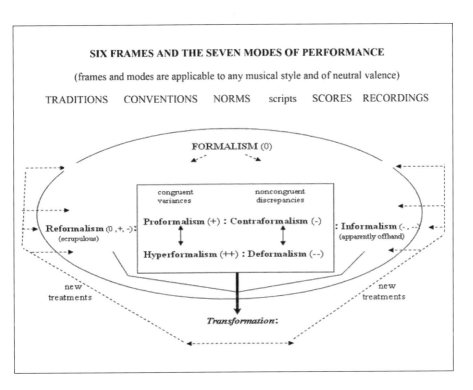

down (in prose or personal shorthand), or notated in one form or another. They are post-sketch. In many cases, written scripts (s) eventually morph into formally notated scores. Scores (S) tend to dominate interpretations more strongly than any of the other *material* frames (s and R), given their degree of *notated* specificity, which accurately symbolizes the foreground of a musical

performances (a synchronic progression would be sk, unwritten s, written s, S, and R.). Each of the six frames (TCNsSR) is independent, but frequently operates in tandem.

work from start to finish (recordings are highly specific, but they lack the imaginal prospects of notation).

The dashed arrows in Figure 1 pointing to modes inside the continuous oval indicate that interpretive modes are never static, but rapidly swirl about, changing the expressive content from moment to moment. If, however, we examine the seven modes as momentarily frozen in time (like a single strip from a film), we can posit two positive modal variations in the left sector of the box—namely, *proformalism* (+) and hyperformalism (++), which congruently stem from, build on, and yet go beyond standard formal interpretations formalized in S. Proformal (*pf*) and hyperformal (*hf*) remain faithful to TCNsSR, whether in part or in whole.

Counterpoised across from these two in the right sector, and similarly derived, are noncongruent *contraformalism* (–) and deformalism (– –), whose realizations are discrepant to the notation and may or may not negatively deviate from the contingent T, C, and N.[4]

Both deformalism (*df*) and its counterpart hyperformalism (*hf*) champion the performer as co-creator, maximizing attention to the interpretation and thus to the individual responsible for its execution. Deformalism (*df*), however, skirts the edge of recomposition. But it has its liabilities—empty exaggeration, impulsive over-emoting, and aesthetic narcissism. Right-sector expression is thus self-directed and tends to be indifferent toward the score.

In terms of a chosen interpretive mode the score itself is neutral in quality (o), regardless of whether the mode involved is congruent with the notation (left sector) or noncongruent with it (right sector). Any mode, including the formalist (*fm*) mode (top of oval), can generate good, mediocre, or bad interpretations,[5] just as any T, C, or N can be either congruent or noncongruent relative to the S's notation.[6] All seven modes possess aesthetic potential and

[4] In an earlier article I demonstrated how an *fm* approach toward performing S could generate logical critiques of interpretations in classical music. See "On the Relationship of Analytical Theory to Performance and Interpretation," in *Explorations in Music, the Arts, and Ideas: Essays in Honor of Leonard B. Meyer*, ed. Eugene Narmour and Ruth Solie (Stuyvesant, New York: Pendragon Press, 1988), 317–40. Now I am much more receptive to nonformalist S-based practices and N-based interpretations, both of which partly derive from hearing too many *fm* performances that are alike. Thus readers will find here a more liberal and more nuanced theory than that found in my earlier article, yet I shall still stress the importance of *fm*-S as the beginning point in the evaluation of performance, particularly in classical music.

[5] As *theoretical* concepts, modes are neutral and unvalorized (neither bad nor good) because, as we shall see, performances are also constituted by varying interpretive *norms* (Ns).

[6] To a French harpsichordist living during the Baroque, *notes inégales* (unnotated rhythms) function as CN and were thus unconsciously executed. However, such rhythms are *noncongruent* and *cf* (right sector) in terms of the isochronous notation of the score. Yet *notes*

must be treated as conceptually equal. Thus the theory of seven modes fails to identify anything like *the* definitive interpretation or *the* authentic performance of any piece of music.

As the arrows in the oval of Figure 1 show, most performances admix modes in a highly fluent manner to characterize the different expressions symbolized by individual parameters in a given S (e.g., in Chopin's music, melodic lines are often interpreted quite freely as regards the written S, while underlying harmonic rhythms are played more formalistically with respect to the notated duration, meter, texture, tempo, etc.).[7] Simultaneous interpretive modes are often functionally mismatched; that is, they noncongruently clash, which means that performance choices inextricably induce musical moods, affects, and emotions, as pointed out in the introduction. Given that nonclosure is the default case in music (without which there is no implication, only closural realization, and thus no processual music), the most commanding interpretations tend to be the ones that simultaneously and noncongruently mix and merge right and left sectors with or against whatever *fm*s are currently in vogue vis-à-vis TCNsSR (the frames at the top of the oval).[8]

Reformalism (*rf*), outside the box and to the left of *pf* and *hf* (see Figure 1), recaptures, reconstructs, and restores historically discredited formalisms (whether T, C, N, s, S, or antiquarian R). With regard to valorizations, *current* TCNsSR is agnostic as to whether an historic restoration is congruently neutral (o), congruently positive (+), or noncongruently negative (−). Although in the last few decades *rf* has had an immense (and largely salutary) influence in changing performance practices in earlier music, it is compromised by the difficulties of successfully recapturing or reinvigorating sonic eras gone by. Consequently, many *rf* interpretations acquire a kind of "restomod" quality[9]—some

inégales are *congruent* with respect to French Baroque C at the time of their emergence. If such *notes inégales* were omitted and replaced by a performance adhering to the actual notated rhythms, Baroque French listeners knowledgeable about the style might regard such omissions as "violations" of N and therefore be in "*mauvais goût*," despite S *not* symbolizing them.

[7] Many experimentalist modernist works mix analog S, s, and digital graphs. See Nelson Goodman, "Fictions," in *Languages of Art: An Approach to a Theory of Symbols* (Indianapolis: Bobbs-Merrill, 1968), 21–26. For a critique of Goodman, see Kari Kurkela, *Note and Tone: A Semantic Analysis of Conventional Music Notation* (Helsinki: Musicological Society of Finland, 1986). For the analog and digital properties of the score, see Morris, this volume.

[8] Critics are known to describe performers' interpretations as predominantly one mode or another (e.g., Weingartner's *cf* liberties with tempo or Toscanini's rigid *fm* metronomy). See Raymond Holden, *The Virtuoso Conductors: The Central European Tradition from Wagner to Karajan* (New Haven: Yale University Press, 2005).

[9] I borrow the term from the field of car restoration, where a vintage car appears impeccably

customs of the past are restored (e.g., adding unwritten ornaments or unnotated rhythms to Baroque sonatas), while others remain resistant to change (e.g., playing Baroque works on modern violins with steel strings and modern bows or performing dance suites originally for harpsichords on modern grand pianos).[10]

With reference to *informalist* (*if*) performances (outside the right box, Figure 1), these are indifferent to present-day TCNsSR and are thus noncongruently negative (−). However, as we shall see in norm-based frames (N), which are indifferent to S and written s (and which accounts for musical cultures without written S or s), *if* interpretations *can function as standards* (as can contraformal [*cf*] or deformal [*df*] ones).

Indifferent *if* performance settles for what happens on the spot. Even if working within S, it is apathetic to the S's claims on interpretation. Disregarding partially formalized S, notated s, and the current Ts and Cs associated with them, unplanned and unintended *if* interpretations create easy-going, self-assured Ns. In opposition to score-based culture, *if*-Ns display qualities of nonchalance, off-handedness, whim, and blasé impulse.[11] Recordings (R) are frequently the source for learning *if* practices, and this medium thus firms up the inherent laxity of *if* disregarding the operative *fm*-S from which it came (i.e., popular culture is *if*, but certain Rs function as Ns of a given style).[12]

Informalism (*if*) has an inherently regressive quality: over time it can devolve and degrade carefully made S music into a kind of unnotated s (such as in the debasement of national anthems, stately hymns, and other S-*fm* music).[13] The phenomenon of retrogression is what enables *if* to produce profound

authentic on the outside, but underneath the hood, the engine and chassis are strictly modern.

[10] The more modest pianoforte, which Bach apparently liked, is more acceptable to *rf* enthusiasts

[11] How to make an interpretation sound utterly *if* is studied by Broadway and pop singers (and their agents) down to the last detail. Attend any concert where a singer performs a Vegas night club act, and you will witness almost exactly the same *if* performance year after year, including meticulously choreographed body movements which have the look of being "offhand." Such performances are prefabricated Ns lying within *if* modes that succeed in tricking us to think that we are hearing a performance made exclusively for our entertainment just this one time.

[12] Although there are many subclasses of *if* (from low to high), the most comprehensive Ns seem to come from (1) interpretations by genuine amateurs (natural folk music), (2) casual interpretations by determined performers who attempt to turn *if* into an art form (and a lifelong paycheck), and (3) indifferent or careless interpretations by inartistic pseudo musicians (wannabees who are insensitive to their lack of musical talent).

[13] Many kinds of *notated* musical genres, which we have historically inherited—folksongs,

interpretive transformations, leading to new compositions where a presumed synchronic history (TCNsSR) reverts back to its origin.[14]

By far the largest mode of interpretation, *if* cuts a very wide swath through musical culture. It is constituted by a murky mixture of intentional and unintentional practices and of notated and unnotated TCNsSR. Only within the last generation or so have scholars begun to take musical *if* seriously as a subject worthy of musicological research.

TRANSFORMATIONAL INTERPRETATION (NEW *FM*)

Interpretations defining the currently reigning *fm* standards are never permanent.[15] Innovative, exciting performers consciously create aesthetically compelling novel treatments that gradually transform current Ts and Cs associated with a given S or s. Because the seven modes of interpretation are conceptually independent, we must therefore conceptualize them as being interconnected, interacting, and having the potential to displace the reigning *fm*.

Transformational interpretations (in bold at the bottom of Figure 1) lie outside the oval and the box (see the thick downward arrow). But as the dashed arrows penetrating the sides of the oval illustrate, any one of *fm*- or non-*fm* modes can create new Ns (whether through variance, scrupulousness, discrepancy, or indifference). A transformational interpretation may move circularly, may progressively travel up or down successive modes (boxed arrows), may leapfrog across modes, or for that matter take any course of action. We simply do not know enough about modes of interpretation to determine how systematic, planned, or random transformation is.

Transformational interpretation has no exact *conceptual* parallel to the

---

nursery rhymes, national anthems, church hymns, military marches, etc.—have long since yielded to *if* treatment.

[14] African American gospel music is a perfect example of how church hymns are transformed into improvisatory s's, which in turn create new compositions. See Catherine Chamblee, "Didactic Performance: Cognitive Processes of Improvisation in Contemporary Gospel Solo Singing," in *Musical Implications: Essays in Honor of Eugene Narmour*, ed. Lawrence F. Bernstein and Alexander Rozin (Hillsdale, NY: Pendragon Press, 2013), 73–98.

[15] Everything said in this section about the concept of *fm*, which is a *score standard* that measures *pf*, *hf*, and *rf*, applies to the concept of N, which is a *central tendency standard* defining *cf*, *df*, and *if*. For the sake of space I will use these abbreviations hereinafter in the text to stand for the seven modes. Such abbreviation can stand for either the noun (*fm* = formalism or formalisms), the adjective (*fm* = formalistic), or the adverb (*fm* = formalistically). Because the single abbreviations s and S in this article stand for script and score (respectively), I will symbolize both their plural and possessive cases with apostrophes: s's, = the plural (scripts) or the possessive (script's); S's = the plural (scores) or the possessive (score's). Context will always clarify the intended function. I take up the topic of N below.

seven modes of performance, such as the oppositions in Figure 1 (colons), which is why it is set apart from the core variants and discrepancies (boxed). In sum, transformation *is not a mode* (hence its italicization in the Figure) but rather an indication of localized and transitory interpretations (within and without the box) that can gradually come to transform performing Ns— replacing current *fm* with new *fm*.

Transformational performances need not involve numerous parametric changes or parametric omissions, although aggregated alterations to a score frequently undermine previously dominant interpretations. But a single parametric modification in a score, if strikingly original and strong enough to gain the attention of influential performers and their audiences, can cause a rival transformative interpretation to depose a prior *fm*. *Fm* renditions of S create the standards for congruent performances of *pf, hf,* and *rf* (left sector of Figure 1).

But performance standards restricted to S are not the sole source of transformation. Coupled with N that reflects the central tendencies characterizing different styles and genres, noncongruent *cf, df,* and *if* (right sector of Figure 1) can also function as the causes of transformation (as captured in Figure 6). Indeed, *cf, df,* and *if* often define the standards for N, which rival the *pf, hf,* and *rf* of S (left-sector, Figure 1).

No one quite understands the social and psychological pressures that turn incongruous and unique performances into newly favored norms of music-making while converting prior esteemed interpretations originating in S into lackluster anachronisms. Perhaps it is because we are engulfed by modern mass communications where types of media rapidly recede to ground, forcing us to seek novelty, regardless of the dubious value of hasty choices.

Generally speaking, it is primarily the *cognitive* processing of performers and listeners that accounts for the acceptance of change, with performers choosing to map new interpretive realizations onto previously rendered sSR while undermining current Ts, Cs, and Ns. Depending on the cultural status of a work and how over-entrenched its SRN, when listeners become weary of hearing the same interpretation over and again (live or via recording), many will come to seek novel variety—although conservative audiences may regard a rival *fm* as a passing fancy (new standards always cause tensions). The causes of transformation are the great unknown in the history of performance practice. The theory of modes discussed here offers one way to sort out the historical vicissitudes of interpretation.[16]

[16] Artistic reasons for performance change emanate from (1) discovery, experimentation, and radical interpretation in the hopes of opening up new conceptions (Glenn Gould is a case in point); (2) impatience with constant overexposure to an existing state of affairs; (3)

The Six Frames of Performance

In the discussion of Figure 1 I abbreviated the six frames as a single unit, TCNsSR. The top of Figure 2 shows how individual frames (T, C, N, s, S, R) become increasingly more specific from left to right. The middle of the Figure displays various contiguous and discontiguous pairs, illustrating that not all frames are simultaneously operative all the time. For example, the premiere of an extremely original piece might lack T, C, and N and rely mostly on S or s; a modern concerto might employ S in the orchestra, while, above the accompaniment, the soloist's s improvises in terms of N. Likewise, many post-modern works mix R and S (the reader can easily think of other combinational examples).

Conceptual frames are dynamic in nature and more stable than modes and N-based frames adapted for specific use. They are, moreover, externally unaffected by transformations, that is, by interpretive changes (see Figures 3 and 6 below). With aggregated frames (TCNsSR), a transformational interpretation may thus create complex challenges for performers and listeners. For instance, in a transitional period of *fm* performances, a given interpretation can simultaneously evoke waning *fm*, current *fm*, and rival *fm* all at once. And these can conflict with one another (bottom of Figure 2).[17]

Figure 3 shows the descending hierarchical relationship stemming from frames (level 5) to modes (4), to norms (N) and its seven modes (3), to s and S (2), and to R and individual works (1). Each T, C, N, s, S, and R is independently shaped by all seven nested modes, as is each nested N, each nested s and S, and each nested idiostructural interpretation of a work. In sum, seven common interpretive responses are possible *throughout the various levels* of music: *fm, pf, hf, rf, cf, df,* and *if*. Because the amount of combinatoriality between levels is immense, I confine myself in this article to the six frames and the

being bored with standards that have grown stale; (4) willfulness to defy what is accepted as a cultural rule; and (5) a desire for self-attention. Also playing a part are entrepreneurial wishes (and budgetary needs) to sell more tickets by presenting concerts that exaggerate novelty or provoke the status quo (e.g., the Ballets Russes in the early twentieth century). Music itself offers reasons for change: too many pieces sound stylistically alike, and their constant repetition begs for varied differentiation (witness the current pop scene).

[17] As units, contiguous individual frames (T, C, N, s, S, or R) can develop synchronically or discontiguously with only a modicum of feedback, as in Figure 2. As pairs (TC, TN, Ts, TS, TR, Cs, CS, CR, sS, Ss, SR), triplets (TCs, TCS, TCR, CNR, CsS, CsR, sSR), or quadruplets (TCsS, CsSR, TCSR, TsSR), such sequences with increased specification will tend to generate incrementally dense cross-pollination. Thus, when we ascribe, analyze, trace, or historicize any kind of performing mode to a particular interpretation, many interconnected frames have to be taken into account.

seven modes. Because frames are cognitive adaptations, they display different kinds of modal projections: T, C, N, and s range from *if* to *fm*; S projects from the *pf* to *hf*, whereas Rs, being fixed, are always *hf* by definition.

Figure 2. The six frames of music (TCNsSR) and their interrelationships. Observe the synchronic development and increased fixedness from left to right: having to be thought about, conscious traditions (T) are more open and less fixed than unconscious conventions (C), which are automatically applied; norms (N) in the middle lay the groundwork for writing and catalyze the emergence of written scripts (s), which are less formalized than scores (S); recordings (R) are the most fixed frames of all. Contiguous and discontiguous pair possibilities are illustrated in the middle of the Figure. All frames can be simultaneously active, and those from the recent past, the current present, and rivals on the horizon provide multiple possibilities for interpretations that refresh the listening experience.

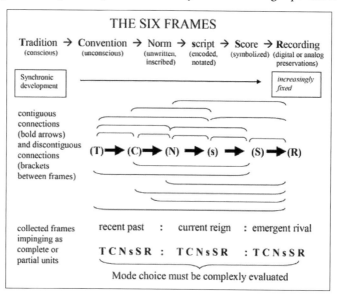

I borrow the word *frame* from the distinctive definitions found in psychology, which point to differences among cognitive schemas, plans, scripts, procedural knowledge, and so forth. I also rely partly on AI concepts, which are concerned with generalizability, openness, syntax, data values, categories, global versus local meanings, and the like.

Frames can be thought of as six diverse conceptual adaptations necessary for the contemplation and discussion of musical interpretation. T, C, and N belong to prototypical concepts that lay the groundwork for the material objects of S and s. I have already discussed the puzzling status of R as a frame, which itself is both an aesthetically finished performance and simultaneously an observational point of view of earlier and current preservations from which performers can craft rival interpretations without consideration of original S or s (recall Figure 2).

Figure 3. The seven herarchical modes from T and C to N (central tendencies), s, S (compositional styles), and R (interpretations of works). Each level is independently subject to all seven nested modes: (fm), (pf), (hf), (fm); (cf), (df), and (if). Like the score-system, the unwritten norm system (N) also organizes itself around standards (see Fig. 6).

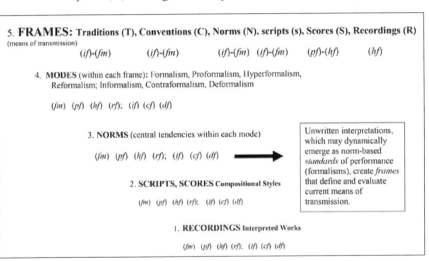

Each of the six frames is flexibly invoked. Frames enable performers to access interpretive creativity by providing imaginative *fms*. For classical musicians the jumping-off point is a partial *fm*, the S. For jazz musicians the quest often begins with an iconic R along with s, either unwritten, notated, or a combination of the two, a rich trove of unwritten N, and perhaps also a passing knowledge of S. For the *if* musician it is usually an imaginal s, rather than a written one, plus loose collections of Ns that function as the entry points for interpreting a popular piece of music. For folklore traditions (notated or unnotated music) the interpretive springboard begins with a deep knowledge of, affection for, and commitment to the cultural Ts, Cs, and Ns in which a given song was nurtured.[18] Once a performance is initiated and learned through

---

[18] To underscore the importance of T, C, and N consider that if an *hf* expression is essential to

numerous presentations, any or all of the six frames (TCNsSR) can simultaneously come into play, as we saw in Figure 2.[19]

The inherent flexibility of frames accounts for why they are constant yet
transitive and both cohesive and yet persistently open. All frames are typical
in certain ways, unique in others, and deterministic in signs and gestures while
providing instructions, interactions, and concrete stylistic information. They
can be loosely defined (as in s) or extremely detailed (as in a modern S or R).

Score (S) and Written or Unwritten Script (s)

Although S is a powerful frame of consideration in categorizing and evaluating a given performance (not to mention in planning an interpretation), s
is equally important. The latter can range from the fully written to the partially notated, to the completely unnotated (oral or aural) and yet still com-
petently indicate or imply interpretive content—for example, the sparsely
rhythmicized, untextured, notated s found in some early seventeenth-century
monodies (bare-boned melodies, figured basses, little else) or in quasi-notated
improvisatory keyboard music from the same era.[20]

Readable without being performed, S and s are *partially* formalized and
thus provide the novel possibility of both mentalistic interpretation and observational learning.[21]

---

an implied genre or an implied style, then the realization of a deadpan or literal performance
of S could sound noticeably *cf* or even *df*.

[19] A classical pianist might play the initial motives in a Mozart sonata strictly according to
fm-S, but then in the recapitulation add *cf* ornamental variations to the motives while being
conscious that such limited additions were generally common in Classical Ts and Cs. Pianists become cognizant of *rf*-Ns from the many *rf* recordings available today (such as those
of Robert Levin or Malcolm Bilson).

[20] See Susan McClary, this volume. Scripts vary greatly in the precision of their notation.
This ranges from proto-sk to sk to proto-s to s to proto-S to S. And these do not necessarily coincide with written or unwritten usages. I symbolize s with a diminutive, lower-case
letter to remind us that it carries much less information than S. Scripts deserve much more
study and are an important artistic media in and of themselves. What unites *S* and *s* is that
both representations are committed to temporal syntactic functions, driving toward finished
aesthetic experiences. With more attention given to notational precision and symbological
consistency than to sk, s frequently forms the foundation for the development of S. But we
still need more study of s's as artworks in their own right.

[21] I regard any inscribed or printed artifact that represents sound in symbolic form as a
musical S or a written s regardless of the number of lines or staves or the timbral setting (the
verb forms "scoring" or "scored" can be contextually reserved to refer to the orchestration
of scores). By "notation" one can mean not just the note symbols but also all other written

Recording (R)

Performers calculating interpretations also depend on Rs, which elevate certain performances to standards worthy not only of preservation but also of emulation and continuous evaluation.[22] Because of their fixedness (like s and S), Rs are invoked by performers as frames for not only studying T, C, and N but also for evaluating current performing styles in order to plan alternative interpretations.[23] This is particularly important in improvisation. Indeed, in many genres of music, R, rather than S or s, serves as the model of choice for deciding how to perform a work. In short, in the modern world, we must acknowledge that Rs, quite apart from their aural aesthetic pleasures, are no less a source of observational learning (and thus a means of social transmission) than N, s, or S.[24]

Even musicians who are highly proficient in reading S will seek out R to supplement their interpretive conceptions. Moreover, R makes all kinds of compositional interpretations accessible to notationally illiterate musicians. Ultimately, the availability of R—whether antiquated, still current, or brand

or printed markings, abbreviations, signs, numbers, words, and linguistic phrases common to S or s .

[22] R has built-in limitations. Although we cannot actually *read* music from LPs, tapes, or disks, through psychophysical means we can acquire partially formalized representations of them through spectrographic transcription, as shall be shown below.

[23] Used in this essay as more or less synonymous terms, the words "perform" and "interpret" perhaps require some clarification. We frequently use the word "performance" to refer to formal concerts of orchestral, chamber, or choral ensembles—public occasions that closely follow selected musical S's. For less ceremonial events, many invoke the term "interpretation" or "treatment" because rendering the music is more *if*-s and less circumscribed by *fm*-S. To distinguish musical presentations this way is, however, misleading and too simplistic because, as we shall see, *fm* rules S and yet affords interpretations that strongly deviate from it (e.g., *pf* and *hf*). In addition, *if* has its own way of performance—in the central tendency standards of N. Hence I use "perform" and "interpret" more or less interchangeably. Strictly speaking, prescribed electronic music is a "presentation," not a performance or an interpretation even though it can be notated, i.e., represented in S, s , or otherwise (schematics, graphs, charts, etc.).

[24] See Michael Chanan, *Repeated Takes: A Short History of Recording and its Effects on Music* (London: Verso, 1995); Nicholas Cook, *Beyond the Score: Music as Performance* (Oxford: Oxford University Press, 2013); Peter Johnson, "The Legacy of Recordings," in *Musical Performance: A Guide to Understanding*, ed. John Rink (Cambridge: Cambridge University Press, 2002), 197–212; Robert Philip, *Performing Music in the Age of Recording* (New Haven: Yale University Press, 2004) and *Early Recordings and Musical Style: Changing Tastes in Instrumental Performance, 1900–1950* (Cambridge: Cambridge University Press, 1992). The journal *Musicae Scientiae*, 11/2 (2007) and 14/2 (2010), devotes two issues to the subject of recordings.

new (recall Figure 2)—adds more scholarly complexity into determining the multiple means of transmission and the assorted T, C, and N associated with S or s. Although R obviously presents more vivid auditory realizations than s or S, and although R is a finished interpretation, it lacks, as said, the imaginal potential *symbologically* embedded in written or printed music.

Composer Performer, and Listener

The relationships between individual S, R, and s vis-à-vis the composer, performer, and solitary listener always exist in a state of flux. The constant variability among the three participants is never fixed, quite apart from the ongoing impingements emanating from current Ts and Cs. Perfect equilibrium among TCNsSR and composer, performer, or listener is never static or predetermined.[25] Nevertheless, S's have always functioned as main channels through which performers understand composers and their works.

In this connection, consider Figure 4. In terms of sSR the seven configurations here illustrate the ongoing changeability among composer, performer, and listener. I have symbolized this variability spatially with regard to the circle according to extent of mental focus (symbolized by the length of the arrows).[26] Equilibriums do occur (far-left configuration, top row), but composers can dominate the musical experience by writing self-absorbed or unreasonably difficult works (e.g., Stockhausen, Babbitt, et al.) such that the receptive distance of the music fails to engage both a listener and an over-worked performer. Similarly, improvising virtuosos can expend so much energy drawing attention to preparation and technique that both composers and listeners become distanced from the interpretive meaning driving the composition.

The dynamic quality of musical experience is not dependent only on the composer or the performer but also on the listener, who can easily suppress self-centered works by simply not paying attention. Even in equilibrated circumstances, listeners can contribute powerfully to the musical experience by

[25] All too many discussions in music theory, musicology, and philosophical criticism deal with musical interpretation in the light of either composers and S's or performers and their s interpretations. Input from ordinary individual listening is frequently overlooked altogether unless it plays into an historical audience, a ritualistic social occasion, or a religious service. The investigation of normal individuals takes place largely in the field of psychology (music perception, cognition, and affective science). To incorporate individual, ordinary listeners into philosophical conversations about music, the various fields of music need to become more interdisciplinary.

[26] See Eric F. Clarke, "Listening to Performance," *Musical Performance: A Guide to Understanding*, ed. John Rink (Cambridge: Cambridge University Press), 185–96.

Figure 4. Variable temporal relationships among composers (C), performers (P), and listeners (L) in terms of script, score, and recording (the sSR circle). Given an equillibrated norm, the three ensuing displays of the first row constrast concepts of C-, P-, and L-dominance. The second row contrasts three kinds of listening. A live experience of a work based on s or S would be different from one based on R (not shown in the circles). Nor would the types of attentive arrows (bold, dashed, squiggly) be exactly the same. In addition, s would ordinarily command less authority than S or R, and thus the C of s would be more distal from the locations of P and L, where interpretive encoding would tend to be less precise.

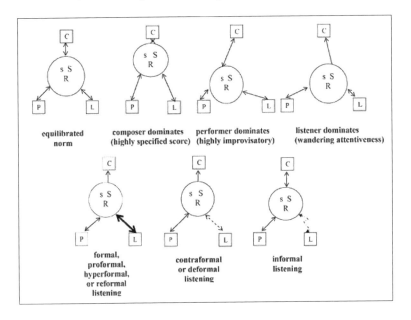

bringing intense attention to bear, in effect maximizing the strength of the musical signal (the thickness of the shaft, bottom row, Figure 4), whether such concentration is *fm*, *pf*, *hf*, or *rf* (recall Figure 3). One can also listen in a very casual way (thin dashed line), or with an erratic tuning in and out of what is being presented (symbolized by the crooked, meandering line). The high variability between composer, performer, and listener is always an intervening concern in the analysis of TCNsSR. This adds immeasurable richness, depth, and complexity to researching how adopted interpretative modes later become social adaptations.

Figures 1–4 displayed hierarchical conceptions of frames (TCNsSR or some combination thereof), nested modes of interpretation (*fm*, *pf*, *hf*, *rf*, *if*, *cf*, *df*), and nested N (proto-standards or central tendencies within modes). But it should not be overlooked that all these operate underneath the meta-levels of psychology, history, culture, and aesthetics.[27]

> Figure 5. *The triarchy among composer, performer, and listener surrounding s, S, and R amid the swirling supra-domains of psychological processing and social communication. Despite their stability, sSR are only partially formalized due to the complexity of concert music as a system of communication that is individually decoded (as opposed to performative, participative, communal music). Fm, pf, hf, fm, cf, df, and if define S, s, and R in each part of the triarchy and for all levels and interactive members that constitute a given experience of music. Composition itself employs all these modes within TCNsSR frames; performers present them; and listeners perceive and cognize them.*

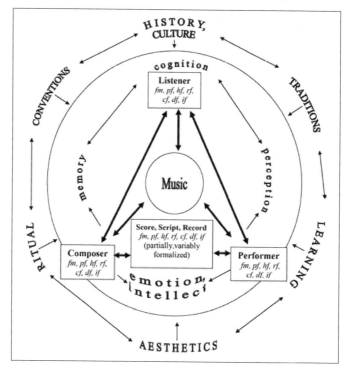

[27] For a discussion of this with reference to the study of music and music theory in the pantheon of knowledge, see Eugene Narmour, "Our Varying Histories and Future Potential: Models and Maps in Science, the Humanities, and in Music Theory," *Music Perception* 29/1 (2011), 1–21. For an extended discussion of performance and culture, see Cook, *Beyond the Score* (and his contribution to this volume).

To theorize about the vast world of musical interpretation with any certainty we need clarity concerning all the initial conditions. It is obvious that Ts, Cs, and Ns are mutable, less fixed, and much more fuzzily defined than s, S, and R and are thus less reliable as starting points in the construction of a *theory* of performance. In addition, as the name implies, s itself is much more variable and thus "noisier" than S, whose notations and signs tend toward much more detail. Thus, of the six frames, S and R produce the most reliably encoded signals.

Much of the world's music survives, of course, without any written representation and is transmitted solely by unconscious C, conscious T, and learned N. Throughout music history, even as written representations emerged, oral or aural C and T always remained important in the interpretation of unwritten mental s, and to this day are of crucial necessity to the understanding of music even when relying on the most meticulously inscribed S's that ever existed. For that matter, Rs themselves, no matter how carefully produced, will always depend on the unwritten Ts, and Cs of Ns in order to be interpreted and understood correctly.

Norms (N) as Frames and as Formalist Standards Behind the Seven Modes of Interpretation

Ns have always functioned as central tendency standards for societies without written s or S. As a practice within oral cultures, N nevertheless cultivates and displays the same kinds of performance enhancements and discrepancies found in S. But instead of S as the *fm* standard, selected Ns function as the *fm* basis of comparison. Thus N, which by definition does not initially rely on inscription, produces the same kinds of artistic sophistications found in S-literate cultures.

Even though the invention of musical notation resulted in s and S that transliterated many unwritten Ns into written ones, N-based cultures have in most cases retained Ns as the interpretive standards. And these continue to function as such for musicians today who are either musically illiterate or literate but do not wish to rely on S or s. After all, not all musics are amenable to S's *fm* notation. However, S-based music and N-based music are not dichotomously independent. Whether literate or illiterate, both S- and N-based frames emanate from the same, unified musical mind and thus function according to prevailing *fm* standards while generating six modal derivatives (*pf, hf, rf, if, cf,* and *df*).

N-based frames with their own *fm* standards provide literate musicians with alternative ways of making and listening to music. There are many such people who are disinterested in reading S and yet live in S-driven societies and reject the S-frame : (1) those who for whatever personal reasons are simply indifferent to inscribed music and thus prefer to ignore it; (2) those who are most comfortable with *if* and want to commit themselves only to this mode of interpretation, which disdains the written S; (3) those who find music with *fm* S as a standard either too unforgiving or too demanding; (4) those who balk at any kind of *fm* S authority and who, whatever the origin of the music, choose a contrarian musical life exploring only noncongruent modes (*if, cf,* and *df*); and (5) cultures that for religious, political, or sociological reasons have no choice but to rely on *unwritten* s in order to generate music via given N as the *fm*-standard (whether transmitted orally or conveyed aurally).

Whatever the circumstances, *fm* standards from N-based music are cognitively structured in much the same way as standard *fm* S, the main difference being that standard *fm* N tends to create less complex *models* of the sonic world than S- or s-generated musics (which rely on *both* models and theories). By this I mean that *fm* S leans toward richer and thus theoretically more abstract, complex, intellectual music (e.g., complex counterpoint) than that of N frames.

But this does not mean that the music or the aesthetic that the fm S-standard produces is more valuable than that of the N-standard. As emphasized in Figure 5, all music is circumscribed by concentric rings of culture, ritual, learning, and aesthetics. Therefore, value or meaning is not wholly constrained by inscribed S-frames *or by* N-frames but rather by what a given culture extrinsically projects in toto onto various musical conceptualizations. Written music is not to be valorized *a priori* as greater than unwritten music. But the *study* of unwritten TCN is better comprehended by written sSR than by oral or aural culture just as the *interpretation* of sSR is best understood in the context of TCN.

Figure 6 outlines the N-frame: a reigning *fm*-standard N (top) is followed in the left sector by congruent *pf, hf,* and *rf* N. In the right sector, noncongruent *if, cf,* and *df* N sit in opposition. Both sectors have the ultimate potential to generate transformalism ("transnormalism") and concomitantly to produce rival *fm*-standard Ns (arrows), some of which over time will gain the upper hand. The seven modes embody structural functions within the TCNsSR-frames (top of Figure 6), which is obvious and needs no extended discussion.

Every style depends on frames and modes, but these are not genre-constrained. It so happens that S-*fm* is the most common interpretative mode in classical music, and classical T, C, and N are frequently congruent with classical music's *fm*-S. On the whole, it is also true that interpretive Ns in classical music—how we expect performances of this music to be performed—closely follow S (relative to other styles). Thus interpretive *fm* modes and the musical content of the N frame are closely correlated in classical music (recall the earlier remark about mode and S).

Figure 6. The unwritten N-system (an emulation of Figs. 1 and 7). Unwritten Ns are imaginal, not conceptual (like T and C), but because they are frequently converted and absorbed into s and S, I have shown the phenomenon in two parts, the first being unwritten and constructed wholly through cultural dissemination and the second ultimately emerging as an artificially constructed notational standard of a rising central tendency. But in cultures that prefer unwritten N, the implied notation system may never take hold. Observe also that with today's technology N-based systems are more easily framed by R, making a developmental notation of a given N seem less necessary.

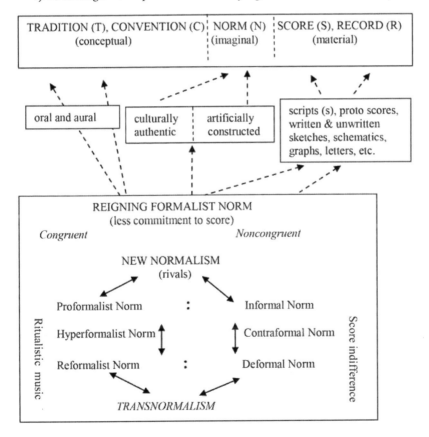

Fm, however, is not an interpretation only applied to classical music. Music that accompanies bodily movement (e.g., marches, waltzes, polkas, tangos, etc.) is often performed in close accordance to S-notation (i.e., to the *fm* mode). So are ceremonious works of N (e.g., chants, hymns, anthems and other ritual music). In all cases, we recognize that the modes of performance are faithful to expectedly congruent S's or Ns. Were this not so, we would not be so alert to *cf* or *df* realizations when noncongruent styles and discrepant genres suddenly appear. Consequently, we wince when mode and N are flagrantly breached (as when two amateur pianists attempt to sight-read a four-hand classical work lying way beyond their capability, or when a *basso profondo* operatically misinterprets the quiet naïve charm of a nursery rhyme).

However, in the N-based frame, certain modal interpretations may or may not closely adhere to S. In country-western music S- or s-frames are almost always played in *if* mode (vis-à-vis S). Numerous noncongruent Ns of interpretation in *if* mode exist because it has developed many potential strategies to contravene the notation of printed S and s. For example, the reigning N of country-western music in the 1930s versus today's over-polished Rs are noticeably deficient in terms of comparative expression. That is, the older N is interpretively inbred and sounds more authentic to the style, whereas in today's stylistic idiom, the reigning N sounds highly calculated and thus loses much of its inherited naturalism. There is no confusion about the same usage of similar *if modes*. But the Ns in the former (i.e., genuinely folksy) are noticeably different in content than the Ns of the latter (i.e., manipulative).

Every mode embodies an interpretive N-frame, prototypical ways of differentiating one given performance from other Ns. The important point is that with noncongruent modes (*if*, *cf*, and *df*) Ns function as simple *models* (and not just as *standards*) for evaluating interpretation. This often renders the S frame less relevant as regards the performance at hand. A critical analysis of an interpretation is thus not only based on S (or written s) but also on the central tendency standards of an expected N, as framed by the relevant T and C (recall Figure 3). Put another way, N is to noncongruent *if*, *cf*, and *df* (right sector) what S (or s) is to congruent *fm*, *pf*, *hf*, and *rf* (left sector). Imagine how any style or genre sounds, and you will not only simultaneously project the T and C governing it but simultaneously project its auditory N (or Ns) and its mode of interpretation. The S-frame is always buffeted about by the kinds of noncongruent interpretations that swirl around it. *If*, *cf* and *df* of N is always indifferent to S—which has a strong theoretic and abstract score—and independent of it. To survive, the *fm* components of S (or s) must be flexible and strongly appealing to audiences. What this means is that *fm* S-culture (literacy) is easily stamped out by *if* N-culture (indifference and illiteracy). All this is by way of saying that theoretic, abstract writing, scripting, or scoring of any musical sort are of bedrock importance to the study of culture.

Modeled Norms (Unwritten Scripts) and Theorized Scores (Inscribed Musics)

Thus for many genres and styles, violating the written S on which a piece is based is common in N. In *if*, S *deviation* is often N, and *noncongruent* Ts and Cs with respect to S are frequently *congruent* with discrepant right-sector frames.[28] So certain kinds of *cf* or *df* create Ns within stipulated non-*fm* modes as regards the performance of S (e.g., casual Broadway melodies and indifferent pop tunes of all sorts, all of which are carefully notated but whose standards often follow N and not S). What this means is that *cf*, *df*, and *if* Ts and Cs can hold *more* N-sway as interpretive standards than the notational standards of S or s (the original published frames of the work). Indeed, that is one manifestation of N: a modeled interpretation where discrepant T and C within a given style or genre outweigh the notated stipulations of S even though S is the originally copyrighted source of the music. Such interpretive cultural noncongruence is partly why today's performers want to copyright their actual performances and not just their scores.[29]

What, then, is the purpose of S where mode is not congruent and where unwritten *cf*, *df*, and *if* Ns are the models? The answer is that S, however transgressed, ignored, and degraded, remains a fundamental comparative frame for understanding modes and unwritten Ns that are noncongruent with it (analyzing and explaining level-comparisons between different S's and noncongruent modes and Ns are also necessary). In short, S (and written s) *allows for an abstract theory of interpretation*, where modeling the musical input from mode, N, style, genre, and individual work create for the listener enriched mental concepts for fully evaluating their experience. Without S or s, one is left only with an N framework, which is a model of the musical input *without* a written

---

[28] Because of the hierarchical nature of performance, it is possible to have congruence on one level while noncongruence occurs on another level (recall Figure 4). Such possibilities offer a key to understanding the interleveled complexities of performance.

[29] Interpretive swing rhythms routinely applied to isochronous notations in S are cases in point of how Ns can outrank S (and how T and C can be noncongruent with S but congruent with the *if*, *cf*, and *df* standards of N). *Cf* interpretations are prevalent in big band music so that when composers want to have the instrumentalists actually play the isochronous notes as written, they mark the score with additional symbols (dots, tenutos, accents, etc.), so as to *rf* the score to communicate what it already contains. See fn. 6, also Butterfield, this volume.

theory. Scholars who study unwritten music frequently turn N-based frames into inscribed s or S so that they can theoretically and abstractly analyze such music. That way, they move from a hypothesized *model* to an analytical *theory*: no unwritten interpretive N ever relegates the inscribed *fm*-S to irrelevance. This is because S and s—both high-level frames—implacably retain properties of partial *fm* no matter how much input from unwritten lower-level modes, Ns, and styles lines up against the standards of *fm*-S.

Ordinary listeners recognize the styles and genres of pieces, and these enable them to evaluate interpretations *by recognizing deviations from interpretive Ns* across all seven modes of performance. This is made much easier by the advent of standard Rs of influential pieces inasmuch as modern listeners tend to be more familiar with Rs than with S or s frames. Indeed, R has fundamentally changed the way we listen, evaluate, and respond to musical interpretations.

The theory that I expostulate here appears largely tied to Western tonal art music (I will explain below how the theory deals with popular styles). My assertion about there being TCNsSR and seven modes of performance is a contextual, cultural, historical, and dialogical paradigm that is constrained by that scholarly slice of time wherein we live and eke out our personal research. Art music is more concerned about adherence to S—whether *fm, pf, hf,* or *rf* (the congruent left sector of Figure 1)—than any other type of interpretation. So situating *fm* with sSR at the top of an oval of seven modes is not unreasonable. After all, the modern S is the closest historical model we have to a more-or-less reliable symbolic representation of performed music, and with period R (from the gramophone onward), the *unnotated* Cs, Ts, and contemporaneous Ns associated with earlier performances of historical S are now available for all to hear and learn from. Therefore electing S as a theoretical point of departure is efficient. As an artifact, it has proved to be an economical and intuitive representation of musical sound (whatever its transient deficiencies are).[30] However, ethnographers and others studying unwritten music may wish to rely only on unwritten and independent *fms* of N, as shown in Figure 6.

---

[30] As many different editions of classical S are readily available, we must contend with the question, whose S or what kinds of S's are we talking about? Important considerations here are obviously whether S is a reliable or an unreliable scholarly edition, a reliable or an unreliable performing edition, a first edition, a second edition, a German edition, a French edition, an authorized or unauthorized print by the composer, and so forth. We must also determine the contextual circumstances surrounding the contemporaneous TCN of any s or S.

A Methodology for S-frames

A critical theory of performance and interpretation requires a methodology, which I hypothesize in Figure 7 (based on Figures 1 and 6). Here variant and discrepant modal interpretations (large enveloping boxes) generate different kinds of outcomes; in the left box (*pf, hf,* and *rf*) we find new composition (via development, improvisation, developmental variation, etc.), and in the right box (*cf, df,* and *if*), we find recomposition (via non-developmental variations, transcriptions, adaptations, etc.).

Graphically conceived, interpretive realizations (dashed arrows pointing to the rectangles) feed downward into the historical transformation of musical style. This occurs because independently emerging transformational interpretations gather strength (increasingly ascendant bold arrows). As we saw in Figure 1, they then feed their novel interpretations upward with the purpose of eventually establishing new *fm*. All this progressively culminates in permanent changes to both performance and historical style. Thus the performing modes, each in its own way, co-create along with the composer the development of musical composition.

Inside the center of Figure 7 I list the evaluative criteria I invoke in order to define the degrees of enhancement (*pf, hf, rf*) and discrepancy (*cf, df, if*). I employ both parametric and formal heuristics (Figure 7, vertical middle), both of which remain open to the possibilities of contextual circumstance. Some single parametric changes are so bizarre as to make the *form* (shape) of a whole passage sound highly differentiated (*ab* or *AB*), with little need for other-parametric interference). In the positive left sector (+) a distinction between *pf* and *hf* is possible because parametric dimensions can functionally and subtly coalesce while still concording with S's notation.

For example, a written *piano* dynamic could be played *pp* while a *poco ritardando* was noticeably lengthened by strongly cumulating the duration. From this, one would sense a *pf* interpretation because just three dimensions are affected (dynamic, tempo, and duration). In other words, in an enhancement context, to cause the difference between *pf*, a single plus (+), and hf, two pluses (++), six or more parametric dimensions are required to achieve the hyper mode. The analytical rules between *cf* and *df* in the right sector are defined in exactly the same way. (Of course, the most reliable criterion in N is form because its aggregative parameters have already formally realized a shape toward a differentiated, negatively valenced *B*.)

In addition to a differentiated formal heuristic (*ab* or *AB*), the parametric heuristic in Figure 7 is formulated in terms of the percentage of musical

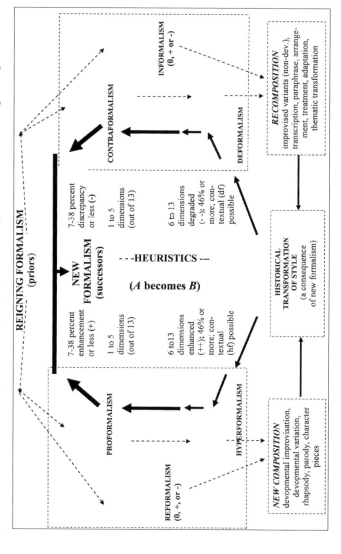

Figure 7. A variation of Fig. 1, Figure 7 shows (1) how different kinds of congruent (left side; +, ++) and noncongruent (right side; -, - -) interpretations move away from reigning fm (center priors) toward creating new compositions and changes in style (bottom of diagram) and (2) how new fm arises from these changes (ascending arrows growing progressively thicker) until various successors transform and ultimately displace prior preferences. Heuristics (center box) provide guidelines for defining pf, hf, rf, if, cf, and df from one another. Different modes are methodologically ascribed by the number of dimensions (12) or parameters (26; see Narmour, 2015, Fig. 1) that are interpretively altered according to a given standard (whether T, C, N, s, S, or R; see Fig. 2 above). The heuristics allow for the possibility of contextual differentiation and (most important) for perceived auditory changes in ongoing aggregate form (e.g., a scored A becoming an experienced B).

dimensions that undergo change. The methodology behind this is that there are at least thirteen parametric dimensions: melody, harmony, timbre, mode/ scale step, rhythm, duration, meter, dynamic, tempo, rate, texture, silence [rests], and location.[31] If 46% or more (roughly half) of the notationally speci- fied parametric relationships are *violated* (6–13 parametric dimensions), then the interpretation of the score is changed sufficiently so as to be *df*. Analo- gously, if more than 46% of the parameters are *heightened*, then the perfor- mance is *hf*.

I stress again that the ascription of positive (+, ++) or negative (−, − −) valences is purely a conceptual/analytical heuristic. The good/bad typically evoked by such signs has absolutely nothing to do with the inherent musical value of the performances to which these terms are attributed. Tones symbol- ized in S are commonly replaced or discarded in opera arias, jazz improvisa- tions, and popular songs to satisfying aesthetic effect. Conversely, *pf* and *hf* can produce disappointing effects. As we saw in the discussion of Figure 1, the seven interpretive modes are not only theoretically equal in conceptual impor- tance and potential value but are in fact also musically ubiquitous. After all, interpretations in classical music would never change if *fm* were the mode of greatest value. The fact is, the standards of classical music, despite being stylis- tically tethered to the printed S, are forever changing, which, at least theoreti- cally, is potentially a good thing. Otherwise, audiences might become bored and seek aesthetic entertainment elsewhere.

ANALYSIS (PART 2): FORMALISM

Fm can function as a standard inasmuch as its interpretive realizations, so it is believed, neither add to, nor subtract from, anything that is notated in S—or that is associated with it by virtue of C or T. *Fm* is, so to speak, the *de jure* case of interpretation, legalized by the notation and by contingent usage. In a psy- chological sense, however, *fm* as a practice is not this simplistic. Because our nervous systems find exact replication difficult, if not impossible to achieve, slight interpretive perturbations in terms of a given notation are a biologi- cal given, unconsciously and permanently integrated into our auditory and

---

[31] Location refers to the sound source (left, right, or center; above, below, or center; in front, behind, or center) and how faraway it is. S often indicates that solos or ensembles are to play off stage, but it is not unusual to see this written directive ignored (a *cf* or *df*). Opera direc- tors often move weak singers closer to the apron to intensify their singing (*pf* or *hf*) even if that violates S. American orchestras rarely play Viennese music with cellos and first violins to the left of the conductor (contra T and C). Location has a strong effect on the musical experience, which is partly why concertgoers are so fussy about where they sit.

muscle memories. That is, no one plays S literally, as symbolized, though some come closer than others (and musicians with the right charisma can make you believe they are playing S exactly as written). Categorical perception wipes out physiological jitter and takes us directly to interpretative intention.[32]

Fm's motto is to "let the notes speak for themselves." Deference to past authority is its interpretive mindset. Beholden more to the composer than to the listener, *fm*'s hands-off reverence to S aims for minimal personal expression and avoids overt subjective display. The attitude is that of consummate artistry in the service of acknowledged creative greatness, the music deserving of a scrupulous *reproduction* with nominal elaboration rather an *interpretation*. *Fm* performers thus keep their personalities at bay and attempt coherent, intellectual "objectivity." They strive to channel S directly to the listener-connoisseur by remaining absolutely faithful to the notation—above and beyond the jitter—to mediate faithfully all of S's markings (notes, symbols, signs, words, numbers, etc.).

Two Interpretations (Bach)

A beautiful example mixing both *fm* and *pf* can be heard in Nathan Milstein's highly regarded R of the Bach solo violin sonatas and partitas. Example 1 excerpts four measures from the first movement of the composer's second partita in D minor, and Milstein's interpretation is contrasted with the performance of Rachel Podger.[33]

A good deal of research has shown that musical structure has a definite effect on manifest-level interpretive decisions[34] even though at higher levels

---

[32] In its search for general truths, the scientific method tends to emphasize behavioral averages. Unlike that approach, I am interested here in using scientific techniques (chiefly spectrographic analysis) to shed light on analytical criticism—that most humanistic behavior—specifically to analyze interpretive differences and project evaluations between *individual* performances and interpretations that lie outside of averages. Nevertheless, common behaviors (averages) are very important for deducing interpretive T, C, and N, but here again only to the extent that they impinge on the critical analysis at hand.

[33] The data extracted for the following discussion come from performances by Nathan Milstein, *Bach: Partitas for Unaccompanied Violin*, ©1998, 1954 by EMI Classics, EMI 5668702, CD, and Rachel Podger, *Violin Sonatas and Partitas Vol. 1*, ©1999 by Channel Classics, CCS 12198, CD, from Bach's Partita no. 2 for solo violin, mm. 1–4. I urge the reader to consult these recordings while reading the analyses.

[34] See Eric F. Clarke, "Structure and Expression in Rhythmic Performance," in *Musical Structure and Cognition*, ed. Peter Howell, Ian Cross, and Robert West (London: Academic Press, 1985), 209–36; "Levels of Structure in the Organization of Musical Time," *Contemporary Music Review* 2/1 (1987), 211–38; "Generative Principles in Music Performance," in *Generative*

Example 1. Bach, Partita no. 2 for solo violin, Allemande, mm. 1–4.
Nathan Milstein's, Rachel Podger's, and Gideon Kremer's contrastive
interpretations are described in terms of fm and pf. Pitch and durational
elements are shown in lower-case letters. Brackets above the staff mark
structural groupings; exclamations represent moderate (!) to strong [!]
surprise. Revised analytical symbols from the I-R model (Narmour, 2015)
show melodic processes (P) and reversals in m. 1 (R) (the tilde sign [P~]
stands for intervallic implicative similarity; the plus sign (R+) for escalating,
implicative intervallic difference; the minus sign (R-) for diminishing
implicative intervallic difference; roman type = ascent; italic type = descent).
Capital letters point to similarly enumerated forms of sequential repetition
(A° A² . . .) with noticeable variation (superscripts). Pent-up implications
"break out" in the last bar (hence the formal differentiation, B) which
begins a new, varied, sequence (again noted by letters and superscripts).

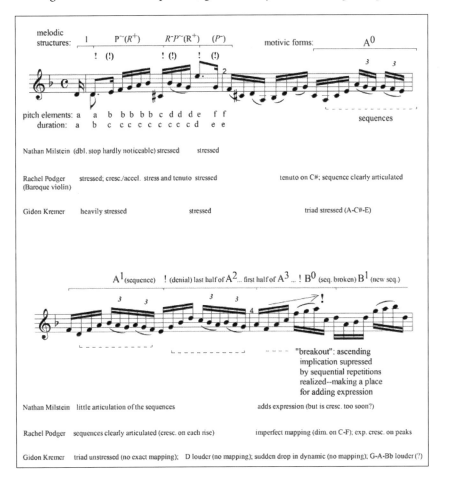

such effects may be minimal[35] and thus not represent a coherent grammar.[36] In other words, interpretive choices may not be systematic. In order to define and critique how accurately a given interpretation represents a specific mode, we must analyze how scaled functions and forms of individual parameters interact.[37]

For instance, in terms of composition, Milstein performs the durational rate of the ongoing running sixteenth notes in m. 1—symbolized in S in

Processes in Music, ed. John A. Sloboda (Oxford: Clarendon Press, 1988), 1–26; and "Expression and Communication in Musical Performance," in *Music, Language, Speech and Brain*, ed. Johan Sundberg, Lennart Nord, and Rolf Carlson (London: Macmillan, 1991), 184–93; Anders Friberg and Giovanni U. Battel, "Structural Communication," in *The Science and Psychology of Music Performance*, ed. Richard Parncutt and Gary E. McPherson (Oxford: Oxford University Press, 2002), 199–218; Caroline Palmer, "Mapping Musical Thought to Musical Performance," *Journal of Experimental Psychology: Human Perception and Performance* 15 (1989), 331–46; "The Role of Interpretive Preferences in Music Performance" and "On the Assignment of Structure in Music Performance," *Music Perception* 14 (1996), 23–56; L. Henry Shaffer, "Musical Performance as Interpretation," *Psychology of Music* 23/1 (1995), 17–38; L. Henry Shaffer and Neil P. Todd, "The Interpretive Component in Musical Performance," in *Action and Perception in Rhythm and Music*, ed. Alf Gabrielsson (Stockholm: Royal Swedish Academy of Music, 1987), 139–52; Sloboda, "The Communication of Musical Meter in Piano Performance."

[35] Heidi Gotlieb and Vladimir J. Konečni, "The Effects of Instrumentation, Playing Style, and Structure in the Goldberg Variations by Johann Sebastian Bach," *Music Perception* 3/1 (1985), 87–102; Mitchell Karno and Vladimir J. Konečni, "The Effects of Structural Interventions in the First Movement of Mozart's Symphony in G Minor, K. 550 on Aesthetic Preference," *Music Perception*, 10/1 (1992), 63–72; Barbara Tillmann and Emmanuel Bigand, "Does Formal Structure Affect Perception of Musical Expressiveness?" *Psychology of Music* 24/1 (1996), 3–17.

[36] Roger A. Kendall and Edward C. Carterette, "The Communication of Musical Expression," *Music Perception* 8/2 (1990), 129–63.

[37] I rely here on the I-I-R model described in Eugene Narmour, "The Implication-Realization Model," in *Music in the Social and Behavioral Sciences*, ed. William Forde Thompson (Thousand Oaks, Calif.: SAGE Reference, 2014), 588–93. For the formalized analytical theory behind the analyses, see Narmour, *The Analysis and Cognition of Basic Melodic Structures: The Implication-Realization Model* (Chicago: University of Chicago Press, 1990); "The Top-Down and Bottom-Up Systems of Musical Implication: Building on Meyer's Theory of Emotional Syntax," *Music Perception* 9/1 (1991), 1–26; *The Analysis and Cognition of Melodic Complexity* (Chicago: University of Chicago Press, 1992); "Analyzing Form and Measuring Perceptual Content in Mozart's Sonata K. 282: A New Theory of Parametric Analogues," *Music Perception*, 13/3 (1996), 265–318; and "Music Expectation by Cognitive Rule-Mapping," *Music Perception* 17/3 (2000), 329–98. For an explanation of the newly revised symbols used in Figures 1 and 2, see Narmour, "Toward a Unified Theory of the I-R Model (Part 1): Parametric Scales and Their Analogically Isomorphic Structures" *Music Perception* 33 (2015), 32–69. For another analytical use of the new, revised symbology, see Alfred Cramer, "Moments of Attention: Function, Coherence, and Unusual Sounds in Works by Anton Webern and Richard Rodgers," in *Musical Implications*, 99–130.

successive elements of *bbb* and *ddd* in melody and *ccc* and *eee* in duration—
almost exactly as printed.[38] As shown from a spectrographic analysis of duration in m. 1 (Figure 8 below), Milstein renders the rising E-F-G-A-B♭ line
almost isochronously, producing percentage differences within a very narrow range (between 0 to 10%), lower than necessary for millisecond discrimination at this tempo.[39] (In addition, he plays the sixteenth-note E4 after the
initial double-stopped long note almost a quarter of a half-tone sharp (+23
cents), thereby subtly strengthening the melodic implication of D-E to rise;
this would be a *pf* decision—to make the E more implicative than symbolized
in the notation.)

To take another revealing event, in m. 1 the skip from B♭ down to C♯
(Example 1) is highly nonclosural in terms of melody (the largeness of the
reversal interval implies a strong change of direction and is structurally symbolized in the analysis as PR+; the preceding P ~ stands for a process of similar
intervals). Nonclosure is also the case in terms of scale step (the leap to the
mobile leading-tone of C♯). Here Milstein adds a slight dynamic stress on this
C♯ (beat 3), which increases its *nonclosure*; simultaneously he inserts a slight
tenuto, which increases the metric *closure*. Such parametric noncongruence
(nonclosure vs. closure) creates functionally mismatched, though subtly transient affect.

But are the two together *cf*? No, because in terms of the accepted, associated, and unwritten Ts, Cs, and Ns of Baroque style, which encourage stress-
ing leading tones, bringing out leaps, and emphasizing unexpected events,
Milstein's interpretation may be regarded as "canonic" *fm* in that he carefully
obeys what performers have come to associate with melodic notes in tonal
style. This is why I stress throughout this essay that any critical analysis of how
a performance mode is applied vis-à-vis a notated *fm* standard—be it from
S, s, or R—must always in addition be considered in the light of S's currently
associated Ts, Cs, and Ns.[40]

In the last measure of Example 1 (bottom staff), Milstein inserts a slight
crescendo on the rising F-A-C triad (arrow), disrupting the ongoing sequence

[38] The analytical plus signs (+) used in the structural symbols of the I-R model are not to be
confused with the plus signs signifying interpretive congruence in the left-sector modes of
fm, *pf*, *hf*, and *rf* (Figure 1).

[39] Eric F. Clarke, "The Perception of Expressive Timing in Music," *Psychological Research* 51/1
(1989), 2–9; "Expression and Communication in Musical Performance."

[40] Operative Ts and Cs do not always render analytical criticism mute. That is, not every T
and C, no matter how long-lived, is forever worthy. If that were so, interpretive T, C, and N
would change infrequently, but we know from the discussion that they do change; indeed
they must do so if music is to retain aesthetic creditability.

intently mapped by the listener (begun in m. 2, continued into m. 3, and momentarily continued into m. 4 before the "breakout" to the high A). The negative effect of this decision is to anticipate (arrow) the coming breakout and undercut in advance the continued perceptual following of the sequence, which in m. 4 was composed so as to surprisingly continue to rise. To my ears, Milstein's early reveal of this continuing rise is a small but interpretive miscalculation. As we see in Example 1, Podger's performance does something of the same thing but in the opposite dynamic direction by creating a diminuendo on the rising C-F, a premature "broadcasting" that also unwittingly announces the breakout. But it is less misguided (in terms of a *cf* concept) because by playing the high A suddenly softer, she makes the expression easier to hear.[41]

Proformalism and Concurrent Reformalism (rf)

Pf does not slavishly follow S, but its functional variances are congruent with the notation (recall the left sector of Figure 1).[42] *Pf* basically preserves yet heightens notated *fm*'s similarity and difference. A *pf* performer believes that S both needs and deserves improvement, provided such is congruent with S's associated T,C, and N. Like *fm*, *pf* does not omit relationships of S, but *pf* performers feel free to supplement, intensify, or magnify S, provided such improvements strengthen the written or unwritten Ts and Cs. By calling attention to the interpretation, *pf* thus actively elevates the performer to the status of co-creator.

  Pf regards S *not* as a faithful representation of the composer's every intention but rather as a challenging cultural artifact in which added enhancements are an inherent responsibility of any hands-on co-creator. Notated relationships are "recruited" and significantly strengthened—whether formal or functional—but not to the degree of violating the inferred written intent of S or negating S's correlated Ts, Cs, and Ns. Rather, *pf* decisions escalate congruence in a positive way (+). Such contributions are not added willy-nilly but are systematically mapped onto the musical structure. They are treated as essential to a re-creation of what the composer's S actually implies but does not or cannot clearly symbolize or convey.

---

[41] See Carolyn Drake, "Perceptual and Performed Accents in Musical Sequences," *Bulletin of the Psychonomic Society* 31/2 (1993), 107–10; Bruno H. Repp, "Detectability of Duration and Intensity Increments in Melody Tones: A Partial Connection between Music Perception and Performance," *Perception and Psychophysics* 57/8 (1995): 1217–32.

[42] Space does not permit me to discuss *hf*, but that mode is easily conceptualized: it is *pf* pushed to the extreme.

S's carry many possibilities of structuration, so it is up to performers to decide exactly which structures, among many potential ones, are to be realized, highlighted, reshaped, or emphatically confirmed. Of course the choices must also be guided by the outcomes of mood, affect, and emotion. Interpretation is not a game of exhausting the possibilities of how something might be played but rather of maximizing the feeling, the intellect, and the composed aesthetic through a carefully coordinated sequence of events for an assumed audience in a given time and place.

According to the notation in Example 1, the downbeat into m.1 should be three times as long as the upbeat (1/16 to 3/16). But as Figure 8 and its commentary show, with a sixteenth-note of 299ms and a dotted-eighth of 771ms, Milstein's downbeat D falls short of the notated category (1:3) and is thus, strictly speaking, *cf*; that is, its cropped length goes against the notation and weakens the stipulated closural cumulation.

Podger's upbeat gesture, in contrast to Milstein's, does just the opposite. It is more cumulatively closed (−) in that her dotted-eighth downbeat of 1146ms is more than three times the duration of the upbeat sixteenth-note of 317ms. It is thus *pf* because it goes beyond the notated cumulation (1:3).[43]

Her *pf* attitude interpretively plays out in other ways as well. As we see from the commentary on Figure 8, her augmentation of the stretched, cumulative tones of the metric D and high E5, the slight tenuto on the mobile-tone C♯, and the variable U-shaped pace of the running sixteenth-note patterns are significantly different from Milstein's fm. What Milstein's metrically durational presentation subtly provides is thrown into relief by Podger's interpretation, which purposely takes the charged notes (D, C♯, E) and stretches them, in effect slightly slowing the overall tempo (note that most of her tones are slightly longer than Milstein's, despite the occasional acceleration after the tenutos).

More precisely, as discussed, the percentage differences in Milstein's rendition occur within a very narrow range (between 0 to 10%), which is less than the necessary milliseconds at this tempo for discrimination, whereas Podger's performance slowly accelerates and then markedly slows down on the upward curve to the B♭.[44] At differences of 15% or more, the change between her

[43] Such lengthening of initial or accented structural tones is commonplace even though performers are frequently unaware of such actions; see Clarke, "Structure and Expression in Rhythmic Performance" and Palmer, "Mapping Musical Thought to Musical Performance."

[44] Percentages aside, human beings are quite competent in detecting very small timing changes in the neighborhood of 30–50 milliseconds (Clarke, "Listening to Performance," 192), although context impacts this sensitivity (see Bruno Repp, "Probing the Cognitive

sixteenth-notes, at the start of the accelerated increase and at the ending deceleration, lie above a JND of 5–10% and are thus readily perceived.[45] The running sixteenths across previous leaps (B♭-C♯-B♭) do not lead listeners to expect a durational cumulation with the leap to E, so such expressive lengthening is easy to detect and corroborates what others have observed about such rhythms.[46] In addition, Podger's interpretation is overtly *rf* in terms of timbre and pitch height in that she adopts a tuning from Bach's time, a half-step lower. [47]

Representation of Musical Time: Structural Constraints on the Perception of Timing Perturbations," *Cognition* 44/3 [1992], 241–48). See also Clarke, "The Perception of Expressive Timing in Music" and "Expression and Communication in Musical Performance." For a recent summary, see Henkjan Honing, "Structure and Interpretation of Rhythm in Music," in *The Psychology of Music*, ed. Diana Deutsch (San Diego: Academic Press, 2013), 369–90.

[45] Carolyn Drake and Caroline Palmer, "Accent Structures in Music Performance," *Music Perception* 10/3 (1993), 343–78: 374.

[46] Alf Gabrielsson, "Once Again: The Theme from Mozart's Piano Sonata in A major (K. 331): A Comparison of Performances," in *Action and Perception in Rhythm and Music*, 81–103; Palmer, "Mapping Musical Thought to Musical Performance"; Bruno H. Repp, "Detectability of Duration and Intensity Increments" and "Obligatory 'Expectations' of Expressive Timing Induced by Perception of Musical Structure," *Psychological Research* 61/1 (1998), 33–43; Johan Sundberg, "Computer Synthesis of Music Performance," in *Generative Processes in Music*, ed. John A. Sloboda (Oxford: Oxford University Press 1988), 52–69.

[47] Milstein tunes to A444, whereas Podger, playing a Baroque violin with a Baroque bow, tunes to A414 (a common reference tone in eighteenth-century Germany and close to A♭ by today's definition of standard pitch). Employing some equal temperament (ET), Podger also uses just intonation (JI, in seven cases), which, at least in this sample, ignores the supposed violinistic preference for Pythagorean tuning (PT). See Franz Loosen, "The Effect of Musical Experience on the Conception of Accurate Tuning," *Music Perception* 12/3 (1995), 291–306. In contrast, Milstein's execution is more various, incorporating both PT (4) and ET (3) but only two instances of JI. Indeed, in three cases Milstein's intervals stretch slightly beyond PT's target numbers. These stretches still remain closer to PT than JI or ET, so Milstein's tuning in this sample is quite different from Podger's. In his article "Intonation of Solo Violin Performance with Reference to Equally Tempered, Pythagorean, and Just Intonations," *Journal of the Acoustical Society of America* 93 (1993), 525–39, Loosen has observed that professional violinists perform intervals in scales almost identical to the arithmetic mean. Thus in their interpretations of pitch, scale step, and interval, Milstein's and Podger's performances may be characterized as *fm*. The study of tuning is not just a scientific enterprise of global averages but is subtly tied to key context, implication-realization, and scale step; see Jay Dowling, "Pitch Structure," in *Representing Musical Structure*, ed. Peter Howell, Robert West, and Ian Cross (London: Academic Press, 1991), 33–57, and Carol Krumhansl, *Cognitive Foundations of Musical Pitch* (Oxford: Oxford University Press, 1990). But as Andrzej Rakowski reminds us in "Context-dependent Intonation Variants of Melodic Intervals," in *Music, Language, Speech and Brain*, 203–11: listeners "do not judge on the basis of a deviation from any 'ideal' musical scale but on the basis of the use or misuse of the most adequate intonation variant" (203).

Figure 8. Durational similarities and differences between Milstein's formalist and Podger's proformalist performances (m. 1) compared and contrasted in milliseconds (spectrographically acquired). Interonset intervals (IOIs) from the start of one tone to the start of another were marked and measured using Adobe Audition.

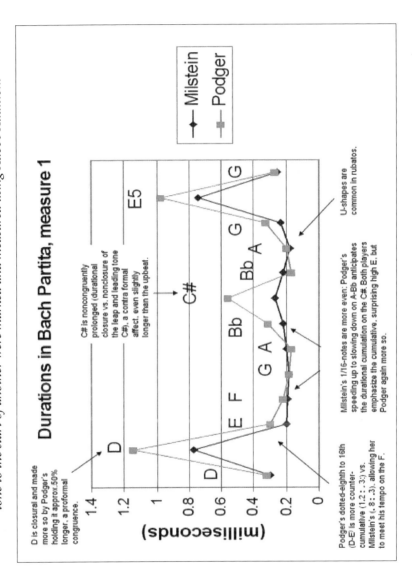

Figure 9. Bach, Partita no. 2 (m. 2)

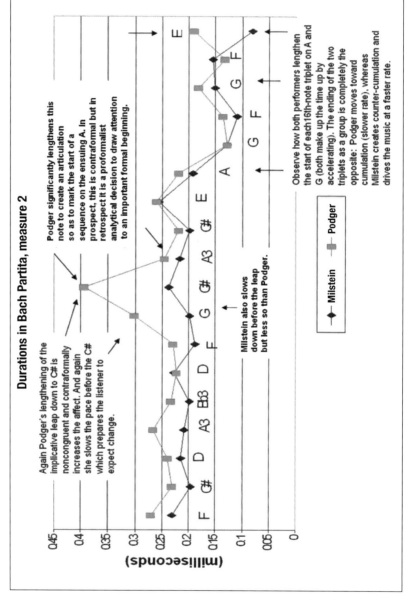

Figure 10. Bach, Partita no. 2 (m. 3)

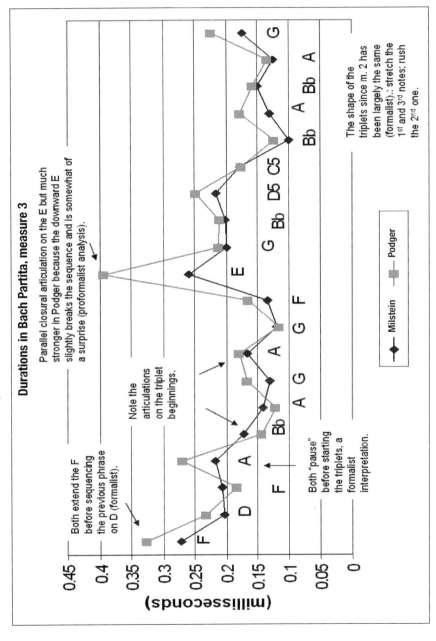

Durations in Bach Partita, measure 3

What, then, of the sequences in mm. 2–3 of Figures 9 and 10 (discussed earlier in connection with the music of Example 1)? For the listener to map a conditioned formal sequence ($A^\circ A^1$ in the music), the analytic performer, after shaping the initial model motive, must conformantly preserve the pitch and rhythm by iterating all the relevant parameters (symbolized by superscripts 1, 2, and 3 at the bottom of Example 1). As Podger's lengthening of the initial tones of each sequence shows (Figures, 9–10, spikes), the durational increases on the C♯ of the third beat of m. 2 (A° in Example 1), on the F and E on the strong metric beats of m. 3 ($A^{1,a}$, $A^{2,b}$, Example 1), and on the downbeat A of m. 4 ($A^{3,o}$, Example 1)—all capture the listener's attention and contribute to the transformal qualities of the sequences (see the commentary on the spikes in both Figures). In addition, Podger gives each ascending triad a crescendo and each pair of descending triplets a diminuendo (Figures 9 and 10). These *pf* expressions, contrasted with Milstein's *fm* (adding less emphasis and letting the sequences speak for themselves), thus enhance the listener's arousal and the mapped expectations onto each rising sequence.

Even the timing of the sixteenth-note triplets between the two performers is varied (cf. Example 1 with Figures 9 and 10) but somewhat consistent (i.e., both the beginning and ending of all six triplets are slightly lengthened). By slight contrast, although Milstein lengthens the first tones of five of the six triplets, his interpretation of the end tones is more diverse (three terminal tones are shorter, swallowed up, and thus somewhat *cf* in nature, whereas three others are longer; see the commentary in Figure 9, bottom right).

Like all things temporal, ascriptions of interpretive mode have prospective and retrospective properties. On first hearing, one may analytically evaluate an interpretation as *cf* (according to the heuristic shown in Figure 7), but in retrospect the event in question may prove to be contextually *pf*, as is the case of Milstein's or Podger's lengthening of the first notes of the sequential motives (Example 1, mm. 2–3). These become the anchor tones of discontiguous formal repetitions yet to be realized (Milstein being less *pf* in this regard than Podger).

In general, Podger is more analytically *pf* than Milstein, whose performance is analytically *fm*. As mentioned, concurrently she is *rf* as regards intonation, bow, violin, and tuning, demonstrating that the mixing of performance modes is common.[48] Very few performances are exclusively one mode or

---

[48] *Rf* attempts to recover previous styles, strategies, and Ns of interpretation that have become literally *out-moded* by contemporary practices (*mode* in the sense used in this essay). *Rf* does not just try to recover the meaning of the notation from S's written centuries ago. Rather, by invoking inactive Ts, Cs, and Ns and inserting them into current aesthetic and artistic aims,

another. Observe, however, that deviation from *fm* requires advance planning: Podger's tempo has to be relatively slower than Milstein's in order to allow her the time to apply *pf* expressions on the affective leaps and to emphasize the groupings of the larger sequential motives.

Contraformalism (cf) along with Contextual Deformalism (df)

We have only seen only one brief case of overt *cf*, but its use is utterly common. What performer has not willfully changed what is printed in S or ignored what is traditionally associated with it? In contrast to congruent enhancements, *cf* adds noncongruent interpretations or omits notated compliance altogether. Its insertions or deletions are thus somewhat "transgressive." Unlike *fm*, *pf*, and *hf* modes, *cf* is not bound to adhere to current Ts and Cs even if these learned behaviors are *cf* in the notation, as in Milstein's interpretation.

Cf (or *df*) becomes a mode of choice when *fm*, *pf*, or *hf* interpretations sound superannuated through overplaying. Listening to unimaginative *fm* interpretations of the same pieces by conductors and soloists (or hearing the same R) is a chief cause of *cf*. Through overexposure, audiences come to know a mode of performance so well that they rapidly map their conditioned learning with great accuracy. Thus a live interpretation or new *cf*–R will deny such learned expectations and produce a distinctively welcome (and perhaps challenging) aesthetic affect. Conservative programming that consists of the same pieces year after year clearly fosters the need for *cf* (or *df*). However, this can lead to quirky and erroneous interpretations as objectionable as the *fm* boredoms they attempt to alleviate. Even as a purposeful digression from the score, however, *cf*, carries a risk: to sophisticated listeners a misjudged *cf* gesture may be perceived simply as an interpretive error.

---

rf performers are able to resurrect new interpretations from older readings, long forgotten. Seemingly unviable interpretations can regain previous interpretive dominance via *rf* performances that frequently seem more animated than those of the status quo. *Rf* is particularly interested in *unwritten cf*, *df*, and *if* that conflict with today's modal renditions vis-à-vis S and written s. In contrast, *rf* attempts to recover *unnotated* and currently ignored interpretations that were initially part of what contemporaneous composers would have expected from an earlier standard (whether S or N), or at least from acceptable Ts and Cs at the time the work was written. We can analyze and critique *rf* performances in the same way that we assess any of the seven modes of interpretation (as we did in discussing Podger's performance, which mixed *fm* and *pf* along with *rf*). The theory formulated here, however, attempts to enlarge the possibilities of mode choice rather than to dictate what to execute.

Figure 11a. A spectrographic analysis (using Adobe Audition) comparing and contrasting Judy Garland's durational interpretation of Arlin's and Harburg's 1939 Oscar-winning song "Over the Rainbow" against the score (mm. 1–4). Rows 7 and 9 provide the analytical description.

Contraformal Treatment of the Durational Notation as Found in the Sanctioned Sheet Music of "Over the Rainbow" (performance from the film *Wizard of Oz*)

measure numbers	1		2					3			4	
pitches	C4	C5	B4	G4	A4	B4	C5	C4	way	up / A4	high / G4	[rest]
	whole-note = circa 2.400; half = 1.200; dotted quarter = .900; quarter = .600; dotted eighth = .450, eighth, = .300 (approximate values)	actual notation (written categories)										
text	Some-	where	o -	ver	the	rain-	bow.	[rest]	way	up	high	[rest]
			high register tone-paints the text, defining "somewhere" as "over the rainbow", and "way up"									
spectrographic analysis via mm:ss ms (approximate values)	1.360	1.271	.621	.336	.531	.993	.891	427 (l)	588 [C4]	1.203 [A4]	2.209 (voice)	+ 945 (orch) (ritard)
desription and critique of performance	generally a formalist beginning but with a tenuto on first tone		the word "the" is stretched almost to a quarter-note (contra the textual semantic) as is the first quarter of "rainbow" (being .more than a dotted quarter-note)					compensation: the extension of the previous third beat is repaid by a shorter quarter-note rest, the two ensuing notes are almost formalist			the overlength of the cadential bar (3.154) is explained by the additional duration of the ritard (a typical +30 %)	
metric span (notated as cut time)	2.631		3.372					2.218			3.145 (cf m 8)	
RATE (RUBATO)	- - - - - - - SPEEDING UP - - SLOW-DOWN - - - FASTER - - - - SLOWER - - SLOWEST - - - - (rit)											

Figure 11b. "Over the Rainbow" (mm. 5–8). By ignoring the written rhythmic motives, mm. 6–7 border on being df.

5		6						7					8
A3	F4	E4	C4	D4	E4	F4	[rest]	D4	B3	C4	D5	E4	C4
there's	a	land	that	I	heard	of	[rest]	once	in	a	hull-	a -	by
.828	1.19	.851	.148	.328	.533	.584	.591	.820	.200	.202	.344	.304	1.719 (voice) + 1.449 rest (orch) = 3.168
	breath taken												ritard [σ]
2.018		2.444						2.461					3.168

both tones are shortened (the 1st more than the 2nd), an *a tempo* to balance the m. 4 ritard, but the word *a* sounds as a tenuto by contrast

the quarter-note here is also shortened, while the abrupt sixteenth-note is just as abruptly converted to an additively gradated slow-down by the eighth-, dotted eighth-, and putative quarter-note, the whole phrase semantically pointing to the penultimate measure where the rest "compensates" slightly for what has been lost before "once" takes up the thought

because of the unwritten breath (a parenthetic intrusion), the middle-to-end of the bar is again rushed with two ensuing dotted sixteenth-notes and then slightly slowed by two eighth-notes (at odds with the word "lullaby"). In sum, the 2nd phrase (mm. 5–8) is more "quickened," than the more "relaxed" first phrase (1–4). Indeed, the metric span of mm. 5–8 is 1.277 shorter, but mm. 5-7 is by comparison to mm. 1-3 almost 2 sec shorter!

the slow vocal rate strengthens the closure, and the meter goes beyond the expected span because of the ritard

RATE (a tempo)- - - - RAPID PACE - - SLOWER - - - - - - - - SLOW - -RAPID- - - -LESS SO- - ABRUPT SLOWDOWN
(RUBATO))- - -
(tenuto)

Middle bars of these two subphrases are very close to being deformal.

Informalism (if), Contraformalism (cf), and Deformalism (df) as Professional Artifice

One consequence of impersonal mass communication (and of our blowback insistence on the absolute value of subjective, individualistic expression) is the ubiquitous emergence of professional *if*, *cf*, and *df*. As in stage and film acting, the usage of right-sector modes in musical interpretations sounds convincingly spontaneous, though, of course, it is anything but. S-noncongruent interpretations are particularly widespread in artificial N that is indifferent to S's precise notation (Figure 6). (For example, the national anthem is routinely and artificially subjected in public to indifferent *if*, *cf*, and *df*.)

Although lyrics are usually preserved in songs, in the world of popular music *ca.* 1930–70 many "crooners" conceptually sought to construct musically relaxed *if*, *cf*, and *df*, though not just in terms of indifference to S. Rather, there was a vigorous attempt to create stand-alone musical treatments so far removed from the original frames of S that artificial individual performances themselves come to function as constructed N-standards (think of the hit songs that Frank Sinatra "owned," but also think of the forgotten composers that originally notated these songs as *fm* and the creative studio orchestrations that recontextualized the original Ss as *if*, *cf*, and *df*). In short, many pop performers of romantic songs and ballads set out to construct unique *if*, *cf*, or *df* interpretations while willfully re-inventing and absorbing the original coded music from S in order to willfully construct a compelling, albeit relaxed, interpretively artificial culture. From a musical point of view, such modal usages rarely rose to the improvisatory art found in the great jazz developments of 1930–70.

Because of its objectivity, spectrographic analysis nevertheless remains a useful technique to gain insight into the interpretative artificial *if*, *cf*, and *df* Ns of popular music. Consider Figure 11a-b, Judy Garland's performance of the Oscar-winning song "Over the Rainbow" (from the 1939 MGM movie, *Wizard of Oz*). Omitting the opening verse, which became the performing norm, her performance at age sixteen established a childlike *if* interpretation of this melody that was imitated by generations of singers after her. There is much to say about how she deploys the pitches of the melody, but let us concentrate just on the timing parameters—duration, rate, meter, and rhythm.

Figure 11a-b shows the pitches and written rhythms in separate rows (as most readers are familiar with this ubiquitous song, I will not display the score). The melody is typically cast in two four-bar phrases. The durational motivic forms (row 3) are subtly laid out by the composer Harold Arlin. Figure 11a is *ABA¹* (motivic lengths of 1-1-2), whereas we find in Figure 11b a surprising $A^2B^2B^3$ (also 1-1-2). Moreover, the sequence of pitch intervals is artful, the tone-painted upward leaps functioning as beginnings and endings of both four-bar phrases.

Concerning Garland's performance itself, the considerable cadential extensions (in mm. 4 and 8), though absent in the published S, are neither *cf* nor *df* because such ritards, albeit noncongruent with S, are utterly common in pop songs, indeed a fixture of the TCN, and hence completely expected. The rubatos (tracked in the last rows of Figure 11a-b) call for more discussion. Despite the common use of rubato in popular music and the symmetrical repetition of the song's form, Garland's rate of speeding up and slowing down in each four-bar phrase does not display the same shape. The length of each measure in terms of aggregate milliseconds (row 11) shows this: from mm. 1–4 (11a) the aggregate speed up to the first cadence oscillates (row 9), whereas the overall bar rate in mm. 5–8 (11b) gradually increases in speed up to the second cadence (row 9). Given the symmetrical composition of both phrases, this suggests the absence of attention—indeed an indifference—to S (recall Figure 6) and a presence of *if*, *cf*, and perhaps even *df*.

To what do we attribute this S-noncongruent N-deviance? The answer becomes clear when we inspect Garland's actual realization of duration (row 6) versus what S inscribes (row 3). The five durations in m. 2 as performed by Garland (11a) are not commensurate with Arlin's written quarter-eighth-eighth-quarter-quarter (row 3). Furthermore, her rendition of exactly the same repeated rhythm in m. 6 (11b) is differently organized. In both motives Arlin's simple rhythmic distribution on two levels (quarters and eighths) becomes something that in both cases (m. 2, m. 6) she processively *ritards* over three beats. But if we examine in m. 7 (11b) the most unexpected subtle rhythmic change in the melody (as analyzed earlier), we find a *processive* series of durations that grow steadily *quicker* (notated ratios: 4:3:2) in contrast to the previous parallel rhythms that progressively slowed down.

How would we depict this change according to the theory of *if*, *cf*, and *df* as hypothesized in Figure 1? Methodologically referring to the heuristics theorized in Figure 7, we see in Figure 11a-b that only four parameters are modified (duration, rate, tempo, and rhythm, i.e., 31% of the thirteen available dimensions). However, the S-*form* is changed in all three motivic rhythmic instances (mm. 2, 6, and 7). This suggests that Garland's performance with respect only to N is probably *cf*—much more than *if* but not crossing the threshold into *df*. Should we conclude that "Over the Rainbow" is a better piece when each phrase is sung according to Arlin's score rather than when the structural differences between each phrase are smoothed out and ignored? Not necessarily. As argued earlier, too much *fm* can become tiresome, and there is something exciting about hearing Garland navigate mm. 6–7 as rubato quintuplets rather than as two embedded motives on a lower level (as written). In particular *if* interpretive Ns admit many kinds of non-standard performances that are satisfying.

To put this in context, Sylvia McNair's R of "Over the Rainbow" with André Previn as pianist is *fm* and a bona fide attempt to achieve an N-crossover (both musicians being classically trained)[49].And as might be expected, McNair respects Arlin's motivic differentiation and yet professionally constructs the persona of a spontaneously relaxed singer. Her vocal ability is superb, reflecting many years of training, with a flawless artistic technique and a vocal performance of recital quality. In contrast, Ray Charles's R (You Tube) adopts a strong *df* posture inasmuch as he drops the opening leap of Arlin's song each time it recurs, which is a clear violation of the motivic signature of the composition and a puzzling decision in terms of the melody and text of the S.

A much more convincing journey into *df* is Sarah Vaughn's virtuoso improvisational R (Japan, 1973) alluding to Arlin's original melody (and developing Harburg's lyrics to serve her alliterative purposes).[50] Vaughn's interpretive melodic artifice is truly transnormal (recall Figure 6) and demonstrates how her constructed N transformed the standard of jazz singing and the interpretation of slow ballads (like "Over the Rainbow") for many years to come.

Communal Singing (the Left Sector of Figures 1, 6, and 7)

Many have pointed out that the outlook of classical musicians toward meticulously following a chosen TCNsS along with the devoted attention of a concert audience (no talking, no bodily posturing, and no applause until the work ends) is strongly ritualistic. Indeed, there are many left-sector musical interpretations with noticeable T and C that generate Ns with ritualistic properties but sans reference to s or S—orally learned communion hymns, sacred plainchants, and collective choral response songs in gospel music, for example.

These display participatory Ns that depend on *fm*, *pf*, *hf*, and *rf*. Secular rites (e.g., "war songs" at athletic events) and events of public singing (such

[49] Sylvia McNair with André Previn and David Finck, *Come Rain or Come Shine: The Harold Arlen Songbook*, ©1996 by Philips, Philips 4468182, CD.

[50] Sarah Vaughn, *"Live" In Japan*, ©1988, 1973 by Mainstream Records, Accord 557302, CD.

as the social slogans chanted at protest rallies) fall in the same categories. To repeat, such performative collectivities depend not on knowledge of s or S but on multiple experiences with T and C and a shared learning of a common N. Unlike performances of art music, communal singing does not aim for newly unified standards of performance because communal standards and group Ns are one and the same. In addition, venue (cathedral, athletic arena, public space) and text play a major role in determining the performed rhythm, tempo, and loudness. And rarely does a prior agenda exist for elevating or choosing one mode over another in order to dethrone a previously reigning N.

CONCLUSION

The seven modes of performance infuse all levels of music, whether motivic, phrasal, sectional (main theme, improvisation), different genres (Viennese waltzes), or works in their entirety (symphony). Modes can interpret any part of the texture, whether a single parameter (melody), a single voice part (the basso continuo), or an instrumental conglomerate (*soli, tutti*). They shape styles (from essential Leitmotifs to "throwaway" *secco* recitatives in opera). They characterize timbral nuances (Russian brass vs. Italian wind sections). Modes of performance can be covert or overt, self-effacing (Milstein) or attention-getting (Podger). They can even characterize whole careers (George Szell, an *fm* or *pf* conductor with a deep respect for S vs. Glenn Gould, a quintessential *cf* or *df* experimentalist for whom S was often a mere starting point).

Behind all such interpretive decisions is the modern musical S, a highly articulated, complexly networked, dynamically multiplicative, symbolized schematic system of hierarchical discourse. It carries an astonishing quantity of interpretive knowledge, and when performed, both induces and models human moods, affects, and emotions. As a detailed cognitive frame from the top down, S involves numerous higher and lower-level relationships: written and unwritten s, limited modes of performance, some but not all interpretive N, and infinitely learned styles and idiostructures. From the bottom up, S lies thoroughly embedded below cultural Ts and Cs and is thus only partially formalized, requiring many sources to realize its full potential. As such, S is a modern marvel, one of the Western world's greatest intellectual achievements.

Part III

The Passage of Time, Holding Time Still

On the Last Measure of
Schubert's String Quintet

SCOTT BURNHAM

In the Classical style that Franz Schubert inherited, the rhetoric of closure is always recognizable. Endings in this style are heavily marked, overde-
termined, especially the ending of the last movement in a sonata or symphonic
cycle, which is almost always energetic and often made to sound as if bearing
great weight. Sometimes this final ending empties out to a single pitch class, as
though to conclude with the elemental origin of it all. Beethoven, at the end of
his First Symphony, runs permutations of the tonic triad and then closes the
door with its root alone; at the end of his Ninth Symphony, a clamorous race to
the finish concludes with a single iteration of the tonic root, after four repetitions of the fifth above. In endings like these, we always *drop* to the tonic, as to
the fundament. And while a full triad at the end is like an embrace of sound,
a bare tonic at loud levels is more of a concussion—this allows the very end to
be more like a naked rhythm. A single pitch class, a single downbeat, creating
a kind of implosion back into our default sense of Time, a shuddering deliv-
erance that is hard to resist: even the most stoically immobile listener would
find it hard not to twitch along with some of Beethoven's symphonic endings.

What does it mean to be the last sound? It can mean everything, That final
downbeat can be heard to contain, or to carry, the entire piece; our experience of the work is caught in this final bit of musical presence, not in some
"life flashing before the eyes" sense, but in the simple sense of hearing a long
process, a long presence, come to an end. We hear the genie go back into the
bottle—and the bigger the genie, the more momentous the reentry. What a

moment ago was vivid presence is now lived experience (*Erlebnis*); the piece turns into the past in an instant. Few complex and extended experiences are transformed to the past tense with such emphatic, instantaneous intensity. "There it goes!"—"It" being the piece, and "it" being the event of the ending, which becomes a sonic synecdoche, in that it can seem to sound for the whole.

Example 1. Schubert, String Quintet finale, last measure

SCHUBERT'S LAST MEASURE

In the ongoing lore of musical endings, the final measure of Schubert's String Quintet cuts a singular figure. Several features distinguish this ending. First, the last sound is a held note. More than just a downbeat, this is a duration, and it is governed by a fermata.[1] Held notes like this are less common than you might imagine in this style (a famous one happens at the end of Beethoven's Fifth Symphony). And then there is the grace note. One of the most gravid grace notes in Western chamber music, this one not only displaces the C from the downbeat, it is almost always held for a full quarter note in performance,[2] a tradition that seems to acknowledge its gravitas through agogic privilege.

---

[1] In the old Schubert edition, the last note is marked with a decrescendo, hardly ever observed in performance. When I first heard the decrescendo, in Rostropovich's 1990 *Deutsche Grammophon* recording, it sounded like a tire deflating—but once you get used to it, it bears thinking about, especially given the dynamic hairpin at the end of the first movement.

[2] I thank cellist (and music theorist) Joseph Straus for drawing my attention to this.

This heaviest of grace notes also justifies, even demands, the extended C that follows: an abrupt C would sound absurdly clipped.

A number of metaphors come to mind when trying to describe the effect of this gesture of D♭ moving to C: a heavy hammer or pile driver, burying the C firmly into the ground like a railroad spike; an aggressive fist pump or other triumphant flourish along the lines of "voilà" or "ta-daaa" (this last echoes the short-into-long durational gesture of the last measure); the way one gives a screw or bolt a final snug twist, providing assurance that it will never loosen again; a venomous stinger striking the final C "with extreme prejudice"; a bolt of lightning running to ground, as if carrying the energy of the entire piece into its final sound.

All these metaphors suggest a play of force, not syntax as usual, not "the end" as convention, but something more directly sonic, directly material. The D♭ behaves like a *downward* leading tone, suitable for the gravity of finality—that is, when you want your final note to be the floor, rather than the ceiling. (Imagine how poor the effect would be with a rising leading tone as the grace note!) We hear the sound of the entire quintet funneling down into the ground, into the lowest open strings of the ensemble via the lowest stopped notes (in both cellos, as well as viola). This emphasizes the materiality of the string quintet ensemble, because it emphasizes the sonic limit of the ensemble, the absolute bottom of its sound. The result is more a material resolution than a syntactic resolution.

Many analysts and critics crowd around that D♭ as a marked pitch class, and more than a few have invested it with a heavy interpretive load. Here is Peter Gülke: "Schubert plays no triumphant trump card with his ending. Instead, with the grace note D♭, Schubert holds the manner and the weight of what has happened through to the very end."[3]

And Brian Newbould: "In the final throes of exaltation, a D♭ weighs down upon the keynote C as a last reminder of earlier tensions."[4] John Gingerich spells out those tensions, in his narrative of lost innocence and Schubert's brave shedding of the false consciousness of heroic style. For Gingerich, the

---

[3] "In diesem [Schluss] hält er, fern von allem affirmative Auftrumpfen, in der plaga-len Kadenzierung und im vorschlagenden *Des* Art und Gewicht des Abgehandelten bis zuletzt gegenwärtig." Peter Gülke, "Zum Bilde des späten Schubert: Vorwiegend analytische Betrachtungen zum Streichquintett op. 163," in *Musik-Konzepte Sonderband: Franz Schubert* (Munich: text+kritik, 1979), 162.

[4] Brian Newbould, *Schubert: The Music and the Man* (Berkeley: University of California Press, 1997), 362.

very end is "egregiously transgressive in its narrative disjunction combined with its willful assertion." He continues:

> The last two notes of the piece emphatically reiterate this Phrygian cadence with the D♭-C resolution unharmonized, still *fff*. This ending comes as a brusque and brutal reminder of the conflicts between the constituent sections of the two middle movements, and nothing within the last movement itself prepares or justifies this ending.[5]

Finally, Misha Donat of the BBC concludes his engaging program note on the Quintet by mentioning the "foreign" D♭ as signifying nothing less than death itself: "And so, for all the music's apparent high spirits, the work ends with a sudden shadow falling across its surface, as though Schubert were aware that his life was about to be cut short."[6]

All these authors hear the D♭ as a concentrated reminder of various contrastive forces at large in the Quintet and more—as an aggressive refusal to settle those disquieting forces. It is certainly true that, as a pitch class, the idea of D♭ in the context of C major is extremely unsettling. The combined effect of such baldly outrageous dissonance—a flat second in the final measure!—and the downward driving, material resolution discussed above creates a sonic *non plus ultra*.[7] No other available chroma would have such maximal dissonance yet also be able to make such a charged linear move to the final tonic. This is why it is hard to resist hearing the D♭ as a cumulative gathering of tension, a final flashpoint, as well as a sound that makes the loudly extended low C into an unequivocally final term. It is impossible to imagine anything happening beyond the C: after that D♭, there is no going back.

MEASURES 424–430

There is more to the force of the final measure than what is generated by the D♭. The last measure is the final term of a threefold closing gesture: a complete C-major triad in measure 428, then the drop to C alone (in octaves), then the D♭ stinger with a held C. This makes the final bar the last of two echoes, or afterbeats, sounding on the heels of the big C-major chord and diffusing

---

[5] John Gingerich, *Schubert's Beethoven Project* (Cambridge: Cambridge University Press, 2014), 333.

[6] Misha Donat, liner notes for Takacs Quartet with Ralph Kirschbaum, *Schubert, String Quintet and Quartettsatz*, ©2012 by Hyperion Records, CDA67864, CD, 6

[7] Of course, one could deflate such a reading by thinking of the D♭ simply as a folk-like final inflection—after all, the movement is commonly taken to be Hungarian in flavor.

the energy of Schubert's remarkable resolution onto that chord. Schubert sets up the tonic triad in m. 428 with an augmented-sixth sonority built on D♭, marked *fff* with jangling trills in the cellos, which means that the D♭ of the final measure, however much we may hear it as a reminder of earlier tensions throughout the Quintet, is also a local reminder of this unconventional

Example 2. Schubert, String Quintet, Finale, m. 371 to end

Example 2, continued

Example 2, continued

resolution to tonic. Leaning into a resolution by half step from above and below is of course the usual job of the augmented-sixth configuration—the chord with the double leading tones, the contrary-motion leading tones that both lead to the same pitch class. But whereas the augmented sixth is the Classical style's most direct way to mark a dominant, here Schubert deploys it to mark a tonic.[8]

This is not the first time in the Quintet that Schubert puts the weight of an augmented-sixth chord onto a non-dominant triad. Non-dominant resolutions of the augmented sixth happen at key spots in the first movement. On the very first page of the first movement, Schubert builds up an augmented sixth step by step and then resolves it to the leading tone (!), which subsequently drops a major third to the dominant.

Example 3. Schubert, String Quintet, First movement, mm. 20–27

This seems an even more radical move than the resolution onto the tonic at the end of the finale, for one thinks of the leading tone as neither a load-bearing scale degree, nor as a likely recipient of such a weighty resolution (not to mention that it is odd to use leading tones to approach the leading tone!). The entire process is a potent way of defamiliarizing the approach to the dominant, making a conventional harmonic destination (the midpoint caesura in a periodic utterance) sound anything but.[9]

[8] John Gingerich connects this augmented sixth on the flattened supertonic to a similar occurrence at the end of Schubert's late song "Der Atlas." See Gingerich, *Schubert's Beethoven Project*, 335. The progression also occurs at the very end of the first movement of one of Schubert's final piano sonatas, the A-major sonata D. 959.

[9] Suzannah Clark observes that " . . . Schubert opens up tonal space by recontextualizing a conventional gesture." The moveable augmented sixth can be regarded as a strong example

At the corresponding moment in the recapitulation of the first movement, Schubert does something even more extraordinary. He again allows an augmented sixth chord to emphasize the pitch B, but then splits this B into B♭ and C, creating a dyad that will impel the harmony into the subdominant F.

Example 4. Schubert, String Quintet, First movement, mm. 286–295

This splitting of B into B♭ and C is syntactic only in an elliptical sense. Its immediate effect is as a strongly material move, which is why it is so striking. One hears a heavily accented tone do the astonishing thing of splitting into two, or perhaps one hears a charged pitch moving outward to its two chromatic leading tones as though the energy of C moving down to B and A♯ moving up to B keeps driving, turning the augmented sixth interval inside out, into a diminished third/major second. However one chooses to construe it, the move has the riveting effect of an electric shock.

Finally, at the end of the first movement, Schubert approaches his final big dominant with an astonishing proliferation of augmented-sixth resolutions. He leans into each step of the descending tetrachord to the dominant (C–B♭–A♭–G) with an augmented sixth, putting an enormous amount of accumulated force onto the dominant.

This series of augmented-sixth resolutions makes the ground give way each time, an effect that helps clarify why the end of the finale deploys the augmented sixth with D♭. This final augmented-sixth move emphasizes that the ground has finally been reached that cannot give way, cannot be undermined. The result is a new, material way to emphasize the finality of the tonic—as a material final term, not just a functional final term. After all, a conventional

of this tendency. See Clark, *Analyzing Schubert* (Cambridge: Cambridge University Press, 2011), 270.

Example 5. Schubert, first movement, mm. 422–428

functional resolution of dominant to tonic has already taken place, in measure 424. It is as though Schubert needed to ratify this functional resolution with a more material resolution, nailing down the tonic once and for all, with two leading tones, the B on top and the D♭ on the bottom. On the other hand, a much different functional reading of the augmented sixth and final tonic is also possible here: the augmented sixth could be heard as unsettling the tonic by investing it with an air of dominant function. But this would be to cling to functional categories in the face of overwhelming sonic evidence. The C at the end of Schubert's Quintet is fully settled, even to the degree of shedding its conventional tonic-hood for something even more elemental: as lowest open string, that final C is the material bottom of the Quintet, its ultimate resonant grounding.

Such sonic materiality sets the music of Schubert's last style apart. Listening to this style often means focusing on what is immediately in front of us rather than what may be arriving in the near future. To resolve an augmented sixth to something other than the dominant is to make that move less transparent functionally, to make it more materially opaque. A related effect can be heard in Schubert's often unconventional modulations, as when he enters a new key from its mediant, or even from its leading tone. The middle sections of each of the Quintet's middle movements are a half step away from their respective A sections—E-f-E and C-Db-C—and both work their modulations in striking ways: the Adagio simply trills the final E of its opening section up into the tonic F of its F minor middle section; the Scherzo takes the long way from C to Db, through a slow lamenting descent into the heart of its valedictory Trio section.

Other non-syntactical, material half steps occur at the hectic outset of the finale. After the bass bounces up from the home dominant G (under C minor) to a Bb (under Eb minor) it then moves to B (under E minor) and then C (now as tonic major). This is modulation by fiat—again a more material, less syntactic, operation. These upward moves to C (via Bb and B in the bass, and with foreshortening phrases) are perhaps answered at the very end of the finale when Schubert resolves to the final tonic C downward through D-flat. Thus the first tonic in the bass and the last tonic in the bass are approached with material resolutions rather than functional resolutions (from B to C and from Db to C).

MEASURES 418–430

At the upbeat to m. 418 the action begins to coalesce around the pitch class C. First we hear two measures worth of the stomping neighbor note figure (D–C) featured in the main thematic strand of the finale, now as a kind of final ratification brought down to the middle and lower registers. Then, in mm. 420–24, Schubert offers a four-bar cadential progression (in a 2 + 2 configuration) that resolves to C in the same mid-to-low register, as though offering a husky resolution that can be felt in the diaphragm, complete with $b\hat{6}$ inflections (Abs) from the minor mode that perhaps open the door for the Db to come.

In m. 425, the first violin shoots an almost two-octave arrow up to the leading tone of the jangling *fff* augmented-sixth chord, bringing the energy back to the higher register for one last time before the closing drop to the bottom of the ensemble. The section from m. 418 to the end arranges its action two measures at a time; these short phrases can be consolidated either into two 6-measure groups that extend to the downbeat of the next, incomplete group, or three 4-measure groups that do the same. The 6-measure grouping follows the cadential progression from mm. 418–24; the 4-measure grouping follows the prevailing 4-measure groups of the preceding section.

MEASURES 402–430

At *più presto*, Schubert locks into his final tempo. The frantic activity of the first three measures snaps into a hasty cadential salute in the fourth bar. This bar speeds up the cadential progression that began in m. 402 with the second cello's C (tracing the notes preceded and emphasized by the trilling figures in the second cello, we get C, then D, then E, then F-D-G-G-C). The first 4-measure phrase initiates a drama of foreshortened cadential progressions: we hear two 4-measure cadences on C (402–9), then two 2-measure cadences (mm. 410–13), then three 1-measure cadences (mm. 414–17). The process of foreshortening may be said to continue even further, because the neighbor-note figures in mm. 418–419 pound on a C every half bar. But these same two measures also begin a longer, slower cadential progression of six measures: two measures of tonic, then of subdominant, then of dominant. So after all those shorter and shorter cadential progressions, the harmonic action broadens into an expansive 6-measure cadential progression. And now those stomping neighbor notes in mm. 418–21 could be heard in a converse sense, as tapping the brakes, slowing into the cadential figure ($\hat{7}$-$\hat{1}$-$\hat{1}$-$\hat{7}$) in the "diaphragm" register, which is followed in turn by that final registral expansion up to the jangling *fff* augmented sixth, then the last tonic triad, the leap down to octave Cs, and the D♭–C stinger.

MEASURES 371–430

The *più presto* at m. 402 is actually an intensification of the *più allegro* that began back in m. 371. Schubert's *più allegro* marks the final appearance of the opening theme of the finale, which now comes on with hard charging, bass-driven intensity. Flung around in wild sequences, the music takes a stand in B minor, feverishly exulting over F♯ in the bass, until the F♯ gets hiked back up to G (the home dominant) only to be hijacked further into a B♭ (the dominant of E♭ minor), from which it continues chromatically through B (the dominant of E minor) and into C. The entire line dramatically extends the action at the outset of the finale, providing yet another material move by "fiat" into C.

The *più allegro* itself comes on as a local arrival that culminates the steady increase of intensity after the cello duet back in mm. 321–36. Moving into the *più allegro* is like crossing the continental divide—everything will now flow downhill. Then the *più allegro* funnels into the *più presto*, with its drama of foreshortened cadential progressions; all this rambunctious intensity floods forward at a faster and faster pace, until the final broadening, from m. 418 to the end.

LAST SOUNDS

Each movement of Schubert's String Quintet has a distinctive ending, emblematic for the life of the movement it concludes. The first movement's final sustained tonic triad swells and recedes with a dynamic hairpin, reminiscent of the movement's opening C-major sound that grows into a diminished seventh and then returns to C. The Adagio brings back the F minor from its middle section at the very end, as a shocking apparition that then allows the ultimate cadence in E major to sound as an act of grace (the minor third of F is resurrected enharmonically as the major third of E, while the F itself moves down a half step to E). Moreover, a trill brings on that reminder of F minor, and a trill confirms E major—these trills look back toward the earlier transition to F minor within the Adagio. The brimming C-major chord at the very end of the Scherzo locally answers a buzzing *fff* dissonance, all trill and tremolo, while echoing the fullness of the Scherzo's opening, a sonorous festival of open strings.

The broadening at the end of the finale encourages an effect of gathering that extends to these previous movements. In addition to absorbing the furious velocity of the finale's coda and to providing various registral resolutions on C, the last section of the finale gathers the ♭6̂ inflections in the coda of the first movement, it gathers the trill and crucial half step at the end of the Adagio[10] and gathers the *fff* dissonant trilling harmony at the end of the Scherzo. That jangling chord four measures before the very end of Schubert's Quintet churns all this up one last time, opening up the space of the ensemble, setting everyone into the loudest kind of commotion. And then the final resolution, with

---

[10] Gingerich connects these trills as well. See Gingerich, *Schubert's Beethoven Project,* 333.

its rooted and confirming echo, drives to the very bottom of the ensemble. The last measure signs off with a final flamboyant signature, as though underlining it all with a flourish of electric immediacy. When one considers that this is also the last bar of Schubert's last big piece of instrumental chamber music, one could be forgiven for hearing it bring much more than the String Quintet to an end that cannot be undone.

In Time with Christopher Hasty: On Becoming a Performer of Robert Schumann's *Davidsbündlertänze*, op. 6

JANET SCHMALFELDT

My RECENT WORK has drawn upon the early nineteenth-century Hegelian concept of "*becoming*," as a point of departure for probing the idea of *form as process* in music of the Romantic generation. For Hegel and his follow-ers, we might say that "becoming" is the transformative moment in thinking about thought. My efforts to explore the philosophical notion of "becom-ing" did not extend beyond Hegel and beyond the mid twentieth-century writers Theodor W. Adorno and Carl Dahlhaus—guardians of what I have called a "Beethoven-Hegelian" tradition. "Becoming" has, however, remained a buzzword in philosophical thought to this day. For our purposes, witness the provocative tenth chapter in *A Thousand Plateaus* (1980) by philosopher Gilles Deleuze and psychoanalyst Félix Guattari; the chapter is entitled "1730: Becoming-Intense, Becoming-Animal, Becoming-Imperceptible . . . "[1] In the 2010 collection of articles about Deleuze's theory and philosophy of music, and in other recent essays, Christopher Hasty's critique of the discipline of music theory has engaged the work especially of Deleuze but also of other process philosophers—for example, William James, Bergson, and Whitehead.[2] Hasty's goal has been to remind us that music, like everything else, is inescapably

[1] Gilles Deleuze and Félix Guattari, *A Thousand Plateaus: Capitalism and Schizophrenia*, trans. Brian Massumi (Minneapolis: University of Minnesota Press, 1987), 232–309.
[2] Christopher F. Hasty, "The Image of Thought and Ideas of Music," in *Sounding the Virtual:*

temporal and always "in motion." He urges us to shift our attention from the objects or products of analysis to the "dynamic becoming" of music in time[3]—music as an ongoing experience, "music in the process of being made," whether through listening, composing, speaking, reading, writing, or performing.[4]

Hasty's challenge might at first seem daunting, if not unfeasible and highly idealistic (a term he may well reject). Like me, most readers of this volume have probably been listening to music since they were children. When hearing recordings, or listening silently to what we hear when studying scores, or attending live performances, or simply reliving music in our minds, how often can we claim that we are utterly, and continually, hearing the musical process *in time*—"living with and through sound"[5]—without distractions of any kind? The click of a fast-forward or -backward button allows us, should we wish, to move "backward and forward" within the music, as Adorno actually recommended.[6] Likewise, composers and writers about music are free to "to make, remake and unmake," as Hasty concedes.[7] What about the work of music analysts and theorists? We give names to "things," to concepts behind or beyond the passage of music—harmonic progressions, types of cadences, forms, structures, operations, schemata. These are Hasty's "objects and products" and Carolyn Abbate's "gnostic," as opposed to "drastic," satisfactions, usually arising from score-based analyses.[8] Our objects are discrete and quantitative—static in Henri Bergson's negative sense of time as "spatialized pseudo-time,"

Gilles Deleuze and the Theory and Philosophy of Music, ed. Brian Hulse and Nick Nesbitt (Farnham, U.K.: Ashgate, 2010), 1–22.

[3] Christopher F. Hasty, *Meter as Rhythm* (Oxford: Oxford University Press, 1997), vii–viii.

[4] Christopher F. Hasty, "If Music is Ongoing Experience, What Might Music Theory Be? A Suggestion from the Drastic," in *Zeitschrift der Gesellschaft für Musiktheorie* Sonderausgabe (2010), 200, http://www.gmth.de/zeitschrift/artikel/546.aspx.

[5] Ibid., 202.

[6] Theodor W. Adorno, *Hegel: Three Studies*, trans. Shierry Weber Nicholsen (Cambridge, MA: MIT Press, 1993), 136: "Highly organized music too must be heard multidimensionally, forward and backward at the same time. Its temporal organizing principle requires this: time can be articulated only through distinctions between what is familiar and what is not yet familiar, between what already exists and what is new; the condition of moving forward is a retrogressive consciousness. One has to know a whole movement and be aware retrospectively at every moment of what has come before."

[7] Hasty, "If Music is Ongoing Experience," 210. Within a different context, see Gilles Deleuze, *Difference and Repetition*, trans. Paul Patton (New York: Columbia University Press, 1995): "I make, remake and unmake my concepts along a moving horizon [. . .] which repeats and differenciates them [sic]. The task of modern philosophy is to overcome the alternatives temporal/non-temporal, historical/eternal, and particular/universal" (xxi).

[8] Carolyn Abbate, "Music—Drastic or Gnostic?" *Critical Inquiry* 30/3 (2004): 505–36.

in which "the juxtaposition of before and after replaces the fluid intricacies of becoming and real distinctions of present, past, and future."[9] Even live speakers about music, having revised and finalized their scripts, might decide to skip a paragraph or repeat a line.

It would seem, then, that the only musicians whose activity calls for creating continuous musical passage, ongoing musical experience, are live performers. They have no choice. From the moment they publicly begin a piece until its conclusion, they are expected not to stop, jump ahead, or turn back. And so my essay takes on Hasty's challenge by exploring a different kind of "becoming" of importance to me; I examine what it has meant to become a live performer of a particular work that I have long adored. I choose Robert Schumann's piano cycle *Davidsbündlertänze*, op. 6, not just because of my long-term involvement with it, but also because this might be the work in which Schumann himself creates his most striking evocation of the ongoing passage of time. I want to consider how an awareness of that evocation affects my temporal engagement with this music.

To remind readers about Schumann's *Davidsbündlertänze*, let me provide some background. Its title, usually translated as "Dances of the League of David," refers to the "half-imaginary band of crusaders against philistinism in music."[10] Several members of the league were collaborators with Schumann in the years leading to his founding in 1834 of the journal *Neue Zeitschrift für Musik*. To his friends and fellow journalists he gave fanciful nicknames. For himself, as early as 1831, the twenty-one-year-old Schumann conjured names for "two of his best friends"—Florestan, a fiery, rambunctious improviser, and Eusebius, introverted and poetic. These two diametrically opposite "friends" were clearly meant to be poetic self-projections—Schumann's solution to the problem of his divided self. All of the eighteen dances of the *Davidsbündler*, originally appearing in two books of nine each, were "composed" by Florestan, Eusebius, or the two of them together; in his first edition, published in early 1838, Schumann inscribed their initials at the end of each dance—as F., E., or F. & E.[11]

As is well known, shortly after Robert and the much younger Clara Wieck declared their mutual love (in 1835), Clara's father enforced their separation.

---

[9] Hasty, "If Music is Ongoing Experience," 205.

[10] John Daverio, *Crossing Paths: Schubert, Schumann, and Brahms* (Oxford: Oxford University Press, 2002), 135.

[11] For further background on the inception of the "Davidsbündler" and on the work that carries this title, see John Daverio, *Robert Schumann: Herald of a "New Poetic Age"* (Oxford: Oxford University Press, 1997), 112–15, 158–59.

A renewed alliance in August of 1837 served as the primary inspiration for the *Davidsbündlertänze*. "In the most wonderful state of excitation" that he could ever remember, Schumann completed a draft of the work in less than a month.[12] About the cycle, Robert wrote to Clara in 1837 that there are many "wedding motifs"; in February 1838 he told Clara that the dances are dedicated to her "more than anything else" of his, that "the story is a bachelor's party" (a *Polterabend*, on the eve of a wedding), and that she will surely "imagine the beginning and the end."[13] He might also have mentioned that, as in several of his earlier piano works, he borrowed two ideas from her own compositions. First, the very opening of the cycle, labeled "Motto by C[lara] W[ieck]" in the first edition, quotes the opening of a mazurka by her, the fifth piece within her *Soirées musicales*, op. 6 (1835–36). In fact, Robert gives his work the same number, op. 6, and begins his cycle in the same key—G major. Example 1 displays the motto, followed by Robert's explosive continuation.[14]

As uncovered by Berthold Hoeckner, a central motive of the cycle, first heard most clearly in Dance No. 3 (Example 2a) and already appearing in Schumann's *Carnaval* (published in 1837) but now always beginning on F♯, can be understood as a sly reference to the opening idea from the first waltz in Clara's Wieck's 1835 *Valses romantiques*, op. 4 (Example 2b). In the second part of her waltz, Wieck's tenaciously repeated F♯s will not be missed.[15]

John Daverio proposed that the "bachelor's party" does not get underway until the beginning of this "rough," boisterous third dance,[16] after which follows a madcap, maybe even manic, series of often wildly exuberant, sometimes dreamy dance-types—for example, waltzes (nos. 1, 2, 4, 14, 15, and 18), a tarantella (no. 6), and various brands of polkas (nos. 8, 12, and 13). If these dances are not entirely recognizable as such, it may be because, as Charles Rosen has shown, "hardly one of them does not distort the traditional rhythm."[17]

---

[12] Robert and Clara Schumann, *The Complete Correspondence of Clara and Robert Schumann*, vol. 1, trans. Hildegard Fritsch and Ronald L. Crawford; ed. Eva Weissweiler (New York: P. Lang, 1994), 76 [no. 42]. Letter begun on December 31, 1837; the reference to the *Davids-bündler* is entered on January 5, 1838. 1:94–95.

[13] Robert and Clara Schumann, *Complete Correspondence*, vol. 1, 95 [no. 44].

[14] I heartily thank William O'Hara, doctoral candidate in the Music Department at Harvard University, for transcribing this and the following music examples into computer notation.

[15] Berthold Hoeckner, *Programming the Absolute: Nineteenth-Century German Music and the Hermeneutics of the Moment* (Princeton: Princeton University Press, 2002), 88–93.

[16] Daverio, *Crossing Paths*, 135.

[17] Charles Rosen, *The Romantic Generation* (Cambridge, Mass.: Harvard University Press, 1995), 224.

Example 1. Robert Schumann, Davidsbündler,
no. 1 (adapted from Edition Peters)

For example, not a single sustained tone of the soprano melody falls upon a downbeat in the opening waltz (see Example 1).

Inspired by the seminal work of Peter Kaminsky, analysts have noted that both the large-scale form and the overall tonal plan of the *Davidsbündlertänze*

Example 2a. Schumann, Davidsbündler, *no. 3, opening*

break entirely new ground.[18] Here is a series of dance "fragments," or minia-tures, whose individual roles within the complete cycle only become recog-nized over the progressive experience of the complete work—a formal and tonal "becoming" on the grandest scale. From the very first dance, allusions to the key of B minor arise again and again. Five of the eighteen dances (nos. 2, 4, 11, 12, 13) and the "Trio" of no. 16 are actually in that key. In fact, the first dance quotes Clara's motto in G but immediately pushes beyond it to a chord on B (see Example 1). And yet, the last dance of Book 1 (no. 9) is in C major, and this is the key in which Eusebius's hushed, "superfluous" final waltz (no. 18) will reside.

If the "real," fundamental tonal center of the cycle rests in B, then here is a piece that ends in the "wrong" key. But now perhaps Schumann's insis-tence that Clara will imagine the beginning and the end of the cycle becomes fathomable. The bachelor party has been "framed" by the first and last two

---

[18] See Peter Michael Kaminsky, "Aspects of Harmony, Rhythm and Form in Schumann's *Papillons, Carnaval*, and *Davidsbündlertänze*" (PhD dissertation, University of Rochester, Eastman School of Music, 1989). See also Peter Kaminsky, "Principles of Formal Structure in Schumann's Early Piano Cycles," *Music Theory Spectrum* 11/2 (1989), 207–25.

Example 2b. Wieck, Valses romantiques, *op. 4, no. 1*

movements, both of which unquestionably belong to Clara: Eusebius speaks to, or for, her in Dance no. 2—the slow, poignant *Ländler* in B minor shown at Example 3—and in its heartbreaking return within Dance no. 17. Finally, C major is the key of the *valse* by Clara from which Robert borrowed its opening idea. Eusebius's final waltz transforms the bachelor party into a dream—Robert's blissful dream of Clara.

As I have been eager to acknowledge, Schumann's *Davidsbündler* has served as an attractive object of analysis for a host of distinguished writers. In each case, special attention has been given to the return of the soulful *Ländler*, Dance no. 2, as an interruption within the ravishingly beautiful penultimate movement, in B major. As we shall see, the *Ländler*'s return does not serve as a "recapitulation" in any formal or other sense of the term. Rather, at first it reappears completely unaltered; and yet, within its new context, it expresses the greatest difference, or "unrepeatability," in Deleuze's sense. Rosen could not have put it better: "Schumann does everything possible to make the return of the *Ländler* sound like the involuntary resurfacing of a buried memory, the rediscovered existence of the past within the present."[19] How can the pianist "pretend" not to know that the return will come but then physically produce it? That question has profoundly affected my ongoing experience of the cycle. By "pretending," I do not mean that I hold it necessary to adopt a "pianist persona" in the performance of this work—the kind of "knowing" persona that Edward T. Cone hears in the pianist's music for, say, Schumann's *Dichterliebe*. Nor do I view the pianist's role as a "channeling" of the composer's voice. I simply mean that, over the course of complete performances of the cycle, I have wanted both to experience and somehow to convey how Schumann suggests, over *musical* time, the potential for the past to emerge within the present.

To prepare my discussion of the *Ländler*, let me first take on Christopher Hasty's view that all of life's experiences, including the experiences of hearing and performing music, must be understood as temporal processes, "becomings" that extend over the complete span of our past and into our present. Hasty's outlook emboldens me to reflect upon what he is fond of calling our "personal past," our "cultural past," our "biological past"—all "massive in [their] bearing on the creation of any new event," and thus inevitably bearing upon our live performances in the present.[20]

Here are a few personal memories. Truth be told, I cannot recall what motivated me to program the *Davidsbündlertänze* as the very first large work by Robert Schumann that I would perform publicly; it's quite possible that a very fine performance of the cycle by a fellow graduate student in the Yale School of Music both drew me to the work and sparked a touch of competition. Perhaps my piano teacher, Ward Davenny, assigned the work to me; if so, I eagerly complied. His characteristic instructions remain in the Peters edition to which I still refer; for example, next to Schumann's "Nicht schnell" for Dance no. 7, Davenny writes, "auch nicht *langsam*"(!) In that same score can be found my own first, crude "analytic" observations, along with suggestions I took down while reworking the cycle for subsequent performances with two

<hr />

[19] Rosen, *The Romantic Generation*, 235.

[20] Hasty, "If Music is Ongoing Experience," 209, on "incompleteness or indeterminacy in becoming"; or, on the performing of a phrase: "All our past (*biological, cultural, personal*) is there to be brought into play," 210 (my italics). See also Hasty, "The Image of Thought and Ideas of Music," in *Sounding the Virtual*, 8. And on the same page, "The new, actual experience when past (passed) will, because of its irreducible novelty, change the composition of the virtual . . . This change, however minute and imperceptible, is real—it is *organic* (neural, chemical), *cultural*, and *personal*, and will be passed on to countless individuals" (my italics).

of my most trusted pianist friends. One of these is my long-standing colleague Charles Fisk, for whom I rehearsed the piece prior to a performance at Tufts University in 2011. By then Fisk had himself presented the *Davidsbündlertänze* several times, and his exquisite performance of the *Ländler* had even been videotaped for a 1977 film by Bruno Monsaingeon about Nadia Boulanger.[21] In short, my battered score marks the site of my first and subsequent engagements with the piece. It is only an "object"—some *thing* that I can hold in my hands; but this object is the repository of countless memories, ideas about playing the *Davidsbündler* that have accumulated and changed over many years.

Shortly after my first effort to perform the work, two extraordinary "cultural" events greatly impelled me to want to try again. Within what may have been my first year as a Yale doctoral student in music theory, Charles Rosen came to campus to present a full-length concert, and this included an impassioned performance of the *Davidsbündler*. Years later, it thus came as no surprise that Rosen's writing about this work in his *Romantic Generation* struck me, and still does, as perhaps his most inspired, and most inspiring, discussion—luminous, deeply insightful, and unabashedly devoted to the piece. Then came Murray Perahia's début recording—his dazzling 1973 Schumann album, with the *Davidsbündlertänze* and the *Fantasiestücke*, op. 12. Young musicians are often discouraged from studying professional recordings of pieces they are preparing to perform. To this attitude I emphatically object; pianists who wish to become performers of the *Davidsbündler* would be fools to deny themselves the opportunity of hearing this work in the hands of a young prodigy.

Are these the kinds of "personal, cultural, and biological" past experiences to which Hasty alludes, rarely with amplification? They were for me. My experience as a graduate pianist in the lap of academia clearly reflects the opportunities and biases of my generation. The idea of the *Urtext* had taken hold. When I began studying the *Davidsbündler*, little did I know the extent to which Schumann had himself revised this and other early piano works during his last years; long before then, he had come to dismiss those early pieces as "immature and unfinished."[22] Some of his revisions within the *Davidsbündler* seem lamentably conservative: for instance, in the first dance, he deletes the sustained B♮ at the end of his introduction, thus abandoning the beautiful effect of a solo horn emerging from within an orchestral texture—the magical

---

[21] Released in DVD format as *Nadia Boulanger: Mademoiselle*, directed by Bruno Monsangeion (1967; Paris: Idéale Audience International, 2007).

[22] F. Gustav Jansen ed., *Robert Schumanns Briefe: Neue Folge* (Leipzig: Breitkopf und Härtel, 1904), 227 [no. 250]; as cited in Nicholas Marston, *Schumann: Fantasie, Op. 17* (Cambridge: Cambridge University Press, 1992), 98.

link into the melody of the dance proper. As Schumann and especially Chopin scholars know, scores by these composers, and by all others, cannot be regarded as fixed objects, as single definitive texts. In fact, Adorno argues that "the musical score is never identical with the work; devotion to the text means the constant effort to grasp that which it hides."[23] Performers of the *Davidsbündler* should be especially free to observe or ignore Schumann's numerous added repeat signs, and perhaps they will even make these decisions in the very moment of performance.[24]

I turn now to the second dance, the slow *Ländler* that will return (Example 3). In a segment within Monsaingeon's film about Boulanger, the great teacher is asking her students to sing the *Ländler*'s melody at mm. 1–8, towards the apparent goal of helping them to discover how the second four-bar phrase differs from the first. In formal terminology we might claim that this opening section alludes to the thematic convention of an eight-bar antecedent-consequent, in which the requirement of a stronger cadence at the end of the consequent calls for a reshaping, a telescoping, of the antecedent upon its repetition. Boulanger clearly wanted her students to discover, in this case, that the immediate repetition of the plaintive opening one-bar gesture has been omitted within the consequent phrase. This is "difference" in the most obvious sense, but it "multiplies" the difference already expressed in the exact repetition at m. 2 of the gesture in m. 1. Within its new context, the repeated gesture is no longer a beginning; its different role is to reinforce the opening idea, to give it greater urgency, and to propel the phrase forward to its goal at m. 4.

What makes this Eusebian-inspired periodic design so completely *post*-classical, relative to earlier paradigms of the same? We can hear that the movement begins off-tonic and that the entire passage rests upon a dominant pedal, all the way until the authentic cadence at m. 8. But the delay of the pedal until the third beat within each bar allows the *Ländler* to seem as if it opens on the distinctly unstable dominant $^4_2$-chord, with the soprano melody creating unprepared dissonant suspensions on the downbeats at mm. 1–2. Within the key of B minor, these suspensions represent the scale degrees $\hat{3}$–$\hat{2}$, answered by the descent from $\hat{5}$ at m. 3. I think that Rosen overstated his case in claiming that *all* of the eighteen *Davidsbündler* dances are derived from Clara's

[23] Theodor W. Adorno, "Bach Defended against his Devotees," in *Prisms*, trans. Samuel and Shierry Weber (Cambridge, Mass.: MIT Press, 1981), 144. Cited in Susan McClary, "Adorno Plays the *WTC*: On Political Theory and Performance," *Indiana Theory Review* 27/2 (2009), 111.

[24] On the repeat signs that Schumann added in his revised edition, see Rosen, *The Romantic Generation*, 705.

Example 3. Davidsbündler, *no. 2: the Ländler*

motto.[25] But of course his point is well taken here: Clara's $\hat{3}$–$\hat{2}$–$\hat{6}$-$\hat{5}$ melodic shape in G major has become the same in B minor, much disguised, and minus the neighbor $\hat{6}$, except within the "accompaniment" texture. Clara's buoyant

---

[25] Ibid., 223. Rosen simply asserts that Wieck's motto "becomes merely an excuse for writing melodies that emphasize initially the third degree of the scale, and then the fifth." See also ibid., 235.

introduction to the first dance has here become an expression of intense long-ing—wistful and melancholy; Eusebius, representing Clara, or longing for her, has turned inward ("Innig"). As Rosen notes, the Ländler "pits a clear duple time in the melody against the traditional $\frac{3}{4}$."[26] In the "present" moment, as in past performances, my focus is on how technically to capture this metric ambiguity—this tension between holding back and pressing forward: I attempt to play the initial, repeated idea of the *Ländler* as if in duple time (that is, in $\frac{6}{8}$).

The contrasting middle section of the *Ländler* turns briefly to the tonic B *major*, as if the dream of fulfillment for and with Clara might become a reality. Lingering within the dream, Schumann repeats his B-section, thus distorting the conventional rounded-binary form that he has promised, and exemplifying his often unruly transformations of classical forms. When the reprise of the minor-mode A-section returns at m. 17, with deeper dominant bass pedals, we know that the dream was only that—a wish not yet fulfilled. Already within this second movement, a deeply reflective moment has been introduced; as a slow dance, the *Ländler* will find its companion only within Dance no. 14, the slow waltz marked "tender and singing" ("*zart und singend*"). Perhaps, by presenting the *Ländler* so early within the cycle, Schumann forecasts its hold over the cycle—even signals the inevitability of its return.

The dénouement of Schumann's cycle already gets underway in Dance no. 16 (Example 4). With "good humor," this scherzo-like dance begins, tellingly, in the opening key of the cycle, G major. A pianistically wicked canon in octaves at the unison takes up a rant on the dance's initial idea to serve as the B-section of what promises to be an unusually straightforward rounded-binary form. But like the ending of the A-section, its return as A' (at m. 16) refuses to close in G major, instead again only reaching an authentic cadence in the dominant (at m. 24, not shown).

Given this detail, we would not conventionally be ready for a "Trio," but that is how Schumann marks the next section (Example 5). Shifting onto the dominant of B minor, the *real* key of the cycle, he now offers the most disturb-ing passage of the complete work—a slower, *pianissimo* chordal progression that is brutally interrupted by the *forte* return of those insistent F♯s in octaves, from Dance no. 3, now stentorian, oracular in character. The octave intrusions grow more frequent, where a dispute over G♮ versus G♯ erupts. As if in exhaus-tion, the two contenders cede to a reconciliation at m. 33, and then they join forces toward an emphatic cadence in B minor.

---

[26] Ibid., 224.

Example 4. Davidsbündler, *no. 16*

Codettas bring the return of the F♯ octaves in the bass, but now a most breathtaking transformation occurs: just when we might have expected a modulating retransition into a da capo reprise of the scherzo, the F♯ takes on a syncopated, offbeat rhythm that creates the segue—no pause—into Dance no. 17. As shown at Example 6, the Clara-associated F♯ becomes the pervasive, pulsating internal dominant pedal within what must be regarded as one of Schumann's most astonishing creations—his portrayal, in B major, of how music, composed by both F. and E., can sound "as if from the distance" ("Wie aus der Ferne").

How does Schumann do this? Distance itself seems to be represented by the great registral space between treble and bass throughout most of the movement, with echoes in the tenor voice of each of the initial two-bar ideas giving middleground depth to the space. I turn again to Charles Rosen, because, as a pianist, like Schumann himself, he especially understood the composer's achievement. Rosen writes: "The passage must *swim* in pedal, so that the bass and treble notes are sustained against the inner ostinato. This is not merely a price to be paid for a pretty effect but the whole point of the music: a soft, widely spaced texture blurring tonic and dominant harmony together in a single mist."[27] When I play the opening of this penultimate no. 17, I must focus on how subtly, but not completely, I can clear the pedal at the dominant-to-tonic changes of harmony. My "biological past," to use Hasty's expression, becomes a factor here: because my hands cannot reach a tenth, I must concentrate on how gently to break the right-hand chords without losing the syncopated pulse of the inner F♯.

[27] Ibid., 26. Emphasis mine.

Example 5. Davidsbündler, no. 16, Trio

Example 6. Davidsbündler, *no. 17*

As with the scherzo of no. 16, the first part of the "Wie aus der Ferne" movement ends on the tonicized dominant, and its reprise will do the same. Spanning these parts is a contrasting middle section that begins by warning us of an impending catastrophe: over a dominant pedal in effect for eight measures, the stinging G♮s—clearly serving as a long-range neighbor to the prominent F♯ of the opening—now unambiguously invoke B minor. On Schumann's piano, it might have been possible to play the entire passage with the dampers raised; on today's Steinway, this doesn't quite work, but the effect of the sustained dominant pedal simply must be achieved, if only in the performer's imagination. Relief comes with the stunning shift, at m. 25, onto the dominant of F major; and then a free imitative exchange, as if among violas, cellos, and basses, leads to the reprise of the opening section, at the end of which, without a break and arising directly from the pulsating F♯s, the B-minor *Ländler* returns (Example 7).

Example 7. Davidsbündler, *no. 17, the* Ländler

Here is the moment where distance, space, and *time* merge. Here is Rosen's "involuntary resurfacing of a buried memory." Because he is centrally concerned to portray Schumann's miraculous recreation "of the sense of time and memory of Romantic landscape," he compares the return to a *Rückblick*—"a looking-back, as the Romantic travelers delighted to look back to perceive the different appearance of what they had seen before, a meaning altered and transfigured by distance and a new perspective . . . the *Ländler* is apparently unaltered, transformed simply by distance in time and space, by the preceding sonorities, by everything that has taken place since the opening."[28] In short, Rosen's "looking-back" analogy captures within the *Davidsbündler* precisely what Hasty, through Deleuze, describes as "unrepeatability"; the past, within this music as within all of life, intrudes upon the present and transforms it.

Rosen was either unaware or dismissive of Schumann's private allusion to the story of a "bachelor party," but he was right to assert that the *Davidsbündler*

---

[28] Ibid., 236.

has "no visible program"; Schumann's letter to Clara was strictly private, and he even removed the initials F. and E. in his revised edition. Has the memory of the *Ländler* resurfaced over a great span of time and distance, or does it arise simply at the end of a long celebratory *Polterabend* evening? And if we imagine the latter, then what does this poignant return tell us of the outcome of the celebration? I offer no answers here, especially in light of the upheaval that follows. The reprise of the *Ländler's* opening section, marked *Nach und nach schneller*, leads without pause into a Coda of devastating magnitude—one that ends with a tumultuous, climactic cry of anguish (Example 8).

In his early, seminal study *Difference and Repetition* (1968), Deleuze reinforces his argument that repetition cannot be generalized—that repetition is always difference—by introducing ways in which the comprehension of a concept and its representation can be "blocked"; for one of those "blockages," he draws upon Sigmund Freud's psychoanalytic theory of repression.[29] Here, in Schumann's return of the *Ländler*, it is as if the hitherto blocked memory, and now its remembrance, gradually unleash an affective pain, or conflict, that was associated with the memory but repressed, along with the memory itself—a moment of great longing but perhaps also of the fearful pain of loss. The affect now rushes in: the dreamer awakes; the present reality recaptures the pain.[30] The end of the Coda, with its passionate outpouring of grief, is where first-time listeners would surely assume that the cycle has ended.

From various recordings, I have discovered that roughly twenty-nine minutes in "real," or "clock," time usually transpire between the first appearance of the *Ländler* and its return. Within that passage of time, technical obstacles face even the finest pianist—for example, the finger-twisting tarantella of Dance no. 6, and (for me) the exhausting octave stretches in both hands throughout the "Wild und lustig" (wild and joyous) no. 13. Respite follows with the slow and tender no. 14, and within the core of no. 15. In these movements, it is as if time stands still, or at least slows down. But with no. 16, the pianist moves hastily into the beginning of the end—the finale that leads to what must be made to sound like a shattering conclusion. When the *Ländler* returns, the pianist simulates the effect that she is conjuring a memory of the movement she has

---

[29] Deleuze, *Difference and Repetition*, 15–19.

[30] Schumann and Heinrich Heine portray a comparable psychological state within Song 13 of Schumann's *Dichterliebe*, "Ich hab' im Traum geweinet": the musical setting reaches its wrenching climax in the last strophe, where the protagonist has dreamt that his beloved is still fond of him; after he awakes, his tears, now a flood, keep flowing. ("Ich hab' im Traum geweinet, / Mir träumte, du wärst mir noch gut. / Ich wachte auf, und noch immer / Strömt meine Tränenflut.")

Example 8. Davidsbündler, *no. 17, the Ländler, continued*

already played, not so long ago in clock time, but, from the perspective of her "inner" time, perhaps almost as if in an earlier life experience.

Performers of the *Davidsbündler* will agree, I hope, that such a simulation cannot be achieved without at the same time a good deal of mental "multitasking." For example, if the *Ländler* is to return as though unaltered, then perhaps it should return in roughly the same tempo heard earlier; this means that performers might want to retain the memory of their original tempo and find it again. But given that the "Wie aus der Ferne" movement leads seamlessly into the return of the *Ländler*, marked *a tempo* after a short *ritard.*, the pianist might also want already to have remembered her original tempo and establish this from the outset of the movement (Schumann's first edition contains no metronome markings). Then there is the problem of the pianist's foreknowledge that the *Ländler* is about to lose all its original stability and head, faster and faster, into the devastating Coda. Just how much faster one should dare to play the Coda is a crucial question. From the recording of my 2011 performance, I can hear precisely where, in the heat of excitement, I suddenly shot ahead in tempo and then lost control of the difficult pre-cadential passage.

Hasty thoroughly understands this kind of situation: "Music in its making or actual passage involves so many things, so much more than abstract images of objects occupying position. It involves imagining, thinking, remembering, forgetting, discovering, expecting, waiting, moving, being moved, feeling, and valuing, among other processes."[31] But he cannot speak for me when he claims that "the wrong note we played a minute ago or last year is not there now for us to hear."[32] Yes, of course this is empirically true; but for some performers, remembering, even when the memory is painful, can trump forgetting—the memory of the wrong note can be hard to overcome. Hasty puts a bright spin on the phenomenon of the botched passage: "It may (or perhaps must) have an enduring, lasting effectiveness. We may, without noticing it, approach this spot in the piece differently when we play it again, differently than if we had not so botched it before."[33] I certainly now approach the coda of no. 17 differently; but I am aware that, in an effort not to rush, it would be just as foolish to play with too much caution. Either way, I can assure you that, unlike Carolyn

---

[31] Christopher F. Hasty, "Rhythmicizing the Subject," in *Musical Implications: Essays in Honor of Eugene Narmour*, eds. Lawrence Bernstein and Alexander Rozin (Hillsdale, NY: Pendragon Press, 2013), 170.

[32] Hasty, "If Music is Ongoing Experience," 211.

[33] Ibid.

Abbate in her live piano performance of a Mozart aria, I cannot be thinking that *"doing this really fast is fun."*[34]

No matter what happens to the pianist within the coda of no. 17, the last, slow, heart-wrenchingly tender waltz of no. 18 —clearly a postlude, or post-script—offers the opportunity for *redemption* after a botched performance. It would also seem to bestow a blessing, a benediction, upon the complete cycle, as the curtain now descends. At the top of the score for this last dance, as shown at Example 9, Schumann wrote: "Quite superfluously [or "flowing over," "*Ganz zum Überfluss*"], Eusebius added the following, and his eyes spoke of great bliss."[35] Through the agency of her F♯, Clara has been quietly present for Robert from the beginning of the "Wie aus der Ferne"; now the key from her own *valse*—C major—confirms that his final, blissful thoughts are of her.

Example 9. Davidsbündler, *no. 18*

To conclude, I raise the question whether *even performers* can sustain the illusion of being single-minded in ongoing musical time during the act of per-formance. Cultural historian and memoirist Eva Hoffman, in her 2009 study entitled, simply, *Time*, reports the following about recent experiments on mul-titasking: "It seems that the shift from one activity to another literally takes brain-time—up to seven-tenths of a second."[36] This does not sound like a lot of time; but, for example, even less time is available to the pianist for establish-ing the opening tempo of the "Wie aus der Ferne" movement, while also (in my case) managing to roll unreachable chords and maintaining a syncopated

---

[34] Abbate, "Music—Drastic or Gnostic?" 511.

[35] "Ganz zum Überfluss meinte Eusebius noch Folgendes; dabei sprach aber viel Seligkeit aus seinen Augen." This epigraph complements and transforms the one at the top of the score for Dance no. 9, the final movement of Book 1: "Hierauf schloss Florestan und es zuckte ihm schmerzlich um die Lippen" ("Hereupon Florestan concluded, and his lips quivered with pain").

[36] Eva Hoffman, *Time* (New York: Picador, 2009), 71.

pulse. In short, perhaps many, if not most, performers inhabit multiple temporal domains—some from the distant or split-second past, some in anticipation of the future—all while striving to give their listeners the experience of an ongoing musical present. I thank both Robert Schumann and Christopher Hasty for provoking me to probe this possibility.

Shaping Time

JEANNE BAMBERGER

The same returns not, save to bring the different. Time keeps budding into new moments, every one of which presents a content which in its individuality never was before and will never be again.

—William James[1]

The past is consumed in the present and the present is living only because it brings forth the future.

—James Joyce [2]

Making time;
  Keeping time;
    Losing time;
      In time;
        Out of time;
          In no time;
            Take your time.

What time is it? It's about time.

---

[1] William James, "The Problem of Novelty," in *Some Problems in Philosophy* (Cambridge, Mass.: Harvard University Press, 1979), 76.

[2] James Joyce, *A Portrait of the Artist As a Young Man* (New York: Viking Press, 1960), 251.

INTRODUCTION

MUSIC, OF ALL our creations, is about time. Music, shaping time, brings time's transient presence into consciousness—making time palpable, as if hand-held.

We necessarily experience the world in and through time; our body actions, the flow of objects and events around us are experienced as successive and contiguous. How and why, then, do we step off these temporal action paths to selectively and purposefully interrupt, stop, contain, and measure the natural passage of continuous actions/events?

The episodes with children that I follow here recapitulate in innocent form efforts of philosophers and scientists throughout history to hold time still so as to reflect upon it, to digitize, count, and notate its passing presence. Here is Aristotle:

> [Time:] First, does it belong to the class of things that exist or to that of things that do not exist? Then secondly, what is its nature? One part of it has been and is not, while the other is going to be and is not yet.
>
> ... Time, on the other hand, is not held to be made up of "nows." Again, the "now" which seems to bound the past and the future—does it always remain one and the same or is it always other and other? It is hard to say.[3]

In contrast, dictionary definitions ignore these elusive issues by depending on calmly putting time into space:

> Time: A space or extent of time. A limited stretch or space of continued existence. "A long time. A short time."[4]
>
> —Oxford English Dictionary

> Time: The period between two events or during which something exists, happens, or acts; measured or measurable interval.[5]
>
> —Webster's New World Dictionary

[3] Aristotle, *Physics*, 4.10. Translated by R.P. Hardie and R.K. Gaye in Robert Maynard Hutchins, ed., *Great Books of the Western World*, vol. 8 (Chicago: Encyclopedia Britannica, Inc., 1952), 297.

[4] *Oxford English Dictionary*, 1972 edn., s.v. "time."

[5] *Webster's New World Dictionary*, 1957 edn., s.v. "time."

How, then, do we learn to turn the moving flow of our complex, organized bodily actions—like clapping, drumming, or bouncing a ball, swinging on the park swing, or rollerblading—into discrete, static entities that we believe represent our experience of those objects and our sensory mastery of them?

Children, in seeking to make descriptions of objects (or themselves) in motion, also find ways to hold time and motion still, to contain and bound it, to make bits and pieces of their *going on.* I will argue that in their efforts to describe organized rhythmic actions (clapping, walking, drumming), children give us a window into our everyday assumptions. In particular, into those assumptions that hide the poignant complexity of how we have learned to make, understand, and to use descriptions of continuous motion that have been compiled into common symbolic expressions. Studying children's efforts to make descriptions of themselves as well as things in motion also provide us with insight into the critical (silent) transformations through which the *know-how* of familiar action becomes the selective *know-about* that is expressed in symbolic conventions that compress, consolidate, and hold time's evanescence still.

But to study children's spontaneous productions, to take them seriously in search of answers, we need to become something like cultural anthropologists. Like the anthropologist entering a new culture, we need to begin with the assumption that what is found there—rituals, myths, modes of representation—no matter how strange, incomprehensible, or meaningless they may initially seem, make sense to the inhabitants of that culture. Once we make that assumption, the task becomes mutual and reciprocal: we must learn to understand our own belief systems, our own deeply internalized intuitions for making sense, even as we learn to understand the sense-making of the other. As Clifford Geertz has said of the practice of anthropology: ". . . progress is marked less by a perfection of consensus than by a refinement of debate. What gets better is the precision with which we vex one another."[6]

PART I

What Develops in Musical Development?

Influenced initially by traditional cognitive developmental theory, I saw the children's inventions and wrote about them as exhibiting a clear developmental progression based in Piagetian theory. Reflecting on the typology from a

---

[6] Clifford Geertz, *Interpretation of Cultures* (New York: Basic Books, 1973), 29.

greater distance in time, I now see the children's work quite differently and in this broader context, perhaps more interestingly. To begin with, I am troubled by Piaget and others who propose that achieving a later stage in development requires *overcoming* features that characterize an earlier stage. Vygotsky, in taking issue with Piaget's view of "progress," puts it perhaps a bit starkly:

> For Piaget the child's mental development consists of the gradual *replacement* of the unique qualities and characteristics of the child's thought by the more powerful thought of the adult. . . . With age, the characteristics of the child's thought begin to disappear. They are replaced in one domain after another and ultimately disappear entirely. . . . One must be done away with so that the other can take its place. . . . We must understand it in the same sense that we understand an enemy."[7]

On this view, "progress" implies, for instance, gradually giving up a response to context where properties may shift and change their meanings. Heinz Werner, in contrast to Piaget, makes what I now believe to be the critical point: "As a rule the lower level is not lost. In many instances it develops as an integral part of a more complex organization."[8]

Following Werner, I no longer see the children's drawings as illustrating a process of *giving up* aspects that are thought to characterize "earlier stages." Instead I see the typology as if it were an *accumulating palette of useful and provocative sensory organizers*—emergent possibilities that gather and evolve throughout a musical life. Thus, as I shall show, the mature musician is responsive to shifts in meaning of the properties of events as they change their function in response to activity and context, while also recognizing that properties *as* properties remain invariant in spite of situation and function.

But, as I shall show, the scope of possible sensory organizers as revealed in the children's drawings also predicts the emergence of an essential tension—one that begins early on in musical studies, and continues to pervade and also enliven mature musical life. In its most potent form, it is the tension that we experience as we move back and forth between *action and symbol*. Perhaps the typology suggests, in practical form, the philosophers' quandaries as they

---

[7] Lev S. Vygotsky, *Thinking and Speech,* in *The Collected Works of L.S. Vygotsky,* vol. 1, ed. Robert W. Rieber and Aaron S. Carton, trans. Norris Minick (New York: Plenum Press, 1934/1987), 175–76. Emphasis mine.

[8] Heinz Werner, *Comparative Psychology of Mental Development* (New York: International Universities Press, 1973), 216.

contemplate parsing continuous time. Christopher Hasty helps to make the tension explicit with "the opposition of meter and rhythm," most particularly in the role played by notation and pedagogy:

> Now it must be granted that in our elementary training we do not reflect on the issue of homogeneity or on what metrical homogeneity must mean for our conception of musical rhythm and time in general. But it must also be granted that the practice and pedagogy of metrical notation are not detached from theory. Since we have little reason to reflect on the conceptual framework we accept in learning to read, with long familiarity we can come to accept certain customary notions of meter and rhythm simply as matters of fact . . . Indeed, I would argue that all our systematic theories of meter draw upon a conceptual framework grounded in the technology of *metric notation*. . . . And yet, for all the subjectivity and vagueness that the idea of rhythm seems to present, it may serve as a reminder of the real complexity of musical experience and perhaps also as a reminder of the inadequacy of our conception of temporality.[9]

In his recent book, *Time Reborn*, Lee Smolin makes the argument with respect to physics:

> By succumbing to the temptation to conflate the representation with the reality and identify the graph of the records of motion with the motion itself, these scientists have taken a big step toward the *expulsion of time* from our conception of nature. . . . They [Descartes, Galileo, Kepler, and Newton] showed us how to display the records of these motions in simple diagrams whose axes represent the positions and times in a way that is frozen and hence amenable to being studied at our leisure.[10]

With all of this in mind, I have come to see the children's drawings as a display of our emergent efforts to hold motion and time still. In that cumulating process one is also tempted to see "progress" as a move towards the expulsion of time—*motions frozen and hence amenable to being studied at our leisure.*

[9] Christopher F. Hasty, *Meter As Rhythm* (Oxford: Oxford University Press, 1997), 5–7. Emphasis mine.
[10] Lee Smolin, *Time Reborn* (New York: Houghton Mifflin, 2013), 34–38.

PART II

A Typology of Children's Invented Notations

Figure 1a. A Developmental Typology

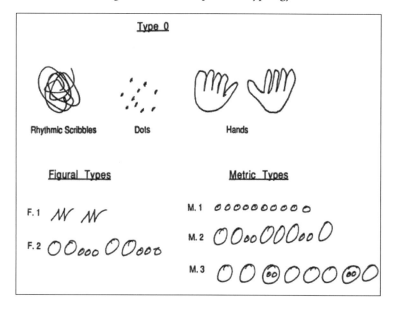

Figure 1b. The given rhythm

I begin with an analysis of the invented notations as I originally organized them—a developmental typology. I interweave this with comments and examples of how the particular qualities of each type are expressively integrated into mature analysis and performance.

The original typology, shown in Figure 1a,[11] derives from 186 drawings made primarily by children between the ages of 6 and 12. During their regular music classes, the children were asked to listen to a clapped rhythm, to clap it

---

[11] Taken from Jeanne Bamberger, *The Mind Behind the Musical Ear* (Cambridge, Mass.: Harvard University Press, 1991), 46.

back, and then: "Put something on paper that will help someone else who isn't here today clap the rhythm that you just clapped." I have chosen one of the six rhythms the children worked with and copies of a selection from the drawings of it to illustrate how the inventions typically change as children grow older.[12]

The typology has two global dimensions reflected in the labels I have assigned: one is what I have called the figural-metric distinction that is seen in the drawings labeled F for figural and M for metric; and within each of these are the characteristics related to age, development, and learning (0; F.1 -F.2; M.1 - M.2 - M.3). I will argue that the figural-metric distinction refers to differing organizing aspects of music, *all of which are inherent in the structure of even such simple rhythms;* it is their interaction that gives a rhythm pattern its particular coherence. It follows that developmental distinctions should not be seen as representing a single linear "progression," but rather as an interacting evolution between two complementary ways of understanding or "hearing a rhythm, each of which enriches the other.

Type 0 Drawings

Figure 2. Type 0

Rhythmic Scribbles

Type 0 drawings were made only by the very youngest children, ages three to five. These children were interviewed individually and given only this one rhythm. Initially I labeled these drawings "scribbles" and I saw them as just that—simply meaningless scribbles. But by making the assumption that, like members of another culture, there might be reason in what the children were doing, the drawings revealed an aspect of rhythm that is lost entirely in its conventional notation. The scribbles were a trace of the children's *continuous clapping motions:* the children were *re-playing their clapping using their pencils on the paper.*

Once I noticed the relation between a child's actions and the trace she

---

[12] The children actually used many different kinds of shapes in their inventions. I have chosen drawings that were similar with respect to graphic objects in order to make comparisons simpler.

left behind, I saw it as live evidence for the disjunction between action and symbol—between *continuous action* and *discrete notes*. Conventional notation symbols actually represent only the momentary *stop* in the continuous motion of the performer's two hands as they collide. By notating only the stop in the continuous motion, we give credible existence only to the public, acoustic element of the event. And since we cannot, or do not, "note" spontaneous, continuing motion disappearing in time, the *actions* of performing a rhythm become invisible to our glance. Making their actions visible, the youngest children's drawings "liberate" from discrete notation-space the continuousness of living performance. Nowhere do we find in the score the subtlety of the violinist's arm moving his or her bow continuously across the strings, making the discrete pitches marked by his or her fingers continuous as well. To escape into notation is to escape notice:

> The aspects of things that are most important for us are hidden because of their simplicity and familiarity. (One is unable to notice something because it is always before one's eyes.) . . . And this means: we most often fail to be struck by what, once seen, is most striking and most powerful.[13]

Figural Inventions

Figure 3. F.1 drawing

The term *figural* is used here to refer to the clarity of *groupings and boundaries* of clapped events. I have borrowed the term "figure" from music terminology where it refers to brief musical patterns that form and function as *meaningful structural entities*. A figure is a bounded musical structure perceived as organizing continuously unfolding sound as it goes on through time. *Figural* is thus meant to characterize drawings in which one can see the child's effort to *parse* her clapped events into small, structural gestures; the boundaries of these *figures,* in turn, reflect momentary goals of motion. Grouping (or figural)

---

[13] Ludwig Wittgenstein, *Philosophical Investigations*, trans. G.E.M. Anscombe (Oxford: Blackwell, 1958), 50 (§129).

structure in music has more formally been described as: " . . . the most basic component of musical understanding," "expressing a hierarchical organization of the piece into units such as motives, phrases, sections[, etc.]"[14]

These structural entities as they are happening in time and motion have also been called "temporal gestalts" in analogy with the more familiar spatial configurations or spatial gestalts. Temporal gestalts are:

> . . . distinct spans of time . . . each of which is both internally cohesive and externally segregated from comparable time-spans immediately preceding and following it.[15]

The F.1 drawings were made typically by children aged five to seven.[16] Like those who made Type 0 drawings, these children are still playing the rhythm on the paper with their pencils. However, the process and the result were quite different from that of the youngest children. Unlike the Type 0 drawings, these children's claps are distinct and clearly seen in the up and down, undulating lines; but there is still no trace of the changes in pace, no differentiation among them save succession. The children moved their pencils first slowly (/\), then proportionately faster (/\/), then paused, pencils suspended in the air; then made an exact repetition of their previous actions. The trace left behind almost magically reflects back the larger and more articulated *figural* structure of the rhythm. One sees the two like figures, their boundaries marked by the pause which is transformed into a space, an "in between."

F.2 Drawings

Figure 3. F.2 drawing

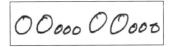

The more fully developed F.2 drawings were made by children beginning at about eight years of age.[17] These older children's inventions have become more

---

[14] Fred Lerdahl and Ray Jackendoff, *A Generative Theory of Tonal Music* (Cambridge, Mass.: MIT Press, 1983), 13 and 18.

[15] James Tenney and Larry Polansky, "Temporal Gestalt Perception," *Journal of Music Theory* 24/2 (1980), 205–41: 205.

[16] However, in a recent class of adult students, this F.1 drawing appeared again.

[17] F.2 drawings were commonly made by subjects up to and including musically untutored adults.

discrete, thus merging toward common practice and also more useful communication—a measure of "progress" within the figural dimension. In contrast to
the children's F.1 drawings, which were still played on the paper, F.2 children
are no longer simply transporting their actions directly onto paper (playing/
drawing). Making distinct and differentiated big and small shapes, the shapes,
in turn, show both *changes in pace and also more fine-grained inner groupings.* The continuous lines of F.1 drawings have become discrete, differentiated
graphic shapes that *stand for and refer to* actions rather than being the *direct
result of the actions* themselves. These are *thought actions.* In this sense, F.2
notations move away from action towards symbol.

But the F.2 drawings present an intriguing puzzle: the relation between
size of shape and actually performed durations is not consistent.[18] As seen in
Figure 4, Clap 5 is *drawn* with a smaller shape like the faster Events 3 and 4 that
immediately precede it, but actually *performed* as an event of longer duration,
like Events 1 and 2 or 6 and 7.

Figure 4. Figural functions

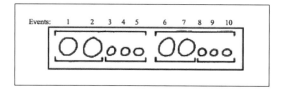

We can account for why Event 5 is drawn as a small circle by noticing that
it is the last of the inner, faster figure, 3→4→5. Moreover, even though Clap 5
is "longer," like Clap 6, it is apprehended as different because it has a different
figural function. Clap 5 functions as the *ending* of the figure, 3→4→5, whereas
Clap 6 functions as the *beginning* of the figure, 6→7. In contrast, conventional
notation, always notating consistent *properties,* naturally represents Clap 5 the
same as Claps 1 and 2 or 6 and 7. Once again we confront the essential tension
between action and symbol and also between *property and function.*

The F.2 drawer is still, in effect, inside her performance, moving with it to
the boundaries of structural goals as she re-enacts the experience. In performing a simple rhythm or even a large complex piece, the experienced performer

---

[18] "Duration" as used here, is more accurately termed "attack time"—i.e., the time from the
attack of one event to the attack of the next event.

is continuously responding to the unique *situation* of events as they occur, and also the particular *function* of an event within the figures of which it is a member. The F.2 drawing is a graphic reconstruction of experienced actions—what I have called a player's *felt path*.

As an example, one child who made a metric drawing, in looking at the typical F.2 drawing said, "It's hard to play it like that. There should be a big circle there" (and he pointed to Clap 5). With his focus on properties rather than function, he played the F.2 drawing as:

Figure 5. A property focused rendition of F.2

The child who had made the original F.2 drawing responded with, "It doesn't matter how long that one is; you just stop and start again."

Seen in the light of conventional developmental theory and conventional notation, we would have to conclude the child's F.2 invention is inadequate, something to overcome. But as an expression of an evolving sensory organizer, the invention makes visible a living, even cherished aspect of an artist's performance: two events that are represented symbolically as sharing an invariant property (here, duration), can be performed differently in response to their changing function within the contexts in which they occur. This is not something that we overcome, that disappears with growing maturity; rather, it can be seen as a sign of growing musical sophistication.

David Soyer, the cellist in the Guaneri Quartet, in describing his own performance, gives a powerful example:

> Soyer: [. . .] The passage begins in the key of G♯ minor; the G♮ in measure 216 is clearly a simplified way of writing F♯♯, which, as the leading note, has an upwards attraction towards the tonic G♯. For this reason I'd avoid using the open G string and would play the passage on the C string. When G♮ comes again (m. 224), its harmonic function is altered; it is now the fifth degree of C major and thus not sharpened. The subsequent G♯ (m. 225) is no longer the tonic but acts as the leading note in A minor and *should* be sharpened. This is the explanation from the harmonic standpoint, but your hearing once

sensitized to such things, will often be able to put you there quite of itself without your needing to think it out.[19]

Figure 6. Beethoven String Quartet, op. 59, no. 2, first movement, coda

Metric Inventions

Comparing the metric drawings, M.1, M.2, and M.3, with the figural drawings, the focus of attention has obviously changed. One might see these drawings as "progressing" as they become closer and closer to conventional notation, if looking only within the three metric drawings. However, as a group, I now see them as another contribution to the *accumulating palette of useful and provocative sensory organizers.*

M.1 Drawings

Figure 7. An M.1 drawing

As with the F.1 drawings made by the six- to seven-year-old children, one really needs to have been there in order to understand what the children have left behind as "product." As we watched the children who made M.1 drawings correctly clapping the rhythm to themselves, we saw them also slowly and laboriously *counting up each clap* as it went by—ten claps in all. It was as if

---

[19] Quoted in David Blum, *The Art of Quartet Playing: The Guarneri Quartet in Conversation With David Blum* (New York: Alfred A. Knopf, 1986), 33. First emphasis mine.

they were trying to "extract" from their continuous motions each separate and discrete clap sound.

With the count-up in mind and ignoring the changes in pace they actually clapped, the children carefully drew a row of ten separate, ungrouped and undifferentiated circles. Each of their claps thus became an item in a *count-up*, with the clapping translated into a line-up of all-alike shapes going left to right across the page.

The drawings seem to be a first emergent attempt to homogenize time and motion so as to hold it still. Perhaps this was in the service of making action events become externally "noteable." While the count-up drawings suggest a primitive form of metric, the critical feature of a metric notation, *an invariant unit of measure generated by the varied durations*, is not yet realized.

In contrasting the earliest figural and metric drawings (F.1 and M.1), we see, even in these early drawings, the emergence of the potential tension between meter and rhythm: M.1 drawings show the child's focus on differentiating clap from clapping, counting them up to form the beginnings of *discrete units*. In contrast, F.1 drawings show the child's focus on differentiating within and bounding his or her continuous clapping motions so as to form the beginnings of *figures*. Thus we have on one hand, *rhythm* as the figural response to motion and to situated function, and on the other, *meter* as a search for the stability of calculated, measured, and *noteable* invariance. Both become critical elements in the cumulating *palette of sensory organizers*. Hasty captures the essence:

> The notion of time *meter* evokes is that of classical scientific doctrine—a homogeneous, evenly flowing time that serves as a receptacle for events while remaining unaffected by the events it comes to contain. It is a conception of time modeled on number. . . . [20]

Dewey uses quite different terms to suggest a similar contrast but without the advantage of the more tangible and practical case of music:

> Temporal quality is however not to be confused with temporal order. . . . Order is a matter of relation, of definition, dating, placing, and describing. Temporal order is a matter of science; temporal quality is an immediate trait of every occurrence whether in or out of consciousness. Every event as such is passing into other things, in such

[20] Hasty, *Meter as Rhythm*, 7.

a way that a later occurrence is an integral part of the *character* or *nature* of present existence.[21]

M.2 Drawings

Figure 8. An M.2 drawing

With the M.2 drawings, this tension grows more serious. The children who made M.2 drawings were about the same age as those who made F.2 drawings. However, in contrast to both M.1 and F.2 drawings, each clapped event is consistent with respect to duration. And this is irrespective of where it falls in the course of the rhythm pattern, and irrespective of its figural membership and function. Rather than going along the temporal felt path of the rhythm, these children step off the path to compare events with respect to duration, even events that are distanced from one another in their order of occurrence. And as in all metric notations, the figural groups that are so clear in both F.1 and F.2 drawings *have disappeared entirely* in M.2 drawings.

The contrast between F.2 and M.2 drawings can best be understood by considering the meaning of "group" or "go together" in each. An F.2 group is a *figure*—events go together as *a sequence of unique, necessarily contiguous and functionally bounded events.* An M.2 group is a *class*—its members are single events that go together because they *share a particular property,* here, the property *same relative duration.* It is this focus on *classifying* events in contrast to a focus on situation and function of actions within figures that most particularly distinguishes F.2 from M.2 drawings. In terms of consistency and the greater objectivity of classification, the M.2 drawings take on strong value within traditional developmental theory, but also in the cumulating palette of sensory organizers. William James has doubts about the very value of classification, however:

When, for example, we think that we have rationally explained the connection of the facts A and B by classing both under their

[21] John Dewey, *Experience and Nature* (New York: Dover, 1958), 110.

common attribute x, it is obvious that we have really explained only so much of these items as *is* x. . . .

We are thus led to the conclusion that the simple classification of things is, on the one hand, the best possible theoretic philosophy, but is, on the other, a most miserable and inadequate substitute for the fullness of the truth. It is a monstrous abridgment of life, which, like all abridgments is got by the absolute loss and casting out of real matter.[22]

Before going on, I would like to sympathize with readers who may feel, by this time, a little like they are in Alice's Wonderland, where the most ordinary things seem to come to life in confusing ways. And this is even worse when we are naming things—what do we give names to and what do the names mean? Or as Humpty Dumpty and Alice put it in *Through the Looking Glass*:

"Don't stand there chattering to yourself like that," Humpty Dumpty said, looking at her for the first time, "but tell me your name and business."

"My *name* is Alice, but . . . "

"It's a stupid name enough!" Humpty Dumpty interrupted impatiently. "What does it mean?"

"*Must* a name mean something?" Alice asked doubtfully.

"Of course it must," Humpty Dumpty said with a short laugh: "*my* name means the shape I am—and a good handsome shape it is, too. With a name like yours, you might be any shape, almost."[23]

M.3 Drawings

Figure 9. An M.3 drawing

The shift in focus found in M.2 drawings is further developed in M.3 drawings.

---

[22] James, "The Sentiment of Rationality," in *The Will to Believe and Other Essays in Popular Philosophy* (New York: Dover, 1956), 67–69.

[23] Lewis Carroll, *Alice's Adventures in Wonderland and Through the Looking Glass* (New York: Penguin, 1960), 28.

While M.2 drawings classify events with respect to their *relative* duration (longer or shorter), M.3 drawings show *how much* longer or shorter. The underlying beat in the M.3 drawings is represented by the larger circles—eight beats in all. The shorter (2:1) durations are represented by the two smaller circles inside the larger circles. As the child who made the M.3 drawing said of Events 3 and 4, "You can see there's two for one, there."

Indeed, the M.3 drawing comes very close to conventional notation. The notated rhythm, is ♩♩ ♩, equivalent to the child's ⊙⊙○. However, the child's invention has the advantage of consistently showing the beat, the regularly occurring ○, and the varied performed events in relation to it ⊙. M.3 children have invented what might be called the beginnings of a formal symbol system.

But notice that just as M.1 children lose the marking of the large figural boundary found in F.1 in their singular focus on counting, so M.2 and M.3 children, in their focus on measuring, obscure figural boundaries as well as the changing function of events in response to context. Thus metric graphics, like standard notation, leave the performer with the problem of "putting in the interpretation"—that is, finding the figures, the *phrasing* now hidden in the carefully denoted metric units.

Neither standard notation nor the children's inventions adequately captures the many faces of a fully apprehended or performed rhythm. For practicing musicians, it is these multiple views that create the generative tension and the complexity that continues to inform and influence a performer's developing "hearing" and its projection in sound and time.

Coming full circle, I argue that the children's spontaneous inventions provide evidence that the typology illustrates a *palette of useful and provocative sensory organizers*. In turn, rather than assuming that progress, as described by Piaget and others, means *giving up* characteristics associated with earlier stages of development, progress means appropriating the array of sensory organizers made visible by the children's inventions, using them as vehicles when, where, and in ways that the particular (often unique) situation demands.

PART III

Varieties of "Fastness"

I turn again to "now" and the exclusion of time in our analytic and notational discourse. The examples that follow again illustrate that if, in observing children, we can assume the stance of an anthropologist entering a new culture, we may encounter our own internalized assumptions.

We may, for instance, reveal and make explicit aspects of our own experience of time and music that previously remained tacit.

The linguist B. L. Whorf sets the stage for this discussion of time and "fastness" in his seminal study of the Hopi Indians. Whorf compares the meanings implicit in our ways of speaking of time with the meanings given to time implicit in the language of the Hopi. He says:

> Instead of our linguistically promoted objectification of that datum of consciousness we call "time," the Hopi language has not laid down any pattern that would cloak the subjective "becoming later" that is the essence of time.[24]

An eight-year-old child, as if echoing both Whorf and Hasty, put it this way in response to a question about the "sameness" of a repeated musical event. She said: "But it will never be the same because it's *later*."

Example III.1 Formal Fastness Distance/Time

It was through finding reason in the children's inventions that my attention was alerted to the following question: What are the means that composers use to generate the effect of "going faster" within the unfolding of a musical composition? Are these means in some ways related to the figural/metric or the property/function tensions?

The triggering situation was this: Working with a group of eight- to nine-year olds, I played a two-octave chromatic scale starting on middle C. After a brief pause, I played *at the same tempo*, a whole-tone scale, also over two octaves starting on middle C. I asked the children what the difference was. I was, of course, expecting them to say that the second one, the whole-tone scale, had bigger steps (or something to that effect). But to my surprise, the children all agreed that the second example was *"faster!"* I was puzzled; how could this be, since I had kept the beat, the *tempo*, the same for both the chromatic and the whole-tone scales?

Later in the day I played the same examples for a group of college music students and reported the children's view. The students responded simply that

---

[24] Benjamin Lee Whorf, *Language, Thought, and Reality*, ed. John B. Carroll (Cambridge, Mass.: MIT Press, 1956), 140.

the children were just wrong—the beat stayed the same. But taking the advice of the anthropologist, Geertz, I urged the group to let the children's view "vex" us: Let's assume that there is reason in the children's view and go in search of it.

Figure 10. Chromatic and whole-tone scales

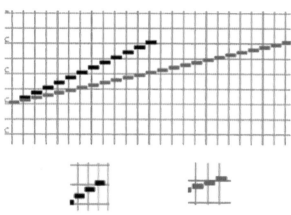

Whole tone   Chromatic

To help, I translated the scales as I had played them into static, graphic space. Looking at the graphics, the children's "hearing" suddenly made perfect sense; it was a simple instance of the classical definition of "faster": the whole-tone scale goes the same *distance* as the chromatic scale but in *half the time*!

Figure 11. They now come out together

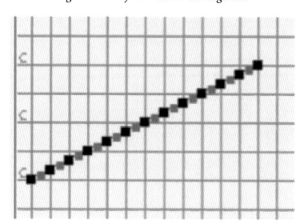

But what if I play the chromatic scale twice as fast as the whole-tone scale? They now come out together not only in pitch-space but in time.

What does twice as fast mean, here? It means that now there are two chromatic events for each whole-tone event—or that each chromatic event is "half way" between each whole-tone event in both space and time. Thus, the total time is now equivalent because the chromatic scale is both twice the number of events (frequency) as the whole-tone scale and also half the duration—"size" in space compensates for "size" in time.

With this in mind, I designed an activity to follow what was initially meant as an opportunity for children to explore relations among time, space, and motion. However, it turned into an exploration of how children would respond to confronting an emergent paradox. What follows is an analysis of a moment of learning that occurred in an environment that encouraged children to confront such complexities rather than eschew them.

Equidistant lines had been drawn on the floor in preparation for participating in an activity that we described to the children as follows:

> You are going to walk in pairs. One person is going to step along each of the lines drawn on the floor in time with a drumbeat. The other person will go along taking two steps for each drumbeat, two steps for each line, and also two steps for each of the other person's steps. *The two people have to come out together at the end of the lines.*

Sidney, one of the nine-year-old participants, chose to carry out his version of the experiment with Jeanne. Rose, another child, watched closely. Sidney made a variation on the original directions.

> SI: I skip a beat. You're here on my first beat. And then you take another one. And by the time you're here, I'll be here.
>
> J: So two beats are going to go by for each of yours. But we have to end up together.

Following Sidney's special instructions to Jeanne, the walk along the lines developed as follows: Sidney and Jeanne start together on the first line. Jeanne moves ahead, stepping on each line together with the drumbeat (chromatic scale). Sidney, waiting a moment, moves ahead by *skipping every other beat and then jumping ahead over every other line* (whole-tone scale).

Figure 12. ". . . by the time you're here, I'll be here."

So while Sidney was momentarily standing still on the first line, Jeanne, following the drumbeat, was moving ahead to the next line. Sidney then leaped ahead, skipping over the line Jeanne was now on, and landed together with her on the next line and on the same beat. Even though Jeanne was actually taking twice as many steps as Sidney, they ended up together at the same time on the last of the lines.

Figure 13. Ending up together

As they arrived, Jeanne posed questions that intentionally created a puzzle:

> J: So who was going faster?
> Rose: You.
> Sid: You.
> J: But we ended up together.
> Rose: But you were still going faster.
> J: What if... [brief pause]
> Sid: No, we were going the same *pace* ...
> Rose: She took more steps, though ...
> Sid: *... because when I was going faster she was going slower; and when she was going slower, I was going faster.*

In response to my question, "So who was going faster?" both Rose and Sidney agree that Jeanne was going faster. My next comment, "But we ended up together," intentionally presented them with a problem: How could I be going faster than Sidney if we both started together and arrived together at the end? Sid, after a moment's reflection, engages the problem and countering both himself and Rose says, "*No, we were going the same pace.*" But Rose continues to focus on more steps, "She [Jeanne] took more steps, though." Engaging the paradoxical problem, Sidney changes his view of our walk and offers an explanation for his new view. He explains: "Because when I was going faster she was going slower; and when she was going slower, I was going faster."

At the outset, Sidney's instructions had been local, discrete, and pointing to relevant *places:* "You're here ... and then you take another one... and by that time, I'll be here." But presented with the paradox, it was as if watching himself and our interactions from a distance. He sees our walk as continuous and interactive, a relational scheme of compensating movements. But despite my question, "Who was going *faster*?" Sidney uses the term "same *pace*"—a more continuous and more malleable expression.[25] And, on the way, Sidney has intuitively reconstructed a basic physics principle—*average velocity*. This is an explanation from experience in contrast to explanations in terms of discrete proportional measures of time and pitch-space.

Rose, continuing to focus on more steps (*She took more steps, though*) is

[25] It is probably relevant that Sidney was a serious hockey player. And as in all sports, "pace," with its connotation of flexible change, is probably the more useful term as compared with faster (for instance, "Change your pace as you approach the goal").

still describing "faster" as "frequency"—i.e., more steps per unit of time. Out of the paradox comes emergent distinction.

Example III.2 Frequency

With Rose's sense of faster (more events per unit time or frequency), I recognized a familiar meaning for musically "going faster." An example is seen in Figures 14a and 14b, excerpts from the beginning of Vivaldi's "Winter" movement of the *The Four Seasons*. While a clear and abrupt change in *frequency* occurs, the *tempo* (rate of the beat) stays the same. This *faster* is clearly seen in the notation. I have noticed, however, that beginning music students, in listening, often fail to distinguish frequency from a change in *tempo*—more events per unit (beat) is taken to be a faster *tempo*.

(A good example of faster in the conventional sense of tempo or an *increase in the rate of the beat*, is the Bartók *Sonata for Two Pianos and Percussion*, first movement, mm. 21–32. The passage is marked *poco a poco accelerando e sempre più agitato*.)

Figure 14. Vivaldi, "Winter," mm. 9–10, 12

Example III.3 Figurally Faster

Once I became alert to possible varieties of "getting faster," specifically figural types emerged. For example, Haydn gives a distinct feeling of getting faster as he moves into the B section of the Minuet, op. 76, no. 5. By truncating the little cadential figure heard repeatedly in the preceding A section, he creates a perception of "speeding up." That is, by shortening the figural grouping, Haydn effectively speeds up the repetition of groupings. In turn, accents occur more frequently, which also shifts the meter from triple to duple (Figure 15). However, Haydn continues to notate bar lines to show triple meter. I'll call the sense of speeding up by shortening of the motive, *figurally faster*.

Figure 15. Haydn, String Quartet op. 76, no. 5, Minuetto. Cadential figure with truncated figure; shift to duple meter.

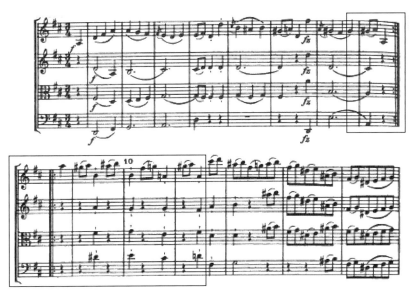

As the passage goes onward, building toward the return of the A section in m. 12, Haydn further shortens the cadential motive making the eighth-note motion continuous (mm. 14–15, Figure 16). The resulting "faster motion" comes to a rather sudden slow-down with the return of the A section and triple meter in mm. 16–17.

As Fig. 16 shows, *figurally faster*, together with an increase in frequency, serves Haydn as an effective compositional means helping to generate what we hear as the *structural functions* of the Minuet. The contrasting B section, beginning with the truncated cadential motive (mm. 9–11), followed by the continuing build-up of temporal intensity (mm. 12–13; mm. 14–15)—deposits us (as it were) neatly into the return of A at the upbeat to m. 17.

And, of course, many examples of *figurally faster* occur in the works of Bach, perhaps most noticeably in the compositions for solo cello and solo

Figure 16. Haydn, String Quartet, op. 76, no. 5, Minuetto

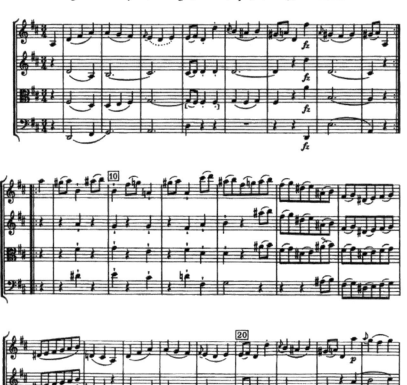

violin. Looking at the score, one often *sees* continuous 16th notes. But attending to the figural grouping, the constant 16th-note motion gives way to moments that project a sense of speeding up and slowing down within it. Figure 17 shows an example from the Gigue of the Bach Partita No. 2, for solo violin.

Notice that in mm. 11–13, the sequential figure is always two beats long. However, in measure 14, the sequential figure lasts only one beat, thus half the time of the preceding figures. This results in the figural rhythm becoming twice as fast—from a two-beat figural grouping to a one-beat figural grouping. Moreover, the *rate of passage* through the pitch-space is also quickened in measure 14: in measures 12 and 13, the sequential figures move stepwise through a pitch space of a perfect fourth in seven beats—**Bb** (E), **A** (D); **G** (C), **F**. While in the fourth measure the sequential figures skip through a greater pitch space—a minor seventh—in just four beats—**Bb** -**G-E-C.** And yet, this sense of *figurally faster* is hidden from view since the rate of surface events, the notated 16th notes, remains the same throughout.

Figure 17. J. S. Bach, Partita No. 2, Gigue. Figurally faster
and also a quicker passage through pitch space.

The example of quickening the rate of passage through pitch space recalls the children's hearing of the whole-tone scale as "faster" than the chromatic scale. And it was that surprising event that set off my hunt for examples where composers might have used similar means for uniquely-generating structural functions.

PART IV

Coda

In the musical examples discussed in Part III, I have tried to exploit further my re-thinking of the developmental typology. In particular, the examples of *figurally faster* are meant to provide further evidence for the children's figural inventions, as a legitimate type in a *palette of continuing useful and provocative sensory organizers.* But I also proposed that the typology predicts the potential emergence of an essential tension as we move back and forth between continuous but disappearing *action* and discrete, static *symbol.*

Noticing alternative modes of "getting faster" illustrates but a single instance of this generative tension between action and symbol. *Figural faster* is shaping time in an internal, structural way, unique to a particular situation and moment. For instance, in the Haydn and Bach excerpts, transformation of germinal motives generating *figural faster* served as a means towards creating a particular structural function. In the Haydn, the function was building up for the "let down" into the return. In the Bach, *figural faster* was a means for structurally moving onward after rhythmically slower melodic motion.

The tension implicit in the typology itself was seen starkly in the children's metric M.2 and M.3 inventions, in contrast to the figural F.2 inventions. On the one hand, the metric drawings show notational availability and certitude of invariant properties (as in the notes specified in a score). On the other hand, the figural inventions show the unique *situation* of properties as they occur, and in particular, the *function* of those properties as events within the figures of which they are members. I argue, then, that the typology reveals a musical tension experienced by performer and composer as they, too, learn to move creatively between the stable invariance of properties as represented in conventional notation, and the passing presence of figural functions created towards the goal of uniquely shaping time.

Finally, it was through adopting the stance of the anthropologist that the broader significance of the typology emerged: making the assumption that whatever performances were found in the children's culture, no matter how strange or surprising, they were making sense to the inhabitants of that culture. So the challenge became mutual and reciprocal. Confronting our own deeply internalized assumptions, our sensory organizers, we not only come to understand the sense-making of the other, but we liberate for reflection intuitions and know-how that we use and believe in, but rarely if ever make quite so explicit. In such moments, our worldly musical experience seems to be sharing the philosophical enigmas of Aristotle, James, and Wittgenstein. And Piaget comes back into favor when he proposes:

> Rhythm characterizes the functions that are at the junction between organic and mental life.[26]

---

[26] Jean Piaget, *The Psychology of Intelligence* (Totowa, N.J.: Littlefield, Adams & Co., 1960), 69.

Part IV

Finding Time: The Body and Parsing Rhythm and Meter

Meter, Entrainment, and Voice
in *The King's Speech*

EUGENE MONTAGUE

INTRODUCTION

WHAT, IF ANY, is the significance of musical meter beyond its potential for entrainment? Many recent studies of musical rhythm, especially those rooted in cognitive perspectives, characterize meter in terms of its potential to regulate and inspire synchronous movement. Such potential for movement is considered to be grounded in the quasi-mechanical notion of entrainment, which thus becomes a defining concept for all types of meters and for much of what is rhythmic in music.[1] Such definitions are both plausible and useful, yet they

---

[1] For examples of such approaches to meter, see Roger T. Dean et al., "The Pulse of Symmetry: On the Possible Co-Evolution of Rhythm in Music and Dance," *Musicae Scientiae 13* (supplement 2) (2009), 341–67; W. Tecumseh Fitch, "Rhythmic Cognition in Humans and Animals: Distinguishing Meter and Pulse Perception," *Frontiers in Systems Neuroscience 7/68* (2013), 1–16; Marc Leman and Luiz Naveda, "Basic Gestures as Spatiotemporal Reference Frames for Repetitive Dance/Music Patterns in Samba and Charleston," *Music Perception: An Interdisciplinary Journal 28/1* (2010), 71–91; Rosalee K. Meyer and Caroline Palmer, "Temporal and Motor Transfer in Music Performance," *Music Perception: An Interdisciplinary Journal 21/1* (2003), 81–104; Luiz Naveda and Marc Leman, "A Cross-modal Heuristic for Periodic Pattern Analysis of Samba Music and Dance," *Journal of New Music Research 38/3* (2009), 255–83; Jessica Phillips-Silver, "On the Meaning of Movement in Music, Development and the Brain," *Contemporary Music Review 28/3* (2009), 293–314; Petri Toiviainen et al., "Embodied Meter: Hierarchical Eigenmodes in Music-Induced Movement," *Music Perception 28/1* (2010), 59–70.

also inevitably circumscribe metrical experience. If the whole import of meter resides in entrainment, then there is a clear division between what entrains and what does or can not, and meter, like entrainment, becomes necessarily a binary phenomenon, wholly defined by the separation between the synchronous and asynchronous. This conclusion leaves no room for situations in which meter has relevance for sounds that are not entrained. In this essay, I examine such a situation through a discussion of the role of music and meter in the film *The King's Speech*.[2] This film, particularly in the context of the King's final address, presents a case study for the influence of musical meter beyond entrainment, as the music that accompanies this speech exerts an important influence on its success, even while the King's words are not entrained to the musical meter. I develop this study through an analysis of the ways in which the film creates this musical influence, and, as a consequence of this analysis, suggest that the concept of entrainment does not exhaust the function of musical meter. While the majority of this chapter eschews theoretical speculation in favor of careful analysis of *The King's Speech* and its music, the implication of my argument is that meter does not function solely through the precise operation of entrainment but also creates a future of temporal opportunity for expression and action, whether entrained or not. Thus, it is through the creation of such a context that the music accompanying the King's speech supports the fluency of his spoken words: a support that operates through the regularity of meter but without the particular synchronicity that characterizes entrainment. These theoretical implications, I believe, fit well with the general theory of projection and the creative function of meter developed in Christopher Hasty's work.[3]

MUSIC IN *THE KING'S SPEECH*: CONTINUITY AND FLOW

The film *The King's Speech* is an elaborately produced semi-fictional period piece set in 1930s Britain. It chronicles the relationship between Prince Albert, Duke of York and later King George VI, and Lionel Logue, an Australian speech therapist without formal qualifications or training who treats the future king's debilitating speech disorder. Eventually, through the unorthodox techniques

[2] The King's Speech, DVD, directed by Tom Hooper (2010; Beverly Hills, Calif.: Weinstein Company Home Entertainment, 2011).

[3] Christopher F. Hasty, *Meter as Rhythm* (Oxford: Oxford University Press, 1997); "If Music is Ongoing Experience, What Might Music Theory Be? A Suggestion From the Drastic," *Zeitschrift der Gesellschaft für Musiktheorie* Sonderausgabe (2010), 197–216, http://www.gmth.de/zeitschrift/artikel/546.aspx.

and friendship offered by "Lionel," "Bertie" is able to overcome most of his disability and, at the crux of the film's plot, deliver a vital speech to his subjects on the cusp of the Second World War.[4]

The themes of the film include the significance of words, the difficulty of expressing them, the importance of "finding one's voice," to quote a phrase that is prominent in the advertising for the film, and the consequent differences between public and private speaking. In exploring these themes, music plays an important part in several ways, despite, or indeed because, of the somewhat restricted use of music in the film. No music is more important in this than the excerpt from the second movement of Ludwig van Beethoven's Symphony no. 7, op. 92, which is heard as the King makes the speech that functions as the culmination of the drama. In this scene, the music seems to share the burden of narrative, assuming a dominant position in the soundscape. Through this dominance, music plays an important role in ensuring the success of the speech, allowing the King to overcome his stutter and discover his own voice. With this achievement, music develops and to an extent resolves several of the main themes of the film, in particular those concerning the problems of speech.

Compared to many contemporary movies in which music plays an almost constant part in the film, *The King's Speech* employs music in a rather restricted fashion. Many of the film's scenes employ dialog against a silent background, and where music is used as underscoring, it is often quite understated; functioning as a background part of the film's sound. Suitably, Alexandre Desplat's score for the film is rather spare in tone, often using only piano and strings, and developing small repetitive motives to fashion a music that conveys a quietly fluid temporal passage, while only rarely communicating any dramatic intensity. Apart from Desplat's score, there are four places where music from the Western classical canon is given prominence, all of these using excerpts from large-scale orchestral pieces from the First Viennese school.[5] These mostly appear as non-diegetic, though one is at least partly diegetic, as I discuss below. The fully diegetic music of *The King's Speech* is limited to two

---

[4] When the then-Duke of York comes to him for treatment, Logue insists on being called "Lionel" and on calling his patient "Bertie" in the therapeutic context. These names resonate throughout the film, and come to characterize the relationship between the two men. I will, therefore, often use these names as referents throughout this essay, particularly when the situation under discussion implies a therapist-patient relationship.

[5] There is a fifth brief diegetic occurrence of related music when a news reel of a speech by Hitler ends with a band performing "Deutschland über Alles." This, however, does not have either the length or the weight of the other extended musical quotations.

jazz numbers from the 1930s. Both of these are visually sourced to recordings, with the medium of playback, a record player, clearly displayed on screen. Therefore, the only live performance of music takes place when the King and Logue explore singing as a therapeutic technique, leading to brief excerpts from popular tunes being sung by both men. This singing has particular significance in developing the notion of music as an aid to fluency of speech, a vital trope of the narrative and one that is emphasized each time that music takes a prominent role in the film.

The general absence of background underscoring in *The King's Speech* reflects the importance of speech as the central concern of the film, and in particular the importance of verbal fluency. The sparse use of music, so often a continuous sonic presence in film, tends to emphasize continuity in speech, highlighting any hesitations or repetitions, such as those produced by Prince Albert. Of course, the act of speaking may in one sense be understood as the act of producing words without music, in contrast to singing. Such an opposition is useful in considering the problems of fluency: if music so often provides and supports continuity, then in the absence of music it is up to the spoken word to provide the experience of flow, smoothly connecting each moment of speech. For Prince Albert, however, such flow is out of reach. His speech, temporally pockmarked by a disabling stutter, can only aspire to emulate the continuous metrical flow of music.

The connection between continuity in music and speech is demonstrated at the very start of the film, where we encounter Prince Albert waiting to make a public speech, to be broadcast over the radio, at the close of the British Empire Exhibition at Wembley Stadium. The Prince, brother to David, Prince of Wales, and thus second in line to the throne, is clearly becoming increasingly nervous and gloomy as the time for the speech approaches. By contrast, we witness a professional BBC announcer making practiced and confident preparations through gargling, reciting tongue twisters and establishing an exact distance from the microphone. Throughout these preparations, nondiegetic music plays: a gently repetitive piano piece from Desplat's score, music that seems to mark time without drawing attention to itself. As the announcer begins his broadcast, however, this music rather suddenly vanishes, and his dulcet, measured tones dominate the suddenly vacated aural space. Here, it is clear, is someone who can speak, who has found his voice, and for whom music can and perhaps must vanish as spoken fluency replaces musical meter. The contrast with Prince Albert's situation is made painfully obvious as the announcer completes his introduction and the reluctant duke approaches the microphone. Music returns gradually as he ascends the stairs to the podium in the outdoor arena, but now the music is hesitant and uncertain. As he climbs, a single high-pitched string sound develops into repeated chords, but the piano intervenes, destroying any hint of meter or sense of forward motion. A static, lamenting music in strings and piano continues to underscore the Prince's abject failures as he attempts to deliver his speech; this music marks him as someone who has not achieved fluency, and therefore cannot control either speech or music.

Introduced in this way, both music and speech are related through their connections to temporal continuity. The Duke's failure to become fluent is comparable to a music that has no temporal flow, i.e. one without rhythm or meter. Indeed, Desplat's underscore to the failed speech shares an absence of flow with the Duke's words. This is music that does not interrupt the speaker—it is not loud or disruptive—but continues because his attempts at speech are so weak. What seems out of reach at this stage is any consistent flow in the Duke's speech, such as that displayed by the announcer. Thus, at the start, the continuity and metric flow that music may achieve are set up as something to be admired and emulated in the activity of speaking. For Prince Albert, such emulation will not occur until his final speech at the end of the film.

MUSIC AND CAMERA IN ENTRAINMENT

In the speech that lends the film its title, Albert, now King, succeeds in delivering a crucial live radio speech to his subjects on the topic of the newly declared war with Germany. As with his failed speech at Wembley, this speech is also accompanied by music, but this is now not an underscoring but an aural presence that takes over the scene, even appearing to organize the succession of visual images on the screen. In this, the penultimate scene of the film, musical continuity becomes both a practical experience of, and a metaphor for, temporal flow. Thus, the excerpt from Beethoven's symphony creates the temporal context for the successful delivery of the King's words: an experience of (metrical) continuity through which the spoken words can emerge. Beethoven's music, therefore, is both a model and a catalyst for the king to discover fluency of speech.

As mentioned above, the music played in this scene is the first large section of the second movement from Beethoven's Symphony no. 7, op. 92. What is played represents a slightly altered version of the published score: the opening chord is sounded twice, in a manner that imitates a stutter, and the second large phrase group, from mm. 27–50, is also repeated, probably for reasons of timing. This music, through its rhythmic structure, becomes an essential element of the viewer's experience.[6] The effect of the orchestral movement is motivated by the long-term themes of the film, as suggested above, as well as the immediate visual context for the delivery of the speech. This context is defined by an unusual synchronization between the alternation of camera changes and the musical meter. To set the scene: after some last-minute preparation and rehearsal, the time for the speech arrives with the King and Lionel Logue together inside a specially decorated back room of Buckingham Palace. Besides the desultory conversation of the two men, of which more later, there is silence. However, as the radio technician's countdown ends and the microphone goes live, music is heard: an orchestral chord. This chord, which we later understand as the opening of the symphonic movement, initially seems to provoke no response, but then it is repeated, and the music, familiar in genre if not title to many viewers, continues on, forming a steady meter of two-measure units. These units provide the temporal basis for the rhythmic succession of images on the screen. This succession goes from the audience waiting immediately outside the room to Logue's face, and then to the face of the King, and back to Logue, each image changing in synchrony with the musical meter.

Figure 1 shows how the changes in camera shots entrain to the two-measure phrases of the music over the course of the first eight measures. Through the development of this entrainment, a dynamic relationship develops between the three visible elements of this scene. This relationship is enhanced by the double duration of the third shot in the sequence, which focuses on the King for four measures. The length of this shot increases the sense of anticipation—he does not begin to speak until the fifth measure—and also gives the image of the King a quality of temporal resolution in the context of the rhythm of shots.

While the sense of entrainment between camera and music is unmistakable, the effect of this interplay is not quite mechanical, as indicated by the small discrepancies in the figure between measure lines and lines indicating a shot change. At the start of the relationship, the camera seems to anticipate the metrical change just slightly, but by m. 19 the musical meter has caught up. This imprecision gives an impression of a lifelike playing with meter, rather than a

---

[6] The impact of the symphony is mentioned by many commentators in online discussions about the film, as well as in several more formal reviews by journalists. See, for example, David Stabler, "Beethoven's Music in 'The King's Speech': a Magical Match," *OregonLive. com*, last modified February 7, 2011; Joe Morgenstern, "The King's Speech: Wit, Warmth, and Majesty," *The Wall Street Journal*, November 6, 2010, (http://www.wsj.com/articles/SB10001 424052748703572404575634483293371478.

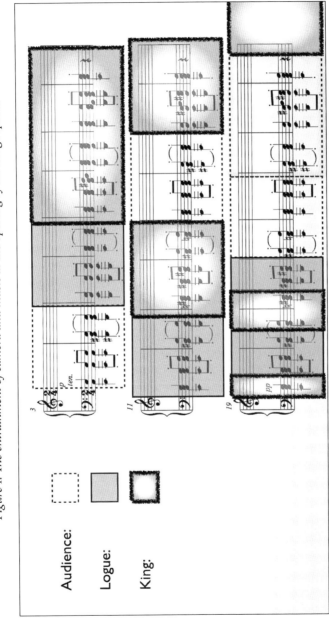

Figure 1. The entrainment of camera and music at the opening of the King's speech

Audience:

Logue:

King:

metronomic mickey-mousing between image and sound, but does not weaken the overall quality of entrainment between music and camera.

The relationships between meter and camera rhythm demonstrate a systematic interaction between the musical meter and its environment. This type of interaction is characteristic of the regulative relationship between entrained systems. Entrainment is sometimes conceptualized in a general way as the product of human action, involving coordinated movement to a shared sense of periodic rhythm. Thus, the ways in which music can provide such a periodic rhythm serves as grounds for Justin London's psychologically based understanding of meter.[7] Moreover, writing from a general cognitive stance, Silver et al. have used the notion of coordination of movement to argue for a wide, interdisciplinary function for entrainment.[8] While this cognitive understanding of entrainment has been useful, it is also worthwhile to remember that the notion of entrainment fundamentally involves systems rather than necessarily being connected to human action. Thus, in ethnomusicologist Martin Clayton's recent definition, entrainment "refers to the process by which independent rhythmical systems interact with each other. . . . In order for interaction to take place some form of coupling must exist between the rhythmical systems, and this too can take many forms. This process of interaction may result in those systems synchronizing, in the most common sense of aligning in both phase and period, but in fact entrainment can lead to a wide variety of behaviors."[9] Clayton's usefully broad definition opens up many rhythmic phenomena to the concept of entrainment, including the audience's perception of the relationship between camera shot and musical meter in this scene.

This entrainment is not merely a structural conceit but consists in a setting of the rhythmic scene for the success of the speech. This argument rests, of course, on a metaphorical understanding of the film and the logic of the plot. That is, I am not arguing for a physical connection between the succession of images and the speech, but rather that the entrainment between music and camera provides a fundamental condition for our belief in the success of

---

[7] Justin London, *Hearing in Time: Psychological Aspects of Musical Meter* (Oxford: Oxford University Press, 2004); Justin London, "Rhythm," *Grove Music Online, Oxford Music Online*, http://www.oxfordmusiconline.com/subscriber/article/grove/music/45963, accessed April 9, 2015.

[8] Jessica Phillips-Silver et al., "The Ecology of Entrainment: Foundations of Coordinated Rhythmic Movement," *Music Perception* 28/1 (2010), 3–14.

[9] Martin Clayton, "What is Entrainment? Definition and Applications in Musical Research," *Empirical Musicology Review* 7/1–2 (2012), 49–56.

the speech. For this entrainment, founded on the local relationships between camera and meter, also functions as an element in the long-term relationships between music and speech, played out over the course of the film.

The notion that musical meter may support speech was already suggested in the analysis of Prince Albert's first speech above. The central difference between the situation of the first speech and that of the last is, of course, the presence of Logue. It is Logue who, more than any other character, demonstrates and utilizes the flow of music throughout the film, and it is Logue who finally provides the music that allows the King's speech to flow. To understand how this happens, and its import in the context of the film, I will return to examine earlier uses of music in the film and how Logue, in particular, manipulates music for his therapeutic purposes.

MUSIC IN LOGUE'S THERAPIES

As already argued, the opening scene of the film demonstrates the relationship between continuity in speech and music. This is a relationship in which flow in one can be replaced by the other, as when the radio announcer's voice cuts off Desplat's music, or in which absence of continuity can be manifest in both together, as in the failure of Albert's speech. The first time we witness hints of continuity in both speech and music together involves the presence of Logue and the sound of an orchestra playing canonical Western art music, a combination that will, of course, recur at the climax of the film. In the first case, however, there is no long and fluent speech; instead, we see a long montage of short clips comprising of shots of "Bertie" and "Lionel," sometimes with the Duchess, practicing physical and vocal exercises of very varied types, all interspersed with the Duke seeming to complete, albeit with considerable hesitations, a public speech at the opening of a factory. The Duke's actions during this montage do not actually demonstrate spoken fluency of more than a second or so, but they do represent such fluency, within the context of these specific exercises. There is no question, however, of the musical fluency on show: the whole sequence is bound together by the regular metrical flow of the orchestral opening section of the first movement of Mozart's Clarinet Concerto K. 622. Musical continuity is, again, both a metaphor for verbal fluency and, equally important, an actual sonic presence that ensures and regulates forward motion through the scene.

It should be said that such use of music to create a sense of continuity in film is by no means novel or particular to *The King's Speech*. Music has been an important element in the creation of cinematic continuity since the earliest days of film, as several studies attest.[10] What is special about this use of musical continuity, however, is its close association with verbal fluency in a film that deals with the problems of continuous speech. Moreover, in both symbolizing and creating fluency, the music of the *The King's Speech* grounds the idea of continuity in metrical flow, driven by both Desplat's score and the selection of pre-composed music. Thus, the concept of musical fluency developed in the course of the film is a specific one, a concept that serves to supplement and call forth fluency in speech through a regularity in meter.

If music may function as continuity to elicit fluency in speech, such continuity contains within itself a certain amount of diversion or even deception. This is the case, in particular, when musical flow acts as a cover for verbal expression, obscuring a lack of regular motion. A certain amount of this deception is present in the montage to the Clarinet Concerto, discussed above, given that the flow of the music is not truly matched by speech. An earlier scene, however, provides a stronger example of music's potential to deceive. At Lionel's first meeting with Bertie he finds the Duke prickly, reluctant to speak or engage in any way. As a ruse, the therapist takes out a copy of the famous soliloquy from William Shakespeare's *Hamlet*, and makes a bet with Bertie that he can read it aloud. After Bertie grudgingly accepts the bet, Lionel places headphones over his patient's ears, headphones that are playing the overture from Mozart's *Marriage of Figaro* from a recording, while at the same time using a second turntable to record Bertie's voice reading the soliloquy. As Bertie's ears fill with music, music heard also by the film's audience, he cannot hear his own voice and as a consequence his speech becomes free and fluent, under the cover of Mozart's music. The same music also functions as a cover for the audience, for the soundscape is switched from Logue's room to the location between Bertie's ears where the music sounds. The overture, therefore, functions not only as catalyst for the spoken word but at the same time as a cover for it, even to the point of casting doubt on whether any speech is in fact sounding. It is not until much later, after the Duke has left Logue's office with a determination not to return, that the prince decides to listen to the recording of his voice given to him by Logue. On finding that his speech sounds continuous and rhythmical, both he and the audience realize the power of music to support and sustain speech, and in addition become aware of its

[10] See, for example, James Buhler, "Wagnerian Motives: Narrative Integration and the Development of Silent Film Accompaniment, 1908–1913," in *Wagner & Cinema*, ed. Jeongwon Joe and Sander L. Gilman (Bloomington: Indiana University Press, 2010), 27–45; Rebecca Leydon, "Debussy's Late Style and the Devices of the Early Silent Cinema," *Music Theory Spectrum* 23/2 (2001), 217–41.

deceptive qualities: its capacity to distract and divert both the semantics and the prosody of language.

This trope of music as deception is developed further through Logue's therapeutic techniques involving singing. Early in their first meeting, Lionel asks whether Bertie stutters when he sings—he does not—and later we see him using singing and chanting as part of his exercises. The significance such singing can have is revealed when Bertie pays an unexpected visit to Lionel following the death of his father, King George V. Logue attempts to draw the Duke out on the problems of his childhood, which the therapist believes lie at the heart of his disability. To voice these unpleasant memories, Lionel challenges Bertie to sing what he wants to say, using the popular melodies of "Swanee River" and the "Campdown Races." Bertie complains initially, but then follows instructions, singing the details of his abuse at the hands of a family nanny. Music, simultaneously, is revealed not just as the provider of temporal flow but also as balm for the expression of difficult truths. Again, then, music acts as a kind of veil or shield, somewhat like the headphones, which obscures the meanings of words.

Logue's use of music, then, includes its operation as a means to provide temporal flow, and also as a way to obscure semantic content. Both of these functions promote fluency, one by creating an experience of flow, the other by obscuring the expression of unpleasant topics. These related qualities come together through the operation of musical meter in the climactic scene of the King's speech on the outbreak of war. And in this scene, it is Logue once more who introduces the music that accompanies and facilitates the speech, allowing the new King to find his own voice.

LOGUE AS MUSIC-MAKER

Logue brings music to the King in his hour of need in two distinct ways: by demonstrating the actual production of musical meter through his own speech, and also by assuming the role of a conductor for the musical context and support for his speech.

First, prior to the beginning the speech, Lionel and Bertie stand together in the small dark room, in the presence of the microphone. The tension is obvious, and both men engage in small talk, attempting to relax. As the moment of going on the air approaches, Lionel addresses words of advice to Bertie, words that thicken the association between spoken word and musical meter by establishing their own metrical qualities. Thus, Logue moves even closer toward the musical, providing an intimation of the forthcoming metrical qualities of Beethoven's music and establishing a connection between the content of his words and his manner of delivery: "Forget everything, and just say it to me. Say it to me as a friend." These two sentences, already evocative of some musicality through the extended anadiplosic connection between them, are strongly suggestive of a particular metrical organization, shown in Figure 2.

Figure 2. A metric interpretation of Logue's words to the King before the speech

For-get e-ve-ry-thing   and just   say it to me.   Say it to me___ as a friend.

Logue's prosody creates an immediate metric rhyme between "everything" and "say it to me," and the first syllables of each word initiate metric projections, as shown in Figure 2. The repetition of "say it to me," set to a similar rhythmic motive, comes a beat too early, interrupting the suggestion of a quadruple meter, by implying that a triple meter already began, as shown in the analysis. This creation of musical flow in words sets the stage for the King's successful speech through both semantics and rhythm; in this context the change from quadruple to triple meter suggests a heightening of anticipation for the speech itself. Moreover, in establishing the possibility of creating flow through his words, Lionel sets up an intimate space between himself and Bertie, a space where music may cover what the speaker finds uncomfortable, including, of course, the subject of the forthcoming war.

The second way in which Logue brings music to the King's speech is through a rather theatrical gesture, which functions both as an invitation to speak and as an apparent summoning of musical sound. Through this gesture, Logue creates an alliance between image and sound, an alliance which bears immediate fruit in the entrainment between camera and meter discussed above. The gesture itself comes in perfect synchrony with the slow, sustained sound of the first of the repeated chords that sound at the opening of the orchestral excerpt. It consists of a slow raising of both arms in an upward and outward semi-circular motion, from a vertical, hanging position in front of the torso to a lifted and extended ending, as shown in Figure 3.

Coinciding as it does with the start of this music, it is easy to see this movement as a conductor's gesture to bring together a group of players. Such a gesture comes before any measurement of meter: it is an call to attention, an invitation to alert all to the prospect of playing together, to the potential for action inherent in entrainment. In this instant, it turns the therapist into a conductor, transmitting the conditions for speech through his gestures just as surely as through his therapies.

Figure 3. Logue's "conductor's" gesture as the music
starts just before the King begins to speak

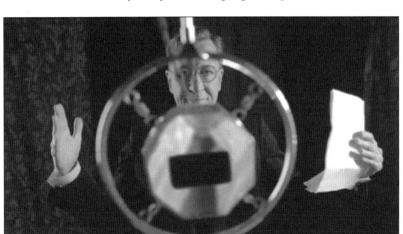

As a movement, Logue's gesture perfectly matches the opening chord of this music: an A-minor triad in second inversion, in harmonic terms isolated and incomplete so that it is "barely grammatical," according to semiotician David Lidov.[11] As such, the syntactical oddness of the chord demands some sort of response, just as does Logue's gesture, and the odd grammatical status of the chord makes the substance of the response unclear. Thus, neither gesture nor chord demand a particular answer, both may be answered by a range of possible responses. They invite the auditor and viewer to engage with the music, inspiring an encounter with meter. This is an invitation that the King will, indeed must, accept.

In the film music, as noted above, this chord is repeated, apparently due to Bertie's lack of immediate response. This echo repeats Logue's summons but, as the camera shows us, the invitation now comes from outside the room:

[11] David Lidov, "The Allegretto of Beethoven's Seventh," *The American Journal of Semiotics* 1/1–2 (1981), 163.

from the waiting, listening audience of the royal family, the political elite, and a radio engineer. This audience evokes a reponse from the stately and determined strings, and thus becomes the first image of the visual series that entrains with the meter of the music (see Figure 1). It is this meter that, with slow inevitability, becomes the temporal context in which the King achieves his speech.

The King's response to Logue's invitation is made in halting terms at first but gradually gathers continuity through the course of the scene. As it does so, it persuades the viewer of the music's power to support and sustain the King's fluency of speech. Lionel's gesture is, in the end, not just to Bertie, but includes the totality of the film's audience as he invites us to believe with him that the speech will continue, and that this music both represents and creates the conditions for its success.

THE INDEPENDENCE OF SPEECH, MUSIC, AND IMAGE

As the King, and his voice, grow into the challenge of the speech, Logue with-draws from his role as coach and conductor. After first encouraging Bertie, miming his words and gesturing to aid his fluency, Lionel gradually becomes silent, content to watch and admire the speaker. This gradual withdrawal of Logue, the summoner of music, from involvement in the speech marks both the King's growing confidence and the separation of the music from its entrainment with the camera. At the start of the speech, the synchronization of music with image tends to relegate the King's words to a background from which they emerge only gradually.[12] As the speech takes on fluency, however, the entrainment dissolves, and music establishes an independent voice against those of images and words, respectively. This counterpoint, to use the cin-ematic sense of the word advanced by Sergei Eisenstein, develops through the growing prominence of the King's speech as words, a prominence that allows his voice to establish its own temporal continuity in counterpoint with the flow of images and the metrical progress of sound.[13] As the rhythm of the camera

---

[12] As Neumeyer and Buhler argue convincingly, the redundancy of synchronous sound materially transforms the image, creating a much starker divide between those elements in the image that are associated with a synchronized sound (foreground) and everything else (background). In this case, the divide separates the spoken word from the entrained music and image. James Buhler and David Neumeyer, "Music and the Ontology of the Sound Film: The Classical Hollywood System," *The Oxford Handbook of Film Music Studies*, ed. David Neumeyer (Oxford: Oxford University Press, 2014), 17–43.

[13] For Eisenstein's concept of counterpoint, see Julie Bess Hubbert, "Eisenstein's Theory of Film Music Revisited: Silent and Early Sound Antecedents," in *Composing for the Screen in*

moves away from the meter of the music, sound, image, and words all take part in a dynamic of growth. As part of this growth, there is an increase in the number and variety of scenes included in the montage of the King's audience, as the camera wanders more broadly to scenes outside the palace and beyond. This growing expansiveness is echoed in the shifting sound quality of the King's voice, as his words, heard as coming through a wireless transmission, match how they might have sounded in each visual location. A similar sense of growth is also clear in the dynamic rise of the music, as a slow crescendo shapes the excerpt as a result of the gradual increase in instrumentation specified in Beethoven's score. This crescendo participates in the general metaphor of growth and a widening range; a metaphor that suits the trope of "finding a voice." The details of the interaction between music, image, and words are contrapuntal, as each strand of music, image, and words develops its own forward motion.

Within this counterpoint, the independence of the King's voice emerges as a vital quality of the speech, one that is produced through the lack of entrainment between voice and music. Indeed, an entrainment with music is not available for the King in both practical and metaphorical terms. In earlier scenes, we witnessed the power of singing—the personal expression of words synchronized with the rhythm of music—to liberate Bertie from his stutter. Indeed, just before making his speech, the King, at Logue's direction, seeks to to gain movement while he speaks by singing the words of his speech to the tune of the waltz from Tchaikovsky's *Sleeping Beauty*. But this attempt breaks down: singing, the absorption of speech by musical continuity, is not what a king wants or needs for a public address. Such singing is private, intimate language, a means of sharing secrets, but not what the task of public speaking requires. Musical meter can, therefore, have no direct relationship with the King's words: it remains separate as a counterpoint to the speech.

METER, SINGING, AND PUBLIC SPEECH

In addition to its role as counterpoint, the music accompanying the speech can be heard as an echo of a personal sentiment that remains mostly unexpressed in the formality of this spoken language. The quality of the orchestral movement as a public demonstration of grief, a jeremiad, was well established through much prominent public commentary and criticism in the nineteenth century, thus the use of this music suggests an emotional counterpoint, perhaps a hint

Germany and the USSR, ed. Robynn Stilwell and Phil Powrie (Bloomington: Indiana University Press, 2008) 125–47

at the King's private feelings concerning the upcoming war.[14] Such sentiments, however, must be kept apart from his public voice, and it is this latter voice which requires the temporal surety of meter to speak.

The sense of a certain future, a future that permits and encourages action, is central to the relationship between music and speech throughout the film. Logue, by channelling music's potential to provide such a future, is therefore instrumental in providing the temporal foundation for the success of the speech. In this success, however, it is the absence of entrainment that is key to its delivery. As viewers, we see the introduction of meter through Logue's voice and gesture, and hear how this music invites the King to speak. In making this metaphorical jump, we as viewers see meter as producing the King's fluency: it is by following the forward arch of meter that he gains the requisite flow to speak. To follow this meter into the future is to hear it as providing a temporal opportunity for action. The knowledge that the opportunity is there is itself enough without the necessity for entrainment. The King does not entrain his gestures or voice to the meter, but borrows from it a general sense of a future opportunity for action. It is in this sense that meter operates in this film and, more broadly, that meter may have function and relevance beyond the mechanism of entrainment.

This distinction between entrainment and a general sense of future may be taken even further to emphasize the function of entrainment would be to miss the general sense of a directed future that is vital to the metrical effect of the music in this film. Thus, the dissolution of the entrainment between camera and sound is a part of the overall success of the speech. In the end, the King has succeeded in treating the music as an independent factor, not one that drives his words or the succession of images. Thus, he has proved his capacity to act in an individual way. The meter of the music has had a vital effect on his speech *because* of the lack of entrainment between word and sound.

METER BEYOND ENTRAINMENT

This analysis of the role of the music in *The King's Speech* suggests that meter may affect actions, words, and other sounds through a context of projection that is outside the concept of entrainment, although perhaps related to it. In this case, the power of meter operates as a general force for action without

---

[14] For a survey of critical interpretations of this orchestral movement through the nineteenth century see Lidov, "The Allegretto of Beethoven's Seventh."

the necessity of an entraining relationship, and so there is metrical function beyond the limits of entrainment, beyond the regulation of oscillating
relationships.

It is clear that such a function operates on a symbolic plane, operating as
the sort of constructive one-among-many media element identified in Nicholas Cook's insightful typology.[15] And so, it might be argued, I have invented
the importance of the music for the speech rather than reporting on empirically observable connections between music and words. But when, as audience
members, we understand music as a generative force, we accept the invitation
of conductors such as Logue to interpret music as a field for action and creativity. And this acceptance includes an understanding of the power of music and
its meter to generate and affect other elements of sound. Such power is not limited to entrainment, if this is understood as a fixed oscillation through empty
duration. For the lived experience of metric projection creates the potential
to move as a general future possibility, not merely as and with an oscillation
that repeats a regular duration. Thus, to conclude, the role played by meter
in situations such as those in *The King's Speech* suggests a wider and more
potent notion of what meter is than that conveyed in most theories of entrainment. Such a notion will include reference to the power of meter to attract and
inspire movement beyond repetitive regulation, and this in turn will permit a
deeper engagement with the particular temporal qualities of musical events.

[15] Nicholas Cook, *Analysing Musical Multimedia* (Oxford: Oxford University Press, 1998).

Doing the Time Warp in Seventeenth-Century Music

SUSAN MCCLARY

TOWARD THE END of his pioneering book, *Meter as Rhythm*, Christopher Hasty includes analyses of a couple of early seventeenth-century pieces.[1] Like many composers of that era, the artists Hasty discusses—Claudio Monteverdi and Heinrich Schütz—often indulged in wildly contorted temporalities, with pieces that careen between simulations of rational speech, paralyzed stasis, free-falling spirals, and extravagant teleological trajectories. Although these composers had available to them the combination of devices later consolidated as "tonality," they clearly preferred to exploit such rapidly changing qualities of motion.

This essay considers the predilection of seventeenth-century composers for what I will call "the time warp." Our desire to see the incremental development of tonal harmonic grammar has sometimes led us to push many such pieces to the side as unfortunate throwbacks or else to minimize their strangeness. Yet for a good fifty years after the hierarchical arrangement of harmonic tonality had become viable, many composers chose to approach the shaping of time in ways that differed fundamentally from the strategies favored by later musicians. They did so in the service of cultural priorities—simulations of Divine Love, performances of mercurial and spellbinding virtuosity, expressions of

---

[1] Christopher F. Hasty, "Problems of Meter in Early-Seventeenth-Century Music," in *Meter as Rhythm* (Oxford: Oxford University Press, 1997), 237–81.

abnormal affective states such as erotic trance or madness—quite alien from those for which eighteenth-century tonality was designed.[2]

I learned how to deal with temporality in music in Harvard's Paine Hall, in which the conference dedicated to Christopher Hasty took place. In the spring of 1970 I took an analysis seminar with the late Earl Kim. It was, broadly speaking, the Sixties: in the wake of the Cambodia bombings and the Kent State shootings that year, students occupied President Pusey's office; riot policemen indiscriminately clubbed even relatively innocent bystanders such as composer John Adams and myself; the building next to Paine Hall was burned to the ground; and the university shut down—right around the time the undergraduate music history survey reached (appropriately enough) *The Rite of Spring*. For the most part, we musicology graduate students remained oblivious to all this chaos. But we were required to take an analysis seminar, and since Leon Kirchner was on leave that semester and Hasty had not yet arrived on the scene, we had no choice but to sign on with Kim.

Widely rumored to be eccentric, Kim lived up to his reputation by spending the first half of the semester having us recite passages from Samuel Beckett's television play, *Eh Joe* (1965). Like I said, it was the Sixties, and Beckett loomed large in the counterculture's pantheon as well as in Kim's own compositions. In class, bewildered musicology students would dutifully read from Beckett and then face interrogation concerning the reasons they had placed emphasis on a certain word, whether or not they regarded that moment as a downbeat, and how they would locate it within an implied hierarchy of upbeats and downbeats within the speech in question. Much grousing transpired in the halls afterwards, along with anecdotes about Kim's favorite question for General Examinations: "Why are early pieces of music short and later pieces long?" But I was entranced.

After weeks of Beckett, Kim turned to a piece of *real* music: Donna Anna's recitative leading up to "Or sai chi l'onore," the narrative in which she recounts to Don Ottavio the events of that fateful night when Don Giovanni invaded her bedroom and then murdered her father. All listeners wait with bated breath, along with Ottavio, to learn whether or not Giovanni succeeded in violating Anna. Following the pedagogical model he established with Beckett, Kim now had us spend whole sessions contemplating why Mozart had chosen to put a particular chord in first inversion. He would have us recite the

---

[2] See my *Desire and Pleasure in Seventeenth-Century Music* (Berkeley and Los Angeles: University of California Press, 2012).

relevant phrase imagining a range of other chords in that place, then flash his inscrutable Cheshire-Cat grin.

Again, I was entranced. The department's Director of Graduate Studies warned me that I was spending altogether too much time with composers (Harvard did not yet have professional theorists on the faculty) and that I needed to turn my attention back to the archives. But like the flower Carmen tossed to Don José, Kim's perceptions had already worked their spell. I have spent my career pursuing his techniques for parsing out temporalities in music, literature, film, and theater until today; I never returned to the archives. So before going further, I want to express my enormous debt and gratitude to Earl Kim.

But back to the seventeenth century, a period that vexes not only music historians but also those who study virtually any of its cultural practices, even—or particularly—the sciences. For if this period witnessed the appearance of many concepts we like to regard as progressive, contradictory impulses often manifested themselves in the same individual: think, for instance, of Isaac Newton's (to us) embarrassing pursuit of alchemy alongside his celebrated advances in physics and optics. The activities that flourished between the glory of the Renaissance and the brilliance of the Enlightenment qualify to some as a second Dark Age; indeed, eighteenth-century intellectuals branded this interregnum period "baroque," which was not meant as a compliment.[3]

Crucial to most of these enterprises is the phenomenon of change. Whereas many of our theories (musical and otherwise) rely on steady-state, quasi-universal principles, the seventeenth-century penchant for simulations of instability resists uniform methods. Owing in part to the radical upheavals in the political, religious, and intellectual domains of the time, artists and thinkers in all media found themselves drawn to concerns such as discontinuity, decay, and acceleration. It is no coincidence that the mathematics required to account for change—the calculus—was invented simultaneously by Newton and Leibniz, so urgent was the need for such a tool.

In his eccentric yet oddly influential book, *Noise*, Jacques Attali has argued that musicians often take the lead in registering social transformations, in part because sound is so much more malleable than the materials with which, say, architects work.[4] A composer can quickly fan through myriad possibilities offered by a new device: recall, for instance, the fecundity of Joseph Haydn in

---

[3] See the interdisciplinary collection *Structures of Feeling in Seventeenth-Century Cultural Expression*, ed. Susan McClary (Toronto: University of Toronto Press, 2013).

[4] Jacques Attali, *Noise: The Political Economy of Music*, trans. Brian Massumi (Minneapolis: University of Minnesota Press, 1985).

the 1780s or hip-hop in the 1980s and the speed with which their innovations became common practices in a wide variety of genres.

Similarly, musicians in the first half of the seventeenth century took the idea of temporal fluctuations and ran with it. They relied on a number of new techniques, especially monody and basso continuo, which relieved voices or solo instruments of their traditional task of articulating modal functions.[5] This is not to suggest that this music counts as "tonal," for in some ways its logic becomes even less clearly related to the procedures of eighteenth-century repertories. But the security of the newly developed bass line makes possible the acrobatics and radical shifts in qualities of motion that have long puzzled analysts even as they have delighted listeners.

Monteverdi first started publishing his experiments with basso continuo halfway through his Fifth Book of Madrigals (1605) in a setting of Giovanni Battista Guarini's rime "Ahi, com' a un vago sol." In highly mannered and convoluted verse, our baroque Amfortis here laments his long-standing and incurable affliction, even as he seeks to rip off the bandages and renew his anguish. Monteverdi's setting seems at first no less convoluted: he bisects lines and runs others together, extenuates some words and chatters through others.

Ahi, com' a un vago sol cortese giro	Ah, how at a single kind and lovely glance
de due belli occhi, ond'io	of two beautiful eyes—from which I
soffersi il primo, e dolce stral d'Amore,	suffered the first and sweet arrow of Love—
pien d'un nuovo desio,	full of a new desire,
sì pronto a sospirar, torna il mio core.	so ready to sigh, my heart turns back again.
Lasso, non val ascondersi, ch'omai	Alas, hiding is fruitless, for by now
conosco i segni, che'l mio cor m'addita	I know the signs that my heart shows me
de l'antica ferita,	of the old wound,
ed è gran tempo pur che la saldai.	which I thought I had long since cured.
Ah, che piaga d'Amor non sana mai!	Ah, a love wound never heals!

But he punctuates his piece with a homophonic refrain on the rime's final line, "Ah, che piaga d'Amor non sana mai!," thus imposing upon it an overarching architecture, similar to the Alleluia that punctuates Giovanni Gabrieli's *In ecclesiis*. Moreover, he gives his refrain the most powerful of modal progressions, the Romanesca, and it moves in typical sixteenth-century fashion, with

---

[5] For an explanation of modal practice, see my *Modal Subjectivities: Self-Fashioning in the Italian Madrigal* (Berkeley and Los Angeles: University of California Press, 2004).

each bass note supporting each pitch in the mode-bearing voice on a one-to-one basis, thus providing the stable temporality most familiar to Monteverdi's listeners. Only the occasional change in voice-leading or slight embellishment moves this part of the madrigal beyond the bare presentation of the formula itself (though I might mention the wonderful extenuation of the second scale degree on "non sana," made possible by the unexpected appearance of a C♮ that has to be corrected upward); see Example 1.

Example 1. "Ah, com' a un vago sol," Refrain

Romanesca

The refrain presents different performing forces from the principal subject, represented here jointly by two tenors. In its first two iterations, the refrain features two treble voices plus a bass; later the entire five-voice ensemble will join in the admonition. As the refrain enters over and over to wag its moralistic finger at our subject, it may recall the choral platitudes interjected throughout *Orfeo*, for, like the character Orfeo, our subject is enjoined to buck up and develop some discipline. But, as Saint Augustine would say, "Lord, not yet."[6] Otherwise we would miss out on all his delicious backsliding. Only toward the end do the tenors dutifully recite the refrain, thereby admitting the consequences of the failure to resist temptation.

---

[6] Augustine, *Confessions*, 8:7.

As he often does in his continuo madrigals, Monteverdi renders his subject with two equal voices, which affords him the clarity of diction and dramatic immediacy of monody while allowing for the intertwining of lines so crucial to the simulation of divided interiorities and erotic *frisson*. And with the support of his basso continuo, he is able to produce the jagged or ornamented melodies he wants to foreground—the kinds of melodic figures that would be unintelligible within a strictly modal logic.

A tonal musician may see the first few measures as tracing a circle of fifths and will feel relatively safe. But this is not a Vivaldian circle, and although the progression moves systematically by fifth, it should not be trusted (Example 2). Rather than heeding the bass alone, I would suggest understanding it as a second-hand response to a modal line moving slowly through the Dorian species of fifth: from A to G (sustained by G and C) to F, where it stalls, listing back and forth between G and F. This passive descent and its desultory wavering lulls us into a false sense of security, for, along with the subject, we are suddenly brought up short with the words "belli occhi." The generating line, which had stretched out in such a leisurely fashion, abruptly reverses course, dumping us unceremoniously on B♮ and a very hard hexachord (Example 3a).

Note that Dorian usually makes use of the flatted version of the sixth degree when operating within the diatonic diapente (Example 3b). For although the Dorian scale does indeed include B♮, that pitch occurs primarily when a piece is exploring other regions. Consequently, the B♮ here comes as a very rude shock. I am reminded of the moments in *Being John Malkovich* (1999) when individuals ejected from Malkovich's mind get plunked down beside the New Jersey Turnpike. Yet that chain of fifths is so compelling that Monteverdi simply returns to it, leading us down the garden path once again, only to spike us back to B♮ at "desio."

A third chain of fooling occurs, but this time the twice-tricked heart acknowledges its unwilling acquiescence on an extended cadential preparation to the long-delayed cadence on D. Notice that the composer has not yet really revealed his mode, for the slippage by fifth required that each sonority include the leading tone to the next, causing even the chords based on the final to include F♯ rather than the F♮ upon which this mode will ultimately depend. An interpreter who sticks with the concept of madrigalisms can easily explain the elaborate intertwining melismas preceding the cadence as painting the word "turn." I would not deny this, but I would also argue that the strategy up until this point has presented a condition of lazy complacency disrupted twice by that wound the subject has tried to forget. The flurry of ornamental

Example 2. Monteverdi, "Ah, com' a un vago sol," mm. 1–24

pitches before the cadence simulates a last-ditch effort at denial, delaying his surrender to the inevitable.

It is here that our stern, chordal refrain enters for the first time, not only with its no-nonsense, unexpanded statement of truth but also with the hitherto missing F♮ planted firmly in the bass. For the rest of the madrigal, the subject tries repeatedly to fabricate that carefree zone that drifts by fifth. Now, however, it is faced with a B♭ that will not allow it to reconstitute its previous condition. When it does manage to achieve a cadence away from reality, the refrain hauls it back, even replicating itself at the level of the fifth degree in order to block all exits. The soloists' attempts become truncated: thirteen measures, then two of only four measures each. The cautionary refrain takes over the piece, reducing the subject to a whisper. Indeed, the final iteration of the refrain even appropriates the *seconda prattica* harmonic violence that would seem to have belonged to the soloists, crushing the breath out of any last protests.

Example 3a. Reduction of "Ah, com' a un vago sol," mm. 1–6

Example 3b. Dorian diapente descent with usual sixth degree

What Monteverdi grasps in this and his other continuo madrigals is his new-found ability to work time as if with a zoom lens. He can still wield the one-to-one relationship between each pitch in the modal line, as in his refrain, but he can also allow the bass thus generated to maintain a single function while the melodic lines frolic luxuriously over it—most clearly in the five-measure extravaganza on "core." This temporal elasticity becomes, then, one of his principal techniques for expression.

I hasten to emphasize that this expressivity operates not only at the service of his texts but, more importantly, as a new and increasingly pervasive "structure of feeling"—a term I borrow from Raymond Williams, one of the founders of Cultural Studies. Williams sought through this concept to connect dimensions of human experience often regarded as unique or subjective with scholarly methods of formal analysis and archival research. In his words:

> For what we are defining is a particular quality of social experience and relationship, historically distinct from other particular qualities, which gives the sense of a generation or of a period. The relations between this quality and the other specifying historical marks of changing institutions, formations, and beliefs, and beyond these the changing social and economic relations between and within classes, are again an open question: that is to say, a set of specific historical questions. . . .
>
> We are talking about characteristic elements of impulse, restraint, and tone; specifically affective elements of consciousness and relationships: not feeling against thought, but thought as felt and feeling as thought: practical consciousness of a present kind, in a living and interrelating continuity.[7]

I would argue that Monteverdi chooses texts like "Ahi, com' a un vago sol," precisely because they allow him opportunities for time warping. In the first years of the Seicento, the certainties of the late Renaissance became attenuated to the point of no return. And even if they continued to serve as points of reference, they stood at the same time as wearisome reminders of parental discipline. The glee with which Monteverdi and his contemporaries transgressed sixteenth-century notions of time is palpable, especially when they launched off into queasy-making territories. These composers were in no hurry to embrace another standard brand of temporal regulation, which would begin to solidify only decades later.

But experiments such as Monteverdi's become perceptible to listeners only if performers know how to respond to his indications. In fact, I have located no recordings that do what I have suggested in my comments.[8] One of my teachers once told me that composers of this period did not really care very

[7] Raymond Williams, *Marxism and Literature* (Oxford: Oxford University Press, 1977), 131–32.

[8] At the Hasty conference, I had to substitute another Monteverdi madrigal, "Non vedrò mai le stelle," so that I would have a performance that backed up my argument. I had already published an account of that madrigal, however, in *Desire and Pleasure*, and I do not want to duplicate that discussion here. I hope that enterprising musicians can use my discussion of "Ahi, com' a un vago sol" as a guide.

much about where they cadenced; they just got to the end of their texts and stopped. Several commercial recordings do just this—they coast along with little differentiation between the chains of fifths and the move to B♮ or between the drawn-out melismas and the tight progression of the refrain. Others grasp the idea of time warping but use it indiscriminately all the way through, even slowing the pace of the refrain so that it sounds as languid as the passages surrounding it. Performers need to develop analytical skills not so that they distance themselves from the music that they sing or play (a common complaint in theory classes) but because familiarity with the grammar of these early repertories can invite or even demand much more shocking renditions than an all-purpose sense of "musicality" will admit. Just as the first page of Monteverdi's "Cruda Amarilli" should sound like a head-on collision rather than the wispy ninth-chord heard in most recordings, so "Ahi, com' a un vago sol" should alternately cajole and jolt listeners, repeatedly slapping us upside the head.[9]

Temporal elasticity appears in nearly all Italian genres of the time, including sacred music. Recall Monteverdi's "Duo Seraphim," which begins with excruciatingly deliberate modal unfoldings and nearly impossible feats of ornamentation, then progresses to wildly careening spirals, simulations of angels circling weightless around the throne of God, rather like George Clooney and Sandra Bullock in the 2013 film *Gravity*.[10] Heinrich Schütz caught the bug during his sabbaticals with Giovanni Gabrieli and Alessandro Grandi in Venice, and he brought the contagion home to Germany with him. As Christopher Hasty's rhythmic analysis of "Adjuro vos, filiae Jerusalem" reveals, the principle of time warping deeply influenced Schütz, who used it to simulate fluctuating states of mystical ecstasy.[11]

Moreover, composers of instrumental music made full use of such devices, producing the same kinds of phenomenological experiences without the assistance of verbal texts. Dario Castello's solo and trio sonatas frequently depart from linear exposition to revel in the kind of lavish, protracted spiraling developed by Monteverdi for his explorations of space.[12]

---

[9] See the discussion of "Cruda Amarilli" in *Modal Subjectivities*, 181–88.

[10] See my discussion in *Desire and Pleasure*, 94–96.

[11] Hasty, *Meter as Rhythm*, 243–57. I deal extensively with this piece as well as its first half, "Anima mea liquefacta est," in *Desire and Pleasure*, 148–58.

[12] Many excellent recordings of Castello's sonatas now exist. Listen, for instance, to Andrew Manze with Romanesca, *Phantasticus*, 1998 by Harmonia Mundi, HMU 907211, CD or to Quicksilver, *Stile Moderno*, 2011 by Acis Productions, APL72546, CD.

My title alludes to *The Rocky Horror Picture Show* (1975), and the "Time Warp" led by Riff Raff seems tame and even stodgy next to these seventeenth-century experiments. But not all of Europe embraced these erratic qualities. The French famously resisted Transalpine influences, sometimes even going so far as to prohibit the playing of Italian music. They did so not primarily out of nationalist zeal, however, but rather because such willful eccentricities offended the Neoplatonic ideals that regulated most aspects of Louis XIV's court, which greatly preferred the discipline of orderly dance.

Yet the seicento time warp did manage to infiltrate France in the guise of a uniquely French genre: the unmeasured prelude. Indeed, the first ones of these, produced by Louis Couperin around 1650, were explicitly modeled on the toccatas of Johann Jacob Froberger, who learned this part of his craft from Girolamo Frescobaldi in Rome. French lutenists and keyboardists had long preceded their dances with relatively free improvisations, some of which survive as sketchy or fully fleshed out scores. But capturing temporal elasticity in notation posed both technical and conceptual problems. The Italians chose to write out their extremely intricate rhythms, with strings of thirty-second notes, and then to indicate in their prefaces that performers were to play freely, avoiding at all cost a rigid reproduction of the note values that appeared on the page. Good Italian that he was, J. S. Bach followed this precept in his toccatas and fantasias. Performers were expected to bend the meticulously indicated rhythms.

Louis Couperin and his successors, including most prominently Jean-Henry d'Anglebert and Elisabeth-Claude Jacquet de la Guerre, chose a radically divergent means to a similar end: they simply tossed the mostly undifferentiated pitches onto the page and invited players to arrange them in whatever shape they liked. This encouragement to a kind of performative anarchy seems antithetical to the usual French modus operandi; recall that this was a moment when ornaments and dance steps were being codified and controlled to an unprecedented degree.[13] Yet performers get to exercise extraordinary, nearly unparalleled agency in unmeasured preludes.

Not everyone regards this kind of license as welcome. My harpsichord students, most of whom hesitate even in the face of fully realized French dances, cannot be coaxed to venture into the preludes. At least the Italians provided precise sets of instructions for their extravaganzas; Louis Couperin left only

---

[13] See my discussion in *Desire and Pleasure*. For a broader cultural analysis of this moment in French history, see also Michel Foucault, "Docile Bodies," in his *Discipline and Punish: The Birth of the Prison*, trans. Alan Sheridan (New York: Vintage Books, 1977), 135–69.

a vague trace of his own noodling and then expected us to make it up for ourselves.

Never less than perverse, I love wallowing in these things, for they demand everything I know concerning voice leading, formal backgrounds, and everything in between. During the first read-through, I try to locate the centers of relative gravity—the places where the restless energies seem (or can be made to seem) to land. This was the period during which Galileo and Kepler attempted to calculate the orbits of the planets, with Newton later supplying the mathematical means to account for and measure the phenomena of attraction, repulsion, and acceleration, what he called "the science of fluxions."[14] Monteverdi was drawn to lyrics concerning circling stars and angels for some of his most dazzling experiments, though he indicated with great precision how to go about realizing his effects.

But when one plays an unmeasured prelude, one gets to invent an entire cosmology. It is as if we are there before Time began, before the Big Bang, confronted with mere blobs of unarticulated matter, and we have to determine the extent to which each potential point of release exerts a gravitational pull, the ways the surrounding pitches submit to or resist that magnetic force. And what could be more fun than playing God?

I want to turn now to Louis Couperin's Prélude in what I would term G Hypodorian. The score presents us only with bunches of whole notes and lines that suggest something about voice leading. And that is all.

Like most such pieces, this one opens with an unfolding over a tonic pedal (Example 4). Notice how nicely Couperin points up the tenor line's Schenkerian unfolding from G to A to B♭, as the top line moves through anguished intervals, even pausing briefly on VI♭. But for all the apparent stability afforded by the sustained pedal in the bass, it is not entirely clear where the next pillar in this suspension bridge is located. Whenever a cadence on G seems within grasp, something happens to skew the harmonic vectors.

Here is where my training with Earl Kim comes to mind. For in working through this piece, I have to decide where to put my points of rhetorical emphasis and where to imply downbeats, just as we did with Samuel Beckett's play. How might I parse this stream of blobs in ways that will sound effective? Choosing not to interpret does not seem to me an option; Couperin did not construct his score this way so as to produce nonsense.

---

[14] See Isaac Newton, *The Method of Fluxions and Infinite Series*, trans. John Colson (London: Henry Woodfall, 1736); the translation was from a posthumously published Latin text.

Example 4. Louis Couperin, Prélude in G Moll

Example 4, continued

Example 4, continued

Example 4, continued

I see two possible places for at least momentary repose on the first page. The first occurs in the second system just after the second low G. The right hand's C appears to stand alone, and if it is marked in performance as preparatory to the B♮, then B♮ can serve both as a quasi confirmation of the G mode and a new impulse forward. If this does not allow for release, it may at least allow us to catch a breath.

A more complicated situation appears in the fourth and fifth systems, and I can propose two possible solutions. Most of system 4 is taken up with written-out pre-cadential ornaments—something one sometimes finds in Frescobaldi and Froberger toccatas. But however emphatic this build-up might be, it is not entirely clear where to put its arrival. We can treat the D that occurs seven pitches from the end of the line as a downbeat, thus eliding the arrival with a new forward-moving gesture. Or we can perform that D as continuing the upbeat quality that precedes it and allow the lower G at the bottom of system 5 to serve as the arrival, nicely sealed up with the ornamented B♭ in the right hand. That solution allows the E♮ to begin a new impulse.

My point is not that one of these is somehow correct and the other not; rather, it is precisely these sorts of quandaries that make unmeasured preludes so challenging and also endlessly variable. If Couperin had wanted to require one of these or the other, he could have indicated as much—as he does, perhaps (or perhaps not), with the barline halfway through the second page. With that barline he may signal a discontinuity following the upward sweep in the right hand and also makes explicit a link between the C in the bass with the B♭ in the preceding system. But some expert performers just barrel through that spot, basing their decisions on other patterns or other musical impulses.

This particular moment presents another set of questions as well. Near the end of system 5, the right hand has a 7-pitch configuration that unfurls some kind of seventh chord against the bass, and this figure persists throughout the next page. Should one play these as if they are not related? Or make their similarities audible through rhetorical emphasis? Or perhaps even create a rhythmic pattern that gives it a motivic profile? I happen to like emphasizing the dissonances of each cocktail chord (i.e., the fifth note in the figure), holding it quite a bit longer than the surrounding pitches. Again, it is up to the performer to decide whether such features should emerge from the surrounding chaos as continents rising from the sea or planets from the firmament.

The prelude never strays far from G, its point of reference, but it manages to touch briefly on C minor, D minor, and F major before ending on G. And then Couperin switches to something completely different, announced in the score as a "Changement de mouvement." The eccentric energies of the opening give way to the Neoplatonic order of social dance. After a page of regular rhythms, the dance disintegrates and lapses back into unmeasured conundrums for the conclusion. The stable metric foundation offered during this reassuring section is withdrawn, the rug unceremoniously yanked out from under the feet of our simulated dancers.

In a last parting shot, Couperin stages a passage of dissonant stagnation near the end of his prélude. A pattern in the right hand gets stuck at the top of page 4, becoming increasingly strident against the bass. Here voice leading is paramount: which pitches link with which others to provide a plausible contrapuntal framework? How might the performer harness the energy of the various linear vectors in order to achieve the greatest dramatic effect?

Our ability to deal effectively with seventeenth-century music has been hampered by its considerably different sense of harmonic syntax—an aspect we can overcome if we take the trouble to learn about late sixteenth-century modal procedures and the mechanisms for expansion developed in the 1600s. But the greater obstacle is its very alien constructions of temporality. Of course, these two dimensions are tightly related to one another. Yet if we concentrate too much on the pitches, we will miss the reasons these composers deployed them in such erratic ways in the first place.

I prefer to understand pitch *in all musical repertories* as raw material to be pushed around and arranged in order to produce particular qualities of motion and experiences of time. The pitches give us something concrete to analyze, but it is finally the construction of temporality that matters culturally and aesthetically, that offers us traces of bodies, emotions, subjectivities, and structures of feeling from other moments in history. And our honoree for this volume, Christopher Hasty, has done a great deal to provide tools for interrogations of this most crucial sort.

For it is not only seventeenth-century music that foregrounds radical transformations in temporality. Indeed, this erratic treatment of time occurs throughout music history, especially in moments of extreme style change. Think, for instance, of how Leonin shifts back and forth so thrillingly between free organum and measured discant, of the dizzying superimpositions of layers in isorhythmic motets, of the eccentricities of Beethoven's late quartets, of Mahler's montages, of the shocking simplicity of Miles Davis's "So What" or early Philip Glass.

My decision to concentrate in my own career on how seventeenth-century music works has required me to focus on this inescapable element. But we should all, regardless of the repertories we study, pay much more serious attention to temporalities, especially those whose radical fluctuations stymie our well-behaved linear theories. Even if we want to understand the cultural work associated with the emergence of eighteenth-century tonality, we have to recall the great age of the Time Warp, against which it was reacting. So let's do the Time Warp again.

When Swing Doesn't Swing: Competing Conceptions of an Early Twentieth-Century Rhythmic Quality

MATTHEW BUTTERFIELD

To learn from Wundt that "no series of impressions is possible that can-not in some way be comprehended as rhythmic" is a matter of small concern until we suddenly discover that by listening for rhythm in irregular sequences, in the criss-cross lapping of many waves upon the shore, in the syncopating cries of a flock of birds, in the accelerating and retarding quivers of a wind-blown tree, we have found a new form of pleasure that embraces in its field every moment of our conscious life. [1]

—William Morrison Patterson

IN THE SPRING of 1995, I was one of a privileged few graduate students at the University of Pennsylvania to take a seminar on rhythm with Christopher Hasty. The manuscript of his epic volume *Meter as Rhythm* was actually due to the publisher that spring, but Hasty informed us one day in class with a sly

---

[1] William Morrison Patterson, *The Rhythm of Prose: An Experimental Investigation of Individual Difference in the Sense of Rhythm* (New York: Columbia University Press, 1916), 1–2. Quoting William Wundt, *Grundzüge der physiologischen Psychologie*, vol. iii (Leipzig: Engelmann, 1911), 53.

and mischievous grin that he had been given an "extension."[2] We were, consequently, amongst the first to read through a complete draft of that profound work, prior to its publication. The experience was indescribably breathtaking. It is no understatement to say that it prompted me to rethink the entirety of everything I thought I knew about music. My dissertation, begun that summer and completed in 2000, represented the first stage in that process. My subsequent research has continued to work through the implications of *Meter as Rhythm*, most specifically in an effort to account for the mysterious rhythmic quality we refer to as "swing." Indeed, most of my work since graduate school has stemmed from the paper I wrote for Hasty's seminar that spring.

That paper was largely a critique of Gunther Schuller, whose explanation of swing in the opening pages of *Early Jazz*, published in 1968, I found to be profoundly unsatisfying. Schuller had identified two characteristics that distinguished jazz rhythm from "classical," namely: "(1) a specific type of accentuation and inflection with which notes are played or sung, and (2) the continuity—the forward-propelling directionality—with which individual notes are linked together." "Swing," he contended, is "a force in music that maintains the perfect equilibrium between the horizontal and vertical relationships of musical sounds; that is, it is a condition that pertains when both the verticality and horizontality of a given musical moment are represented in perfect equivalence and oneness."[3]

Schuller states this matter-of-factly, of course, but I must confess I have always found it completely baffling. It is essentially a claim that pitch and rhythm are of equal importance in jazz performance, and their "perfect equilibrium" in the execution of any given phrase will generate a quality we call swing. But it relies on an untenable assertion that, in the performance of classical music, "it is often sufficient to play the notes at exactly the right time (the vertical aspect) without becoming involved in the horizontal demands of the passage."[4] Surely, good classical performers are always mindful of the "propulsive flow" of a given series of tones in relation to harmony, and they do in fact respond sensitively to the rhythmic impetus of each note in the becoming of a phrase—they would be terrible musicians if they did not! Where, then, does classical rhythm leave off and swing begin, and why must an explanation of the latter require the misrepresentation and disparagement of the former as its foil?

---

[2] Christopher F. Hasty, *Meter as Rhythm* (Oxford: Oxford University Press, 1997).
[3] Gunther Schuller, *Early Jazz: Its Roots and Musical Development* (Oxford: Oxford University Press, 1968), 7.
[4] Ibid.

In Hasty's theory of metric projection, I found what I thought was a better framework for explaining the motional qualities of good jazz rhythm—specifically, the forward-propulsive quality Schuller had identified as its basis. In brief, the theory I proposed in that seminar paper and have worked out in detail in a series of articles since then is that this forward-propulsive quality emerges from the operation of anacrusis in the projection of duration at multiple levels of rhythmic structure. The "power of anacrusis," I believe, is then either enhanced or tempered by expressive microtiming in a variety of ways.[5]

The process of developing this theory of jazz rhythm has prompted me to explore how others have defined "swing" and explained both its origins and effects. I have been particularly interested in early uses of the term in relation to African American music, and the historical processes by which it acquired a distinct racial meaning. When did "swing" emerge as a meaningful term for designating a specific rhythmic quality found in music? How did it come to be understood not merely as the rhythmic foundation of good jazz, but also as an explicit rhythmic manifestation of a black racial essence? Part of that larger project, this essay examines the empirical studies of two Columbia University scholars published in the early twentieth century. Warner Brown's *Time in English Verse Rhythm* (1908) and William Morrison Patterson's *The Rhythm of Prose* (1916) rely on "swing" to explain the subjective rhythmic behaviors of readers of poetry and prose, respectively.[6] Their understanding of the term is quite peculiar from a current perspective, but as I will show, it was entirely consistent with its broader usage in relation to rhythm in their day. My aim, then, is to reconstruct the context in which their use of the term "swing" had meaning.

Today, there are a few fairly specific things we typically mean by "swing." We use it to refer to music of the Swing Era, of course. We also use it to designate uneven eighth notes—what Don Knowlton in 1926 called the "*um*-pa-*tee*-dle"

---

[5] This theory is elaborated in Matthew W. Butterfield, "The Power of Anacrusis: Engendered Feeling in Groove-Based Musics," *Music Theory Online* 12/4 (2006) <http://www.mtosmt. org/issues/mto.06.12.4/mto.06.12.4.butterfield.html>; "Participatory Discrepancies and the Perception of Beats in Jazz," *Music Perception* 27/3 (2010), 157–76; "Race and Rhythm: The Social Component of the Swing Groove," *Jazz Perspectives* 4/3 (2010), 301–55; and "Why Do Jazz Musicians Swing Their Eighth Notes?" *Music Theory Spectrum* 33/1 (2011), 3–26.

[6] Warner Brown, *Time in English Verse Rhythm: An Empirical Study of Typical Verses by the Graphic Method* (New York: The Science Press, 1908); and Patterson, *The Rhythm of Prose*. Brown had training in both psychology and philosophy, and *Time in English Verse Rhythm* appears to be his PhD dissertation in the latter. Patterson was an English instructor at Columbia at the time of the publication of *The Rhythm of Prose*, which appears to be his PhD dissertation in literature. His experimental method and his handling of data and statistical analysis, however, suggest considerable training in psychology.

pattern.[7] And we use it to refer to the underlying rhythmic groove of what is by now understood to be mainstream jazz: the ding-CHICK-a-ding, CHICK-a-ding pattern played by the jazz drummer on the hi-hat and ride cymbals, accompanied by a walking bass line.

Swing also refers to a more general rhythmic quality, however, akin to another sense of "groove," where it designates something beyond a specific musical style or rhythmic pattern. Pinning this meaning down with any precision is quite difficult, but I think Gunther Schuller actually makes the gist of it fairly clear: "In its simplest physical manifestation swing has occurred when, for example, a listener inadvertently starts tapping his foot, snapping his fingers, moving his body or head to the beat of the music."[8] Swing, in this sense, is about the engagement of the body's motor response systems. It prompts an almost involuntary response from the listener, manifested in physical movement of some sort.

Schuller's phrasing, "swing has occurred," invokes a common theme in writings about the phenomenon since the 1930s: you know it when you hear it, but you cannot necessarily say what it is or what produced it; its essence is simply too mysterious and somehow transcends explanation. This idea is clearly evident in André Hodeir's effort to explain swing as a manifestation of something he called "vital drive," a quality that "resists analysis," and involves "a combination of undefined forces that creates a kind of 'rhythmic fluidity' without which the music's swing is markedly attenuated." He was nevertheless at a loss to explain its cause. "If I weren't afraid of straying too far afield," he writes, "I would suggest that this drive is a manifestation of personal magnetism, which is somehow expressed—I couldn't say exactly how—in the domain of rhythm."[9]

Hodeir's perspective on swing owes a great deal to his predecessor, Hugues Pannasié, who I believe is most responsible for mystifying the concept and tying it most explicitly to a black racial essence. For Panassié, the "essential element of jazz" is "the Negro 'swing.' All true jazz must have swing; where there is no swing, there can be no authentic jazz." No one has successfully explained swing, of course, but it is an "entirely *objective*" phenomenon: "there is almost always complete agreement among competent critics on whether swing is

---

[7] Don Knowlton, "The Anatomy of Jazz," *Harper's Magazine* (April 1926), 580.

[8] Gunther Schuller, *The Swing Era: The Development Of Jazz, 1930–1945* (Oxford: Oxford University Press, 1989), 223.

[9] André Hodeir, *Jazz: Its Evolution and Essence*, trans. David Noakes (New York: Grove, 1956), 207–8.

present or not, and on its intensity."[10] Swing, moreover, "is 'a gift'—either you have it deep within yourself or you don't have it at all," and "neither long study nor hard work will get you anywhere in jazz if you do not naturally know how to play with a swing. You can't learn swing."[11] With some practice, "you can acquire bit by bit a metronomic regularity of rhythm, but that doesn't mean that you can acquire swing. It is a thing untaught"—this last is Panassié quoting his contemporary Stéphane Mougin, who goes on to observe that swing depends on a sense of natural facility and ease. One must feel the musician "free from any constraint, even though his rhythm, his time, is marvelously exact and marked."[12]

Evident in Panassié's perspective is the more or less modern conceptual framework that has governed most commentary on jazz rhythm since the 1930s: 1) the notion that swing is something special, something distinctive that sets rhythm in jazz apart from rhythm in other forms of music—indeed, it is the very essence of good jazz; 2) swing approaches what we might call "metronomicity," but in some mysterious way, it avoids being mechanical; and 3) though it resists a precise definition, swing is a phenomenon that must be addressed or accounted for in some way—and virtually every jazz critic or historian since the publication of *Hot Jazz* has endeavored to do so. Though Hodeir, Schuller, and others have taken different approaches and emphasized different features of jazz rhythm, few have departed appreciably from this basic foundation.

This was not the case earlier in the century. It took some time for "swing" to become linked explicitly to jazz and to be understood as its rhythmic essence. Earlier uses of the term are more general and apply to a rather broad range of musical styles and other rhythmic phenomena. In this context, it is not surprising to find it used by Warner Brown and William Morrison Patterson to account for a coherent rhythmic framework governing the production and perception of speech rhythms outside the musical setting of texts. In their respective empirical studies of English verse rhythm and the rhythms of prose, both find a tendency of readers to project an underlying meter that makes possible the expressivity of a given text's rhythmic organization. Crucially, however, this meter is not made up of isochronous temporal intervals between clearly defined "beats." Rather, it is more flexible—it emerges from "a series of

---

[10] Hugues Panassié, *Hot Jazz: The Guide to Swing Music*, trans. Lyle Dowling and Eleanor Dowling (New York: M. Witmark & Sons, 1936), 4.

[11] Ibid., 6–7.

[12] Stéphane Mougin, quoted in ibid., 7.

motor performances of alternate vigor and relaxation," inducing perception of a more or less regular "swing."[13] Consider Brown's first use of the term:

> Thus I hear the rhythm as dactylic when the verse affects me so as to stimulate me; I hear it as anapestic when it depresses me. I notice and emphasize the stress or time factors according to my interest or prejudice in favor of one or another theory of versification. The rhythm is smooth or rough to me according to the degree, perhaps, in which I enter into the swing of the verse and make it my own; or perhaps the roughness is only the result of poor muscle tonus which prevents a good motor response.[14]

What he means by "swing" is a sense of periodicity in verse rhythm that is measured not objectively in terms of isochronous temporal intervals, but felt subjectively through a regular alternation between states of strain and relaxation. As he puts it elsewhere, "The regularity becomes a matter of recurrence of strain at the end of a definite cycle. The muscles may take a longer or shorter time to accomplish their cycle and the strain may not come at equal intervals of time but the swing is there and from one place to the next like place is one definite mental state held together by the continuous circular process."[15]

What is remarkable here is that Brown, writing in 1908, is not using "swing" as a technical term. He does not enclose it in quotation marks, nor does he appear to feel any need to explain its meaning. Rather, he takes for granted that his readers will understand him, indicating that his use of the term is fairly colloquial.

And in 1908, it was. By that time, the word "swing" had been used in numerous song titles of the ragtime era. Most often, of course, this was in reference to an actual swing, typically hung by rope from a tree, and the lyrics concerned either romantic courtship or childhood play (often nostalgically remembered).[16] On at least a few occasions, however, "swing" appeared in march, piano-rag, or song titles with a meaning that referenced dance. The

---

[13] Brown, *Time in English Verse Rhythm*, 76.

[14] Ibid., 6.

[15] Ibid., 75.

[16] "Swing" songs concerning children at play from this era include L. M. Lester's "Swinging, Swinging" (1898), and the "coon" song "Swinging on de Golden Gate," by Paul Barnes (1894). Songs that employ the swing image in the context of romantic courtship include "Swing Me High, Swing Me Low," by Victor Hollaender and Ballard MacDonald (1905); "Swinging," by Will J. Harris and W. R. Williams (1909); and "Swinging Together," by E. J. Gardner and Mary Emerson Miller (1913). These and others can be found in the Lester S. Levy Collection

earliest such use that I have found is "'The Popular Swing' March, or Two Step Dance," composed by T. P. Brooke, director of the Chicago Marine Band, in 1894.[17] Others include Harry H. Mincer's "Virginia," which was published in 1899 and described on the sheet-music cover as a "Two-Step and Hot Rag Swing."[18] Shortly thereafter, Will Marion Cook's popular tune "Swing Along" served as the opening chorus for the musical comedy *In Dahomey*, which premiered on Broadway in February 1903.[19] Cook's lyrics urge young black "chillun" not merely to walk, but to "swing along de lane," seemingly as though dancing, with head and heels lifted "mighty high" and "pride an' gladness beamin' from yo' eye." In 1908, the Edison Military Band recorded Henry Frantzen's "Society Swing Two-Step," a bouncing march tune in $\frac{6}{8}$ time, and in the same year, an obscure composer named Oswald Thumser published "Real Swing Rag," though unfortunately the music seems to be lost.[20]

In *writing* about rhythm in music, the term "swing" was certainly in use very early in the century. John Stillwell Stark, who was Scott Joplin's publisher, used it in the May 1905 issue of *The Intermezzo*, the monthly magazine of his music publishing house: "[T]here are many fairly good players and many teachers," he wrote, "who cannot by any possibility get the swing of the Joplin

---

of Sheet Music at the Milton S. Eisenhower Library of the Johns Hopkins University, https://jscholarship.library.jhu.edu/handle/1774.2/2085 (accessed April 16, 2015).

[17] T. P. Brook, "'The Popular Swing' March, or Two Step Dance" (1894), available in the Lester S. Levy Collection of Sheet Music, http://jhir.library.jhu.edu/handle/1774.2/10307 (accessed on April 16, 2015). Many two-steps of the day were written in $\frac{6}{8}$, as was this one, and the anonymous author of the entry "History of Ragtime" in the Performing Arts Encyclopedia of the Library of Congress (August 29, 2006) notes that such pieces "were often referred to as 'swings' as were the steps danced to them" (http://memory.loc.gov/diglib/ihas/loc.natlib.ihas.200035811/default.html, accessed April 16, 2015).

[18] Mincer's "Virginia" is included in Trebor Jay Tichenor, *Ragtime Rediscoveries: 64 Works from the Golden Age of Rag* (New York: Dover Publications, Inc., 1979), 181–84.

[19] "Swing Along" was also published in a version for men's vocal quartet with piano accompaniment in 1912. See Will Marion Cook, "Swing Along!" (New York: G. Schirmer, 1912).

[20] A 1908 recording of the Edison Military Band's "Society Swing Two-Step" is presently available online in digital format on the website for the Cylinder Preservation and Digitization Project of the Donald C. Davidson Library of the University of California, Santa Barbara (http://cylinders.library.ucsb.edu, accessed April 16, 2015)website for the Cylinder Preservation and Digitization Project at the University of Santa Barbara (http://cylinders.library.ucsb.edu/, accessed on April 16, 2015). Oswald's "Real Swing Rag" is listed in "Appendix 3: Published Rags in America," in David A. Jasen, *Ragtime: An Encyclopedia, Discography, and Sheetography* (New York: Routledge, 2007), 526. It was evidently published in 1908 by Bafunno Bros. Music in St. Louis, Missouri, but I have been unable to locate a copy of the composition.

ragtime."[21] Joplin himself echoed this language three years later in his pedagogical text *School of Ragtime* (1908), in which he famously admonished students to practice his exercises "slowly until you catch the swing, and never
play ragtime fast at any time."[22] Like Brown, neither Stark nor Joplin seems
to have sensed any need to define or explain swing. What they meant by it,
however, is clear enough. Joplin's use of "swing" is presented in the context of
instruction regarding practice strategies. The proper execution at the piano of
any complicated rhythmic figure, be it a complex syncopation in a Joplin rag
or a challenging cross-rhythm in a Brahms intermezzo, requires the student
to practice slowly until the underlying meter can be felt without conscious
counting. To "catch the swing," then, seems to indicate something like "to get
the hang of it," to internalize the pulse and convey it clearly to listeners, such
that the rich syncopations of the melodic line can be experienced to maximum
effect. In this respect, "swing" seems to designate little more than a danceable
rhythmic cadence, consistent with its occasional use in song titles of the era.

Use of the term "swing" at this time, however, was not at all specific to
popular or African American music. Donald Francis Tovey used it several
times in an essay on the distinctive violin playing of Joseph Joachim, particularly in reference to his remarkable use of rhythm.[23] Tovey first observes the
undesirability of playing with "stiff and mechanical rhythm," but then notes
some confusion over what exactly that means. We tend to think of a stiff performance as one that is metronomic and mathematically exact. To the contrary, Tovey claims that a scale played mechanically actually sounds as shown
in Example 1, with the commas representing very slight pauses between the
ticks of the metronome.[24]

Example 1. A Scale Played Mechanically (Tovey)

[21] John Stillwell Stark, *The Intermezzo* 1/5 (1905); quoted in Trebor Jay Tichenor, "John Stillwell Stark, Piano Ragtime Publisher: Readings from 'The Intermezzo' and His Personal
Ledgers, 1905–1908," *Black Music Research Journal* 9/2 (1989), 201.

[22] Scott Joplin, "School of Ragtime," *Music Educators Journal* 59/8 (1973 [1908]), 65.

[23] Donald Francis Tovey, "Performance and Personality, Part III," *The Musical Gazette* (July
1900), 33–37.

[24] Ibid., 33.

Stiff or mechanical rhythm, then, is not mathematically exact, with all sixteenth notes being equal; rather, for Tovey, it is a matter of exaggerated grouping: "Every group begins on the beat," he writes, "but no group properly fills out the beat."[25] "Stiff rhythm," then, "is always smaller than its own main beats."[26] By contrast, for Tovey "true artistic rhythm must be at least equal to its own beats," and consequently, it always seems "unexpectedly large for its pace."[27]

Enter Joachim. His playing, according to Tovey, gives an impression of "breadth and detail" because he allows each note to sound for its full duration. This causes some listeners to interpret Joachim's tempos as unusually slow; this is an illusion, however, for as Tovey asserts, "those who have had the thrilling experience of accompanying him have testified that while he can play extraordinarily slowly without losing swing and coherence, his quicker tempi are really unusually fast."[28]

"Swing" here, as with Stark and Joplin, is used without quotation marks, without qualification, without definition. It refers, quite clearly, I think, to the clarity of the underlying rhythmic cadence. The same is true elsewhere in the essay, where Tovey praises the subtlety of Joachim's use of accent. One does not typically notice it in his playing because of his tendency to give "full measure" to even the smallest note values.[29] And yet, in a passage like that shown in Example 2, from the first movement of Brahms' B♭ string quartet (op. 67), "played by Dr. Joachim and his Berlin colleagues with the utmost smoothness and an intense pianissimo," the accents "unimaginably delicate and unobtrusive as they are, are so strong that after all that rhythmic swing, there is no mistaking the fact that the tied notes at the end [under the arrows in example 2] are on the sixth, and not the first beat of the bar."[30] Again, "swing" here can only refer to the underlying rhythmic cadence, the sense of meter that emerges clearly despite the downplaying of metric accents and the full measure given to each note in its performance.

[25] Ibid.

[26] Ibid., 33–34.

[27] Ibid., 34.

[28] Ibid.

[29] Ibid.

[30] Ibid., 35. Tovey reproduces only the second violin part of mm. 50–51 and the first violin part of mm. 55–57; the complete passage is provided here for convenience.

*Example 2. Johannes Brahms, String Quartet no. 3
in Bb, op. 67, I, mm. 50–57 (Tovey)*

Finally, Tovey praises Joachim's sensitive use of portamento. In a passage like the one shown in Example 3, from the recapitulation of the first movement of Beethoven's Violin Concerto, an ordinary violinist "will begin caterwauling down long before one can possibly take that highest note for a minim." But the "supremely great player," i.e., Joachim, "will hold it for two good beats, and then swoop deliberately but swiftly down the great drop on to the equally large lower note. The mathematical result may be that that bar is a little larger than the normal; but that will be reconciled with the context by imperceptible gradation and swing."[31]

[31] Ibid.

Example 3. Ludwig van Beethoven, Violin Concerto,
op. 61, I, recapitulation (Tovey)

This, then, is the context in which we must understand Warner Brown's use of "swing" in his monograph on the rhythms of poetry. Brown, however, puts the term to a slightly different use than Tovey, Stark, and Joplin. In his study of time in English verse rhythm, he sets out to identify metrical patterns or norms in the recitation of poetry. He describes in exhaustive detail the mechanical apparatus he used to record several different readers, each reading lines first of nonsense syllables organized into iambs, trochees, and the like, and then reading lines of actual poetry.[32] This apparatus generated graphic representations of the timing of each reader's rhythms, as shown in Figure 1, allowing him to make very precise determinations of durations down to the hundredth of a second. Finally, he undertook a comprehensive statistical analysis of his data.[33]

Brown's conclusion was ultimately negative: "The empirical facts leave no room for a theory of verse rhythm based merely on time."[34] He found no evidence of any sort of metric regularity underlying the recitation of English poetry. Observing, however, that verse nevertheless generates rhythmic impressions—that, in his view, is what makes it verse after all, and not prose— he proposed what he called a "non-temporal theory of rhythm."[35] The feeling of rhythm in poetry, he claimed, arises not out of durational equality between accented syllables, but rather "out of a series of motor performances of alternate vigor and relaxation," which produces "the illusion of equality in time," an equality "not of time, but of kind, between the elements."[36]

[32] Brown, *Time in English Verse Rhythm*, 14–20.

[33] Ibid., 38–73.

[34] Ibid., 72.

[35] Ibid., 75.

[36] Ibid., 76.

Figure 1: "Specimens of the Records"; graphic encoding of one reader's timing in the recitation of nonsense syllables and verse[37]

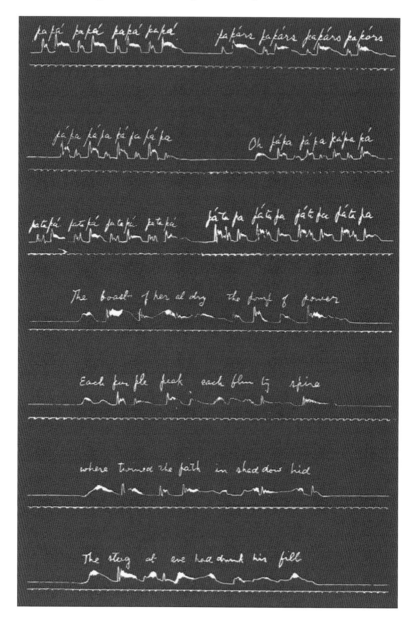

[37] Ibid., 23.

"Time not only fails to account for the regularity of verse rhythm," Brown writes, "it also fails to offer a base of distinction between the different types of rhythm," for instance, anapests and dactyls. The most "satisfactory course" of action in the recitation of poetry, then, "is to fall back upon the swing of the rhythm itself. The different rhythms form distinct kinds of cycles. It is the perseverance of one of these types throughout a verse or stanza that establishes the rhythm. Each beat, or each swing, brings up another of the same general structure and the same total affective value."[38] For Brown, then—and unlike Tovey, Stark, or Joplin—"swing" appears to be the sensation of rhythm *in the absence of isochrony*. It is the sense of cycle, the sense of back and forth, that makes an experience rhythmic, though it might not be explicitly metrical.

Brown's notion of "swing" was more fully developed eight years later in Patterson's work. Like Brown, Patterson regards rhythm as "first of all an experience, established, as a rule, by motor performance, of however rudimentary a nature."[39] "If rhythm means anything to the average individual, it means motor response and a sense of organized time."[40] And yet, Patterson's book *The Rhythm of Prose* begins by lamenting "a lost art of rhythm" brought on by "modern sophistication" and the "conventional dignity" that "usually forbids us to sway our bodies or to tap our feet when we hear effective music." Unlike "contemporary savages," such as the "Kwakiutl" or the "American Indian," the rhythmic facility of modern Westerners has been "thoroughly blunted," according to Patterson, and our efforts to execute syncopated rhythms are "characterized by hesitation and awkwardness."[41]

There are certain individuals, however, with more developed rhythmic skills—particularly professional musicians—and Patterson describes their reactions to music and other stimuli as "aggressively rhythmic":

> Such persons are capable of feeling a consistent and continuous experience of organized rhythm when confronted with haphazard series of sounds of any nature (within the limits of "time-discrimination thresholds" and "attention spans"). The impressions of accented and unaccented "syllables" in freely uttered prose usually suggest haphazard arrangement. To the aggressively rhythmic person a passage of spoken prose, whose measured intervals (between accents) display the utmost objective irregularity, can be organized subjectively and

[38] Ibid., 76–77.
[39] Patterson, *Rhythm of Prose*, x–xi.
[40] Ibid., 14.
[41] Ibid., xix.

give pleasure according to the varying facility of the process and the varying emotional suggestiveness attending it.[42]

Aggressively rhythmic individuals "can keep strict time" if they choose, but they also possess a "confident sense of 'swing,'" which for Patterson is the ability to organize perception of events by means of an "elastic unitary pulse"—elastic in the sense that it accommodates "progressive acceleration and retarding" without difficulty, and "unitary" because these pulses are not necessarily grouped into units of two or three. It is through the "sense of swing," so conceived, that "any haphazard series, by means of syncopation, can be readily, because instinctively, coordinated. The result is that a 'rhythmic tune,' compounded of time and stress and pitch relations, is created, the chief characteristic of which is likely to be complicated syncopation. An arabesque of accentual differences, group-forming in their nature, is superimposed upon the fundamental time-divisions."[43]

Patterson appears to be the first scholar to have put "swing" in quotation marks, but likely not because the term had acquired a fashionable currency in the eight years since the publication of Brown's study of verse rhythm. He does so, rather, because he intends to use "swing" as a technical term, introducing it into the psychological literature on rhythm, where there was as yet no tradition of its usage—in fact, where others had used the term only sporadically and casually, Patterson devotes an entire chapter to explicating "The Sense of Swing."[44] To an extent, he draws the term from Brown, whom he cites, and whose earlier study, also conducted at Columbia University, surely must have had a share in prompting his own.[45] But he gives no one explicit credit for coining the term, suggesting that he was appropriating it from common usage, especially as it was employed in discourse about music. It is telling, for example, that he employs Joplin's phrase "catch the swing" (itself a variant of Stark's earlier "get the swing") at least twice without reference to *School of Ragtime*.[46] Given how comprehensive his citation practice was, it seems clear that he had no reason to believe Joplin's use was extraordinary or original.

---

[42] Ibid., xix–xx.

[43] Ibid., xx–xxi.

[44] Ibid., 47–61.

[45] Ibid., 30–31.

[46] Ibid., 56: Patterson's experiments and statistical analysis provide him "a convenient way of ranking observers with regard to their ability to *catch* and to remember and to reproduce, under the conditions of the experiment, *the 'swing'* of the six intervals [i.e., .7, .6, .5, .5, .6, .7 sec.]" (emphasis mine); and ibid., 60, included in the caption for Figure II: "Test for the

In close proximity to these uses of "catch the swing," Patterson uses two similar phrases, likely for the purposes of elegant variation in his own prose. They appear in a discussion of an experiment intended to gauge individual differences in the sense of swing. Observers were asked to listen to and then reproduce under different memory conditions the "swing of [a] standard series of intervals"—i.e., a sequence of pulses with interonset intervals varying precisely as follows: .7, .6, .5, .5, .6, .7 sec. His concern was to ascertain whether or not the observers could "catch the rate of progression" or "catch the modulus of change."[47] It is difficult not to conclude that these were substitutions for "catch the swing," providing further evidence that his use of "swing" derived from colloquial linguistic practice. But these substitutions help to illuminate further what Patterson understands swing to be. "Swing" clearly refers to the progressive change in the temporal intervals separating events in a given series of events, and the "sense of swing" pertains to one's ability to track any such series by means of some sort of active motor engagement.

In this respect, the "elasticity" Patterson values in his conception of "swing" is largely antithetical to the rhythmic organization of ragtime and early jazz, both of which relied upon the pronounced articulation (or at least the strong implication) of a steady, unvarying beat to facilitate perception of the expressive effects of syncopation. Indeed, Patterson's "swing" better describes the performance practice of Western art music than jazz:

> [T]he sense of swing means nothing unless it be a sense of progressive movement. When a melody is played in strict, unvarying metronome time, swing is at its lowest, and the "psychological moment"[48] for an accent is merely a matter of remembering that two and two make four. What is usually meant by swing is really "elastic" swing, where the simple mathematical relations are complicated for purposes of expression. Compensation figures conspicuously. Time stolen in one place, is repaid in another. What Riemann calls "agogic

sense of 'swing': Graph of the reproductions of three individuals, attempting to *catch the 'swing'* of the standard series of intervals given by the time-sense machine" (emphasis mine).

[47] Ibid., 57.

[48] Patterson provides some idea of what he means by "psychological moment" earlier in the text: "[I]t is universally conceded that there is nothing in the individual performance of a musical composition or the combined effect of an orchestral production that is so vital to its success as the power to achieve what we consider to be 'the psychological moment' for a point of climax. This is the root of all of our discussions about *tempo rubato* (stolen time) . . . .It is in such situations that the mysterious 'sense of swing' is supposed to officiate." See ibid., 50–51.

accent" (the deliberate addition of length to a note, instead of stress, in order to give it prominence) and, of course *tempo rubato* (stolen time), belong to this category; so, though it does not seem to be generally remembered, [do] all effects due to accelerating and retarding the standard tempo.[49]

For Patterson, then, it is the sense of "swing" that enables one to intuit or project a flexible, implicit pulse in order to organize the perception and to shape the expressive quality of any more or less haphazard series of events. As a sort of internal clock, the sense of swing is most active *in the absence of an isochronous pulse* provided from without, because only in such situations is the body itself drawn most explicitly into the process of timekeeping.

To review: Brown offers a "non-temporal theory of rhythm" for English poetry, where the perception of rhythm depends on the degree to which one enters into the "swing of the verse" to make it one's own. Patterson proposes further the notion that swing must be understood in terms of elasticity, as implying or embracing an underlying pulse of progressively variable durational intervals, such that any haphazard rhythmic series can be experienced expressively in terms of some sort of syncopation.

Could any characterization of "swing" be further from the modern understanding of the concept? To be sure, jazz scholars have routinely sought to emphasize deviations from metronomicity as crucial to the production of swing and critical to generating its relaxed, non-mechanical quality. But the insistence upon "participatory discrepancies," as Charles Keil has famously described sub-syntactical expressive microtiming, only attests to the near-isochrony that is the norm of the underlying pulse of good jazz rhythm.[50] Tempo rubato, so central to Patterson's conception of swing, is foreign to the underlying groove on which microrhythmic variation in jazz melody lines depends for its expressive effects. Thus the "swing" referred to by both Brown and Patterson is not at all characteristic of the swing that came to be understood as the essence of jazz rhythm by the late 1930s. Simply put, they were describing a rhythmic quality derived from an entirely different musical practice.

It is particularly intriguing, then, to find Patterson cited as among the first

[49] Ibid., 51.

[50] On "participatory discrepancies" (or PDs), see Charles Keil, "Motion and Feeling Through Music," *Journal of Aesthetics and Art Criticism* 24/3 (1966), 337–49; "Participatory Discrepancies and the Power of Music," *Cultural Anthropology* 2/3 (1987), 275–83; and "The Theory of Participatory Discrepancies: A Progress Report," *Ethnomusicology* 39/1 (1995), 1–19. For a critique of the limits of this theory, see Butterfield, "Participatory Discrepancies and the Perception of Beats in Jazz."

to apply the term "swing" to the rhythm of jazz. The confusion began a year after the publication of *The Rhythm of Prose*, when Walter Kingsley sought to explain "Whence Comes Jass?" in the August 5, 1917 edition of the *New York Sun*.[51] Kingsley drew on Patterson in an effort to explain jazz syncopation, in particular, and for Patterson, as we have seen, syncopation in prose rhythm depends on an aggressively rhythmic individual's projection of an "elastic, unitary swing." "Jazz," wrote Kingsley, supposedly paraphrasing Patterson, "is based on the savage musician's wonderful gift for progressive retarding and acceleration guided by his sense of 'swing.'"[52] But the paraphrase is inaccurate and misleading, as Patterson never once referred to jazz in his study—the word wasn't even in common currency until after its publication—and he mentioned ragtime only twice in passing. And thus Kingsley's conclusion, "There is jazz precisely defined as a result of months of laboratory experiment in drum beating and syncopation," falsely attributes to Patterson a concern that was never a relevant component of his research.

On August 25, 1917, the *Literary Digest* picked up Kingsley's story and reprinted parts of it without clarifying the attribution.[53] This piece led Geoffrey L. and James Lincoln Collier more recently to identify Patterson as one of two "early experimenters [who] attempted to measure certain parameters of jazz."[54] It appears, too, that Robert Walser failed to catch Kingsley's false paraphrase of Patterson. Walser included Kingsley's article in his edited volume *Keeping Time*, and in his introductory remarks, he claims that "when Patterson tries to explain the power of jazz, his theory relies on a contradiction that would plague jazz throughout its history: he refers to 'savage,' 'instinctive' jazz musicians, yet he praises their skills and links their art to modernity."[55] This is indeed a contradiction typical of much early jazz criticism, but the fault here lies with Kingsley, not Patterson, despite the latter's utterly conventional use of primitivist discourse. I suspect that the Colliers' and Walser's misidentification of Patterson as an early theorist of jazz rhythm stems less from carelessness

---

[51] Walter Kingsley, "Whence Comes Jass? Facts From the Great Authority on the Subject," *New York Sun*, August 5, 1917, 6–8.

[52] Ibid.

[53] "The Appeal of the Primitive Jazz," *Literary Digest*, August 25, 1917; reprinted in Karl Koenig, ed., *Jazz In Print (1856-1929): An Anthology of Selected Early Readings in Jazz History* (Hillsdale, NY: Pendragon Press, 2002), 119–20.

[54] Geoffrey L. Collier and James Lincoln Collier, "Introduction," *Music Perception* 19/3 (2002): 279.

[55] Robert Walser, ed., *Keeping Time: Readings in Jazz History*, 2nd ed. (Oxford: Oxford University Press, 2015), 4.

than from an assumption that what Patterson and Kingsley meant by "swing" was the same thing we mean today—and clearly, it was not.

It is nevertheless instructive to consider how Brown and Patterson might have interpreted the swing in a musical performance recorded at an historical moment when "swing" had emerged as the putative rhythmic essence of jazz. Billie Holiday's recording of "I Can't Give You Anything But Love" (1936) will serve as an example.[56] The swing credentials of the men who accompanied her performance are unimpeachable, of course, but my analysis will concern primarily her vocal line.[57]

Example 4 presents three interpretations of the first two lines (i.e., eight measures) of the tune, from the beginning of the vocal entrance. The top staff shows the song in lead-sheet format, more or less as it might be found in a typical jazz fake book. The text setting exhibits a reasonably clever melody line, but it is rhythmically bland—almost unbearably so. One might have heard a fairly "straight" performance of the melody on the vaudeville stage—this seems to be Ethel Waters's objective in the first chorus of her 1932 recording of the same tune, in fact—but most jazz performances involve at least a modest rhythmic transformation of the melody.[58]

The middle staff provides as precise a transcription as I am able to make in conventional music notation of the vocal part Billie actually sings. Though fairly accurate, it is almost unreadable, and I suspect one would have a very difficult time trying to go from this notation to a rendering of the vocal line as graceful and elegant as Billie's. And yet, as Hao Huang and Rachel V. Huang observe, "amid the irregularity of Billie's rhythms vis-a-vis the band you perceive, if you listen long enough, a logic and a coherence *distinct* from those which govern the band. You perceive them in the power of her gestures, in the authority of her phrasing; for gesture and phrasing have rhythmic components."[59]

Accordingly, I have followed Huang and Huang's procedure in re-notating

[56] Billie Holiday, *The Quintessential Billie Holiday, Vol. 3 (1936-1937)*, © 1988 by Columbia Jazz Masterpieces, CK 44048, CD. "I Can't Give You Anything But Love," by Jimmy McHugh and Dorothy Fields, was published 1928. It was originally recorded by Teddy Wilson & His Orchestra, featuring Billie Holiday, in New York on November 19, 1936 (B20291-1).

[57] Pianist Teddy Wilson served as nominal leader of the ensemble, which also included Jonah Jones on trumpet, Benny Goodman on clarinet, Ben Webster on tenor sax, Allan Reuss on guitar, John Kirby on bass, and Cozy Cole on drums.

[58] Ethel Waters, "I Can't Give You Anything But Love," *The Jazz Singers*, © 1998, Smithsonian Collection of Recordings, RD 113–2, CD.

[59] Hao Huang and Rachel V. Huang, "Billie Holiday and *Tempo Rubato*: Understanding Rhythmic Expressivity," *Annual Review of Jazz Studies* 7 (1994–5), 182.

Billie's vocal line as shown in the bottom staff of Example 4. Here, expressive timing has been normalized, such that her part scans relatively easily in conventional music notation. This, however, is not as great a distortion of her rhythm as one might think. When she sings "any" in measure 2, "love" in measure 3, and "baby" in measure 4, for example, she articulates each as though she were singing it on the downbeat, and not after. In other words, each has the metrical meaning and weight of a downbeat, though she times each one expressively late. The bottom staff, then, provides a better representation of what we actually hear.

Example 4. Transcription of Billie Holiday's vocal line in the first two phrases of "I Can't Give You Anything But Love" (1936)

Huang and Huang explain this as a consequence of Billie's sophisticated use of "dual-track time," which they define as "the simultaneous presentation of two different, independent frameworks regulating the passage of time":

> Billie's signature use of dual-track time involves a steady beat for the vocal line, which we might call her "recitation beat," moving at a different tempo from the accompaniment. Not only does Billie

free herself from her band's beat; she goes a step further, ceasing to refer even implicitly to that beat. Her line is based on a beat moving steadily at its own rate. Locally, these dual tempi account for the irregular relationships between her rhythmic placements and the beats in the band. Maintained over an entire performance, Billie's separate beat accounts for our sense of security and order in her line. And our simultaneous experience of the two tempi contributes to Billie's floating, dislocated quality, what Stravinsky called the "giddiness" of jazz.[60]

What Huang and Huang describe here resonates remarkably well with Patterson's point of view. Billie's vocal line depends on her own "sense of swing"— on her individual projection of an elastic pulse layer that is non-congruent with the beat of her rhythm section, but that organizes and clarifies the function of her many subtle syncopations, producing "an arabesque of accentual differences."[61] In sum, Patterson would likely situate the swing of this performance not in the steady, danceable groove provided by the rhythm section, but in the elastic pulse embodied in the vocal line itself.

Similarly, Brown's concern would likely be with the swing of the verse, independent of its musical setting and irrespective of the temporal relationships it may or may not exhibit. If we isolate the vocal part and recite it aloud in as close an approximation of Billie's timing as possible, we might start to experience it, in Brown's words, as "a series of motor performances of alternate vigor and relaxation," where "each beat, or each swing, brings up another of the same general structure and the same total affective value."[62]

This becomes more clear if we think of the two phrases in terms of metric projection, as conceived by Hasty and shown in Example 5. Upon completion of the first phrase, "I can't give you anything but love, baby," I suggest one can feel the realization of what I believe Hasty would call an indefinite projective potential (labeled P in the example)—i.e., there is a feeling of a duration having been achieved and a sense of its availability to serve as a "measure" for a subsequent duration, but its precise durational value is somewhat hazy, as it is likely beyond the range of mensural determinacy.[63] And yet, upon completion of the second line, even as the second "baby" is drawn out in duration

---

[60] Ibid.

[61] Patterson, *Rhythm of Prose*, xxi.

[62] Brown, *Time in English Verse Rhythm*, 76, 77.

[63] On metric projection, see Hasty, *Meter as Rhythm*, 84–95. On mensural determinacy, see 78–83.

relative to the first, one can feel the realization of projected potential (P' in the example), even if the comparative durations of the two phrases is only approximate. Indeed, completion of the projection does not seem to require durational equality from one line to the next (nor, incidentally, must the realization of projective potential coincide with the onset of projected potential). There is thus an "illusion of equality in time" between the two phrases, an equality "not of time, but of kind, between the elements," which, as we have seen, Brown explains as a function of the underlying swing of the verse itself.[64]

Example 5. Metric Projection in "I Can't Give You Anything But Love"

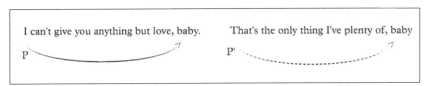

There are, of course, other ways of defining swing and explaining its function in this passage. Gunther Schuller, for example, might situate its swing in the balance Billie strikes between the horizontal impetus of the vocal line and the vertical demands of the harmony. A proponent of the theory of participatory discrepancies might claim that it is precisely the way in which Billie's vocal line resists the syntactical durational categories found in conventional music notation that generates the swing of this performance. Or one could situate swing not in the vocal line at all, but in the steady, danceable groove provided by the rhythm section. I have nothing to say here about which one is most real or authentic swing. The crucial matter, I think, and the way I believe Hasty would approach this, is the effort itself to hear swing in the various ways in which it has been characterized by others, and thereby to leave oneself open to new ways of hearing, to new potentials of rhythmic experience in music with which we might otherwise believe ourselves to be quite familiar.

[64] Brown, *Time in English Verse Rhythm*, 76.

Part V

"Thisness" and Particularities

Off the Grid: Hasty and Musical Novelty in Smooth Time

BRIAN HULSE

> "... *productive repetition has nothing*
> *to do with reproductive meter.*"
> —Deleuze & Guattari[1]

IN THEIR MIND-BOGGLING tome *A Thousand Plateaus*, the French philosopher Gilles Deleuze and his collaborator, the psychoanalyst Felix Guattari, critique forms of representation characterized by striated or metric surfaces. The striated image often works in one, two, or sometimes three dimensions. It expresses spatial relations, evenly distributed so as to produce identical units of difference or distance or duration. Based in this principle of identity, the units are subject to precise computations which, standing in for what the grid represents, produce analyses of meaningful properties or relations which correspond to actual events in the world (such as musical experience).

Deleuze, Guattari, and here I will add Hasty, Whitehead, Bergson, and others, are profoundly skeptical of the striated image as a method of analysis. Its principal problem lies in the empty generality of units and the tendency that these units, configured into elaborate a priori systems, tend to turn attention away from messy actuality. The two types of striated images common to

[1] Gilles Deleuze and Félix Guattari, *A Thousand Plateaus*, trans. Brian Massumi (Minneapolis: University of Minnesota Press, 1987), 314.

musical analysis are the measure of empty and infinitely reproducible units of time, and the measure of a supposed space where the identity of a minimal distance, such as the half step, is subject to calculation. While extolling the advantages for representation of what they call "smooth space," Deleuze and Guattari assert that in actuality both the smooth and the striated exist only in mixture. This is their metaphysical, rather than representational, aspect: smooth space[2] is constantly being overcoded and stratified, while striated space is continuously broken apart by the flows of an anarchic nature. This is a process not unlike the territorialization/deterritorialization dynamic elucidated throughout *A Thousand Plateaus*. What we are interested in here, however, is not so much how the smooth and the striated interact in the world, but rather how one or the other functions as the basis for an analytic approach to music. As anyone familiar with contemporary Western music theory ought to agree, the "reproducible," that is the general, which consists of fixed units, grids, measure or properties, is by far the ruling paradigm. But if we deny the function of reproducible, exchangeable units or properties, the general gives over to the particular. Smooth space is its milieu: where the untamed, lawless flow of intensities is affirmed. Holding the two in tension is extremely difficult because the move toward striation is not given free rein to dominate and ultimately eliminate the rogue, the flux and flow, or the problematic, which is arguably one of the primary functions of the intellect. The main striated systems of musical representation we have are meant to bring order of an objective sort to actuality, but in a unidirectional, or even imperialist, manner. In this sense, music escapes through the back door, as it were, because its flows and ruptures and sonorous becomings will not be tamed or held fast to any concept of identity. The grid is implicated by evenly distributed locations, or quantities of units, or the governing intelligence of a hidden power. These locations, quantities, and reductive schemata seem to take on an actuality beyond that of what is supposedly represented.

If we are to affirm and maintain contact with musical process in analysis, our systems of representation require interrogation. Representation is the attempt to "map" onto the actual, but at a distance, controlled, *stopped*. Of course, there are practical uses for such thought, but as a representation of aesthetic experience I contend that the striated image simply fails to capture reality, a reality that is qualitative, rich, and ultimately indivisible.

At various points throughout his work, Deleuze upholds Bergson's distinction between differences in degree (the metric) and differences in kind

---

[2] Deleuze, *A Thousand Plateaus*, 500.

(the "dividual," or, that in which division produces differences in kind or in nature).[3] The dividual prohibits analytic striation and metrics by thrusting the event/world into experience—where there is no identity, no measure, only dynamic multiplicity. In aesthetic matters the dividual and the metric (or striated space) are incommensurate. 1 + 1 does not equal 2. In describing or analyzing actual, perceived difference one must choose. If, as I am arguing here, the striated image or the grid is a poor representation of musical event(s), then what options does the dividual present? Is music hopelessly lost in proliferate, unrepeatable private experience?

Smooth space is linked to "nomadic" space, while striated space is dubbed "sedentary."[4] Deleuze and Guattari also attribute striated spaces to the "State apparatus," the function of which is to divide, control, and ultimately delete aberration or deviation. Smooth space is by nature open—in it all manner of becomings may be drawn or extrapolated in creative ways. As they put it:

> . . . the striated is that which intertwines fixed and variable elements, produces an order and succession of distinct forms, and organizes horizontal melodic lines and vertical harmonic planes. The smooth is the continuous variation, continuous development of form; it is the fusion of harmony and melody in favor of the production of properly rhythmic values, the pure act of the drawing of a diagonal across the vertical and horizontal.[5]

So even though it is clear that striation is a real thing, and relevant to process, smooth space is the milieu it inhabits, in which it draws and redraws its organizing power. Only in smooth space are processes of striation and smoothness, territorialization and deterritorialization, disclosed *as* processes. Furthermore, it is only in smooth space that process is released from any ground or identity. Deleuze and Guattari make it clear. "Smooth space is directional rather than dimensional or metric."[6] They go on to say "Perception in it is based on symptoms and evaluations rather than measures and

---

[3] See discussions in Gilles Deleuze, "Intuition as Method," in *Bergsonism*, trans. Hugh Tomlinson and Barbara Habberjam (New York: Zone Books, 1991), 13-35; "Asymmetrical Synthesis of the Sensible," in *Difference and Repetition*, trans. Paul Patton (London: Continuum, 2004), 222–261; and "First Commentary on Bergson," in *Cinema 1: The Movement-Image*, trans. Hugh Tomlinson and Barbara Habberjam (Minneapolis: University of Minnesota Press, 1986), 1–11.

[4] Deleuze, *A Thousand Plateaus*, 474.

[5] Ibid., 478.

[6] Ibid., 479.

properties . . . smooth space is occupied by intensities, wind and noise, forces, and sonorous and tactile qualities . . . "[7] It sounds to me like the founding of an aesthetic principle, one where perception—or the phenomenological—cannot be captured or represented "on" the grid.

In smooth space representation is open to imaginative connectivity, rather than being defined in terms of identical units of difference. It is an invitation for inventive, "unbound" thinking—thinking that, in not being confined to measure, can develop and explore events which are repeatable but never identical, *repetition being a differing from what is repeated*, in a world that is always renewing itself. This unbound renewal rewards novelty, which will not be captured or held to any principle of identity or generality. Rethinking music in such terms—terms more adequate to the eternal haecceity of passage—requires much more imagination than wielding weights and measures. The pseudo-complexity of such calculation is based on rather low-level principles: the identity of measure, the identity of distance, the false division between the vertical and horizontal, and so on. Extrapolating meaningful insights, musical insights, founds a new problem in every case. It is much more different than the apparently inexhaustible project of building theories or systems meant to tame the problematic in the name of generality.

Western musical notation itself is an example of striated space (and the extent to which its properties inflect our systems of representation cannot be overstated). The "vertical" axis represents pitch, and the "horizontal" axis represents time. As we know, this symbolic system, accumulated over centuries, has an eminently practical function. It designates actions (depress this key at such and such tempo in a specified series governed by durational ratios). The success of these actions in creating what we call music depends on a common understanding on the part of the performer who must first *decode* the specified actions (recognition) and then *perform* them as unique, singular events. But there are significant issues that obscure the practical function of music notation. One issue is the decoding itself. Decoding is deceptive because, although two people may be "reading" the same symbols, their meaning may vary significantly. For instance, where a performer reads the score as a series of cues for actions, a theorist may translate the symbols differently—as belonging to an order representing *things*. These "things" are often thought of as inhering functions, or belonging to a negative space where what *is* is defined in terms of distances or differences from other things. Another issue is in the performance itself. Of what does performance consist? Is it some transient variation of the

---

[7] Ibid.

ideal truth of the score? Or is performance really the central matter, where notation is useful, but inessential? Of course we all know that the two ways of regarding performance have been blurred, conflated, or minimized. But the actions of performance and the things of music theory are arguably of entirely different orders. They may in fact have no consistent or significant relation to each other at all beyond arbitrary signification.

Take the vertical axis, pitch. In my view, the adequacy of thinking musical sounds in terms of spatial positions on a grid drops significantly beyond its function in directing performer actions and certain simplistic, but useful, pedagogic functions.[8] As I tell my theory students, learn it well, and then *unlearn* it just as well.[9] There is simply a lack of correspondence between positional or functional concepts (i.e., what we already "know") and perceived affects. The qualitative prismatic affects of sounds do not map onto a uniform system of distances or differences. (Splitting the representation of pitch into a pitch-space and a separate pitch-class space hardly calibrates the problem; if anything, it magnifies it). Furthermore, the location of tones in a gridded space implies that the movement from one tone to another is similar to, say, the movement of the hand across a keyboard. But such movement does not actually occur, not even in a purely "physical" conception of sound waves changing in intensity.

Phenomenologically speaking, moving from one position to another across a space implies direction (what we call "up" or "down"). But we cannot know this direction until *after* we arrive at the next position. This means there was never any space crossed in the first place, physical or imaginary. The very idea of tones in a space is highly problematic and should not be allowed to pass un-problematized, as it usually is. Yes, it is useful to speak of "contour," of notes being higher or lower, but this is metaphor owing to a lack in language, not an adequate basis for representation.

The "horizontal" axis (time) embedded in musical notation has its own problematic aspects if it is taken beyond its functional symbolism for performance. In notation, time is also depicted in a striated fashion. What are measures, beats, and the "location" of events relative to these if not a literal time-line, made comprehensible through striation and an implicit even-ness or homogenous identity of time equal to distance? Again, to a performer, this aspect of symbolic notation is straightforward and useful for coordinating

---

[8] It is important here to distinguish between the abstract pitch space of music theory and the real (experienced) spatiality of musical hearing, which cannot be measured.

[9] I adopted this pedagogic perspective from the writings of Hazrat Inayat Khan. See *The Mysticism of Sound and Music* (Boston: Shambhala Publications, 1996).

actions. But for music theory, literally taking this time/space conflation as an actual representation of musical, experienced time is problematic. In a recent essay, Christopher Hasty writes "When we speak of artistic products in terms of representation, that is, as bearers of such things as form and structure, we speak of abstractions removed from time."[10] To be removed from time is to take shelter in a safe, controlled delusion, for there is no escape from time. Hasty (and Deleuze) fearlessly plunge thought into the real, where nothing is safe, and nothing is truly "controlled." A decade and a half after the publication of *Meter as Rhythm*, it seems, to me at least, almost incomprehensible that a distinction between meter and rhythm came to be in the first place. Perhaps it is simply an unfortunate byproduct of thinking of music as a pacified object in a stratified space. But as sensible as Hasty's theory is, it is still considered "radical" by many music theorists. I regard this marginalization as having a lot to do with protecting institutional power and the status quo, and little to do with the merits of the theory itself.

It is unfortunate that Deleuze and Guattari, caught up in the modernist ideologies of Boulez, were unable to sort out the meter/rhythm distinction clearly—that is, they took *musical meter* (the sounding/felt projections of durational quality) to be an example of a striated space—trading, if only for a few pages, all the liberative, nomadic aspects of the varieties of music they themselves celebrate for what turns out to be a weak ideology of an extremely esoteric music. The implication is that musics which are pulse-based are "striated," while modernist music (and presumably any music lacking an audible pulse) is called "smooth." I am not casting dispersions on modernist music here, but rather, pointing out that Deleuze and Guattari seem to have been confused by taking up Boulez's views uncritically. Martin Scherzinger writes: "While Boulez's music and Deleuze and Guattari's philosophy both elaborate the coalescence of vertical and horizontal dimensions in terms of diagonal lines of flight, the unhinging of the interval . . . from historically sedimented coordinates, and the destratification of planes in quest of smooth space/time, their respective attitudes to heterogeneity are in fact vividly contrasting."[11] If the processes and principles described above are held to, striation and destriation are affects belonging to perception. I suspect that if Deleuze had had

---

[10] Christopher F. Hasty, "Rhythmusexperimente—Halt und Bewegung," *Rhythmus – Balance – Metrum: Formen raumzeitlicher Organisation in den Künsten*, ed. Christian Grüny and Matteo Nanni (Edition Kulturwissenschaft, 2014), 160.

[11] Martin Scherzinger, "*Enforced* Deterritorialization, or the Trouble with Musical Politics," in *Sounding the Virtual: Gilles Deleuze and the Theory and Philosophy of Music*, ed. Brian Hulse and Nick Nesbitt (Farnham, U.K.: Ashgate, 2010), 119.

access to Hasty's work, for example, the bodily, phenomenological processes which produce a feeling of meter would not be conflated with the actual notation of meter or any concept of a reproducible unit of time. The manifold qualities of musical time would require an analytic intervention, that is, reviving (or affirming) the intensity of temporal experience that is cancelled out by the empty grid of meter.

The younger Deleuze, the Deleuze before Guattari, would not have fallen into this trap. Even in the introduction to *Difference and Repetition*, Deleuze immediately dispenses with all forms of generality, including the generality of time. He writes: " . . . generality expresses a point of view according to which one term may be exchanged or substituted for another." Instead, repetition, which here refers to the recurrence of interonset intervals, "concerns non-exchangeable and non-substitutable singularities."[12] Without expounding upon the fundamental insight of *Difference and Repetition*, that is, the demonstration of repetition *as* difference and difference *as* repetition (which, by the way, turns practically all of Western philosophy on its head), let us say that Deleuze is concerned with detail, singularity, and novelty, freed from the *a priori* mediation of representation. After all, what is representation if not the technology of the general and the equivalent, or that of science? Instead, Deleuze affirms the primacy of the world forever in a state of actualization, a "dynamic space" which "must be defined from the point of view of an observer tied to that space, not from an external position."[13] This is precisely the point of departure for Hasty's theory of meter. Consider this statement from Hasty's essay "Rhythmicizing the Subject" in which he clarifies what he means by the term "real time": "By 'real time' I mean the ongoing, subjective emergence of music, in contradistinction to the formal, mathematical, or fictional time constructed for an external or objective observer who calculates and classifies from the outside . . . "[14]

The technology of Western music notation has come to us in order to facilitate performance, not analysis. Wherever theory takes the musical score as its object, it does so at its own peril. The governing intelligence of notation is strictly utilitarian, a set of directions. It hardly "shows" everything. In fact, it hardly shows *anything* if music is understood as an indivisible becoming of sound, body, and world. Hasty is well aware of this problem when he writes:

[12] Deleuze, *Difference and Repetition*, 1.

[13] Ibid., 26.

[14] Christopher F. Hasty, "Rhythmicizing the Subject," *Musical Implications: Essays in Honor of Eugene Narmour*, ed. Lawrence F. Bernstein and Alexander Rozin (Hillsdale, NY: Pendragon Press, 2013), 169.

"Music in its making or actual passage involves so many things, so much more than abstract images of objects occupying positions."[15] The objectification of music is no longer sustainable if we recognize, once and for all, that there is no music apart from the body, and no body apart from the world. I believe that in resolving the meter/rhythm problem, Hasty did not simply substitute one abstraction for another. *In specifying the productive role of memory and projection in musical becoming, Hasty relocates the site of musical becoming altogether, that is, internal to the body, a body engaged in a world.* Physical sound waves do not "retain" duration, nor do they project anything. Retention and projection are intuitive functions of the body. Without memory, there would be no continuity (indeed, there would not even be a "subject"). Without projection, there would be no potential to actualize, no differentiation of temporal qualities; none of all those affects that make music so thrilling. These functions of the body are essential to music. Systems of representation designed to hold music still, to hold music *apart from the body*, are hopelessly inadequate, indefensible. Yet a conceptual relocation of music *to* the body, where it has always been in the first place, is not only a relocation of music, it is also a *dis*location of thought. Unfortunately, thought is not nearly as nimble and clear as we might like to believe. Mind and its images form in tandem. Fundamental conceptual change is not simply a matter of persuasive argument, because what needs to occur is the apprehension of something completely outside seemingly fixed coordinates; or, off the grid. This is a "power grid" in multiple senses: it traps thought, channels transmissions, creates the illusion of a stable world, locates subjects, and sustains institutions. Resistance to this power is not merely a matter of lack of imagination, however. I would venture that it primarily comes from what is at stake: the perpetuation of sedentary institutions, a stable commodity exchange, control of "knowledge," and ego.

If we de-stratify our conceptions of musical time, separating out its notation from its experience, then the analytic effort would require a technology of time-representation more adequate to its qualitative differentiations. "Smooth space" becomes "smooth time." It is a conception of temporal becoming where mapping or analysis is released from its stratified representation in notation, where "now" can accommodate a variety of times: past, present, and future, as well as the foldings and unfoldings, depth, and the simultaneous expanding/contracting of planes and qualities of time. Smooth time becomes the effective "center" of an unstable, prismatic multiplicity—living, breathing, becoming. In a word: rhythm. Even Derrida recognized the primacy of rhythm when he

[15] Ibid., 170.

writes: "Everything is summoned from an intonation. And even earlier still, in what gives the tone to the tone, a rhythm. I think that, all in all, it is upon rhythm that I stake everything."[16] One thinks of the shimmering image of the crystal of time, Deleuze's interpretation of Bergson's tripartite division of time in *Matter and Memory*.[17] Here time is no longer a line or homogenous flow extending infinitely into the past and the future, "containing" events in a simple succession. Rather, time is a site of transfer, sonority, memory, projection, actualization—the eternal production of novelty, here, now, and always.

The idea that what we call meter is actually an aspect of rhythm implicitly relies upon a logic of smooth time. Now, Hasty, too, takes Western notation as a point of reference. So how is Hasty's theory any different than others which presuppose the grid of notation? The question again, I think, is one of decoding. I believe that Hasty's interpretive apparatus is much closer to that of the performer than to that of conventional music theory as a whole. With the latter there seems to be an un-problematized and almost universal "first thought" in the direction of reduction. It is as if the truth of music is a kind of essence or unity that can only be accessed through the clearing away of the problematic. Hasty writes: "Music is problematic in many ways, but it is especially problematic in its resistance to representation—it is in this sense a violation of common sense . . . For this reason, music can provide a useful vehicle for criticizing the *doxa* of representation and thus for thinking in unorthodox ways that problematize notions of subject and object, unity and multiplicity, finite and infinite, knowing and feeling."[18] Reduction to unity or identity occurs in proportion to the eradication of plurality and difference. Thus, even though notation plays a practical role in his theory, Hasty's work is inherently *performative*, embracing the problematic, the transitional, the plural; in short, all the messy differences of musical articulation. I believe the difference begins immediately with the direction of the "first thought": for Hasty (and for performance in general) the first thought is in the direction of production. Notation does not call for less, but rather more—much more. This *productive* direction cuts against the grain of *reductive* music theory. But it flows nicely alongside that of performance where music opens to body, and body opens to world.

---

[16] Jacques Derrida, *Monolingualism of the Other: or, the Prosthesis of Origin* (Stanford: Stanford University Press, 1998), 48.

[17] See Deleuze, *Bergsonism* and *Difference & Repetition* for a lengthy discussion of what Deleuze calls the "three syntheses of time."

[18] Christopher F. Hasty, "The Image of Thought and Ideas of Music," in *Sounding the Virtual*, 3.

Example 1. Hasty's theory of meter as projection

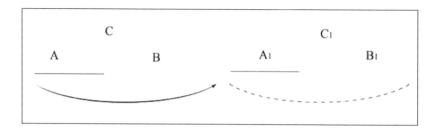

Let us see how this works. Example 1 shows some basic features of Hasty's theory of meter as projection.

During the course of events A and B, a total duration, C, is produced. C stands for what Hasty calls "projective potential," which is "the potential for a present event's duration to be reproduced for a successor."[19] Once a second event determines the duration of C, C is immediately past and its projective potential is established. Projection itself occurs when the duration of C begins to repeat as duration C^1 (the dotted line). The distinction between "projective" and "projected" is this. "Projective potential is . . . the potential of a past and completed durational quantity being taken as especially relevant for the becoming of a present event."[20] In the case of Example 1, after "C" is completed, its potential for repetition is held in memory as a virtual (or "past") image. Projected potential is created by the initiation of an event (the recurrence of A) that calls forth and "throws forward" the duration of the prior event (C), here labeled as C^1. The illustration does not represent static "things," but rather a process of time perception which cannot be accommodated by notation. "Now" in this graphic would be placed somewhere after the recurrence of B^1, but the entire process remains *present* to attention simultaneously. In other words, actualization is but an instant, now, but the virtuality of temporal process spans past, present, and future, all of which are vividly apprehended. Deleuze calls this triple formation the "crystal of time,"[21] because it is always ongoing in multiple registers of experience, its facets reflecting and influencing one another. Hasty's theory is thus a productive one, a complex of temporal

---

[19] Christopher F. Hasty, *Meter as Rhythm* (Oxford: Oxford University Press, 1997), 84.

[20] Ibid.

[21] Gilles Deleuze, *Cinema II, The Time-Image*, trans. Hugh Tomlinson and Robert Galeta (Minneapolis: University of Minnesota Press, 1989), 82.

"folds" invisible to the eye but vivid to the ear. And, notably, it adds richness and depth to our understanding of musical passage, rather than subtracting, reducing away, or subordinating what we are used to calling music's surface to an abstract order (such as the principle of structural unity, or the identity of units of difference or distance in post-tonal theory, and so on). Example 1 is not a reduction. It moves in the direction of production, an attempt to supply thought with avenues of hearing which cannot be notated in a score but which are nevertheless a primary aspect of musical experience.

Because the theory represents a virtuality that is, in effect, simultaneous and indivisible, there can be no overcoding of a rule of measure, or striation. There are no locations on a time line. If some form of successional time were introduced, it could be presented in some sort of relief, say, back to front, with several expanding and contracting images. The process of projection could then be shown to bloom and morph through musical actualization. But even this process, shown to develop progressively, could not be represented adequately by striated measure, or "clock time." The theory is pliable and able to accommodate approximations, transformations, and multiple hearings by virtue of the plasticity that smooth time provides representation. The virtual receives and inflects the process of actualization, just as actualization itself influences the composition of the virtual. None of this suits metric or striated measure, as if musical-temporal passage were something external to the body. This is how we can regard Hasty's theory as mapping in smooth time. It is "smooth" due to it being conducive to imaginative representations of temporal multiplicity which characterize "felt" or phenomenological time. Hasty's theory is one of process and particularity. The affect produced by duration *includes* the supple stratifying and destratifying of complex temporal becomings. What we call pulse, for instance, is produced by events in the passage of musical sound. In every case, no matter how familiar we are with conventions, they require a unique production. There are no shortcuts. Sonorous passage does the work, not ideal structures in an a priori space. These structures cannot rescue music from mediocrity, an issue that is often ducked by a music theory that presupposes the artistry of its objects, imagining that the "coherence" shown by analysis somehow relates to or explains the quality of the music.

But coherence, even in smooth space, is a lifeless generality unworthy of the dynamic fullness of musical experience. We must always turn our attention again and again towards the novelty of music, and think creatively about the complex virtual becomings which inhabit it. I think this is what Deleuze and Guattari meant when they wrote:

" . . . smooth spaces are not in themselves liberatory. But the struggle is changed or displaced in them, and life reconstitutes its stakes, confronts new obstacles, invents new paces, switches adversaries. Never believe that a smooth space will suffice to save us."[22]

Very well, smooth space will not save us. But salvation is not the goal, unless by salvation we mean relevance. What we are after is thought more adequate to musical experience.

[22] Deleuze, *A Thousand Plateaus*, 500.

Theory, as a Music

MARTIN BRODY

It is good to know how not to know how much one is knowing.

—Stefan Wolpe, "Thinking Twice"[1]

REMOTE CONSONANCE

IN THE OPENING of the essay "Composition With Twelve Tones," Arnold Schoenberg flaunted an eccentric argument. "The concept of creator and creation should be formed in harmony with the Divine Model," he proclaimed, adding that "inspiration and perfection, wish and fulfillment, will and accomplishment [would thus] coincide spontaneously and simultaneously."[2] A few paragraphs later, the master executed a more arduous leap of faith, in the guise of an evolutionary explanation of the emancipation of the dissonance:

> The method of composing with twelve tones grew out of a necessity . . . .
> The ear had gradually become acquainted with a great number

---

[1] My thanks to Scott Gleason for his insightful comments on an earlier draft of this essay. Stefan Wolpe, "Thinking Twice," in *Contemporary Composers on Contemporary Music*, ed. Elliott Schwartz and Barney Childs (New York: Holt, Rinehart & Winston, 1967), 297.

[2] Arnold Schoenberg, "Composition With Twelve Tones," in *Style and Idea, Selected Writings of Arnold Schoenberg*, ed. Leonard Stein, trans. Leo Black (New York: St. Martin's Press, 1975), 215.

of dissonances, and so had lost the fear of their "sense-interrupting" effect....

In my *Harmonielehre* I presented the theory that dissonant tones appear later among the overtones, for which reason the ear is less intimately acquainted with them. This phenomenon does not justify such sharply contradictory terms as concord and discord. Closer acquaintance with the more remote consonances—the dissonances, that is—gradually eliminated the difficulty of comprehension and finally admitted not only the emancipation of dominant and other seventh chords, diminished sevenths and augmented triads, but also the emancipation of Wagner's, Strauss's, Moussorgsky's, Debussy's, Mahler's, Puccini's, and Reger's more remote dissonances.

The term *emancipation of the dissonance* refers to its comprehensibility, which is considered equivalent to the consonance's comprehensibility.[3]

In this passage, Schoenberg described a slowly unfolding cultural/cognitive process that complemented spontaneous inspiration: an intergenerational ear-training exercise in which sensitive composers gradually came to hear the high partials of the overtone series more keenly and then transformed these ephemera into equal-tempered dissonances.[4] The creator's audience eventually followed suit, learning to domesticate the disturbing, dissonant sounds that the composer had wrested from evanescent sound colors. Schoenberg suggested that the very expressivity of dissonance was a symptom of a cognitive/psychic frailty, one that was gradually remediated as the "ear" (an organ connected to the psyche as much as the brain in this story) assimilated unfamiliar sounds and overcame the "fear of their 'sense-interrupting' effect."[5] When fear lifted away, so did the impediment to comprehension; and the dissonance, or more accurately remote consonance, moved from the nether regions to the foreground of consciousness. Over the long haul, this mini-drama of the sublime

[3] Schoenberg, "Composition With Twelve Tones," 216–17.

[4] From the *Harmonielehre*: "[Equal Temperament is] a compromise between the natural intervals and our inability to use them—[a] compromise ... which amounts to an indefinitely extended truce. This reduction of the natural relations to manageable ones cannot impede the evolution of music; and the ear will have to attack the problems, *because it is so disposed*" (Italics in original); see Arnold Schoenberg, *Theory of Harmony*, trans. Roy Porter (Berkeley and Los Angeles: University of California Press, 1983), 25. Thus Schoenberg suggested that translating the sounds of the higher partials into equal-tempered intervals was a kind of cognitive/psychic predisposition.

[5] Schoenberg, "Composition with Twelve Tones," 216.

played out repeatedly, as anxious listeners were cured of fear by exposure to therapeutic new music. The expressivity of what was perceptually remote was replaced by the comprehensibility of what had become cognitively near.

As he signaled in "Composition With Twelve Tones," Schoenberg had laid the groundwork for this narrative at the close of his 1910 *Harmonielehre*:

> The distinction between tone color and pitch, as it is usually expressed, I cannot accept without reservations. I think the tone becomes perceptible by virtue of tone color, of which one dimension is pitch. Tone color is, thus, the main topic, pitch a subdivision. Pitch is nothing else but tone color measured in one direction. Now, if it is possible to create patterns out of tone colors that are differentiated according to pitch, patterns we call "melodies," progressions, whose coherence . . . evokes an effect analogous to thought processes, then it must also be possible to make such progressions out of the tone colors of the other dimension, out of that which we call simply "tone color," progressions whose relations with one another work with a kind of logic entirely equivalent to that logic which satisfies us in the melody of pitches. That has the appearance of a futuristic fantasy and is probably just that.[6]

In this passage, Schoenberg prefigured the emancipation of the dissonance by describing a complementary project, which might be called the evocation of the ineffable. In elaborating this futuristic fantasy, he also flaunted his disregard for positivistic solutions to sound's riddles:[7]

> The material of music is the tone; what it affects first, the ear. The sensory perception releases associations and connects tone, ear, and the world of feeling. On the cooperation of these three factors depends everything in music that is felt to be art.... One of the three factors, however, the world of our feelings, so completely eludes precisely controlled investigation that it would be folly to place the same confidence in the few conjectures permitted by observation in this

---

[6] Schoenberg, *Theory of Harmony*, 421.

[7] See Julia Kursell, "Experiments on Tone Color in Music and Acoustics: Helmholtz, Schoenberg, and *Klangfarbenmelodie*," *Osiris* 28/1 (2013), 191–211, for a detailed discussion of the relationship between acoustical theory and compositional practice in the work of Helmholtz, Stumpf, and Schoenberg.

sphere that we place in those conjectures that in other matters are called "science."[8]

He concluded that "it is of little consequence whether one starts with a correct hypothesis or a false one."[9] What mattered was that exploring the sensations of the tone activated the artistic psyche. Schoenberg went on to describe the "analyzing ear," which regulates traffic between the conscious and subconscious zones of the psyche. "Even if the analyzing ear does not become conscious of [the remote partials of the overtone series], they are still heard as tone color . . . recorded by the subconscious, and when they ascend into the conscious they are analyzed and their relation to the total sound is determined."[10] When codified, we call this analysis "harmony," a relationship between pitch combinations and the total sound, which occurs via an "indefinitely extended truce" between equal temperament and the overtone series.[11] Master composers refreshed the pool of available dissonances by returning to the source and transmuting the ineffable qualities of the high partials into palpable, new arrangements of dissonance.

Schoenberg seemed indifferent to the question of whether or not there was a Fourier analysis lurking in the subconscious. Pitch, he emphasized, was the purview of consciousness; tone color (at least until the futuristic fantasy of *Klangfarbenmelodie* would be realized) directed us to the subconscious. The standing wave was a perceptual puzzle addressed repeatedly by artists, but never solved. The subtle and unfamiliar effects that artists produce by combining tones to produce new colors and pitch patterns ("patterns we call 'melodies', progressions, whose coherence . . . evokes an effect analogous to thought processes") simulated and amplified the sensations that have lodged in the unconscious. It follows, then, that ever-new varieties of remote sound need to be conjured to keep the subconscious from going dormant. Given all this, it may not be too fanciful to add that the *Klangfarben* effect produced the melody of the unconscious; and that the compositional projection of fresh dissonances simulated the awakening of consciousness itself.

When reading "Composition With Twelve Tones" and Schoenberg's other late essays, it is tempting to pass over the dodgy psychoacoustics and allegorical imagery and move quickly to the no-nonsense business at hand: the mechanics of sets, set transformations, combinatoriality, and their compositional

[8] Schoenberg, *Theory of Harmony*, 19.
[9] Ibid.
[10] Ibid., 20–21.
[11] See fn. 4.

applications. By lingering on the former, I want to excavate the parable of artistic self-transformation lodged inside his claims on behalf of twelve-tone methods and the supremacy of German music. For Schoenberg, musical creativity was not just a matter of contriving cognitively viable structures out of stable, historically tested materials, and, most certainly, not of elaborating a stable *Naturklang*. Rather, it involved an ongoing exercise of disciplined listening for something new at the border between pitch and color, unimpeded by the resonant/cognitive filters of conventional consonance. Dissonance was not just a symbolic marker in a story about creativity *ex nihilo*; it was the sonic building block for an aesthetics and ethics of contextuality and the expressive residue of form-making on the fly.[12]

The project of making dissonance comprehensible was also linked to the enlargement of freedom. Normative definitions of consonance (and the technical apparatus of resonating consonance: "overtone chord spacings," octave doublings, etc.) constricted compositional exploration of the full sonic spectrum and subordinated the free investigation of structural potential to an obdurate *Tonwille*. Schoenberg's emancipation of remote consonance offered a remedy. His conjuring of the high partials could be understood (under inversion, so to speak) as a way to level the sonic playing field: to use equal-tempered pitch combinations (specifically those formerly known as dissonances) to destabilize the concept and even materiality of consonance—not just the style, so to speak, but the idea.

In sum, Schoenberg's account of the emancipation of dissonance may be read as a story of epistemic shifts and artistic self-transformations, sparked by a meditation on the phenomenology of sound, which, in turn, is inspired by the experience of composing music. Composition thus is always an errand into the wilderness, an exploration yielding new modes of artistic perception and creation that transform our understanding of the meaning of the past and the potential of the future. Something like this may be what Carl Dahlhaus

---

[12] I am using the term contextuality in the sense Babbitt provides in *Words About Music*, where he treats the term as a synonym for "self-referentiality." "*Self-referential* [as a synonym for contextuality] is a very good term, which means that, as much as possible, you make a work self-enclosed. You define its principles—a progression of relatedness—within itself. Now again that's relative; contextuality has to be relative. When you talk about a piece and talk about the relationship between a theme here and a theme there or how something is transformed or how something relates, you're talking about contextual characteristics, characteristics internal to the particular piece. This is a matter of degree—and matters of degree can be crucial where musical intelligibility is concerned." (Milton Babbitt, *Words About Music*, ed. Stephen Dembski and Joseph N. Straus [Madison: University of Wisconsin Press, 1987], 9.)

had in mind in his comment on Schoenberg as theorist: "Aspiring more to
ends than to origins," Dahlhaus suggested, he "follows the consequences that
emerge from a musical idea. His traditionalism consists less in the discovery
of the past in the present than in the discovery of the future in the past."[13] The
relationship between sound and music, if often understood to be an inquiry
into essences with a long history, can never be conclusively resolved. "Composition with twelve tones has no other aim than comprehensibility," Schoenberg
declared, but then went on to list some of the diverse sounds that composers
have harvested from the sonic spectrum in their pursuit of ever-greater comprehensibility.[14] The list moves from sounds that have names (the "dominant
and other seventh chords, diminished sevenths and augmented triads") to
those that are too personal and particular for conventional labels ("also the
emancipation of Wagner's, Strauss's, Moussorgsky's, Debussy's, Mahler's, Puccini's, and Reger's more remote dissonances"), thereby raising the possibility
of an unending taxonomy of new qualities and entities.

The closed set of equal-tempered pitches (the entities produced by Schoenberg's "indefinitely extended truce" with "natural" intervals) might seem to set
a limit, a curb on the movement from phenomenal impressions into fixed
structures. And the method of "Composition With Twelve Tones Related Only
To One Another" might thereby mark a culmination of historical mandates
and a fulfillment of supreme commands.[15] But why stop there? What is the
upshot of turning the ontology of music on its head, resting the full weight of
musical tradition on the delicate qualities of the faint, higher partials rather
than the solid edifice of the standing wave's fundamental? How many paths
might lead from ephemeral qualities to intersubjective communication? How
many dead ends? Where and when is the work of emancipation over?

A DISCOURSE LINKED TO AN EXISTENTIAL CONTEXT

In the following, I will consider some of the ways composers have responded
to the questions raised by Schoenberg's latent parable of ineffability and inter-
subjectivity—not by aiming to settle them decisively but rather by acknowledging their intractability and recording, even aestheticizing, the struggles that
have ensued. In taking this approach, I have been influenced by the work of the
philosopher Arnold Davidson, who, in turn, has written about the ethics and

[13] Carl Dahlhaus, "Schoenberg and Schenker," in *Proceedings of the Royal Musical Association* 100/1 (1973), 215.

[14] Schoenberg, "Composition with Twelve Tones," 215.

[15] Schoenberg, "Opinions or Insights," in *Style and Idea*, 263. See also "National Music (1),"
in *Style and Idea*, 171.

aesthetics of self-transformation, especially in relation to the work of Pierre Hadot and Michel Foucault.[16] Davidson has also been involved in an ongoing dialogue with the composer George Lewis on the theme of "improvisation as a way of life," a phrase they have adapted from Hadot's discussion of ancient philosophy as a way of life.[17]

Taking Davidson's lead, we may reorient Schoenberg's story of emancipated dissonance from ends to means and read it as a parable of composing as a way of life. In his story of emancipated dissonance, Schoenberg set the terms for a poetics of self-transformation: an exploration of intensely cathected sound with a clearly defined limit condition (the closed set of equal-tempered pitch classes as source structure) linked to an ethos of open-ended exploration (expanding perceptual capacities and burgeoning musical comprehensibility). In the wake of Schoenberg's innovations, and in an era of even more fully emancipated sound (dissonance and consonance, noise and silence) and creative practices (of performance, improvisation, composition), composers are likely to confront "the labyrinthine riddle of reason and resonance" every time they revoice a chord or mark an accent.[18] If they have come to involve epistemology and aesthetics in contending with such riddles, they have also rearticulated philosophical problems through the medium of sound. And their compositions model processes of self-transformation by inciting new modes of aesthetic experience. They have created (to borrow a phrase from Pierre Hadot) a "discourse linked to an existential context, to a concrete praxis," engaging in exercises of self-transformation "to make oneself change one's point of view, attitude, set of convictions, therefore to dialogue with oneself, therefore to struggle with oneself."[19] Understood in this way, we may appreciate

[16] See, for example, Arnold I. Davidson, "Ethics as Ascetics: Foucault, the History of Ethics, and Ancient Thought," in *The Cambridge Companion to Foucault* (Cambridge, Cambridge University Press, 2005), 123–48, and Davidson, "Introduction: Pierre Hadot and the Spiritual Phenomenon of Ancient Philosophy," in Pierre Hadot, *Philosophy as a Way of Life: Spiritual Exercises from Socrates to Foucault*, trans. Michael Chase (Oxford: Blackwell, 1995), 1–45.

[17] Davidson's and Lewis's ideas about music, improvisation, and *askesis* have been percolating in a number of public dialogues. See, for example, http://vimeo.com/71972632, accessed June 23, 2015.

[18] "Labyrinthine riddle of reason and resonance": the source of this phrase is the introduction to Veit Erlmann, *Reason and Resonance: A History of Modern Aurality* (New York: Zone Books, 2010). In focusing on composers' self-transformations, I do not intend to downplay the role of ideology or cultural politics in musical life or the development of musical subjectivity. Rather, I want to raise the question of how to explore the changing hydraulics of experience, structure, and creativity in various kinds of critical and analytical studies.

[19] Hadot, *Philosophy*, 91; quoted with modifications to the translation in Davidson, "Introduction: Pierre Hadot," 20.

the metadiscursive swerves taken in the writing of Milton Babbitt, Benjamin Boretz, and Christopher Hasty, among numerous others, as an efflorescence of gritty, quotidian experiments with sound: not a wrong turn into a desert of arid abstraction, but reports from the front in ongoing compositional explorations of pathways from meaning to being.

"ONLY MEANWHILE..."

As Robert Morris has noted, the punctuating chords in the opening of Milton Babbitt's *Composition for Synthesizer* are a bit of a puzzle.[20] These simultaneities do not resolve into "chords of pitches," to use Morris's phrase, because, as he also points out, the strong high partials of the sawtooth waves that Babbitt deploys mask the fundamentals of the chords' notes. A surfeit of quantizing produces a paradoxical effect: it almost completely dissolves perceptions of the discrete entities comprising the composite sounds. What should we call these, then—synthetic *Klänge* or structural chords? Or are they a mix of the two, something liminal, new, and paradoxical? This sonic transformation seems to me a metonymy: a figure for subjective self- transformation by courting indeterminacy via ruthless quantization. Babbitt's funny twelve-note *Klänge/*chords effectively reverse the process that operationalizes the emancipation of the dissonance as described by Schoenberg ("Pitch is nothing else than tone color measured in one direction."[21])

I ask that we keep the sounds of the opening *Klänge/*chords of *Composition for Synthesizer* in mind when reading Babbitt's metatheory. Both incorporated Schoenberg's ideas about the measurement of pitch and color, but in the metatheory Babbitt applied the lessons learned to issues of epistemology. Here is a characteristic sentence:

> Whether one prefers to declare that a theory must be, should be, or is a mere symbolic description, or a structured formulation of statements of relations among observed phenomena, or a collection of rules for the representation of observables, or an interpreted model of a formal system, or still none of these, presumably it can be agreed that questions of musical theory construction attend and include all matters of the form, the manner of the formulation, and the signification of statements about individual musical compositions, and

[20] Robert Morris, "Listening to Babbitt's Electronic Music: The Medium and the Message," *Perspectives of New Music* 35/2 (1997), 88–91. *Composition for Synthesizer* appears on the Columbia recording *Columbia Princeton Electronic Music Center.*

[21] Schoenberg, *Theory of Harmony,* 421.

the subsumption of such statements into a higher-level theory, constructed purely logically from the empirical acts of examination of the individual compositions.[22]

This is both an endorsement of logical positivism and, in its extravagant fussiness, an enactment of and testimonial to structural complexity.[23] The peculiarly unresolved question of the theory's ontological status ("must be," "should be," "is"?) as well as its substance (rules, relations, description, formulations?) also suggests that variability will rule in "empirical acts of examination of . . . individual compositions." If Schoenberg introduced the destabilizing prospect of reciprocal color/pitch relationships, Babbitt raised the ante by focusing on the fluid relationship between "empirical acts of examination" and "questions of musical theory construction."

What I wish to emphasize (and not for the first time) is that Babbitt's metatheory was aimed less at policing our practices than contemplating their diversity.[24] For Babbitt, procedures for clarifying "acts of examination" and "theory construction" are especially critical in an era of new sound technologies, when the ontology of sound and music are intimately intertwined and always volatile. If his metatheory was a Cold War artifact, it was aimed not at Mutually Assured Destruction but rather what we might call Provisional Ontological Stabilization: a program for aiding and abetting the development of diverse, consensual speech communities engaged in experimenting with sound and structure. Babbitt's approach to questions of musical theory construction permits the participants in a communal enterprise to gin up just enough epistemological security to experience, make, and describe things while, at the same time, rendering the things experienced, made, and described, and the process of experiencing, making, and describing, entirely provisional, open to revision and alternatives. This is not to say that Babbitt's integration of high theory and compositional experimentation gave him a free pass on questions of ideology, or that the cultural context of his epistemology is irrelevant; or that he did not muster all of his considerable rhetorical skills and political acumen to secure patronage for a highly circumscribed set of culturally marginal artistic practices. Rather, I am asking that we remember

[22] Milton Babbitt, "The Structure and Function of Musical Theory," in *The Collected Essays of Milton Babbitt,* ed. Stephen Peles (Princeton: Princeton University Press, 2003), 191.

[23] I have discussed this sentence as a kind of verbal performance in my "The Age of Milton," *Perspectives of New Music* 49/2 (2012), 365–71.

[24] See Martin Brody, "'Music for the Masses': Milton Babbitt's Cold War Music Theory," *Musical Quarterly* 77/2 (1993), 161–92.

that his extensive reflections on the epistemology of music theory and the ontology of music had little life independent from his empirical experiments with sound; that what he aimed to do was to keep the relationship of meaning and being maximally alive, productive, and communicative.

It is striking how many times Babbitt concluded a major essay on twelve-tone structures or compositional metatheory with a statement of uncertainty about the limits of human potential. Witness the last sentence of "Twelve-Tone Rhythmic Structure and the Electronic Medium," which is the peroration of a complicated verbal performance. After presenting a mind-boggling collection of propositions about the compositional projection of time-point sets, he ends with a salute to the "unforeseeably extensive domain" of future applications of the systematic relationships he has presented: "Meanwhile, if it is only meanwhile, there is still an unforeseeably extensive domain in which the electronic medium uniquely can enrich and extend the musical systems whose premises have been tested, and whose resources barely have been tapped."[25] And again, at the conclusion of "Twelve-Tone Invariants as Compositional Determinants," he gestures toward the "unforeseeable" and even "unthinkable": "I can state only, without hoping to have done more than intimate the bases for such a statement, that an 'exhaustion' of the resources of the twelve-tone system in the relevant future is not only unforeseeable but unthinkable."[26] Or the final paragraph of "Past and Present Concepts of the Nature and Limits of Music," where the question of perceptual capacities trumps even the inexhaustibility of systems:

> The limits of music reside ultimately in the perceptual capacities of the human receptor, just as the scope of physical science is delimited by the perceptual and conceptual capacities of the human observer. But the recent history of both disciplines, by bearing witness to explosive and decisive extensions of these capacities, constrains us from venturing only into the realm of prediction.[27]

I think it is fair to say that this was Babbitt's most persistent mantra: the

---

[25] Milton Babbitt, "Twelve-Tone Rhythmic Structure and the Electronic Medium," [1962], in *The Collected Essays of Milton Babbitt*, 138–39.

[26] Babbitt, "Twelve-Tone Invariants as Compositional Determinant," [1960], in *The Collected Essays of Milton Babbitt*, 67.

[27] Babbitt, "Past and Present Concepts of the Nature and Limits of Music," [1961], in *The Collected Essays of Milton Babbitt*, 84.

future is unknowable, a site of expanding human perceptual and cognitive capacities and "explosive and decisive" extensions, conceptual and otherwise. The aim of his positivism was not to foreclose on this future but to stabilize the present—just enough to define distinct, viable practices without limiting the potentiality for change.

"WHAT IS ABOUT, IS ALSO OF, ALSO IS"

If Schoenberg's metaphysics conjured a long line of history and Babbitt's epistemology spoke to the possibility of contingent but stable communities of practice, another strain of phenomenological/epistemological inquiry has confronted the nuances and uncertainties of the present moment. Here is an example of a markedly unscientific metadiscursive performance, from Benjamin Boretz's "Language, as a Music."[28]

> ... here, ...
>
> ..., begins ...
>
> ..., attaching, in
> specious increments,
>
> then,
>
> to now,
> as now of then,
> reshadowed,
> as then of now;
> as here of there,
> reechoed,
> as there of here;
> as nowhere,
> emerging,
> as somewhere,[29]

We could paraphrase this: it is about memory, tenuous relationships,

[28] Benjamin Boretz, "Language, As a Music: Six Marginal Pretexts for Composition," *Perspectives of New Music* 17/2, (1979), 137.
[29] In transcribing this excerpt from "Language, as a Music," the original formatting has been maintained but the typeface has been altered.

transience, the past and future in the present; but to say so seems more than a little sad, sadly reductive. Rather, I would note that the enjambment, the scattered verbs without objects, and the place and time nouns enact more than they describe; and that there is a gapped movement, an expressively unfilled gap, between enactment and ideas. In Schoenberg's parable of creative exploration and Babbitt's theoretical response to epistemic instability, a metadiscursive move was required to reconcile theory and practice. Boretz foregoes reconciliation altogether. Rather he treats the theme of ontological instability as a pretext for verbal composition and an opportunity for performance. This yields a particularly taut kind of self-referential exercise, a drastic strategy for purging reified language. Boretz eliminates discursive prose and analytical predicates altogether; he vaporizes music theory, at least below the meta-level. As he put it in an especially taut turn of phrase (one that Dora A. Hanninen has also noticed), "What is about, is also of, also is."[30]

Boretz's approach in "Language, As a Music" could be called "metamusicking." The term, of course, is a play on Christopher Small's already familiar play on words, "musicking,"[31] which Christopher Hasty has cited with admiration. As Hasty has suggested, "'musicking' has entered our lexicon to mark [the] distinction between a substantialized, external form outside the body and an adverbial process of actual and ever changing music-making which is meaningful, embodied, and world revealing."[32] Metamusicking, by extension, would involve self-reflexive, musically enacted descriptions of adverbial musical processes: composed and performed reflections on embodied music making/thinking.

I will say a bit more about Hasty's explicit discussion of "musicking" and his forays into metamusicking below. But first, I should note that Babbitt had an ambivalent, though not-altogether-inimical relationship to this genre. The characteristic hypotaxis of his prose, if not exactly what Hasty means by an adverbial process, nonetheless expresses an irrepressible desire to project musical being in the temporally unfolding syntax of words, and by extension to demonstrate that there are many different ways for music to be.[33] At the same

---

[30] See Boretz, "Language, as a Music," 134 and Dora A. Hanninen, "'What is about is also of, also is', Words, Musical Organization, and Boretz's Language, As a Music Thesis," *Perspectives of New Music* 44 (2006), 14–64.

[31] See Christopher Small, *Musicking: The Meaning of Performing and Listening* (Middlebury, Conn.: Wesleyan University Press, 2008).

[32] Christopher F. Hasty, "If Music Is Ongoing Experience, What Might Music Theory Be? A Suggestion from the Drastic," *ZGMTH Sonderausgabe* (2010), 198.

[33] See my "The Age of Milton" for a discussion of Babbitt's hypotaxis. The hypotaxis of

time, the business end of Babbitt's metatheory, the nuts-and-bolts theoretical principles aimed at locking down the predicative terms of musical qualities, was, if not a repudiation of metamusicking, certainly aimed at gumming up its works. Babbitt doubled down on cognitivity even while affirming ontological pluralism, hedging against semantic vacuity and solipsism, and safeguarding the communal enterprise.

A CHRISTOPHER

I think that Hasty would assent to the short list of disciplinary desiderata that I have just attributed to Babbitt, but for some time now he has been exploring different ways to achieve them. Hasty wants to go further than Babbitt in destabilizing the predicative language of music theory and in asserting the primacy of adverbial processes, but not all the way to Boretz's more radical receptiveness to jettisoning music theory altogether, when the occasion arises. In his recent work, Hasty has reflected explicitly on music theory as an echo and record of his personal experience as a composer, and he has paraphrased a part of the inner dialogue produced by this experience. One form that this self-reflection has taken has been to treat music composition as a kind of performance:

> Let's say you are playing a piece or improvising. You think of, sense, feel, imagine all sorts of things: for instance, you sense your body in all sorts of ways, feel your instrument, value what is happening in light of what has happened and what might. There is no end to the specifics we could think to name. . . .
>
> In our story of playing everything happened so quickly we scarcely had time to notice how it was all happening. To slow things down let's imagine another sort of performance—composing, where we have time to pause and reflect, to make, unmake, and remake. Let's say you've come to a stop and are trying to come up with a continuation . . . .
>
> What is happening in this moment of waiting and in the coming of the next compositional move—or in the faster, less paused coming of the new in our imagined playing of music?[34]

Babbitt's writing was also noted by Scott Burnham in his introductory remarks to a colloquium celebrating the publication of Babbitt's collected writings at Princeton, December, 2004.

[34] Hasty, "If Music Is Ongoing Experience," 207 and 210.

By raising but not resolving questions of extemporaneous creativity in the process of composing, Hasty casts composition as an exercise in self-reflection and transformation in Hadot's and Davidson's sense. As I will suggest in the following, I believe that Hasty's strategy, to reflect on composition as slow performance and an exercise of self-awareness, can be extended to music theory as well.

The uncertain relationship of phenomenal qualities to fixed structures in music has been very much on Hasty's mind. Like Boretz, he finds intense aesthetic and ethical action at the three-way juncture of *about, of,* and *is*— which we might also take to be the juncture of sense and sound. But he is more attached than Boretz to the amenities of discursive prose and traditional musical disciplines. Thus, I propose that we think of him as an exemplar of an under-discussed professional class: a theorist who is interested in sustaining the discipline's traditions while reconsidering its practices in light of the onto-logical and epistemological insecurities of a struggling composer; a (metamu-sicking) theorist-composer who puts self-transformation at the forefront and aims to translate the experience into a disciplinary practice.

In the interest of elaborating his own distinctive rapprochement of mean-ing and being, Hasty finds what may seem an unlikely tool to build a halfway house between Babbitt's scientific language and Boretz's poetic metamusick-ing. When he wants us to change our ways—and he generally does want us to change our ways—his argument often takes a philological turn. Etymology has a subversive authority in his writing. The Latin *per-formare* takes place of pride in his lexicon. It is a condensed homily, a conjuring of the optative mood: no ideas but in things, says William Carlos Williams, but then, Hasty adds, no things but in time.[35] To temporalize things and meanings, Hasty coaxes us to imagine words as performances, both in their origins and use: sounds coalescing phonetically into gestures and qualities, and then merging into syl-lables and roots that sprout a network of sonorous family relations shaping and reflecting experience. When rousing us to subvert music's "fixed, textlike qualities," he invokes the sibling relation between the words "experience" and "experiment," via their irrepressible Latin parent, *experiri,* "to try," and both words' cousinly bond with *periculum,* "danger," via their shared Greek grand-parent, *peira.*[36] He insinuates that this is a corporeal as well as imaginative exercise, implicitly asking us to feel the connections not only ringing in our inner ears but rolling through our mouths, from the unvoiced bilabial plosive,

---

[35] The maxim appears in William Carlos Williams' poem *Paterson* (1927).

[36] Hasty, "If Music Is Ongoing Experience," 198 and 200–201.

"p," to the dropped jaw, unstressed "eh," and on to the rhotic "r," with throat closed and tongue raised: hence *per*, and thence, "experience," "experiment," "peril."

In another example of etymological performance, aimed at repudiating reified language, Hasty hears the English word "term" as a compression of the Latin, *terminus;* and in yet another case listens for an unstable inner voice that links "drama" and "drastic," both outsourced to English from the Greek *dran* (to do and make) and sonorously connected to *drastikos*, which adumbrates an efficacious violence. This to keep us mindful, as he puts it, "of the openness of performing and creating to a novelty that precisely to be new or now cannot be predetermined."[37]

For all his rooting around in the *Ursprache*, however, Hasty is not interested in uncovering a prelapsarian language of pure experience. Nor does he wish to embrace the ineffable; nor start from scratch. He holds no grudge against catechisms, conjugations, or any rote learning, so long as the exercise produces useful, fluent, and, eventually, at least for the most part, tacit knowledge. Rather, as he forthrightly informs, "My motive in all this etymology is to use largely forgotten traces of process as a way of hearing something more in these words so that they might work freshly as tools for thinking about process."[38] He explicitly links this something more heard in words to the patterns imminent in their etymological affinities. These comprise not only an ethics (for example, by strengthening the bond between making and risking), but also an enactment. Philology reanimates musical thought by unveiling the verb forms, infinitives, and gerunds underlying the denotative functions of nouns and adjectives.

We might even imagine a sign language or Dalcroze method for performing the infinitives of Hasty's metamusical keywords. For example, if we hear with etymologically attuned ears, the closing participle in his phrase a "novelty that precisely to be new or now cannot be predetermined," may spark an internal mini-drama. *Pre-determined*: a coming to a term, marking off of a boundary, arriving at a "terminus," and even more, an arriving too soon, a pre-terminus. I will leave it to you to imagine the scene and the mime.

Rather, I am going to suggest one more etymological association, inspired by an image of John Dewey's, one that both Hasty and Jeanne Bamberger have noticed and admired: "Events when once they are named," Dewey suggested, "lead an independent and double life. . . . Meanings having been deflected

---

[37] Ibid., 201.
[38] Ibid.

from the rapid and roaring stream of events into a calm and traversable canal, rejoin the main stream, and color, temper and compose its course."[39] Dewey's image of a rapid and roaring stream explicitly treats Schoenberg's well-worn path from ineffable experiences to quantized structures as a hyperactive, insecure site. The work of the metamusicking theorist-composer, an ongoing exercise of self-transformation, is to dwell in this site rather than lounging in the calm and traversable canal of stable meanings. Thus, the metamusicking theorist is a Christopher, who (like his saintly, eponymous namesake) not only carries people back and forth to the shores on either side of the roaring rapids but also personifies and validates the activity of laboring in the stream. Playing with this conceit, we might call the two shores gnostic and drastic. Or mind and body; or cognitivity and ineffability. In any case, the point is to locate and dwell in the space between.

But after we leap into the stream, what next? How might we convert a theorist-composer's ongoing self-transformation into a paradigm for a communal practice or academic discipline? This is a central question for Hasty. He calls it forthrightly in the title of a recent article, already introduced above: "If Music Is Ongoing Experience, Then What Might Music Theory Be?"[40] There, he offers three fundamental terms for a music theoretical response to this radical question: *duration*, *particularity*, and *indeterminacy*. Hasty urges us to foster a heightened awareness of the unrepeatability of events in time, describing the experience of duration as process (an "adventure of becoming"), but he pointedly abjures fixed agendas.

I want to add a metadiscursive term to his nomenclature of phenomenological alertness and epistemological humility, what Giorgio Agamben has called "exposure":

> Whereas real predicates express relationships within language, exposure is pure relationship with language itself, with its taking-place. It is what happens to something (or more precisely, to the taking-place of something) by the very fact of being in relation to language, the fact of being-called. A thing is (called) red and by virtue of this,

---

[39] John Dewey, *The Later Works of John Dewey*, vol. 1, 1925, *Experience and Nature*, ed. Jo Ann Boydston (Carbondale: Southern Illinois University Press, 1983), 132–33. Quoted in Jeanne Bamberger, "The Collaborative Invention of Meaning: A Short History of Evolving Ideas," *Psychology of Music* 39 (2011), 82–101, and Christopher F. Hasty, "Learning in Time," *Visions of Research in Education* 20 (2012), http://www.usr.rider.edu/~vrme/v20n1/visions/Hasty%20Bamberger.pdf , accessed June 16, 2014.

[40] See Hasty, "If Music is Ongoing Experience," 208–10.

insofar as it is *called* such and refers to itself as *such* (not simply as red), it is exposed. Existence as exposure is the being-*as* of a *such*. (The category of *suchness* is, in this sense, the fundamental category that remains unthought in every quality.)[41]

Considering music theory as an exercise in exposure, we might think of musical analysis as nothing else but performance measured in one direction. And we might define music theory very broadly, as any symbolic or linguistic work that alerts us to the suchness of musical experiences. I ask that we consider the open-endedness of this definition as a good thing. What would bind us together as a musical community, then, would not be law and order, God, country, Schenker, or set theory, however useful any of these might be, but what Agamben calls "a solidarity that in no way concerns an essence," a solidarity in the project of communicating about singularities. As Agamben elaborated, "*the communication of singularities . . . does not unite them in essence, but scatters them in existence.*"[42] I take it that the willful surrender of epistemic authority inherent in Agamben's "solidarity" is at the heart of Hasty's enterprise. What is lost in authority would be counterbalanced by a gain in the exposure and the amplification of individuality.

THE ALMIGHTY'S GIFT

By the time of his late essays on twelve-tone music, Schoenberg seemed to back away from the futuristic fantasy of tone color proposed in the *Harmonielehre*, even while he returned to his discussion of the flickering sensations of the tone to justify the emergence of the twelve-tone method. With the full emancipation of the dissonance achieved, the historical process of extracting dissonances from their origins in the vibrations of the standing wave would, perforce, be a *fait accompli*. Henceforth, the grammar of musical composition would derive from the closed group of the class of pitches, rather than from contemplating the pitch/color symbiosis inherent in the tone. "Justified already by historical development," he declared, "the method of composing with twelve tones is also not without aesthetic and theoretical support. On the contrary, it is just this support which advances it from a mere technical device to the rank and importance of a scientific theory."[43] The patriarch of twelve-tone music thus ordained that reason would prevail.

[41] Giorgio Agamben, *The Coming Community*, trans. Michael Hardt (Minneapolis: University of Minnesota Press, 1993), 96–97. Italics in original.

[42] Agamben, *The Coming Community*, 18. Italics in original.

[43] Schoenberg, "Composition With Twelve Tones," 220.

Nonetheless, the master still strove to keep the subconscious in play in his understanding of aesthetic experience. He now discovered it at work in the rehabilitation of long forms with solid pitch structures, rather than in a futuristic fantasy of tone color melodies. His early compositional experiments, he professed, "forced us to counterbalance extreme emotionality with extraordinary shortness . . . . New colourful harmony was offered; but much was lost." By contrast, "[t]he possibilities of evolving the formal elements of music—melodies, themes, phrases, figures, and chords—out of a basic set are unlimited."[44] In turn, the unlimited potentiality of the basic set held the promise of stimulating the composer's unconscious creativity and lifting him beyond the earthly plane. As he put it in "My Evolution," an essay written some four decades after the *Harmonielehre*, his belated discovery of an occluded pitch structural relationship locked inside two contrasting and temporally remote themes from his own *Kammersymphonie* was providential, a sign of divine largesse:

> This is also the place to speak of the miraculous contributions of the subconscious. I am convinced that in the works of the great masters many miracles can be discovered, the extreme profundity and prophetic foresight of which seem superhuman. In all modesty, I will quote here one example from the *Kammersymphonie* . . . solely in order to illustrate the power behind the human mind, which produces miracles for which we do not deserve credit. . . .
>
> What I believe, in fact, is that if one has done his duty with the utmost sincerity and has worked out everything as near to perfection as he is capable of doing, then the Almighty presents him with a gift.[45]

Schoenberg makes it clear that the Almighty's gift, even if it appeared in the guise of solid forms (organized pitches and pitch classes, motives, and basic shapes) rather than in a fantasy of evanescent tone color, was still addressed to, and would be received in, the artist's subconscious. The inexhaustible possibilities inherent in the basic set thus constituted a kind of mathematical sublime, a new horizon of ineffability to replace acute listening to the sensations of the tone in sparking a dialectic of cognition and indeterminacy.

My point is not to propose that Schoenberg was the once and future godfather of spectralism, or that phenomenology and secularism are good and

[44] Ibid., 226.
[45] Schoenberg, "My Evolution," *Musical Quarterly* 75/4 (1991), 150–1. (Reprinted from *Musical Quarterly* 38/4 [1952], 517–27).

structuralism and religion are bad, or vice versa—but rather to stress that this consummately ambitious composer, both in his early and late years, understood the Supreme Commander's gifts to be few and far between. Even in his final pronouncements on the topic, Schoenberg insisted that these divine gifts were still received in a largely occluded place, the subconscious. The struggle to access this place still produced provisional results. Even as Schoenberg stabilized his ontology of musical elements to explain the full course of his artistic evolution, he found another horizon of uncertainty and potentiality to chase.

I would like to give Carl Dahlhaus the penultimate word in this celebration of indeterminacy, by recalling a beautiful reflection on the difficulty of understanding Schoenberg's artistic development:

> The fact remains—and to have to admit this is rather difficult for a historian—that it is, strictly speaking, impossible to give a reason for Schoenberg's decision of 1907 . . . the theories with which Schoenberg attempted to justify the emancipation of the dissonance are characterised by a helplessness which prevents us from taking them at their word as being motives for compositional decisions. The same holds true, a decade and a half later, for the step to "composition with twelve notes related only to one another."[46]

To which the young Schoenberg might have replied: exactly. "It is of little consequence if one starts with a correct hypothesis or a false one."[47] We need not concur with him altogether to affirm a corollary—the subordination of explanation to experience—and (joining Hasty) to recall the etymology of explanation (*explanare*: to level or smooth out) to suggest that our descriptions of music should serve not to smooth out, not to *explain*, performance, but rather to *emulate* (rival, equal) it.

---

[46] Dahlhaus, "Schoenberg's Aesthetic Theology," in *Schoenberg and the New Music*, trans. Derrick Puffett and Alfred Clayton (Cambridge: Cambridge University Press, 1987), 88.

[47] Schoenberg, *Theory of Harmony*, 19.

Notes on Contributors
Bibliography
General Index

Notes on Contributors

JEANNE BAMBERGER is emerita Professor of Music and Urban Education, Massachusetts Institute of Technology, and currently Adjunct Professor, Department of Music, University of California at Berkeley. She was a student of Artur Schnabel and Roger Sessions and has performed in the US and Europe as piano soloist and in chamber music ensembles. Bamberger attended Columbia University and the University of California at Berkeley, receiving degrees in philosophy and music theory. Her most recent books include *The Mind Behind the Musical Ear* (Harvard University Press, 1995), *Developing Musical Intuitions: A Project Based Introduction to Making and Understanding Music* (Oxford University Press, 2000), and *Discovering the Musical Mind: A View of Creativity as Learning* (Oxford University Press, 2013).

STEPHEN BLUM founded the doctoral concentration in ethnomusicology at the City University of New York Graduate Center, and taught there from fall 1987 through spring 2016. He is consulting editor for music of the *Encyclopaedia Iranica* and the author of "Central Asia," "Composition," and "Iran, Regional and Popular Traditions" in *The New Grove Dictionary of Music and Musicians,* second edition. He also contributed chapters to the three volumes of *The Garland Encyclopedia of World Music* devoted to the United States and Canada, the Middle East, and Europe. With Christopher Hasty and Richard Wolf, he is currently editing a collection of essays on *Thought and Play in Musical Rhythm: Perspectives from Africa, Asia, and Euro-America.*

MARTIN BRODY is Catherine Mills Davis Professor of Music at Wellesley College, where he has been on the faculty since 1979. He has also served as Fromm Composer-in-Residence at the American Academy in Rome in 2001, Fromm Resident at the William Walton Estate in Ischia (2004), and Roger Sessions Memorial Fellow in Music at the Liguria Arts and Humanities Center in Bogliasco (2006). Brody was Heiskell Arts Director at the American Academy in Rome from 2007–2010. He has written extensively on contemporary music, serves on the editorial board of *Perspectives of New Music,* and is a contributing editor of *The Open Space Magazine.*

SCOTT BURNHAM is the Scheide Professor of Music History at Princeton University, where he has taught since 1989. Burnham holds degrees in music composition and music theory from Baldwin-Wallace College (BM), Yale University

(MM), and Brandeis University (PhD). His best-known book is *Beethoven Hero* (Princeton University Press, 1995), a study of the values and reception of Beethoven's heroic-style music. His most recent book, *Mozart's Grace* (Princeton University Press, 2013), explores aspects of beauty in Mozart's music and was winner of the Otto Kinkeldey Award from the American Musicological Society in 2014.

MATTHEW BUTTERFIELD is Associate Professor of Music at Franklin & Marshall College. He specializes in American music, particularly jazz and blues. Trained as a jazz pianist, he earned a PhD in music theory from the University of Pennsylvania in 2000. His work has been published in *Music Perception, Music Theory Online, Jazz Research Journal, Music Analysis, Current Musicology, Jazz Perspectives,* and *Music Theory Spectrum.* His current research concerns the history of the term "swing" in relation to African American music and the process of its racialization over the course of the early twentieth century.

NICHOLAS COOK is 1684 Professor of Music at the University of Cambridge. Author of *Music: A Very Short Introduction* (Oxford University Press, 2000), which has been translated into fifteen languages, and *The Schenker Project: Culture, Race, and Music Theory in Fin-de-siècle Vienna* (Oxford University Press, 2007), which won the Society for Music Theory's 2010 Wallace Berry Prize, his latest book is *Beyond the Score: Music as Performance* (Oxford University Press, 2013). In 2014 he took up a British Academy Wolfson Research Professorship, working on a project entitled "Musical Encounters: Studies in Relational Musicology."

BRIAN HULSE is Associate Professor of Composition and Theory at the College of William & Mary. He is a composer and philosopher working primarily on the potential musical extensions of the writings of Gilles Deleuze and Henri Bergson. He has published articles and given papers on topics ranging from musical repetition to improvisation to theories of temporality. With Nick Nesbitt he co-edited the volume *Sounding the Virtual: Gilles Deleuze and the Theory and Philosophy of Music* (Ashgate, 2010) in which he penned the chapter "Thinking Musical Difference: Music Theory as Minor Science." Hulse's compositions are recorded on the Albany (*Stain*) and Centaur (*pseudosynthesis*) labels.

SUSAN MCCLARY is Professor of Music at Case Western Reserve University; she has also taught at the University of Minnesota, McGill University, and UCLA. Her research focuses on the cultural analysis of music, both the European canon and contemporary popular genres. Best known for her book *Feminine Endings: Music, Gender, and Sexuality* (University of Minnesota Press, 1991), she is also author of *Georges Bizet: Carmen* (Cambridge University Press, 1992), *Conventional Wisdom: The Content of Musical Form* (University of California Press, 2000), *Modal Subjectivities: Renaissance Self-Fashioning in the Italian Madrigal*

(University of California Press, 2004), which won the Otto Kinkeldey Award from the American Musicological Society in 2005, *Desire and Pleasure in Seventeenth-Century Music*, and *Structures of Feeling in Seventeenth-Century Expressive Culture* (University of California Press, 2012). McClary received a MacArthur Foundation Fellowship in 1995.

EUGENE MONTAGUE is Assistant Professor of Music at The George Washington University. His research focuses on issues of musical performance, including the interactions between instrumental gestures and musical meaning and questions of agency in performance. He received his PhD from the University of Pennsylvania, studying with Christopher Hasty, Eugene Narmour, and Cristle Collins Judd. Recent publications include essays on the pleasure of playing in Ligeti's "Touches bloquées," on instrumental gesture in Debussy's "La terrasse des audiences du clair de lune," and on the relationships between agency and creativity in musical performance.

ROBERT MORRIS is Professor of Composition at the Eastman School of Music, University of Rochester since 1980, where he has chaired the composition department and served as an affiliate faculty member of the music theory and musicology departments; he has also taught at the University of Pittsburgh, Yale, and the University of Hawaii. Composer of over 180 compositions and author of over 60 articles and books in music theory, composition, and Indian music, Morris was the recipient of the Outstanding Publication Award of the Society for Music Theory in 1988 for his book, *Composition with Pitch-Classes: A Theory of Compositional Design* (Yale University Press, 1987). His most recent book is *The Whistling Blackbird: Essays and Talks on New Music*, (University of Rochester Press, 2010). Morris is presently co-editor of *Perspectives of New Music* and contributing editor of *The Open Space Magazine*.

EUGENE NARMOUR is Kahn Distinguished Professor of Music (emeritus) at the University of Pennsylvania where he conducted the university orchestra, served as Dean of Humanities and Social Sciences, and helped found the Penn Humanities Forum. He received from the Eastman School of Music a Performer's Certificate in 1961 and its Alumni Achievement Award in 2006. He is the author of *Beyond Schenkerism* (University of Chicago Press, 1980), *The Analysis and Cognition of Basic Melodic Structures* (University of Chicago Press, 1990), and *The Analysis and Cognition of Melodic Complexity* (University of Chicago Press, 1992) as well as some two dozen articles. Together with Ruth Solie, he co-edited *Explorations in Music, the Arts and Ideas* (essays for Leonard B. Meyer, Pendragon Press, 1989). He served as President of SMPC, and in 2011 the society honored him with its highest Achievement Award. A Festschrift, *Musical Implications*, was published in 2013 (Lawrence Bernstein and Alexander Rosner, eds.). In 2014 the Journal *Music Perception* hosted a conference at McGill entitled "Milestones in

Music Cognition," which celebrated *ACMS* as one of the most important works in the field of music cognition over the past 25 years.

JANET SCHMALFELDT has taught at McGill University and at Yale, where she was awarded the Clauss Prize for Excellency in Teaching in 1993; she joined the Music Department at Tufts University in 1995. She is the author of a book on Alban Berg's *Wozzeck* (Yale University Press, 1983) and has published widely on late eighteenth- and early nineteenth-century music. Her *In the Process of Becoming: Analytic and Philosophical Perspectives on Form in Early Nineteenth-Century Music* (Oxford University Press, 2011) received a 2012 ASCAP – Deems Taylor Award and the 2012 Wallace Berry Award from the Society for Music Theory. She has served as President of the New England Conference of Music Theorists and as President of the Society for Music Theory. Her performances as pianist have included chamber, concerto, and solo music.

LAWRENCE M. ZBIKOWSKI is Associate Professor in the Department of Music at the University of Chicago, where he has served as chair of the Department and as Deputy Provost for the Arts. He is the author of *Conceptualizing Music: Cognitive Structure, Theory, and Analysis* (Oxford University Press 2002) and *Toward a Cognitive Grammar of Music* (forthcoming). He recently contributed chapters to *Music, Analysis, Experience*; the *Oxford Handbook of Topic Theory*; *Speaking of Music*; *Bewegungen zwischen Hören und Sehen*; *New Perspectives on Music and Gesture*; and *Music and Consciousness*. He has also published articles and reviews in *Music Analysis, Music Humana, Musicæ Scientiæ, Music Theory Spectrum, Ethnomusicology*, the *Journal of Musicological Research*, and the *Dutch Journal of Music Theory*. During the 2010–11 academic year he held a fellowship from the American Council of Learned Societies and was also Fulbright Visiting Research Chair at McGill University.

Bibliography

Abbate, Carolyn. "Music—Drastic or Gnostic?" *Critical Inquiry* 30/3 (2002), 505–36.

Adlard, Emma. "Interior Time: Debussy, *Fêtes galantes*, and the Salon of Marguerite de Saint-Marceaux." *Musical Quarterly* 96/2 (2013), 178–218.

Adorno, Theodor W. "Bach Defended against his Devotees." In *Prisms*, translated by Samuel and Shierry Weber, 133–146. Cambridge, Mass.: MIT Press, 1981.

———. *Essays on Music.* Edited by Richard Leppert. Berkeley and Los Angeles: University of California Press, 2002.

———. *Gesammelte Schriften*, vol. 19. Edited by Rolf Tiedemann et al. Frankfurt: Suhrkamp, 1984.

———. *Towards a Theory of Musical Reproduction.* Edited by Henry Lonitz and translated by Wieland Hoban. Cambridge: Polity Press, 2006.

Agamben, Giorgio. *The Coming Community.* Translated by Michael Hardt. Minneapolis: University of Minnesota Press, 1993.

Allanbrook, Wye Jamison. *Rhythmic Gesture in Mozart*: Le Nozze di Figaro *and* Don Giovanni. Chicago: University of Chicago Press, 1983.

Anonymous. *Literary Digest.* "The Appeal of the Primitive Jazz." August 25, 1917, 28.

Aristotle. *Physics.* Translated by R. P. Hardie and R. K. Gaye. Chicago: Encyclopedia Britannica, Inc., 1952.

Arom, Simha. "La 'mémoire collective' dans les musiques traditionnelles d'Afrique centrale." *Revue de Musicologie* 76/2 (1990), 149–61.

Attali, Jacques. *Noise: The Political Economy of Music.* Translated by Brian Massumi. Minneapolis: University of Minnesota Press, 1985.

Babbitt, Milton. "Past and Present Concepts of the Nature and Limits of Music." In *The Collected Essays of Milton Babbitt*, edited by Stephen Peles, 78–85. Princeton: Princeton University Press, 2003.

———. "The Structure and Function of Musical Theory." In *The Collected Essays of Milton Babbitt*, edited by Stephen Peles, 191–201. Princeton: Princeton University Press, 2003.

———. "Twelve-Tone Invariants as a Compositional Determinant." In *The Collected Essays of Milton Babbitt*, edited by Stephen Peles, 55–69. Princeton: Princeton University Press, 2003.

——. "Twelve-Tone Rhythmic Structure and the Electronic Medium." In *The Collected Essays of Milton Babbitt*, edited by Stephen Peles, 109–140. Princeton: Princeton University Press, 2003.

——. *Words About Music*. Edited by Stephen Dembski and Joseph N. Straus. Madison, Wisc.: University of Wisconsin Press, 1987.

Baddeley, Alan. *Working Memory, Thought, and Action*. Oxford: Oxford University Press, 2007.

Bamberger, Jeanne. "Growing Up Prodigies: The Midlife Crisis." In *Developmental Approaches to Giftedness*, edited by David Henry Feldman. San Francisco: Jossey-Bass, 1982.

——. "The Collaborative Invention of Meaning: A Short History of Evolving Ideas." *Psychology of Music* 39/1 (2011), 82–101.

——. *Discovering the Musical Mind*. Oxford: Oxford University Press, 2013.

——. *The Mind Behind the Musical Ear*. Cambridge, Mass.: Harvard University Press, 1991.

Berger, Harris M. "The Practice of Perception: Multi-functionality and Time in the Musical Experience of a Heavy Metal Drummer." *Ethnomusicology* 41/3 (1997), 464–488.

——. "Theory and Practice 8: Contemporary Ethnomusicology in Theory and Practice." *SEM Newsletter* 47/4 (2013), 5.

——. *Metal, Rock, and Jazz: Perception and the Phenomenology of Musical Experience*. Hanover, NH: University Press of New England for Wesleyan University Press, 1999.

——. *Stance: Ideas about Emotion, Style, and Meaning for the Study of Expressive Culture*. Middletown, Conn.: Wesleyan University Press.

Berger, Karol. *Bach's Cycle, Mozart's Arrow: An Essay on the Origins of Musical Modernity*. Berkeley and Los Angeles: University of California Press, 2007.

Berliner, Paul F. *Thinking in Jazz: The Infinite Art of Improvisation*. Chicago: University of Chicago Press, 1994.

Bernstein, Lawrence F., and Alexander Rozin, eds. *Musical Implications: Essays in Honor of Eugene Narmour*. Hillsdale, NY: Pendragon Press, 2013.

Blasius, Leslie David. *Schenker's Argument and the Claims of Music Theory*. Cambridge: Cambridge University Press, 1999.

Bluedorn, Allen C. *The Human Organization of Time: Temporal Realities and Experience*. Stanford: Stanford University Press, 2002.

Blum, David. *The Art of Quartet Playing: The Guarneri Quartet in Conversation with David Blum*. New York: Alfred A. Knopf, 1986.

Blum, Stephen. "Modes of Theorizing in Iranian Khorasan." In *Theorizing the Local: Music, Practice, and Experience in South Asia and Beyond*, edited by Richard K. Wolf, 207–224. Oxford: Oxford University Press, 2009.

Boehm, Rudolf. "Einleitung des Herausgebers." In *Husserliana: Gesammelte Werke*, vol. 10, edited by Rudolf Boehm. The Hague: Nijhoff, 1966.

Boretz, Benjamin. "Language, as a Music: Six Marginal Pretexts for Composition." *Perspectives of New Music* 17/2 (1979), 131–95.

Boring, Edwin G. *A History of Experimental Psychology*. New York: Appleton-Century-Crofts, 1950.

Brée, Malwine. *The Groundwork of the Leschetizky Method: Issued with his Approval*. Translated by T. Baker. New York: G. Schirmer, 1902.

Brinkmann, Reinhold. "In the Time(s) of the 'Eroica.'" In *Beethoven and His World*, edited by Scott Burnham and Michael Steinberg, 1–26. Princeton: Princeton University Press, 2000.

Brody, Martin. "'Music for the Masses': Milton Babbitt's Cold War Music Theory." *Musical Quarterly* 77/2 (1993), 161–92.

———. "The Age of Milton." *Perspectives of New Music* 49/2 (2012), 365–71.

Brown, Warner. *Time in English Verse Rhythm: An Empirical Study of Typical Verses by the Graphic Method*. New York: The Science Press, 1908.

Buder, Eugene H. "The Representation and Cognition of Rhythm." Unpublished Senior Thesis, Harvard College, 1980.

Buhler, James, and David Neumeyer. "Music and the Ontology of the Sound Film: The Classical Hollywood System." In *The Oxford Handbook of Film Music Studies*, edited by David Neumeyer, 17–43. Oxford: Oxford University Press, 2014.

Buhler, James. "Wagnerian Motives: Narrative Integration and the Development of Silent Film Accompaniment, 1908–1913." In *Wagner & Cinema*, edited by Jeongwon Joe and Sander L. Gilman, 27–45. Bloomington: Indiana University Press, 2010.

Butt, John. *Bach's Dialogue with Modernity: Perspectives on the Passions*. Cambridge: Cambridge University Press, 2010.

Butterfield, Matthew. "Participatory Discrepancies and the Perception of Beats in Jazz." *Music Perception* 27/3 (2010), 157–76.

———. "Race and Rhythm: The Social Component of the Swing Groove." *Jazz Perspectives* 4/3 (2010), 301–55.

———. "The Power of Anacrusis: Engendered Feeling in Groove-Based Musics." *Music Theory Online* 12/4 (2006). http://www.mtosmt.org/issues/mto.06.12.4/mto.06.12.4.butterfield.html.

———. "Why Do Jazz Musicians Swing Their Eighth Notes?" *Music Theory Spectrum* 33/1 (2011), 3–26.

Cage, John. *Silence: Lectures and Writings*. Middletown, Conn.: Wesleyan University Press, 1961.

Campbell, Joseph, ed. *Man and Time: Papers from the Eranos Yearbooks*. New York: Bollingen, 1957.

Carroll, Lewis. *Alice's Adventures in Wonderland and Through the Looking Glass*. New York: Penguin, 1960.

Chamblee, Catherine. "Didactic Performance: Cognitive Processes of Improvisation in Contemporary Gospel Solo Singing." In *Musical Implications: Essays in Honor of Eugene Narmour*, edited by Lawrence F. Bernstein and Alexander Rozin, 73–98. Hillsdale, New York: Pendragon Press, 2013.

Chanan, Michael. *Repeated Takes: A Short History of Recording and its Effects on Music*. London: Verso, 1995.

Clark, Suzannah. *Analyzing Schubert*. Cambridge: Cambridge University Press, 2011.

Clarke, E. F. "Expression and Communication in Musical Performance." In *Music, Language, Speech and Brain*, edited by Johan Sundberg, Lennart Nord, and Rolf Carlson, 184–93. London: Macmillan, 1991.

———. "Generative Principles in Music Performance." In *Generative Processes in Music*, edited by John A. Sloboda, 1–26. Oxford: Clarendon Press, 1988.

———. "Levels of Structure in the Organization of Musical Time." *Contemporary Music Review* 2/1 (1987), 211–38.

———. "Listening to Performance." In *Musical Performance: A Guide to Understanding*, edited by John Rink, 185–196. Cambridge: Cambridge University Press, 2002.

———. "Structure and Expression in Rhythmic Performance." In *Musical Structure and Cognition*, edited by Peter Howell, Ian Cross, and Robert West, 209–36. London: Academic Press, 1985.

———. "The Perception of Expressive Timing in Music." *Psychological Research* 51/1 (1989), 2–9.

Clayton, Martin. "What is Entrainment? Definition and Applications in Musical Research." *Empirical Musicology Review* 7/1–2 (2012), 49–56.

Clayton, Nicola S., and Anthony Dickinson. "Mental Time Travel: Can Animals Recall the Past and Plan for the Future?" In *Encyclopedia of Animal Behavior*, edited by Michael D. Breed and Janice Moore, 438–42. Amsterdam: Elsevier B.V., 2010.

Collier, Geoffrey L., and James Lincoln Collier. "Introduction." *Music Perception* 19/3 (2002), 157–75.

Connerton, Paul. *How Societies Remember*. Cambridge: Cambridge University Press, 1989.

Cook, Nicholas. "Epistemologies of Music Theory." In *The Cambridge History of Western Music Theory*, edited by Thomas Christensen, 78–105. Cambridge: Cambridge University Press, 2002.

———. *Analysing Musical Multimedia*. Oxford: Oxford University Press, 1998.

———. *Beyond the Score: Music as Performance*. Oxford: Oxford University Press, 2013.

———. *The Schenker Project: Culture, Race, and Music Theory in Fin-de-siècle Vienna*. Oxford: Oxford University Press, 2007.

Cook, Will Marion. *Swing Along*. New York: G. Schirmer, 1912.

Cowan, Nelson. "The Magical Number 4 in Short-Term Memory: A Reconsideration of Mental Storage Capacity." *Behavioral and Brain Sciences* 24/1 (2001), 87–185.

———. *Working Memory Capacity*. New York: Psychology Press, 2005.

Cramer, Alfred. "Moments of Attention: Function, Coherence, and Unusual Sounds in Works by Anton Webern and Richard Rodgers." In *Musical Implications: Essays in Honor of Eugene Narmour*, edited by Lawrence F. Bernstein and Alexander Rozin, 99–130. Hillsdale, NY: Pendragon Press, 2013.

Cross, Ian. "Listening as Covert Performance." *Journal of the Royal Musical Association* 135/1 (2010), 67–77.

Dahlhaus, Carl. "Schoenberg and Schenker." *Proceedings of the Royal Musical Association* 100/1 (1973), 209–15.

———. "Schoenberg's Aesthetic Theology." In *Schoenberg and the New Music*, translated by Derrick Puffett and Alfred Clayton, 81–93. Cambridge: Cambridge University Press, 1987.

———. *Esthetics of Music*. Translated by William W. Austin. Cambridge: Cambridge University Press, 1982.

Damasio, Antonio R. *Looking for Spinoza: Joy, Sorrow, and the Feeling Brain*. Orlando, Fla.: Harcourt Inc., 2003.

———. *The Feeling of What Happens: Body and Emotion in the Making of Consciousness*. New York: Harcourt Brace & Company, 1999.

Daverio, John. *Crossing Paths: Schubert, Schumann, and Brahms*. Oxford: Oxford University Press, 2002.

———. *Robert Schumann: Herald of a "New Poetic Age."* Oxford: Oxford University Press, 1997.

Davidson, Arnold I. "Ethics as Ascetics: Foucault, the History of Ethics, and Ancient Thought." In *The Cambridge Companion to Foucault,* edited by Garry Gutting, 123–48. Cambridge: Cambridge University Press, 2005.

———. Introduction to "Pierre Hadot and the Spiritual Phenomenon of Ancient Philosophy," by Pierre Hadot. In *Philosophy as a Way of Life: Spiritual Exercises from Socrates to Foucault,* edited by Arnold I. Davidson and translated by Michael Chase, 1–45. Oxford: Blackwell, 1995.

Dean, Roger T., et al. "The Pulse of Symmetry: On the Possible Co-Evolution of Rhythm in Music and Dance." *Musicae Scientiae* 13 Special Issue (2009–2010), 341–67.

Deleuze, Gilles, and Félix Guattari. *A Thousand Plateaus: Capitalism and Schizophrenia.* Translated by Brian Massumi. Minneapolis: University of Minnesota Press, 1987.

Deleuze, Gilles. *Bergsonism.* Translated by Hugh Tomlinson and Barbara Habberjam. New York: Zone Books, 1991.

———. *Cinema I: The Movement Image.* Translated by Hugh Tomlinson and Barbara Habberjam. London: Athlone Press, 1992.

———. *Cinema II: The Time-Image.* Translated by Hugh Tomlinson and Roberta Galeta. Minneapolis: University of Minnesota Press, 1989.

———. *Difference and Repetition.* Translated by Paul Patton. New York: Columbia University Press, 1995.

Derrida, Jacques. *Monolingualism of the Other; Or, the Prosthesis of Origin.* Translated by Patrick Mensah. Stanford: Stanford University Press, 1998.

Dewey, John. *Experience and Nature.* New York: Dover, 1958.

Dibben, Mark, and Thomas Kelly, eds. *Applied Process Thought I: Initial Explorations in Theory and Research.* Berlin: Walter de Gruyter & Co, 2008.

Dowling, Jay W. "Pitch Structure." In *Representing Musical Structure,* edited by Peter Howell, Robert West, and Ian Cross, 33–57. London: Academic Press, 1991.

Drake, Carolyn, and Caroline Palmer. "Accent Structures in Music Performance." *Music Perception* 10/3 (1993), 343–78.

Drake, Carolyn. "Perceptual and Performed Accents in Musical Sequences." *Bulletin of the Psychonomic Society* 31/2 (1993), 107–10.

Eacott, Madeline J., and Alexander Easton. "Remembering the Past and Thinking About the Future: Is It Really About Time?" *Learning and Motivation* 43/4 (2012), 200–208.

Edelman, Gerald M. *Bright Air, Brilliant Fire: On the Matter of Mind.* New York: Basic Books, 1992.

———. *Second Nature: Brain Science and Human Knowledge*. New Haven: Yale University Press, 2006.

———. *The Remembered Present: A Biological Theory of Consciousness*. New York: Basic Books, 1989.

Ellis, Catherine J. "Time Consciousness of Aboriginal Performers." In *Problems and Solutions: Occasional Essays in Musicology Presented to Alice M. Moyle*, edited by Jamie C. Kassler and Jill Stubington, 149–85. Sydney: Hale and Iremonger, 1984.

Erlmann, Veit. *Reason and Resonance: A History of Modern Aurality*. New York: Zone Books, 2010.

Everett, Walter. *The Beatles as Musicians: The Quarry Men Through* Rubber Soul. Oxford: Oxford University Press, 2001.

Federhofer, Hellmut, ed. *Heinrich Schenker als Essayist und Kritiker: Gesammelte Aufsätze, Rezensionen und kleinere Berichte aus den Jahren 1891–1901*. Hildesheim: Georg Olms Verlag, 1990.

Feldman, Morton. " . . . Out of 'Last Pieces.'" In *Give My Regards to Eighth Street: Collected Writings of Morton Feldman*, edited by B. H. Friedman. Cambridge, Mass.: Exact Change, 2000.

Fitch, W. Tecumseh. "Rhythmic Cognition in Humans and Animals: Distinguishing Meter and Pulse Perception." *Frontiers in Systems Neuroscience* 7/68 (2013), 1–16.

Foucault, Michel. *Discipline and Punish: The Birth of the Prison*. Translated by Alan Sheridan. New York: Vintage Books, 1977.

Fraisse, Paul. *The Psychology of Time*. Translated by Jennifer Leith. London: Eyre & Spottiswoode, 1964.

Friberg, Anders, and Giovanni Umberto Battel. "Structural Communication." In *The Science and Psychology of Music Performance,* edited by Richard Parncutt and Gary E. McPherson, 199–218. Oxford: Oxford University Press, 2002.

Fujita, Takanori. "Structure and Rhythm in *nō*: An Introduction." In *The Oral and the Literate in Music*, edited by Yosihiko Tokumaru and Osamu Yamaguti, 88–95. Tokyo: Academia Music, 1986.

Gabrielsson, Alf. "Once Again: The Theme from Mozart's Piano Sonata in A major (K. 331): A Comparison of Performances." In *Action and Perception in Rhythm and Music,* edited by Alf Gabrielsson, 81–103. Stockholm: Royal Swedish Academy of Music, 1987.

Gafijczuk, Dariusz. *Identity, Aesthetics, and Sound in the Fin-de-Siècle: Redesigning Perception*. London: Routledge, 2014.

Geertz, Clifford. *The Interpretation of Culture*. New York: Basic Books, 1973.

Gell, Alfred. *The Anthropology of Time: Cultural Constructions of Temporal Maps and Images*. Oxford: Berg, 1992.

Gentner, Dedre, et al. "As Time Goes By: Evidence for Two Systems in Processing Space-Time Metaphors." *Language and Cognitive Processes* 17/5 (2002), 537–65.

Giedion, Sigfried. *Space, Time and Architecture: The Growth of a New Tradition*. Cambridge, Mass: Harvard University Press, 1974.

Gingerich, John M. *Schubert's Beethoven Project*. Cambridge: Cambridge University Press, 2014.

Goehr, Lydia. "*Doppelbewegung*: The Musical Movement of Philosophy and the Philosophical Movement of Music." In *Sound Figures of Modernity: German Music and Philosophy*, edited by Jost Hermand and Gerhard Richter, 19–63. Madison, Wisc.: University of Wisconsin Press, 2006.

Goodman, Nelson. *Languages of Art: An Approach to a Theory of Symbols*. Indianapolis: Bobbs-Merrill, 1968.

Gorbman, Claudia. *Unheard Melodies: Narrative Film Music*. Bloomington: Indiana University Press, 1987.

Gotlieb, Heidi, and Vladimir J. Konečni. "The Effects of Instrumentation, Playing Style, and Structure in the Goldberg Variations by Johann Sebastian Bach." *Music Perception* 3/1 (1985), 87–102.

Gülke, Peter. "Zum Bilde des späten Schubert: Vorwiegend analytische Betrachtungen zum Streichquintett op. 163." *Musik-Konzepte Sonderband: Franz Schubert* (1979), 5–58.

Halbwachs, Maurice. "La mémoire collective chez les musiciens." *In La mémoire collective: Édition critique*, edited by Gérard Namier, 19–50. Paris: Albin Michel, 1997.

Hamilton, Kenneth. *After the Golden Age: Romantic Pianism and Modern Performance*. Oxford: Oxford University Press, 2007.

Hanninen, Dora A. "'What is about is also of, also is,' Words, Musical Organization, and Boretz's Language, As a Music Thesis." *Perspectives of New Music* 44/2 (2006), 14–64.

———. *A Theory of Music Analysis: On Segmentation and Associative Organization*. Rochester, NY: University of Rochester Press, 2012.

Harnoncourt, Nikolaus. *Baroque Music Today: Music as Speech. Ways to a New Understanding of Music*. Translated by Mary O'Neill. Wayne, NJ: Amadeus Press, 1995.

Hasty, Christopher F. "Experimenting with Rhythm." Unpublished Manuscript.

———. "If Music Is Ongoing Experience, What Could Music Theory Be? A Perspective from the Drastic." *Zeitschrift der Gesellschaft für Musiktheorie,* Sonderausgabe (2010), 197–216.

———. "Just in Time for More Dichotomies: A Hasty Response." *Music Theory Spectrum* 21/2 (1999), 275–93.

———. "Learning in Time." *Visions of Research in Education* 20 (2012). http://www-usr.rider.edu/~vrme/v20n1/visions/Hasty%20Bamberger.pdf.

———. "Rhythmicizing the Subject." In *Musical Implications: Essays in Honor of Eugene Narmour,* edited by Lawrence Bernstein and Alexander Rozin, 169–189. Hillsdale, NY: Pendragon Press, 2013.

———. "Rhythmusexperimente—Halt und Bewegung." In *Rhythmus – Balance – Metrum: Formen raumzeitlicher Organisation in den Künsten,* edited by Christian Grüny and Matteo Nanni, 155–208. Bielefeld: Transcript, 2014.

———. "Segmentation and Process in Post-Tonal Music." *Music Theory Spectrum* 3 (1981), 54–73.

———. "The Image of Thought and Ideas of Music." In *Sounding the Virtual: Gilles Deleuze and the Theory and Philosophy of Music,* edited by Brian Hulse and Nick Nesbitt, 1–22. Farnham, UK: Ashgate, 2010.

———. *Meter as Rhythm.* Oxford: Oxford University Press, 1997.

Hildebrandt, Carolyn. "Children's Representations of Simple Rhythms." Unpublished Manuscript, University of California, Berkeley, Department of Educational Psychology, 1978.

Hodeir, André. *Jazz: Its Evolution and Essence.* Translated by David Noakes. New York: Grove, 1956.

Hoeckner, Berthold. *Programming the Absolute: Nineteenth-Century German Music and the Hermeneutics of the Moment.* Princeton: Princeton University Press, 2002.

Hoffman, Eva. *Time.* New York: Picador, 2009.

Holden, Raymond. *The Virtuoso Conductors: The Central European Tradition from Wagner to Karajan.* New Haven: Yale University Press, 2005.

Hornbostel, E. M. von. "Die Probleme der vergleichenden Musikwissenschaft." In *Hornbostel Opera Omnia,* vol. 1, 247–70. The Hague: Nijhoff, 1975.

———. "Psychologie der Gehörserscheinungen." In *Handbuch der normalen und pathologischen Physiologie,* edited by A. Bethe et al., vol. 11, 701–30. Berlin: Springer, 1926.

Huang, Hao, and Rachel V. Huang. "Billie Holiday and *Tempo Rubato*: Understanding Rhythmic Expressivity." *Annual Review of Jazz Studies* 7 (1994), 181–99.

Hubbert, Julie. "Eisenstein's Theory of Film Music Revisited: Silent and Early Sound Antecedents." In *Composing for the Screen in Germany and the USSR*, edited by Robynn J. Stilwell and Phil Powrie, 125–47. Bloomington: Indiana University Press, 2008.

Husserl, Edmund. "Zur Phänomenologie des inneren Zeitbewusstseins (1893–1917)." In *Husserliana: Gesammelte Werke*, vol. 10, edited by Rudolf Boehm. The Hague: Nijhoff, 1966.

———. *Vorlesungen zur Phänomenologie des inneren Zeitbewusstseins*, vol. 9 of *Jahrbuch für Philosophie und Phänomenologische Forschung*, edited by Martin Heidegger (Halle: Max Niemeyer Verlag, 1928), 367–496; reprinted in *Husserliana: Gesammelte Werke*, vol. 10, edited by Rudolf Boehm. The Hague: Nijhoff, 1966.

James, William. "The Problem of Novelty." In *Some Problems of Philosophy*. Cambridge: Harvard University Press, 1979.

———. *The Principles of Psychology*. New York: Henry Holt and Company, 1890.

Jasen, David A. *Ragtime: An Encyclopedia, Discography, and Sheetography*. New York: Routledge, 2007.

Johnson, Peter. "The Legacy of Recordings." In *Musical Performance: A Guide to Understanding*, edited by John Rink, 197–212. Cambridge: Cambridge University Press, 2002.

Joplin, Scott. "School of Ragtime." *Music Educators Journal* 59/8 (1973 [1908]), 65–67.

Joyce, James. *A Portrait of the Artist as a Young Man*. New York: Viking Press, 1960.

Kaminsky, Peter Michael. "Aspects of Harmony, Rhythm and Form in Schumann's *Papillons*, *Carnaval*, and *Davidsbündlertänze*." PhD dissertation, University of Rochester, 1989.

———. "Principles of Formal Structure in Schumann's Early Piano Cycles." *Music Theory Spectrum* 11/2 (1989), 207–25.

Karno, Mitchell, and Vladimir J. Konečni. "The Effects of Structural Interventions in the First Movement of Mozart's Symphony in G-Minor, K. 550, on Aesthetic Preference." *Music Perception* 10/1 (1992), 63–72.

Keil, Charles M.H. "Motion and Feeling Through Music." *Journal of Aesthetics and Art Criticism* 24/3 (1966), 337–49.

———. "Participatory Discrepancies and the Power of Music." *Cultural Anthropology* 2/3 (1987), 275–83.

———. "The Theory of Participatory Discrepancies: A Progress Report," *Ethnomusicology* 39/1 (1995), 1–19.

Kendall, Roger A., and Edward C. Carterette. "The Communication of Musical Expression." *Music Perception* 8/2 (1990), 129–64.

Kern, Stephen. *The Culture of Time and Space, 1880–1918*. Cambridge, Mass.: Harvard University Press, 2003.

Khannanov, Ildar. "Line, Surface, Speed: Nomadic Features of Melody." In *Sounding the Virtual: Gilles Deleuze and the Theory and Philosophy of Music*, edited by Brian Hulse and Nick Nesbitt, 249–67. Farnham, UK: Ashgate, 2010.

Kingsley, Walter. "Whence Comes Jass? Facts From the Great Authority on the Subject," *New York Sun*, August 5, 1917, 6–8.

Knowlton, Don. "The Anatomy of Jazz," *Harper's Magazine*, April, 1926, 578–85.

Koenig, Karl, ed. *Jazz In Print (1856–1929): An Anthology of Selected Early Readings in Jazz History*. Hillsdale, New York: Pendragon Press, 2002.

Kramer, Jonathan D. *The Time of Music: New Meanings, New Temporalities, New Listening Strategies*. New York: Schirmer Books, 1988.

Krumhansl, Carol L. *Cognitive Foundations of Musical Pitch*. Oxford: Oxford University Press, 1990.

Kubik, Gerhard. *Theory of African Music*, vol. 2. Chicago: University of Chicago Press, 2010.

Kurkela, Kari. *Note and Tone: A Semantic Analysis of Conventional Music Notation*. Helsinki: Musicological Society of Finland, 1986.

Kursell, Julia. "Experiments on Tone Color in Music and Acoustics: Helmholtz, Schoenberg, and *Klangfarbenmelodie*." *Osiris* 28/1 (2013), 191–211.

Kurth, Ernst. *Musikpsychologie*. Berlin: Max Hesse, 1931.

Lachenmann, Helmut. *Musik als existentielle Erfahrung: Schriften 1966–1995*. Wiesbaden: Breitkopf and Härtel, 1996.

Leech-Wilkinson, Daniel. "Listening and Responding to the Evidence of Early Twentieth-Century Performance." *Journal of the Royal Musical Association* 135/1 (2010), 45–62.

Lefkowitz, David S., and Kristin Taavola. "Segmentation in Music: Generalizing a Piece-Sensitive Approach." *Journal of Music Theory* 44/1 (2000), 171–229.

Leman, Marc, and Luiz Naveda. "Basic Gestures as Spatiotemporal Reference Frames for Repetitive Dance/Music Patterns in Samba and Charleston." *Music Perception* 28/1 (2010), 71–91.

Lerdahl, Fred, and Ray Jackendoff. *A Generative Theory of Tonal Music*. Cambridge, Mass.: MIT Press, 1983.

Lewin, David. "Music Theory, Phenomenology, and Modes of Perception." *Music Perception* 3/4 (1986), 327–392.

———. *Studies in Music with Text.* Oxford: Oxford University Press, 2006.

Leydon, Rebecca. "Debussy's Late Style and the Devices of the Early Silent Cinema." *Music Theory Spectrum* 23/2 (2001), 217–41.

Lidov, David. "The Allegretto of Beethoven's Seventh." *American Journal of Semiotics* 1/1–2 (1981), 141–66.

Lochhead, Judy. "Music Theory and Philosophy." In *The Routledge Companion to Philosophy and Music*, edited by Theodore Gracyk and Andrew Kania, 506–16. New York: Routledge, 2011.

Locke, David. Review of *Dried Millet Breaking: Time, Words, and Song in the Woi Epic of the Kpelle*, by Ruth M. Stone. *Ethnomusicology* 34/1 (1990), 172–74.

London, Justin. "Rhythm." *Grove Music Online. Oxford Music Online.* http://www.oxfordmusiconline.com/subscriber/article/grove/music/45963.

———. *Hearing in Time: Psychological Aspects of Musical Meter.* Oxford: Oxford University Press, 2004.

Loosen, Franz. "Intonation of Solo Violin Performance with Reference to Equally Tempered, Pythagorean, and Just Intonations." *Journal of the Acoustical Society of America* 93/1 (1993), 525–39.

———. "The Effect of Musical Experience on the Conception of Accurate Tuning." *Music Perception* 12/3 (1995), 291–306.

Maconie, Robert, ed. *Stockhausen on Music: Lectures and Interviews.* London: Marion Boyars, 1989.

Mailman, Joshua Banks. "Seven Metaphors for (Music) Listening: DRAMaTIC." *Journal of Sonic Studies* 2/1 (2012). http://journal.sonicstudies.org/vol02/nr01/a03.

———. "Temporal Dynamic Form in Music: Atonal, Tonal, and Other." PhD Dissertation, University of Rochester Eastman School of Music, 2010.

Marston, Nicholas. *Schumann: Fantasie, Op. 17.* Cambridge: Cambridge University Press, 1992.

McClary, Susan, ed. *Structures of Feeling in Seventeenth-Century Cultural Expression.* Toronto: University of Toronto Press, 2013.

McClary, Susan. "Adorno Plays the *WTC*: On Political Theory and Performance." *Indiana Theory Review* 27/2 (2009), 97–112.

———. *Desire and Pleasure in Seventeenth-Century Music.* Berkeley and Los Angeles: University of California Press, 2012.

———. *Modal Subjectivities: Self-Fashioning in the Italian Madrigal.* Berkeley and Los Angeles: University of California Press, 2004.

McNeill, David. *Hand and Mind: What Gestures Reveal About Thought.* Chicago: University of Chicago Press, 1992.

Meyer, Rosalee K., and Caroline Palmer. "Temporal and Motor Transfer in Music Performance." *Music Perception* 21/1 (2003), 81–104.

Montague, Eugene. "Phenomenology and the 'Hard Problem' of Consciousness and Music." In *Music and Consciousness: Philosophical, Psychological, and Cultural Perspectives*, edited by David Clarke and Eric Clarke, 29–46. Oxford: Oxford University Press, 2011.

Morgan, Robert P. "Musical Time/Musical Space." *Critical Inquiry* 6/3 (1980), 527–38.

Morgenstern, Joe. "The King's Speech: Wit, Warmth, and Majesty," *The Wall Street Journal*, November 26, 2010, D3. http://www.wsj.com/articles/SB1000142 4052748703572404575634483293371478.

Morris, Robert. "Listening to Babbitt's Electronic Music: The Medium and the Message." *Perspectives of New Music* 35/2 (1997), 88–91.

———. "New Directions in the Theory and Analysis of Musical Contour." *Music Theory Spectrum* 15/2 (1993), 205–28.

Narmour, Eugene. "Analyzing Form and Measuring Perceptual Content in Mozart's Sonata K. 282: A New Theory of Parametric Analogues." *Music Perception* 13/3 (1996), 265–318.

———. "Music Expectation by Cognitive Rule-Mapping." *Music Perception* 17/3 (2000), 329–98.

———. "On the Relationship of Analytical Theory to Performance and Interpretation." In *Explorations in Music, the Arts, and Ideas: Essays in Honor of Leonard B. Meyer*, edited by Eugene Narmour and Ruth Solie, 317–40. Stuyvesant, NY: Pendragon Press, 1988.

———. "Our Varying Histories and Future Potential: Models and Maps in Science, the Humanities, and in Music Theory." *Music Perception* 29/1 (2011), 1–21.

———. "The Implication-Realization Model." In *Music in the Social and Behavioral Sciences*, edited by William Forde Thompson, 588–93. Thousand Oaks, Calif.: SAGE Reference, 2014.

———. "The Top-Down and Bottom-Up Systems of Musical Implication: Building on Meyer's Theory of Emotional Syntax." *Music Perception* 9/1 (1991), 1–26.

———. "Toward a Unified Theory of the I-R Model (Part 1): Parametric Scales and Their Analogically Isomorphic Structures." *Music Perception* 33/1 (2015), 32–69.

———. *The Analysis and Cognition of Basic Melodic Structures: The Implication-Realization Model.* Chicago: University of Chicago Press, 1990.

———. *The Analysis and Cognition of Melodic Complexity*. Chicago: University of Chicago Press, 1992.

Nattiez, Jean-Jacques. *Music and Discourse: Toward a Semiology of Music*. Translated by Carolyn Abbate. Princeton: Princeton University Press, 1990.

Naveda, Luiz, and Marc Leman. "A Cross-Modal Heuristic for Periodic Pattern Analysis of Samba Music and Dance." *Journal of New Music Research* 38/3 (2009), 255–83.

Neisser, Ulric. *Cognitive Psychology*. New York: Appleton-Century-Crofts, 1967.

Newbould, Brian. *Schubert: The Music and the Man*. Berkeley and Los Angeles: University of California Press, 1997.

Newton, Isaac. *The Method of Fluxions and Infinite Series*. Translated by John Colson. London: Henry Woodfall, 1736.

Núñez, Rafael, and Eve Sweetser. "With the Future Behind Them: Convergent Evidence from Aymara Language and Gesture in the Crosslinguistic Comparison of Spatial Construals of Time." *Cognitive Science* 30/3 (2006), 401–50.

Núñez, Rafael E., and Kensy Cooperrider. "The Tangle of Space and Time in Human Cognition." *Trends in Cognitive Sciences* 17/5 (2013), 220–29.

Ornstein, Robert E. *On the Experience of Time*. Harmondsworth: Penguin Books, 1969.

Palmer, Caroline. "Mapping Musical Thought to Musical Performance." *Journal of Experimental Psychology: Human Perception and Performance* 15/2 (1989), 331–46.

———. "On the Assignment of Structure in Music Performance." *Music Perception* 14/1 (1996), 23–56.

———. "The Role of Interpretive Preferences in Music Performance." In *Cognitive Bases of Musical Communication*, edited by Mari Reiss Jones and Susan Holleran, 249–62. Washington, D.C.: American Psychological Association, 1992.

Panassié, Hugues. *Hot Jazz: The Guide to Swing Music*. Translated by Lyle Dowling and Eleanor Dowling. New York: M. Witmark & Sons, 1936.

Patterson, William Morrison. *The Rhythm of Prose: An Experimental Investigation of Individual Difference in the Sense of Rhythm*. New York: Columbia University Press, 1916.

Peles, Stephen, et al., eds. *The Collected Essays of Milton Babbitt*. Princeton: Princeton University Press, 2003.

Pérès, Marcel. "A Different Sense of Time." In *Inside Early Music: Conversations with Early Performers*, edited by Bernard D. Sherman, 25–42. Oxford: Oxford University Press, 1997.

Philip, Robert. *Early Recordings and Musical Style: Changing Tastes in Instrumental Performance, 1900–1950*. Cambridge: Cambridge University Press, 1992.

———. *Performing Music in the Age of Recording*. New Haven: Yale University Press, 2004.

Phillips-Silver, Jessica, et al. "The Ecology of Entrainment: Foundations of Coordinated Rhythmic Movement." *Music Perception* 28/1 (2010), 3–14.

Phillips-Silver, Jessica. "On the Meaning of Movement in Music, Development and the Brain." *Contemporary Music Review* 28/3 (2009), 293–314.

Piaget, Jean. *The Psychology of Intelligence*. Totowa, NJ: Littlefield, Adams, & Co, 1960.

Polansky, Larry. "Morphological Metrics: An Introduction to a Theory of Formal Distances." In *Proceedings of the International Computer Music Conference*, edited by James W. Beauchamp and Sever Tipei, 197–205. San Francisco: International Computer Music Association, 1987.

Prinz, Jesse J. "Emotions, Embodiment, and Awareness." In *Emotion and Consciousness*, edited by Lisa Feldman Barrett, Paula M. Niedenthal, and Piotr Winkielman, 363–83. New York: Guilford Press, 2005.

Qureshi, Regula Burckhardt. "Exploring Time Cross-Culturally: Ideology and Performance of Time in the Sufi *qawwāli*." *Journal of Musicology* 12/4 (1994), 491–528.

Rahn, John. "Aspects of Musical Explanation." *Perspectives of New Music* 17/2 (1979), 202–224.

Rakowski, Andrzej. "Context-dependent Intonation Variants of Melodic Intervals." In *Music, Language, Speech and Brain*, edited by Johan Sundberg, Lennart Nord, and Rolf Carlson, 203–11. London: Macmillan, 1991.

Reinecke, Carl. *The Beethoven Pianoforte Sonatas: Letters to a Lady*. Translated by E. M. Trevenen Dawson. London: Augener & Co., 1898.

Repp, Bruno H. "Detectability of Duration and Intensity Increments in Melody Tones: A Partial Connection between Music Perception and Performance." *Perception and Psychophysics* 57/8 (1995), 1217–32.

———. "Obligatory 'Expectations' of Expressive Timing Induced by Perception of Musical Structure." *Psychological Research* 61/1 (1998), 33–43.

———. "Probing the Cognitive Representation of Musical Time: Structural Constraints on the Perception of Timing Perturbations." *Cognition* 44/3 (1992), 241–81.

Rink, John S. Review of *The Pianist as Orator: Beethoven and the Transformation of Keyboard Style*, by George Barth. *Journal of the American Musicological Society* 49/1 (1996), 155–161.

Roberts, William A. "Evidence for Future Cognition in Animals." *Learning and Motivation* 43/4 (2012), 169–80.

Rodemeyer, Lanei. "Developments in the Theory of Time-Consciousness: An Analysis of Protention." In *The New Husserl*, edited by Donn Welton, 125–56. Bloomington: Indiana University Press, 2003.

Roeder, John. "A Calculus of Accent." *Journal of Music Theory* 39/1 (1994), 1–46.

Rosen, Charles. *The Romantic Generation*. Cambridge, Mass.: Harvard University Press, 1995.

Rubin, David C. "The Basic-Systems Model of Episodic Memory." *Perspectives on Psychological Science* 1/4 (2006), 277–311.

Schenker, Heinrich. "Abolish the Phrasing Slur." In *The Masterwork in Music: A Yearbook,* vol. 1 (1925), edited by William Drabkin and translated by Ian Bent et al., 20–30. Cambridge: Cambridge University Press, 1994.

———. *Kontrapunkt*, 2. Vienna: Universal Edition, 1922. Translated by John Rothgeb, *Counterpoint*, vol. 2. New York: Schirmer, 1987.

———. *The Art of Performance*. Edited by Heribert Esser and translated by Irene Schreier Scott. Oxford: Oxford University Press, 2000.

Scherzinger, Martin. "*Enforced* Deterritorialization, or the Trouble with Musical Politics." In *Sounding the Virtual: Gilles Deleuze and the Theory and Philosophy of Music*, edited by Brian Hulse and Nick Nesbitt, 103–28. Farnham, UK: Ashgate, 2010.

Schoenberg, Arnold. "My Evolution." *Musical Quarterly* 75/4 (1991), 144–57.

———. *Style and Idea: Selected Writings of Arnold Schoenberg*. Edited by Leonard Stein and translated by Leo Black. London: Faber & Faber, 1975.

———. *Theory of Harmony*. Translated by Roy Porter. Berkeley and Los Angeles: University of California Press, 1983.

Schonberg, Harold C. *The Great Pianists*. London: Gollancz, 1965.

Schuiling, Floris. "Animate Structures: The Compositions and Improvisations of the Instant Composers Pool Orchestra." PhD Dissertation, University of Cambridge, 2015.

Schuller, Gunther. *Early Jazz: Its Roots and Musical Development*. Oxford: Oxford University Press, 1968.

———. *The Swing Era: The Development Of Jazz, 1930–1945*. Oxford: Oxford University Press, 1989.

Schumann, Robert, and Clara Schumann. *Complete Correspondence*, vol. 1. Translated by Hildegard Fritsch and Ronald L. Crawford and edited by Eva Weissweiler. New York: P. Lang, 1994.

Schutz, Alfred. "Making Music Together: A Study in Social Relationship." In

Collected Papers 2: Studies in Social Theory, edited by Arvid Broderson, 159–78. The Hague: Nijhoff, 1964.

Shaffer, L. Henry, and Neil P. Todd. "The Interpretive Component in Musical Performance." In *Action and Perception in Rhythm and Music*, edited by Alf Gabrielsson, 139–52. Stockholm: Royal Swedish Academy of Music, 1987.

Shaffer, L. Henry. "Intention and Performance." *Psychological Review* 83/5 (1976), 375–93.

———. "Musical Performance as Interpretation." *Psychology of Music* 23/1 (1995), 17–38.

Shelemay, Kay Kaufman. *Soundscapes: Exploring Music in a Changing World*. New York: Norton, 2006.

Simmel, Georg. "Die Großstädte und das Geistesleben." In *Brücke und Tor: Essays des Philosophen zur Geschichte, Religion, Kunst und Gesellschaft*, edited by Michael Landmann. Stuttgart: K. F. Koehler, 1957.

Sloboda, John A. "The Communication of Musical Metre in Piano Performance." *Quarterly Journal of Experimental Psychology* Section A 35/2 (1983), 377–96.

Small, Christopher. *Musicking: The Meaning of Performing and Listening*. Middlebury, Conn.: Wesleyan University Press, 2008.

Smolin, Lee. *Time Reborn*. New York: Houghton Mifflin, 2013.

Snyder, Bob. *Music and Memory: An Introduction*. Cambridge, Mass.: MIT Press, 2000.

Spitzer, Michael. "The Metaphor of Musical Space." In *Musicae Scientiae* 7/1 (2003), 101–18.

Stockhausen, Karlheinz. "Structure and Experiential Time." *Die Reihe* 2 [revised English edition] (1959), 64–74.

Stone, Ruth M. *Let the Inside Be Sweet: The Interpretation of Music Event among the Kpelle of Liberia*. Bloomington: Indiana University Press, 1982.

Suddendorf, Thomas, and Michael C. Corballis. "Mental Time Travel and the Evolution of the Human Mind." *Genetic Social and General Psychology Monographs* 123/2 (1997), 133–67.

———. "The Evolution of Foresight: What is Mental Time Travel, and is it Unique to Humans?" *Behavioral and Brain Sciences* 30/3 (2007), 299–351.

Sundberg, Johan. "Computer Synthesis of Music Performance." In *Generative Processes in Music*, edited by John A. Sloboda, 52–69. Oxford: Oxford University Press 1988.

———. "Music Performance Research: An 'Overview.'" In *Music, Language, Speech and Brain*, edited by Johan Sundberg, Lennart Nord, and Rolf Carlson, 173–83. London: Macmillan, 1991.

Sutcliffe, W. Dean. "The Keyboard Music." In *The Cambridge Companion to Mozart*, edited by Simon P. Keefe, 61–77. Cambridge: Cambridge University Press, 2003.

Taylor, Benedict. "Cyclic Form, Time, and Memory in Mendelssohn's A-Minor Quartet, Op. 13." *Musical Quarterly* 93/1 (2010), 45–89.

Tenney, James, and Larry Polansky. "Temporal Gestalt Perception in Music." *Journal of Music Theory* 24/2 (1980), 205–41.

Tenney, James. *Meta+Hodos and Meta Meta+Hodos,* Hanover, NH: Frog Peak Music, 1988.

Tenzer, Michael. "A Cross-Cultural Topology of Musical Time." In *Analytical and Cross-Cultural Studies in World Music*, edited by Michael Tenzer and John Roeder. Oxford: Oxford University Press, 2011.

———. "Temporal Transformations in Cross-Cultural Perspective: Augmentation in Baroque, Carnatic, and Balinese music." *Analytical Approaches to World Music* 1/1 (2011), 152–175.

Tichenor, Trebor Jay. "John Stillwell Stark, Piano Ragtime Publisher: Readings from *The Intermezzo* and His Personal Ledgers, 1905–1908." *Black Music Research Journal* 9/2 (1989), 193–204.

———. *Ragtime Rediscoveries: Sixty-Four Works from the Golden Age of Rag.* New York: Dover, Inc., 1979.

Tillmann, Barbara, and Emmanuel Bigand. "Does Formal Structure Affect Perception of Musical Expressiveness?" *Psychology of Music* 24/1 (1996), 3–17.

Todd, Neil P. McAngus. "The Dynamics of Dynamics: A Model of Musical Expression." *Journal of the Acoustical Society of America* 91/6 (1992), 3540–50.

Toiviainen, Petri, et al. "Embodied Meter: Hierarchical Eigenmodes in Music-Induced Movement." *Music Perception* 28/1 (2010), 59–70.

Tomasello, Michael. *The Cultural Origins of Human Cognition.* Cambridge, Mass.: Harvard University Press, 1999.

Tovey, Donald Francis. "Performance and Personality, Part III." *The Musical Gazette,* July (1900), 33–37.

Tulving, Endel. "Episodic Memory and Autonoesis: Uniquely Human?" In *The Missing Link in Cognition: Origins of Self-Reflective Consciousness*, edited by Herbert S. Terrace and Janet Metcalfe, 3–56. Oxford: Oxford University Press, 2005.

———. "Varieties of Consciousness and Levels of Awareness in Memory." In *Attention: Selection, Awareness, and Control: A Tribute to Donald Broadbent*, edited by Alan Baddeley and Lawrence Weiskrantz, 283–99. Oxford: Clarendon Press, 1993.

———. *Elements of Episodic Memory.* Oxford: Clarendon Press, 1983.

Tunstill, Guy. "Melody and Rhythmic Structure in Pitjantjatjara Song." In *Songs of Aboriginal Australia*, edited by Margaret Clunies Ross, Tamsin Donaldson, and Stephen A. Wild, 121–141. Sydney: University of Sydney, 1987.

Uno, Yayoi, and Roland Hübscher. "*Temporal Gestalt* Segmentation: Polyphonic Extensions and Applications to Works by Boulez, Cage, Xenakis, Ligeti, and Babbitt." *Computers in Music Research* 5 (1995), 1–38.

Varwig, Bettina. "Metaphors of Time and Modernity in Bach." *Journal of Musicology* 29/2 (2012), 154–90.

Vygotsky, Lev S. *Thinking and Speech*. Edited by Robert W. Rieber and Aaron S. Carton and translated by Norris Minick. New York: Plenum Press, 1987.

Wade, Bonnie C. *Thinking Musically*. Oxford: Oxford University Press, 2013.

Wagner, Richard. *On Conducting: A Treatise on Style in the Execution of Classical Music*. Translated by Edward Dannreuther. London: W. Reeves, 1887.

Walser, Robert, ed. *Keeping Time: Readings in Jazz History*. Oxford: Oxford University Press, 2014.

Weingartner, Felix. *On Conducting*. Translated by Ernest Newman. Leipzig: Breitkopf and Härtel, 1906.

Werner, Heinz. *Comparative Psychology of Mental Development*. New York: International Universities Press, 1973.

Whorf, Benjamin Lee. *Language, Thought, and Reality*. Edited by John B. Carroll. Cambridge, Mass.: MIT Press, 1956.

Will, Udo. "Oral Memory in Australian Aboriginal Song Performance and the Parry-Kirk Debate: A Cognitive Ethnomusicological Perspective." In *Musikarchäologische Quellengruppen: Bodenurkunden, mündliche Überlieferung, Aufzeichnung*, edited by Ellen Hickmann and Ricardo Eichmann, 161–179. Rahden: Marie Leidorf, 2004.

Will, Udo, and Catherine Ellis. "A Re-Analyzed Australian Western Desert Song: Frequency Performance and Interval Structure." *Ethnomusicology* 40/2 (1996), 187–222.

Williams, Raymond. *Marxism and Literature*. Oxford: Oxford University Press, 1977.

Williams, William Carlos. "A 1 Pound Stein." In *Selected Essays of William Carlos Williams*, 162–166. New York: New Direction, 1969.

Wittgenstein, Ludwig. *Philosophical Investigations*. Translated by G.E.M. Anscombe. Oxford: Blackwell, 1958..

Wolf, Richard K. Review of *Time in Indian Music*, by Martin Clayton. *Asian Music* 34/2 (2000), 133–139.

———. *The Black Cow's Footprint: Time, Space, and Music in the Lives of the Kotas of South India*. Delhi: Permanent Black, 2005.

Wolpe, Stefan. "Thinking Twice." In *Contemporary Composers on Contemporary Music*, edited by Elliott Schwartz and Barney Childs, 274–307. New York: Holt, Rinehart & Winston, 1967.

Zbikowski, Lawrence M. "Dance Topoi, Sonic Analogues, and Musical Grammar: Communicating with Music in the Eighteenth Century." In *Communication in Eighteenth Century Music*, edited by Kofi Agawu and Danuta Mirka, 283–309. Cambridge: Cambridge University Press, 2008.

———. "Music and Movement: A View from Cognitive Musicology." In *Bewegungen zwischen Hören und Sehen: Denkbewegungen über Bewegungskünste*, edited by Stephanie Schroedter, 151–62. Würzburg: Königshausen & Neumann, 2012.

———. "Music, Dance, and Meaning in the Early Nineteenth Century." *Journal of Musicological Research* 31/2–3 (2012), 147–65.

———. "Music, Emotion, Analysis." *Music Analysis* 29/1–3 (2011), 37–60.

———. "Music, Language, and Kinds of Consciousness." In *Music and Consciousness: Philosophical, Psychological, and Cultural Perspectives*, edited by Eric Clarke and David Clarke, 179–92. Oxford: Oxford University Press, 2011.

———. "Musical Gesture and Musical Grammar: A Cognitive Approach." In *New Perspectives on Music and Gesture*, edited by Anthony Gritten and Elaine King, 83–98.: Farnham, UK: Ashgate, 2011.

———. *Conceptualizing Music: Cognitive Structure, Theory, and Analysis*. Oxford: Oxford University Press, 2002.

General Index

Adorno, Theodor W., 5–6, 14–15
Agamben, Giorgio, 308–309
agogic accent, 11, 156, 271–72
Allanbrook, Wye Jamison, 4
analog notation, 76. *See also* notation
Aristotle, 192
Arlen, Harold,
"Over the Rainbow," 146–50
Attali, Jacques, 239
augmented sixth chord, 159–65
awareness, 39–41

Babbitt, Milton, 300–305
Composition for Synthesizer, 300
Bach, Johann Sebastian,
Partita for Solo Violin no. 2 in D
minor, BWV 1004, 134–45, 213–15
Beethoven, Ludwig van, 14, 155
Piano Sonata in C minor, op. 13
(*Pathétique*), 88–98
Symphony no. 7 in A Major, op. 92,
221, 223–26, 231–32
String Quartet in E minor, op. 59, no.
2, 201–202
Violin Concerto in D Major, op. 61,
266–67
Bluedorn, Allen, 16, 24
Boretz, Benjamin, 303–304
Boulanger, Nadia, 178
Brahms, Johannes,
String Quartet no. 3 in B♭, op. 67,
265–66
Symphony no. 1 in C minor, op. 68,
73–74, 76
Brown, Earle, 84–85
Brown, Warner, 259, 261–62, 267–69, 272,
276–77

Cage, John, 71
Cassidy, Aaron, 78
Charles, Ray, 150
chronometric time, 14–15. *See also* time
circular time, 19–21. *See also* time

clock time, 291. *See also* time
Cone, Edward T., 176
consciousness, 39–41
content-based time, 17. *See also* time
context-sensitive notation, 84–86. *See also*
notation
contraformalism (*cf*), 112, 145, 148–50
conventions (C), 110
Couperin, Louis,
Prélude in G Moll, 247–54
Crumb, George, 87

D'Albert, Eugen, 8–9
Dahlhaus, Carl, 297–98, 311
Damasio, Antonio, 40
dance, 262–63
Davidson, Arnold, 298–99
deformalism (*df*), 112, 145, 148–50
Deleuze, Gilles, 185, 281–84, 286–92
Derrida, Jacques, 288–89
descriptive notation, 77–79. *See also*
notation
Dewey, John, 203–204, 307–308
digital notation, 76. *See also* notation
dual-track time, 275–76. *See also* time

Eisenstein, Sergei, 232–33
Ellis, Catherine, 65–67
emancipation of the dissonance, 293–99,
309–11. *See also* Schoenberg, Arnold
emic notation, 81–84. *See also* notation
entrainment, 28, 219–20, 223–27, 234–35
epochal time, 16. *See also* time
etic notation, 81–84. *See also* notation
Eusebius, 171–75. *See also* Schumann,
Robert
event-based time, 16, 23, 26. *See also* time

Feldman, Morton, 62
Florestan, 171–75. *See also* Schumann,
Robert
flow, 23–24, 88–93, 104–107, 227–30
formalism (*fm*), 110, 133–45

fungible time, 16, 26. *See also* time

Garland, Judy,
  Over the Rainbow, 146–50
Gentner, Dedre, 7
gesture, 47
Gould, Glenn, 5–6
Guattari, Félix, 281–84, 286–87, 291–92

Hadot, Pierre, 299
Harburg, Edgar "Yip" Yipsel, 146–50
Hasty, Christopher, 23–24, 59–60, 62, 63,
  169–71, 176–77, 187, 195, 203, 237, 246,
  257–58, 276–77, 286–91, 304–308
  metric projection (theory of), 26, 220,
  230, 259, 276–77, 288, 290–91
Haydn, Joseph,
  String Quartet in D Major op. 76, no.
  5, 212–14
Hodeir, André, 260
Holiday, Billie,
  I Can't Give You Anything But Love,
  274–77
Hornbostel, Erich Moritz von, 58–61
Huang, Hao, 274–76
Huang, Rachel V., 274–76
Husserl, Edmund, 58–59
hyperformalism (*hf*), 112

informalism (*if*), 114–15, 148–50
inner time, 15. *See also* time
intervals, 73–74

James, William, 204–205
Joachim, Joseph, 264–66
Joplin, Scott, 263–64

Keil, Charles, 272
Kim, Earl, 238–39
Kingsley, Walter, 274
Klangfarbenmelodie, 295–96, 309–10. *See
  also* Schoenberg, Arnold

Lachenmann, Helmut, 62
Larrocha, Alicia de, 4–7, 10–11, 18, 23,
  25–26, 30
Lewin, David, 56

Lewis, George, 299
Ligeti, György, 79–81
linear time, 19–21. *See also* time

McHugh, Jimmy,
  I Can't Give You Anything But Love,
  274–77
McNair, Sylvia, 150
memory, 41–48, 53–54, 176–77, 187
metric projection (theory of), 26, 220,
  230, 259, 276–77, 288, 290–91. *See also*
  Hasty, Christopher
Milstein, Nathan, 134–45
Monteverdi, Claudio,
  "*Ah, com' a un vago sol*," 240–46
Morris, Robert, 300
Mougin, Stéphane, 261
Mozart, Wolfgang. Amadeus,
  Clarinet Concerto in A Major K. 622,
  227–28
  Piano Sonata in F Major K. 332, 3–6
musicking, 304

neutral notation, 84–86. *See also* notation
nomadic space, 283. *See also* space
norms (N), 110, 125–30
notation
  analog, 76
  context-sensitive, 84–86
  descriptive, 77–79
  digital, 76
  emic, 81–84
  etic, 81–84
  neutral, 84–86
  prescriptive, 77–79

Oort, Bart van, 30–31
oral tradition, 125–30
Ornstein, Robert, 17
outer time, 15. *See also* time

Pannasié, Hugues, 260–61
parametric dynamics, 94–107
Patterson, William Morrison, 257, 259,
  261, 269–74, 276
Penderecki, Krzysztof, 79–81

phenomenological time, 14–15. *See also* time
Philip, Robert, 18–19
phrase arching, 27–29
Piaget, Jean, 193–94, 216
piano rolls, 3, 8
Pitjantjatjara, 65–67
Podger, Rachel, 134, 139–45
prescriptive notation, 77–79. *See also* notation
Previn, André, 150
proformalism (*pf*), 112, 133–45
projection, metric (theory of), 26, 220, 230, 259, 276–77, 288, 290–91. *See also* Hasty, Christopher

recordings (R), 110, 121–22
reformalism (*rf*), 113, 140, 144
Reinecke, Carl, 3–4, 7–15, 17, 23, 25–28, 30–31
Repp, Bruno, 13
revision (compositional), 177–78
Rosen, Charles, 176–82, 184–85
Rubin, David, 43–45

Schenker, Heinrich, 9, 12, 29–30
Scherzinger, Martin, 286
Schoenberg, Arnold, 293–98, 309–11. *See also* emancipation of the dissonance; *Klangfarbenmelodie*
Piano Piece op. 19, no. 4, 100–103
Schubert, Franz,
String Quintet in C Major D.956, 155–68
Schuller, Gunther, 258, 260, 277
Schumann, Clara, 171–75, 178–80, 188
Schumann, Robert,
Davidsbündlertänze, op. 6, 171–89
Florestan and Eusebius, 171–75
Schütz, Alfred, 15, 57
Schütz, Heinrich, 246
scores (S), 110–11, 120, 151
scripts (s), 110–11, 120
sedentary space, 283. *See also* space
Small, Christopher, 304
Smolin, Lee, 195

smooth space, 281–84, 291, *See also* space
sonic profile tools, 94–107
South India (music of), 82–83
Soyer, David, 201–202
space
nomadic, 283
sedentary, 283
smooth, 281–84
striated, 281–86
Stark, John Stillwell, 263–64
striated space, 281–86, 291. *See also* space
Stumpf, Carl, 58
swing, 26–27, 257–77

Takemitsu, Tōru, 33–39, 47–50
12 Songs for Guitar, 33–35
All in Twilight, 35–39, 47–52
Tenney/Polansky algorithm, 99–103
texts (T), 110
time
chronometric, 14–15
circular, 19–21
clock, 291
content-based, 17
dual-track, 275–76
epochal, 16
event-based, 16, 23, 26
fungible, 16, 26
inner, 15
linear, 19–21
outer, 15
phenomenological, 14–15
topic theory, 4
Tovey, Donald Francis, 12–13, 264–66
transcription (ethnographic), 83–84, 267–72, 274–77
transformational interpretation, 115–16

Vaughn, Sarah, 150
Vygotsky, Lev S., 194

Werner, Heinz, 194
Whorf, Benjamin Lee, 207
Williams, Raymond, 244–45